D0931628

GROWTH POLE STRATEGY
AND
REGIONAL DEVELOPMENT POLICY

Other titles of interest

BALASSA, B.
Policy Reform in Developing Countries

BLUNDEN, W. R.
The Land Use/Transport System: Analysis and Synthesis

CHADWICK, G. F.
A Systems View of Planning: Towards a Theory of the Urban and Regional Planning Process

COWLING, T. M. and STEELEY, G. C.
Sub-regional Planning Studies: An Evaluation

DARIN-DRABKIN, H.
Land Policy and Urban Growth

DAVIDSON, J. and WIBBERLEY, G.
Planning and the Rural Environment

FAGENCE, M.
Citizen Participation in Planning

FALUDI, A.
A Reader in Planning Theory

FRIEND, J. K. and JESSOP, W. N.
Local Government and Strategic Choice: An Operational Research Approach to the Processes of Public Planning

GOODALL, B.
The Economics of Urban Areas

HART, D.
Strategic Planning in London: The Rise and Fall of the Primary Road Network

LEE, C.
Models in Planning: An Introduction to the Use of Quantitative Models in Planning

LICHFIELD, N. *et al*.
Evaluation in the Planning Process

MAROIS, M.
Towards a Plan of Action for Mankind

MOSELEY, M. J.
Growth Centres in Spatial Planning

NEEDHAM, D. B.
How Cities Work

RAPOPORT, A.
Human Aspects of Urban Form

SANT, M. E. C.
Industrial Movement and Regional Development

SOLESBURY, W.
Policy in Urban Planning: Structure Plans, Programmes and Local Plans

STARKIE, D. N. M.
Transportation Planning and Public Policy

GROWTH POLE STRATEGY
AND
REGIONAL DEVELOPMENT POLICY

Asian Experience and Alternative Approaches

Edited by

FU-CHEN LO
United Nations Centre for Regional Development, Nagoya, Japan

and

KAMAL SALIH
University of Science, Malaysia

Published for the
UNITED NATIONS CENTRE FOR REGIONAL DEVELOPMENT
by
PERGAMON PRESS

OXFORD · NEW YORK · TORONTO · SYDNEY · PARIS · FRANKFURT

U.K.	Pergamon Press Ltd., Headington Hill Hall, Oxford OX3 0BW, England
U.S.A.	Pergamon Press Inc., Maxwell House, Fairview Park, Elmsford, New York 10523, U.S.A.
CANADA	Pergamon of Canada Ltd., 75 The East Mall, Toronto, Ontario, Canada
AUSTRALIA	Pergamon Press (Aust.) Pty. Ltd., 19a Boundary Street, Rushcutters Bay, N.S.W. 2011, Australia
FRANCE	Pergamon Press SARL, 24 rue des Ecoles, 75240 Paris, Cedex 05, France
FEDERAL REPUBLIC OF GERMANY	Pergamon Press GmbH, 6242 Kronberg-Taunus, Pferdstrasse 1, Federal Republic of Germany

First edition 1978

British Library Cataloguing in Publication Data

Growth pole strategy and regional development policy.
1. Regional planning - Asia - Congresses
I. Lo, Fu-chen II. Salih, Kamal III. United Nations Centre for Regional Development
309.2'5'095   HT395.A8   77-30701
ISBN 0-08-021984-5

Printed in Great Britain by William Clowes & Sons Limited London, Beccles and Colchester

FOREWORD

This volume brings together the papers presented at a seminar and symposium sponsored by the United Nations Centre for Regional Development (UNCRD). The focus of the gathering was on a critical review of industrialization strategies and the growth pole approach to regional planning in Asia, but the coverage extended beyond this theme to consider vital issues and alternative development strategies appropriate to prevailing conditions in Asia.

The purpose of bringing these papers to a more global audience is threefold. First, we should like to provide the theoretical and empirical research contained in this volume to planners and policy-makers who are engaged in the continuing process of designing and implementing regional development policies. Secondly, we hope that this collection will stimulate further international collaboration on research into key development issues for regional development. Thirdly, by adding a few papers not originally contained in the proceedings of the seminar and symposium, our intention has been to not only include the results of the Asian experience to date but to also move the theoretical considerations toward a more complete statement of current thinking in regional planning in Asia.

UNCRD's own approach to research into key regional development issues is centred on the philosophy of "cumulative effort", to utilize not only our own past research efforts but to also maximize the utilization of research being carried on in Asia and throughout the world. This approach also attempts to systematically fit relevant case studies together into a broad conceptual framework for policy planning purposes. Such framework building can only be done by sequential, cumulative research fully utilizing the resources of collaborating institutions and the research being carried out by public and private institutions throughout the world.

I am pleased that these papers are being presented to a wide audience. They represent both the richness of regional planning approaches in Asia and the continuing search for fresh approaches to key development issues. This reflects the philosophy of UNCRD and its research efforts.

MASAHIKO HONJO
Director, UNCRD

PREFACE

In November 1975 a Seminar on Industrialization Strategies and the Growth Pole Approach to Regional Planning and Development was organized by the United Nations Centre for Regional Development in Nagoya to review the various Asian experiences in the adoption of the growth pole approach in regional development. The proceedings of that Seminar have been widely circulated under the title, *Growth Pole Strategy and Regional Development Planning in Asia,* published by UNCRD in 1976. The issues raised by the participants of the Seminar, and reflected in the proceedings, have since generated considerable interest beyond the immediate circle of planners and researchers in Asia concerned with regional development planning.

The present volume includes the major papers presented in the seminar, each of which has since been considerably updated and revised for the present book. Together with additional articles not presented at the Seminar, but referring to equally important related issues, the volume as a whole should hopefully form, in our view, a consolidated statement of the theory and practice of growth pole strategy and regional development policy in Asian countries. The papers together reflect both the continuing theoretical and practical issues in regional policy as well as some new thinking regarding alternative analytical and strategic approaches to the problems of regional development and under-development. In this fashion, it is hoped that this book will stimulate further elaboration and discussion by scholars, practitioners and students in this important field of development studies.

The incorporation of the spatial and regional dimension into national development planning in Asian countries is clearly evident in recent years. This is in many ways a reflection of the increasing sophistication in the understanding of the regional structure of their economies and in dealing with problems of regional allocation of public investments, industrial location policy, backward region development, and the role of comprehensive regional development planning in the national context. At the regional level itself, in many of these countries many studies have been undertaken, often with foreign assistance as part of a general technical aid scheme, of particular subnational areas and regional masterplans have prepared to guide the national authorities. Various issues on the ability to aggregate these regional plans into a consistent national development plan are being raised, and major gaps in knowledge are being filled. Through the diffusion and adaptation of new ideas in regional planning the entire effort has been a tremendous learning process. In the process, considerable interest has been created in regional development planning, both as a profession and as a distinct field of study in these countries and has led to the emergence of a new generation of regional planners in Asia.

In all this activity, practice and ideas in regional development and planning become entangled and hence generate conflicting interpretations and possible misapplications. As one of the frontiers of regional development planning is on the historical and socio-economic diversity of conditions in Asia, this book can be seen as a first introduction to the complex problems of regional development in Asian countries and to the dimensions of regional policy subsumed under the growth pole approach in solving them. As a result, new formulations of received regional development theory—and their applications to suit particular Asian conditions—may emerge and hence contribute further to the developing theory of regional policy.

In putting together these articles, we would like to acknowledge the many contributions from persons and institutions which have made this volume possible. Our thanks should first of all be extended to those authors who have directly or indirectly contributed in actual regional policy formulation and to the experience brought together in the collected case studies through active participation in the UNCRD collaborative research. These papers could not have been done without the understanding and assistance of various government agencies and individuals in each respective country. This, in one way, may also be seen as a reflection of the increasing feeling among Asian planners and scholars that their country experience should not be the means to prove or disprove any given theory. Rather, in and of itself it should be useful in the exchange of knowledge for a better understanding of regional planning in the Asian context. In bringing this research together, John Friedmann joined the research project as UN consultant and contributed a significant paper with Mike Douglass. His steersmanship was timely and most stimulating.

We are grateful to Niles Hansen, Benjamin Higgins, and Koichi Mera for contributing their papers in this volume presented at the UNCRD Seminar. These papers, together with Masahiko Honjo's article and Jon Sigurdson's paper on China, reprinted here with the permission of *World Development,* form a wide spectrum of regional planning thinking. As it is our overriding objective that the conflicting views and in-depth concern over alternatives open for regional development in Asia be captured in this volume and delivered to a broader audience, all contributions are deeply appreciated.

In addition we are very much indebted to the able assistance of Mike Douglass and Thasanai Phiriyavithayophas for untiring editing and proofreading of successive drafts of the manuscript, and to Kuniko Kondo for typing and preparation of the entire volume.

September 1977

F.C.L.
K.S.

CONTENTS

CONTRIBUTORS

DOUGLASS, Mike, Research Staff, United Nations Centre for Regional Development, Nagoya, Japan

FRIEDMANN, John, Professor, Urban Planning Programme, School of Architecture and Urban Planning, University of California, Los Angeles, Calif., USA

HANSEN, Niles M., Research Scholar, Urban and Regional Systems, International Institute for Applied Systems Analysis, Schloss Laxenburg, Austria

HIGGINS, Benjamin, Vice-Dean for Research, Faculty of Social Sciences, University of Ottawa, Canada

HONJO, Masahiko, Director, United National Centre for Regional Development, Nagoya, Japan

KIM, An-Jae, Chairman, Department of Urban and Regional Planning, Graduate School of Environmental Studies, Seoul National University, Seoul, Korea

LO, Fu-chen, Chief, Comparative Studies, United Nations Centre for Regional Development, Nagoya, Japan

MATHUR, O. P., Senior Regional Planning Adviser, United Nations Development Programme, Tehran, Iran

MERA, Koichi, Professor, Institute of Socio-Economic Planning, University of Tsukuba, Ibaragi, Japan

PAKKASEM, Phisit, Director, Economic and Social Planning Division, National Economic and Social Development Board, Bangkok, Thailand

PRANTILLA, Ed. B., Regional Executive Director, National Economic and Development Authority, Region XI, Davao City, Philippines

SALIH, Kamal, Dean, School of Comparative Social Science, Universiti Sains Malaysia, Penang, Malaysia

SIGURDSON, Jon, Associate Professor, Scandinavian Institute of Asian Studies, Copenhagen, Denmark

SOEGIJOKO, Sugijanto, Dept. of Regional and City Planning, Bandung Institute of Technology, Bandung, Indonesia

INTRODUCTION

ACCELERATED INDUSTRIALIZATION AND UNEVEN DEVELOPMENT

Since the Second World War so-called developing countries, most of them just emerging from centuries of colonialism, have been advised and have undertaken through foreign assistance a strategy of accelerated industrialization in order to modernize their economies. The prescription has called for careful central planning of resource allocation, the application of technology borrowed from the advanced industrialized countries, injection of international capital for industrial development and resource exploitation through foreign investment and aid, via bilateral or multilateral arrangements, and promotion of trade structures which were to continue to support an elaborate international division of labour between primary producing countries and industrialized nations. In all these the main objective has been the active pursuit of economic growth in order to reduce the gap between the poor and rich countries and eventually to achieve a fairer sharing of development.

Over the past decades, this strategy has been successful in increasing the GNP of some countries, especially those well endowed with resources and those receiving massive foreign assistance which were able to undertake import-substitution industrialization, later expanding into export of cheap manufactures. In most cases, however, in particular the resource poor countries, the record of accelerated industrialization has been dismal, and the gap between rich and poor countries has continued to widen.

Indeed, the strategy had deepened the problems of uneven development. Deteriorating terms of trade and balance of payments problems, increasing national debt and debt service burdens, and the slow down of economic growth in the industrialized countries have all combined to rub the lustre off the dominant development strategy and has increased the dependency of Third World countries on the world metropolitan centres. At home, unemployment, food shortage, mass poverty and lack of basic needs, inflation, and general socioeconomic inequality have made the issue of uneven development very political. Attitudes toward foreign investments and technology are beginning to change, and the role of transnational corporations are being critically re-examined. The importance given to imported technology is now being replaced by efforts to identify and expand the use of more appropriate and indigeneous technology. Unstable and declining relative prices on world markets have given rise to bolder moves toward primary commodity nationalism and collective producer action. Along with pressures for renegotiation of terms of foreign debts and better access of Third World manufactures to Western markets, these have all contributed to the current debate over the form of a New International Economic Order.

In terms of regional development, unevenness is expressed in ever-increasing regional disparities within nations due to the polarization of modern industries in one or a few relatively developed regions established as part of the accelerated industrialization strategy. This polarization is further compounded by the depopulation of lagging regions and massive migration into the congested national core areas, which in turn have led to serious deterioration of urban environments, unemployment and declining real incomes, as well as to increasing costs of urban public services. In the rural areas the penetration of the capitalist industrial and commercial sector has decapacitated the potential growth of towns through competition from the capital regions and in its place created new internal dependency structures of the big city and the stagnant rural sector. This state of regional underdevelopment and unbalanced rural - urban growth is not merely due to structural rigidities within the Third World nation, but rather it in fact arises from the same incorporative process which integrates the national economies into the world capitalist system and contributes to accumulation on a world scale. It is perhaps because this fact has been largely ignored in dominant writings in regional development that the analysis has been essentially ahistorical and that strategies for regional development such as the growth pole approach are inconsistent with the real situation.

THE GROWTH POLE APPROACH

The continued underdevelopment of their peripheral areas and increasing regional disparities through polarized development in core areas have led governments of Third World countries to search for ways for regional decentralization. Development planning became regionalized, large-scale regional projects were identified and rationalized not merely on economic grounds but also for their political demonstration value. Some administrative reorganization was undertaken together with enabling legislations in many countries in order to underscore the seriousness of the government's commitment to regional equity.

In this planning environment, the growth pole approach has become a vital tool of public policy for decentralized development. Since the introduction of the concept by Perroux, the approach has been popularized through theoretical and empirical writings in the planning journals and numerous books by some of the most prominent authors in the field of regional development and planning. Actively promoted as well through international agencies, including the United Nations and its agencies, the private foundations and consultants, the idea quickly spread from Western Europe and the United States to Latin America, first in Chile then Venezuela, Brazil and so on, and finally to Africa and Asia, particularly Japan, South Korea, India and to a lesser extent Southeast Asia. The growth pole or growth centre approach is now incorporated into many national development plans as integral if not the centrepiece of their regional development strategy.

The universal appeal of the growth pole approach is amazing yet understandable. Under the growth-through-industrialization paradigm and the limiting conditions of capital and planning resource scarcities, the approach provides the opportunity to reconcile the goals of equity and efficiency considered central in regional allocation of investments. The theory's intuitive appeal rests on its two major conceptual pillars. First is the notion of agglomeration economies, which will induce concentration of propulsive industries in particularly advantageous locations in which their mutual industrial attractions and sharing of infrastructure facilities will minimize costs in a cumulative fashion to lead to self-sustained growth of the urban centre. Second, the rapid growth of the urban centre is supposed to eventually induce spread effects into the peripheral areas of the region in which the growth centre is located. The first assumption reduces the planning problem to identification of urban centres with some "potential for growth" and the allocation of public expenditure for urban infrastructure development. On the other hand, the second assumption serves as a political palliative to the initial spatially discriminatory policy, which through subsequent expansion of a system of growth centres and hierarchical diffusion progressively it is thought, integrates all the regional economies to the long-run benefit of the entire country and its people.

This model of regional development, along with the linear integration development paradigm mentioned earlier, has in recent years come under severe criticism. Not only have its theoretical foundations been found to be weak and wanting elaboration in order to reduce its terminological and conceptual confusion, but its application to real situations in many cases has also revealed its empirical shortcomings. Besides the practical problem of identification and determining the number, location and time phasing of growth centre investments, which perhaps can technically be solved, the real issues are associated with the impacts of growth centres on regional development. While the role of agglomeration economies remains a thorny issue, and further studies need to be made on their true nature, at least the fact of spontaneous urban growth suggests their existence. But the problem is really not whether they exist or not, rather what other sources of self-sustained regional growth can be generated which do not lead to spatial polarization, for there is hardly any case where the strategy has been implemented in which the spread effects imputed to growth centre development have been demonstrated to operate in reality. Indeed, the situation has appeared to be to the contrary. Namely, that development poles, to the extent that they really exist, in most cases either became an enclave without pole-periphery linkages or merely distort the pattern of regional development in an under-developed economy, and have led, through leakage beyond regional and even national boundaries, to the stagnation of the rural sector.

The adoption of the growth pole approach by many Third World countries reflects two underlying forms of wishful thinking: first, that industrialization with modern technology can be decentralized to the benefit of rural areas, and, second, that national integration through the growth pole strategy can solve the problem of regional underdevelopment. These myths need to be debunked. There is need to reassess the strategy in the particular context of prevailing conditions in the Third World, in this case in Asia, by referring to their level and stage of development, their dependency on the major industrial powers, their resource endowment, demographic situation, and technological requirements. In addition, such a reassessment is necessary in light of the shifting development paradigm and the search for a New International Economic Order.

ORGANIZATION OF ARTICLES

In bringing together the articles appearing in this volume, two organizing principles are followed. First, recognizing that policy emerges from a distinct milieu of experience, practical concerns and development aspirations, an understanding of how the growth pole concept is perceived and defined in the nations of Asia is thought to be critical to any evaluation of the implementation of growth pole strategies. Although all growth pole approaches may be said to have common roots in the idea of "concentrated decentralization", even this basic concept varies from nation to nation. In South Korea and Japan the growth pole approach has been invoked in a style of explicit decentralization of industrial growth and development. Both nations, as have been demonstrated in the Mizushima and Ulsan cases, analysed by Lo and Kim respectively, have registered some success with the decentralization goal. Honjo's article on the Japanese experience illustrates, however, that the growth pole approach, even in these countries, may be appropriate only to a specific historical phase of development, reflecting prevailing conditions and stages of development which are reflected in turn in changing planning objectives.

The Japanese and Korean approaches may be contrasted with the growth pole strategies of the Southeast Asian nations (Indonesia, Malaysia, the Philippines and Thailand), which are at a level of testing the concept as a response to recognized internal development disparities. As demonstrated by the Salih *et al.* paper, in Southeast Asia these nascent schemes have a dual concern: decentralization of polarized economic development and mobilization of latent natural resources in national frontier areas. On the other hand, in South Asia, represented in Mathur's paper on the Indian experience, the emphasis is on reduction of internal disparities from a local regional-based development perspective. Finally, in contrast to these centring policies, the distinction between decentralization from above and resource-based regional development strategies from below is most clearly exemplified by Sigurdson's discussion of regional planning in China, which has adopted an explicit policy of rural-based development with an emphasis on rural industrialization. The Chinese experience may well be compared with the Indian approach to find a clue as to how to solve the problem of uneven development on a mass scale.

The second objective in the organization of this volume is to examine the validity of the growth pole approach from a variety of policy perspectives. Higgins' paper sets the stage for this analysis by questioning different growth pole concepts in relation to their usefulness as policy instruments. Taking one aspect of the manifold growth pole objectives, Mera, on the other hand, uses the Japanese experience to suggest that decentralization can be achieved by the national economic system through the market mechanism at a later stage of industrial development. Mera asserts, therefore, that the efficiency of polarized development should be followed in the early stages of development before any decentralized growth pole policy can be effectively implemented. In also supporting this view, Hansen looks at the settlement system in relation to its role in the development process and as a lever for the solution of the problem of persistent poverty.

Both Mera's and Hansen's views stand in strong contrast to those of Friedmann and Douglass. In introducing an "agropolitan" approach to regional planning, the emphasis is explicitly placed on bottom-up rather than top-down development planning and implementation. This again relates to the distinction made by Sigurdson between decentralization and rural mobilization approaches in Asian regional development. The Friedmann - Douglass approach also emerges as a critique of the urban-biased growth-oriented approaches and their impact on the spatial patterns of development, particularly in the developing countries of Asia. Their recommendations for regional planning thus reflect scepticism of Mera's and Hansen's thesis concerning the nature and role of market mechanisms in reducing disparities in the foreseeable future.

Taking the growth pole approach from the point of view of both an efficiency and a welfare consideration, Lo and Salih use the Asian context to evaluate the experience of industrialization policies under the import-substitution strategy. In explaining the pattern of internal disparities in both their regional and urban - rural forms, which are due to this strategy, the authors introduce the concept of comparative urban efficiency, including its sectoral distinctions, in order to rationalize the differential impact of a growth-centre-based decentralization policy. The analysis is carried further to the identification of regional policy issues related to both regional economic efficiency and the absorption of labour as the major problem of Asian development and recommends a balanced rural - urban strategy of regional development.

PROLOGUE TO AN EPILOGUE

This collection of articles does not necessarily fit into a neat framework aimed at a thorough analysis of experience with the growth pole approach in Asia nor does it comprise a comprehensive study of the alternative approaches. Such organization is not possible from the start with any endeavour involving highly independent contributions and such diverse viewpoints, experience and positions. Thus, a thorough critique of the theory and strategy of growth poles or centres, based on sound empirical and historical impact analysis, is still to be written, although some recent works are worth noting. At the same time, the search for effective alternative approaches—not necessarily amounting to a total rejection of the growth pole thesis—appropriate to the particular national condition and possibly complementary to the growth pole approach, must at the same time await the findings of sound empirical research on internal dependency structures in an open economy, on the leakage phenomenon, on the role of social institutions and formations, and generally on the processes and structures of regional underdevelopment.

Nonetheless, a number of points related to the thread of the argument must be borne in mind when reading this book. First, because of the different levels of development, prevailing conditions and historical stage of growth in relation to the world economic system, there appears to be a notion of the "appropriateness" of the growth pole approach at different phases in the development of a country. In other words, different countries exhibit different capacities to adopt the growth pole strategy and enjoy or suffer its consequences in terms of its position in development on a world scale. Yet the dominant view is that the growth pole approach is context-free and is a universal strategy for the purpose of accelerating industrialization in a spatial welfare context—much to the same extent and sense as industrialization has been advocated as the universal path of Third World economic growth.

The second point is that, having debunked the notion of universality of growth pole strategy, there is a need to consider what complementary or alternative regional development strategies would be required to achieve the different development goals of the underdeveloped countries. In this sense, under certain conditions, the growth pole approach is only a partial solution to the problem of regional underdevelopment.

Third, in order to achieve this it is essential that regional theory and regional development strategy be located properly within the framework of overall national development processes as well as their international economic relations. In addition, with the shift in the paradigm of development, the beginning of which is evident in recent years but which is still not completely defined yet, the role and function of the growth pole strategy in this broad context may have to be re-examined. It follows that we should see what the particular perceptions of Asian countries are toward the growth pole approach and then induce a reorientation of the regional strategy to suit their development needs.

On the other hand, the theory itself must also be reconsidered. To the extent that it will remain useful as a conditional theory of accelerated regional development, its concepts, such as juxtaposition economies, linkages to extra-local entities and their labour absorptive capacities, all need to be tightened and given a sounder empirical basis. At the same time alternative and complementary ideas, such as the agropolitan approach, must be developed and tested. In this connection perhaps it is time to get away from the impasse concerning the efficiency of large cities *per se* and go on to studying and solving the issue in relation to small towns and rural areas in general. We need to correct the urban bias that has crept into regional theory if the problems of regional underdevelopment in the

Third World are to be solved, and in doing this urban and rural structures and processes cannot be separated, but in fact should be analysed in terms of urban - rural relations.

This leads us to the final point. As mentioned earlier, a meaningful consideration of regional development policy cannot be undertaken in isolation of the larger developmental structures and processes. The causal connection between spatial policy and development policy is circular, complex and fundamental to regional development. To develop more effective strategies we must avoid the pitfalls of spatial *naïveté* by not merely considering spatial structures and processes but more importantly by investigating their interface with socioeconomic and institutional change and the broader causes and consequences of uneven development. It is hoped that this collection of readings based on Asian experiences can be seen as a first step toward a better understanding of regional development processes and policy alternatives in the Third World.

PART I

Asian Case Studies in Decentralization Policy and the Growth Pole Approach

1

TRENDS IN DEVELOPMENT PLANNING IN JAPAN

MASAHIKO HONJO

INTRODUCTION

More than thirty years have passed since the end of World War II. Japan has achieved high economic growth through industrial development and has urbanized at a rapid pace. Economic growth and urbanization have brought a greater GNP to the Japanese people but at the same time, as a result of such development, they are faced with a number of domestic problems, such as deficiencies in social development and aggravation of environmental disruption.

The problems should also be observed in light of the international situation. Being a country without resources, Japan had to develop by expanding her international trade. The promotion of exporting manufactured products and the import of necessary raw materials was imperative, and little thought was given to limitations inherent in these expansions. The national land was metamorphosized to accommodate increased involvement in international trade over the decades.

Now the world situation is changing. The imbalance in development between the developed and developing countries is becoming a serious issue. Nations of the developing world, especially those with natural resources, are becoming more aware of national sovereignty over their resources. The energy crisis of 1973 sounded a strong alarm against the exclusive and unlimited utilization of the world's resources by the developed countries.

Those two problems, internal as well as external, are posing to Japan the urgent necessity to seriously seek new ways to fit herself into the new realities of the world.

The purpose of this paper is to examine how national development plans were formulated and implemented at each stage of economic development from the end of the war up to now. It is intended to look into the concepts that underlie such plans as they respond to the emerging situation, rather than to evaluate their content. Since the present situation is so fluid, I would hope to make a further review looking toward the years to come.

Regional planning in Japan is undertaken by government agencies at different levels - central government ministries divided by functions, prefectural governments, and municipal governments - and the scope of planning differs from agency to agency. In this context, it may be said to be pluralistic. However, one point to be mentioned in the Japanese post-war development process is the establishment of a comprehensive planning function

3

at each level of this pluralistic set-up. It first started in the central government under the Economic Planning Agency and gradually became independent of the budgeting and implementation functions as an agency that provides the implementing agencies with guidelines. What the Economic Planning Agency has conceived seems to provide the clearest image of the comprehensive planning ideology in Japan—at least up to recently. Therefore, in the following I would like to try to outline the trends in post-war development, focusing on the plans formulated at the national level by that Agency.

The post-war Japanese economy may be divided into the following developmental periods, and each period will be considered separately below (Fig. 1)[1].

Developmental stage	Period	Per capita GNP ($US at 1965 price)
Period of post-war reconstruction	Late 1940s to early 1950s	150 - 300
Period of industrialization		
First stage	Late 1950s	300 - 500
Second stage	1961 - 7	500 - 1000
Period of post-industrialization		
First stage	1968 - 74	1000 - 2000
Second stage	Since 1975	Over 2000

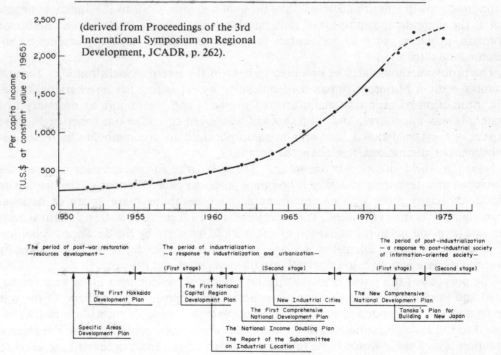

Fig. 1. The trend of *per capita* income

[1]See Noboru Nishifuji, Perspective of regional development planning in Japan, in *The Third International Symposium on Regional Development,* Japan Centre for Area Development Research, 1970; Keizai Shingikai Sogo Bukai (ed.), *Nihon no Keizai Keikaku (Economic Planning in Japan),* Okura—Sho Insatsu-kyoku, 1969; Keizai Kikaku-cho Sogo Kaihatsu-kyoku (ed.), *Shin Keizai Shakai Hatten Keikaku no Zembo (An Outline of the New Economic and Social Development Plan),* Keizai Kikaku Kyokai, 1970.

1. THE PERIOD OF POST-WAR RECONSTRUCTION

1.1. Economic Planning

The first stage was the period of emergency reconstruction. Japan suffered great damage in the Pacific War. Large areas of cities were reduced to ashes and most production facilities were destroyed by Allied bombing; overseas colonies were lost. National land was devastated by the lack of proper maintenance. The national population increased at a rapid rate due to the repatriation of military and civilian personnel from abroad, and employment had to be created for such people. The economy was paralysed; inflation was accelerating. First of all, minimal emergency assistance had to be extended to the devastated cities, and at the same time the measures to check inflation and to resume production of necessities had to be stepped up. Parallel to this, Japan had to do away with militarism and to start herself as a democratic country under the direction of the occupation forces. SCAP (Supreme Command for the Allied Powers) demanded that the Japanese Government enforce a series of measures for the democratization of the country, including the liquidation of *zaibatsu*[2], land reform, and reform of the educational system. Much of the remaining production equipment was taken out of the country as reparations, and the former war industries had to be quickly transformed into industries producing for the domestic market. Several years passed while the state of affairs remained in confusion. It cannot be denied, however, that even in those hectic years foundations were being laid for new political, economic, and cultural development in Japan in the following decade.

The Economic Stabilization Board was created under this situation. It was something like a compact version of the Japanese Government, representing a variety of its functions in contact with SCAP. Therefore, much power was concentrated in this Board, such as the drafting of the comprehensive economic survey, long-range economic planning, allocation of materials, budgeting, and supervision of public works carried out by respective ministries. In view of this importance, ministries seconded well-informed staff to this Board, and this presented a good opportunity of making experts in different ministries work together. As the emergency period passed, the power thus concentrated was taken back to the ministries, but the function of drafting the comprehensive economic (and social) survey and of long-range planning remained with the Board and have become its main functions. This Board is the forerunner of the present Economic Planning Agency.

The Five-year Economic Rehabilitation Plan was drafted in 1948 by the Economic Stabilization Board. It was the first plan of its kind in Japan and served as a model for many later plans. It aimed at bolstering production, keeping inflation under control, and at restoring the Japanese economy to the prewar (1930 - 4) level within five years. In other words, its main strategy was to seek the shortest critical path to "make the pie larger". To begin with it gave highest priority to the reconstruction of the fundamental sectors of the economy. Scarce resources in investment and materials were to be concentrated in these sectors (*keisha-seisan*). Five priority objectives were identified: (1) disinflation, (2) promotion of exports, (3) production of electricity, coal and steel, and strengthening of transportation, (4) increase in food production, and (5) rehabilitation and prevention of natural disasters (especially by flood).

In selecting those objectives, self-sufficiency was one of the main concerns. It was thought very important to improve the balance of international payment by increasing

---

[2]Financial oligopoly.

the amount of home products. Therefore electricity meant hydraulic power generation, food meant the increase in the production of staple food, especially of rice, by reclamation. It is to be noted that coal was one of the priority sectors, although at present it is a declined industry. (The present energy crisis of the world may revive this industry again.) Rehabilitation and prevention of natural disasters had to be stressed, as the lack of maintenance and repair of national land (especially for flood control) had caused so much damage by the successive typhoons that hit Japan during the wartime. It should also be noted that no such priority was given to either the reconstruction of cities which faced a rare opportunity for the implementation of rational planning or housing which everyone thought to be of urgent need. Indeed, it was a straightforward manifestation of austere policy to put stress on economic growth, appealing to the nation to sacrifice its well-being until the "pie" became larger. The plan, however, was not officially adopted by the Cabinet because it did not accord with the SCAP policy of stopping inflation at one stroke through a balanced budget.

Looking into the government investment in public works, we find that still further stress was put on flood control and disaster rehabilitation. Their share occupied nearly two-thirds of the total. Investment in agricultural reclamation, emergency public housing, and the reconstruction of cities, which enjoyed a big share just after the war, met serious compression towards 1950. Road construction, which at present occupies a substantial share of public works budget, was still inactive, enjoying only about 10 per cent of the share. In fact, it was the pressure from the rural areas which suffered from successive typhoon damages that forced the enlargement of the share of government investment in public works exclusively in the sector of flood control.

1.2. National Land Development Planning

The comprehensive National Land Development Law was enacted in 1950. The law stipulates that the national land development plan be formulated at each of the hierarchic levels, national, regional, prefectural, and Specific Areas (*tokutei-chiiki*). The last category is defined by criteria stipulated by the law, such as underdeveloped natural resources areas, natural disaster prone areas, and urban and/or fringe areas which need urgent improvement. National investment is to be concentrated in those areas to meet drastic development needs. From this outlook, the law seems to be structured in quite a logical way. However, the real motive that promoted the enactment of this law was political pressure from the underdeveloped regions to have their areas nominated as one of the "Specific Development Areas" (*tokutei-kaihatsu-chiiki*). The rectifying of imbalances in development between the regions was the main cause of this law, and, therefore, it attracted policy makers of underdeveloped regions to which little attention had so far been given by the central government. A sole ministry, namely, the Ministry of Construction, was promoting this enactment of the law. However, because of the comprehensive nature of this law dealing with the problems of land use, it inevitably provoked disagreement with other ministries who were responsible for sectoral interests. Eventually, the Economic Stabilization Board had to represent the other ministries in counteracting the Ministry of Construction, and in doing so it had to maintain the pursuit of economic efficiency as the natural outcome of the Economic Rehabilitation Plan which it had worked out.

The enactment of the Comprehensive National Land Development Law was the outcome of the compromise of such conflict between the ministries. Under this law, the

Economic Stabilization Board was designated to be responsible for its implementation, and the Ministry of Construction was given the role to represent the interest of the local government. The important fact is that two factors in the national land development planning, namely, economic efficiency and the rectifying of imbalance in development, were put into the spotlight as conflicting positions from the very beginning. The process that followed shows how Japanese policy in national land development swayed in between those two positions.

Following the enactment of the law, nineteen underdeveloped areas were designated as Specific Development Areas at the end of 1951. This set the precedent for the favoured treatment of Specific Areas. In subsequent years, many other areas followed in requesting similar special assistance from the central government, and many such laws as those aiming at the development of remote islands or areas prone to typhoon damage, soil erosion, and/or heavy snowfall were enacted in the same way as this law.

The Specific Areas thus designated came to cover an extremely wide land area, and thus resulted in "spreading the butter thinner over the bread". The central government's assistance to them turned out to be much smaller than expected. On the other hand, economic reality made it imperative to concentrate on rehabilitating the advanced areas for efficiency's sake. To the disappointment of advocates for the rectifying of imbalance in development and of the people in these areas, underdeveloped areas were again left behind.

2. THE PERIOD OF INDUSTRIALIZATION (FIRST STAGE): THE LATE 1950s

2.1. Economic Planning

The Korean War, which broke out in 1950, had great impact on the Japanese economy that was steadily recovering from war damage. The growth rate of the Japanese economy was speeded up, and in 1955 the Japanese economy recovered to its pre-war level. The problem in this period was how to make the Japanese economy a self-supporting one. Up to this period, Japan's favourable trade balance had been maintained by US aid totalling two billion dollars and special procurement by the US Forces totalling three billion dollars. To restore and maintain the favourable trade balance by normal means at the earliest possible date was the immediate task facing the Japanese economy.

The Five-year Economic Self-supporting Plan of 1955 was the first economic plan adopted by the Japanese government. The first objective of the plan was to achieve the favourable trade balance mentioned above. Among the other objectives was the expansion of economic activity and employment in response to the expected increase in the working-age population, a result of the sharp post-war population increase. Needless to say, the plan emphasized industrial development to achieve these objectives. The annual economic growth rate was expected to be 5 per cent.

Subsequent economic development, however, surpassed the projected growth rate of the plan. Increases in industrial production and trade were conspicuous, and the projected goal of the plan was almost achieved two years after the plan was formulated.

2.2. Progress in Physical Development

One of the most striking evidences of rapid progress in industrial development was the construction of coastal industrial complex. Prospects of accelerated demands for heavy and chemical industrial products, as indicated by the economic plans, prompted big enterprises to invest willingly in plants and equipment in heavy and chemical industries. The location of these industries on coastal land offered decisive advantages to Japan which had to import all important raw materials by sea. The shift of energy sources from hydroelectricity and coal to petroleum, and the advance in reclamation technology that made possible the large-scale, low-cost development of coastal land adjacent to large ports, provided additional advantages. The construction of industrial complexes centring on steel and petrochemical industries was begun in the early 1950s in Tokyo and Ise Bays.

In the initial stage, some of these industrial complexes were former military facilities. For example, the fuel supply depots of defunct Imperial Navy in Yokkaichi and Tokuyama were transformed into petrochemical industrial complexes. In some cases it was a venture of enterprise combined with the industrial aspirations of prefectural governments, such as the steel mill at Chiba Port near Tokyo. Agglomeration economies invited related industries into these areas. The areas rapidly expanded and induced drastic transformations of surrounding areas, eventually leading to environmental disruption.

One noteworthy fact in this period was the creation of public corporations as new entities entrusted with executing projects related to social overhead capital. Up to then social overhead capital investment had been carried out exclusively by government agencies. First established was the Japan Housing Corporation (1955). Whereas progress was made in economic recovery, the housing situation showed little progress. The Japan Housing Corporation was created to provide public housing over the region in addition to local governments' public housing within their administrative boundaries. It became a model for public corporations established later. In 1956 the Japan Public Highway Corporation, entrusted with the construction of toll expressways throughout the country, was established. Delay in road construction was as serious a problem as the housing shortage.

These public corporations began to work efficiently as soon as they were established. The scale of their activities accelerated as the years went by. The impact they had on the local communities became too large for the latter to absorb. Since corporations were independent from the local governments, this eventually resulted in raising many disputes.

3. THE PERIOD OF INDUSTRIALIZATION (SECOND STAGE): 1961-7

3.1. Economic Planning

As was mentioned earlier, the growth of the economy in the late 1950s was about 10 per cent per year, much higher than the projected rate. The factors that contributed to the growth were, among others, favourable conditions in foreign trade—an expansion of export and an increase in the import volume due to a drop in import prices—and a sharp increase in gross national fixed capital formation centring on investments in plants and equipment. Reflecting these circumstances, a more positive attitude toward economic development was demonstrated. On the other hand, however, the sustained economic growth came to expose many structural deficiencies such as, *inter alia,* a shortage of social overhead capital, environmental disruption, and a widening of inequality among regions and economic sectors.

The Income-doubling Plan of 1960 was formulated against such a background under the strong leadership of Prime Minister Ikeda with his commitment to economic growth. It was designed to increase the *per capita* income of the Japanese people from about $500 in the late 1950s to $1000 by the end of the 1960s. As its name implied, the plan had great appeal and was quite unlike previous economic plans in its tone. To achieve the goal, the annual growth rate of 7 - 8 per cent was to be maintained, and through such high growth the improvement of the standard of living and full employment were to be realized. In this sense it was again the plan to make the "pie" larger. However, it should be noted that concern was given to the social problems which became evident as a result of economic growth. As the means to achieve these goals, the plan stressed, larger investment in social overhead capital, sophistication of industrial structure, promotion of international trade and economic co-operation, development of human resources, protection and support of low-productivity sectors of the economy, and maintenance of societal stability (in other words, the promotion of social development). As such, it was different from the previous plans that were exclusively concerned with the expansion of economic bases.

The Income-doubling Plan created the concept of the "Pacific Coast Belt Scheme" as its areal expression. To achieve the goal of the plan, it was estimated that in ten years' time industrial production had to be increased fourfold. Since it would be difficult to accommodate such a high level of industrial activity within the four overcrowded industrial areas of Tokyo, Osaka, Nagoya, and Kita-Kyushu, it was considered necessary to disperse industry from the existing industrial areas. It was proposed that industry be dispersed throughout the Pacific Coast Belt connecting the four industrial areas mentioned above and that investment in social overhead capital be concentrated on the belt to improve public facilities such as ports and harbours and highways. As for areas outside the belt, it was proposed that growth poles[3] be selected from among them and that the basic facilities that would enable the development of large-scale industrial areas in such growth poles to be gradually constructed.

Economic planning was further elaborated. The Mid-term Economic Plan of 1965 was the first case in which econometric modelling was applied. This technique has been incorporated in subsequent planning works.

3.2. National Land Development Planning

The Comprehensive National Land Development Plan as stipulated by the Comprehensive National Land Development Law of 1950 was formulated for the first time in 1962. On the one hand, the plan was an application of the concept in the Income-doubling Plan to the problem of national land development, and, on the other hand, it pursued the objective of rectifying regional inequity and eliminating deficiencies arising from overcrowding—ideas dominant in comprehensive national land development from the very beginning.

Japan's regional structure was undergoing radical change in this period due to industrial development. Capital, technology, production, and the labour force came to be concentrated in the advanced areas. For example, the total population of the three largest metro-

---

[3]The word "growth pole" is used here to represent the Japanese word *kaihatsu kyoten* (development base), which means the strategic point where investment will be concentrated to induce the development of surrounding areas.

politan regions, namely those centred at Tokyo, Nagoya, and Osaka,[4] which accounted for 31.2 per cent of the national population in 1955, increased to 33.7 per cent in 1960 and further continued to increase. In large metropolitan areas where such concentrations took place, especially in Tokyo and Osaka, the disadvantages of overcrowding rather than the advantages of agglomerations came to be strongly argued. In rural areas, on the other hand, the population not only decreased but also aged, due to the migration of residents, especially young ones, to cities; in some areas it became difficult to maintain basic community services such as public safety, education, and medical care; thus depopulation intensified. Solutions to both overcrowding and depopulation had to be found in regional terms.

The Comprehensive National Land Development Plan was formulated against this background. The plan aimed at achieving balanced economic growth and dispersing industrial and urban development not only in the Pacific Coast Belt but throughout the country. As a means to achieve this goal, the plan focused on the growth pole scheme and the regional centres scheme. The country was divided into three areas: (1) "overconcentrated areas" (large metropolitan areas); (2) "adjustment areas" (those surrounding "overconcentrated areas"); and (3) "development areas" (underdeveloped northeast, the Japan Sea coast, and southernmost areas). It was proposed that growth poles be designated and fostered as strategic areas for industrial development in areas outside "overconcentrated areas", and that selected local cities were to be fostered as regional centres that would serve as nodes of the national network of central management functions.

The plan was followed by legislative action for implementation. Several ministries competed in taking leadership in the enactment of the law for the designation of the "growth poles". As the result, the Law for the Promotion of Industrial Development (*kaihatsu*) in Underdeveloped Areas (1961), the Law for the Promotion of New Industrial City Construction (*kensetsu*) (1962), and the Law for the Promotion of Development (*seibi*) of Special Industrial Development Areas (1964) were enacted successively for this purpose.

The designations of the "new industrial cities" and "special industrial development areas" became a serious political issue for local interests in candidate areas. Chief executives of local governments in candidate areas vied with each other to receive these designations. Under political pressure, the number of growth poles, which should be few in principle, was increased. Finally, in 1963, fifteen areas were designated as "new industrial cities" primarily in "development areas", six "special industrial improvement areas" were designated mainly in "adjustment areas" along the Pacific Coast Belt; and more than 100 "small-scale industrial development areas" were designated in "development areas" (Fig. 2).

With the designation of these areas, the Law Concerning the Special Arrangement of National Finance for these areas was enacted in 1965, providing for national assistance in the issuance of prefectural bonds for development and to local expenditures incurred by towns and villages in the areas.

3.3. Progress in Physical Development

Together with the growth of the economy, the increase in the role of the construction sector came to be strongly felt. Large-scale projects, started several years before, such

---

[4]Metropolitan regions including neighbouring prefectures, each consisting of four, two and three prefectures around Tokyo, Nagoya, and Osaka respectively, totalling 10.6 per cent of the national land.

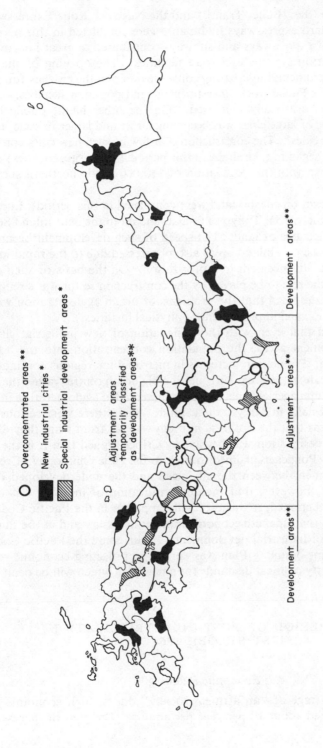

*Designated by specific laws in 1963.
**Classification according to the 1962 comprehensive national land development plan.

Fig. 2. New industrial cities and special industrial development areas (1963).

as the New Tokaido Line (the "Bullet Train") and the Nagoya - Kobe Expressway (the first of the modern standard expressways in Japan), were completed in this period. In Tokyo the construction of expressways and subways contributed to great improvements in intra-urban transportation systems and road facilities. The opening of the Tokyo Olympics of 1964 was instrumental in creating consensus among the citizens for pushing such construction forward. Public works investment in transportation facilities, especially in road construction, was drastically increased. On the other hand, public housing development in the suburbs of large cities was becoming larger and larger in scale, resulting in the development of new cities[5]. The construction of a few of such new cities commenced in the late 1950s and they began to take shape in this period. The largest of these housing projects is Senri New Town with the population of 150,000 in the northern suburbs of Osaka.

Many industrial complexes on coastal land were completed in this period. Located on the Pacific Coast Belt, namely from Tokyo to Osaka, and on to the Seto Inland Sea, they each covered some 1000 hectares of land. The speed of such development became even faster. Industrial development in inland areas also progressed due to the rapid improvement of road systems and advancement in motorization. On the basis of such circumstances, the confidence in the role to be played by the construction sector was strengthened, and the feeling became widespread that the problems of urban agglomeration would be solved through the expansion and improvement of physical facilities.

It should be mentioned that even with the designation of new industrial cities and special industrial development areas, the population concentration into the advanced regions did not slow down. Population increases in metropolitan regions continued, and industries continued to locate in the areas surrounding big urban centres rather than in the designated areas. Central managerial functions even increased in agglomeration in the big metropolitan centres, especially in Tokyo, the capital. Again there were serious claims from those designated areas that the progress in them was far from what they expected and their effort to invite designation was betrayed. Critics argued that it is the failure of the government policy. Politicians claimed to stick to the basic philosophy of rectifying the imbalance in development between the advanced and the underdeveloped regions.

It would be fair to say, however, that the decentralization of industry was actually taking place. As above-mentioned, it was especially apparent in the Pacific Coast Belt. The growth in the scale of the Japanese economy made it necessary and at the same time feasible to expand areas for industrial development. In this sense the Pacific Coast Belt concept of the 1960 Income-doubling Plan was correct in reflecting economic realities. However, it could not satisfy political demands for a new plan which will be dealt with in section 4.2.

4. THE PERIOD OF POST-INDUSTRIALIZATION
(FIRST STAGE): 1968-74

4.1. Economic Planning

Japan entered into the stage of "an affluent society" due to high economic growth in the 1960s which averaged about 10 per cent per annum. The goal of increasing per

---

[5]New cities in this case do not include industrial area development and are predominantly residential.

capita income to the $1000 in the Income-doubling Plan of 1960 was accomplished in 1968, two years ahead of the target year. Japan's international balance of payments became favourable, and she changed from an aid-receiving to an aid-giving nation. Urbanization and industrialization proceeded at a rapid pace; in 1968 about half of the population lived in DIDs (densely inhabited districts)[6]. In this regard, it may be said that Japan has entered into the stage of a highly industrialized society.

In spite of rapid economic growth, however, the structural contradictions in the economy—problems carried over from the preceding decade—remained unsolved. "Distortions" came to be felt even more keenly. The advance of urbanization and the increase in productive activity made more clearly visible such problems as the lag in the improvement of the standard of living, the shortage of social overhead capital, overcrowding in urban areas and depopulation in rural villages, and environmental disruption. The Japanese economy experienced a widespread labour shortage for the first time in its history; at the same time the low productivity of small- and medium-scale enterprises, especially in services and retailing, due to structural deficiencies, became evident. The prices of land skyrocketed due to increasing demand arising from urban concentration and the inadequacy of land policy. All this led to an accelerated increase in commodity prices. Balanced rather than merely quantitative growth of the economy—in other words, emphasis on social aspects—became a key issue in this period.

The Economic and Social Development Plan of 1967 was formulated against such a background. In the plan reflections mentioned above were incorporated, and the name of the plan itself included the term "social development" as well as "economic development". The three major goals of the plan were: (1) stabilization of commodity prices, (2) efficiency of the economy, and (3) social development. Unlike the previous economic plans focused on economic growth, this plan attempted to deal with the problems arising from the internationalization of the economy and from the labour shortage, and to achieve stable rather than rapid economic growth by emphasizing social development.

4.2. Comprehensive National Land Development Planning

In response to the expanded scale of the economy, the New Comprehensive National Land Development Plan[7] was formulated in 1969. Again this was the National Land Development version of the Economic and Social Development Plan, but it could be argued that this plan did not necessarily reflect the latter directly; rather, this was an ambitious application of the concept of growth poles, which had been developed in the Comprehensive National Land Development Plan, to the proposal of creating the new national network. The background of the plan was described as follows:[8]

---

[6]A DID is an area where more than 5000 people cluster in a density of over 4000 per km². Administratively urban areas mean the areas included in cities (*shi*) as designated by law, although this includes areas for non-urban use, such as farms and forests. Following this definition the population in urban areas was about 70 per cent in 1967.

[7]Official terminology used is New National Comprehensive Development Plan. However, for consistency in expression, the word "Land" is still kept in this paper.

[8]Hitoshi Miyazaki (ed.), *Shin Zenkoku Sogo Kaihatsu Keikaku no Kaisetsu (An Explanation of the New Comprehensive National Development Plan)*, Tokyo, Nihon Keizai Shimbun-sha, 1969. Also refer to Economic Planning Agency, *New Comprehensive National Development Plan*, 1969, and Economic Planning Agency, The New Comprehensive National Development Plan (summary), *Area Development in Japan*, No. 3, 1970, pp. 24-29.

A century has passed since the Meiji Restoration that marked Japan's emergence as a modern state. The national structures that supported Japan's subsequent development were all conceived and constructed by the Meiji Government in the early years of the Meiji Period. Since high economic growth in post-war Japan was rapidly achieved on the basis of such old systems (national structures), overcrowding and depopulation problems, problems of regional inequity, etc., have been brought about. On the other hand, Japan's capacity for investment has been tremendously expanded, and there is a need for developing new national structures on a long-term basis.

The plan envisaged new structure to run through the country. It proposed that new networks of trunk railway lines, expressways, and communications be constructed to form the new axis of the country and that central managerial functions and physical distribution structure be reorganized around this axis in such a manner as to lay new foundations for the fullest utilization of the limited national land in the future. It also proposed to locate and implement large-scale projects in agriculture, industry, commerce, recreation, conservation, and urban development in relation to this new network. In this way, the new network was expected to sustain comprehensive development in the future and to guarantee balanced utilization of the national land (Fig. 3).

I would like to argue that this was an attempt to answer the long-standing question of reconciling the basic controversy in national land development: economic efficiency versus balanced development. The plan was based on the forecast that the Japanese economy would continue to grow, and as a result the total land of this small archipelago would have to be fully utilized. It was a proposal to equalize opportunity for development over the whole national land by creating the new network. In fact, with the development of technology such as the "Bullet Train", on the one hand, and the huge scale of economy as against the limited area of the national land, on the other hand, the plan was very persuasive to the policy makers at local level who were still anxious to have more development in their areas, as well as to the industrialists who were looking for new sites of expansion. As the aggregate scale of the Japanese economy grew, so did the scale per unit of industrial complexes. It was estimated that the future size of one such unit would be 5000 hectares with corresponding capacity of water, power, cargo-handling and output. It is impossible to acquire such a site in the already developed areas, while the economics of scale seems to justify the creation of necessary infrastructure. The "large-scale projects" to be related to the "network" included the construction of such big industrial bases in the most remote areas of Japan, where no such development has been feasible so far.

These are the reasons that this new plan was accepted with favourable response when it was made public. In other words, people felt that with this plan the growth in scale of the Japanese economy brought the long-sought answer to a controversial problem in regional development policy.

4.3. Change in the Basic Trend: The Turning Point

EXPO '70, held in Osaka in 1970, was another showcase of concerted achievement in large-scale construction. As in the case of the Tokyo Olympics, many construction projects around the area, including those projects carried over from the preceding period, were undertaken simultaneously and intensively, and were all completed before EXPO '70 opened. As a result, the infrastructure servicing the area—the expansion of the airport, the construction of Expressway System in the Kinki (Osaka, Kyoto, and Kobe) Region,

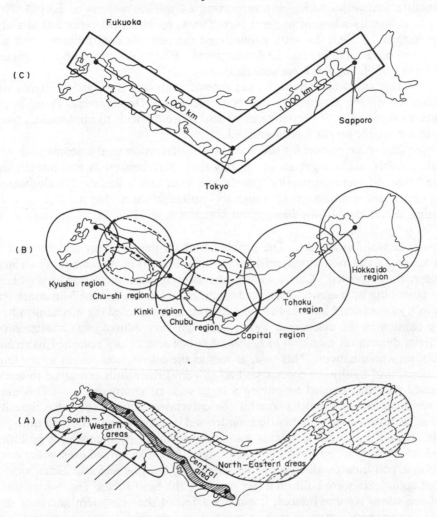

Fig. 3. Idea of the "New Comprehensive National Land Development Plan".

Source: *Area Development in Japan*, No. 3, 1970, p. 29.

(A) Present land use in Japan is polarized in the central area along the Pacific Coastal Belt ▨. The north-eastern areas with heavy snowfall ▨, and the south-western areas with frequent attack of typhoon ▨ are left underdeveloped, notwithstanding their wide land resources. These areas have been very much handicapped by their natural environment, but progress in technology and the expansion of the scale of the Japanese economy is now making their development possible.

(B) In order to disperse the concentrated land use into wider regions, the total national land is divided into seven regions, and the development will be promoted by injecting the central managerial functions into the big urban centres of respective regions, and by connecting them by the new network.

(C) When the new network is fully utilized with intensified communication and high-speed transportation activities, the total Japanese Archipelago of 2000 km in length will function as one whole entity.

and the extension of subway lines—was drastically improved. In fact the whole of this infrastructure was responsible for transporting 64 million visitors to EXPO '70. The EXPO site is directly adjacent to Senri New Town, to which reference has already been made in section 3.3. All this setting illustrated the possible contribution which a large-scale project could make in regional development. EXPO drummed up the consensus of ⁻the people in completing this large undertaking.

However, this might have been the last case of such concerted action. Even with the persuasiveness of the Comprehensive National Land Development Plan, large-scale development projects were becoming more and more difficult to implement. Necessary consensus among the people has diminished.

The most important reason for this was the dissatisfaction of the people with what the economic growth had brought about. Surely the "pie" became larger, but the share of the "pie" was different from what people had expected it to be. Development plans brought up hordes of antagonists through its implementation. Let me pick up the issues underlining the change in the basic trend which was guiding Japan towards a turning point.

(a) Environmental Disruption. The problems which development had brought about, such as air and water pollution, traffic noise and congestion, became more strongly felt as development proceeded. Citizen awareness was even more intensified by such notorious cases as poisoning by mercury, PCB, cadmium, etc. The case of the Minamata fertilizer factory in Kyushu Island became the most famous as it revealed the mechanism by which mercury content in the discharged water, although very diluted, was accumulated as it passed from deposit on plankton to bellies of fishes and finally poisoned fishermen and their families who ate them. This case, as well as the others, was fought a very long time in the courts, and finally the companies had to admit their guilt and come to terms with the damage they had caused by paying a large sum of compensation. This made the people seriously resent the behaviour of the enterprises, but at the same time it made people realize how industry could affect nature and its ecosystem in the long run.

Newly created industrial complexes also spawned many problems. Air pollution was the most sensitive one. As their scale grew larger the effect spread even wider over each area. Water pollution by their waste discharge also became serious. Since most of the industrial complexes were built on a bay or along the Seto Inland Sea, where the movement of sea water is quite limited, it quickly affected the ecosystem and thus seriously damaged fishery production as well as recreational amenities. It was realized that the capacity of the ecosystem of an area had to be considered as one important element in planning.

All these cases roused series of protests and campaigns by citizen's groups to accuse the government and enterprise against the environmental disruption. This led to the creation of the Environmental Agency at the central government level in July 1971, with status similar to that of the Economic Planning Agency. Similar offices were established rapidly in local governments. Regulations concerning prevention, monitoring, and control of pollution as well as compensatory measures were enforced, and total emission control of pollutants had become a practice in the cities in question. In fact the world's strictest standard for the emission of motor-car exhaust has been applied to Japanese car manufacturers. All these efforts seemed to have produced better results, but careful monitoring should be continued. The most important point to be mentioned is that protest by the citizens was the very motivation for this change.

(b) Unawarded Benefits to the Locality. Location of big industries did not necessarily bring expected benefits to localities. In particular, petrochemical industries, being equipment industries, required little manpower and did not bring much employment opportunities to the localities. The output of these industries was mostly brought to factories already established in other developed areas. Companies generally had well established systems of Consumer Co-op, which absorbed most of the purchasing power of the employees. In this way, the trickling effect to the locality was very small. Companies and their employees were alien to the local community.

In spite of this, many favourable conditions had been offered to attract the companies in the beginning, such as abatement and/or reduction of local tax. This eventually made the local authorities suffer from deficits in their financial balance. As industries grew larger after their establishment, they automatically required more external infrastructure, which eventually became a burden to the local authorities.

All this made the localities reluctant to accept the location of industries—especially that of the big industrial complex. People, especially those in the primary sectors, opposed this for fear that their place of work would be lost. Thus industrial sites which used to be in a buyers' market in less-developed areas at least up to the early 1960s turned into a sellers' market after the late 1960s. The market was further tightened by the quick rise in land price and accompanying speculation. The dispersal of industry optimistically laid out in the plan had become much more difficult than envisaged.

(c) Change in Local Leadership. Another important issue was the change in the leadership of political powers at the local level. Governors of prefectures used to be nominated by the central government, but after the war they were elected locally. This made governors become more aware of the local interest in their prefectures and tended to strengthen the autonomy at the local level. Also there was an apparent shift of political power from the Conservatives to the Progressives in most of the major metropolitan regions especially after the late 1960s. One of the main supporting pillars of the Conservatives was the agricultural sector. In spite of the tremendous shift of population from rural to urban areas in post-war years, the number of representatives in the Diet by each electorate district did not change proportionately, giving much less per population in urban areas than in rural areas. This imbalance accounted for the dominance of the Conservatives in the Diet: urban people were feeling that their interests were not properly represented. As a result, the Conservatives became less and less popular in urban areas. As the Progressives gained more power, more radical thinking about the needs of common citizens was pushed forward into the political arena. The problems of environmental disruption gave impetus to this trend. Citizen's participation was called for. The top - down approach in decision making became more and more difficult; new ways had to be sought to promote a down - top approach.

(d) Spectacular Growth of Developers and Accelerated Rise in Land Price. The rapid economic growth in 1960s raised the Japanese economy to the level of one of the largest in the world. The capacity of its investment had been largely increased. In addition, due to the serious fluctuation in international currency situation in 1971 an enormous surplus of Japanese currency flowed back from overseas to home capital markets. New opportunities for investment had to be found.

Private housing development was one of the sectors in which such opportunities were sought. So far it was dominated by small-scale enterprises, but after 1970s entry of big enterprises became conspicuous. The first case of private large-scale housing development was that of Tama Garden City (with planned population of 300,000) which was started since the 1950s by a railroad company along the extension of its line. It took more than ten years to take shape, but towards late 1960s it brought tremendous returns to the company because of the rise in land price. This set an example for others to follow. Also, since the late 1960s, private high-rise apartment-house construction began to boom in inner city areas as the market for higher-income housing developed along with economic growth. This also promised highest return to investment due to the quick rise in land price. The surplus capital rushed into these areas of investment, and housing development has become a booming business since then.

This did not mean that housing for common people was promoted. On the contrary, in the absence of proper land policy, private developers shot up the land price higher and higher through speculation and made it even more difficult for the people to obtain land at moderate cost. The behavioural pattern of housing developers was not an exception to those of private enterprises in general in which pursuit of profit was the most important motivation. Speculation in real estate business spread all over Japan in a frantic manner and created many political scandals to such an extent that serious resentment spread among the people over the results of economic development over the decades.

4.4. Prime Minister Tanaka's Book: Building a New Japan (Retto-kaizo-ron)

Prime Minister Tanaka came into power in 1972 after competing with other leaders of the Liberal Democratic Party (the Conservatives). He wrote this book before he came into power to advocate the policy he would take if he were to become Prime Minister. It advocated a more balanced development all over the Japanese Archipelago through decentralization of urban activities by means of spectacular development in infrastructure.

It seems to me, however, that this was just the extrapolation of successive Government "plans" on national land development. It was built upon the whole of the achievements which Japanese bureaucrats had worked out under the long regime of the Conservative through the past twenty years. It was based on the assumption that the Japanese economy was bound to grow. It assumed that even by a moderate estimate the size of the Japanese economy would reach that of the United States at present in ten to fifteen years. The author went on to say: "The question is how the four main islands of Japan, with a total land area of only one-twenty-fifth of the US, can afford an economy as large as today's US economy."[9]

In fact, this was a very interesting book with dynamic descriptions of the answer to this question, such as relocation of industries to solve the problem of over-congestion versus depopulation, new transportation networks to sustain this relocation, the bullet-train-network over the archipelago, three long bridges over the Seto Inland Sea, creation of quarter-of-a-million cities, etc. It was a best seller when published. At the same time, it was bound to meet serious criticism from his opponents, as it was the manifestation of his policy as the Prime Minister.

I would like to cite the following comment by Kimura[10], the former Senator from the Progressives, as one of the good examples criticizing the most salient issues:

---

[9]Kakuei Tanaka, *Building a New Japan,* pp. 64-5, Simul Press, Tokyo, 1973 (originally published in Japanese in 1972).

[10]Kihachiro Kimura, Open-questionnaire to Prime Minister Tanaka, *Chuo-Koron,* October 1972, pp. 168 - 81.

(i) Absence of the land policy: speculation in land price should be stopped immediately;

(ii) Non-recognition of the responsibility of single-minded growth policy: the "distortion" has been created by the very nature of the capitalistic economy of Japan, putting highest priority on price-mechanism (or market-mechanism) for the pursuit of profit;

(iii) Mistake of (high economic growth = high welfare) formula: no proper thought is given to the fulfilment of welfare in spite of economic growth;

(iv) No proper consideration about agricultural policy: agricultural policy should dovetail with industrial relocation policy;

(v) No thoughts about the stabilization of price: the commercial structure is not taken into account at all.

The first thing Tanaka tried after coming into power was to amend the Comprehensive National Land Development Law in order to provide the basis for the implementation of his plan. This amendment met serious opposition from the antagonist parties at the Diet, but was eventually approved in 1974 with modification by changing the word "Development" to "Utilization". On the basis of this law the National Land Agency was created with the similar status as that of the Economic Planning Agency and the Environmental Agency. The new agency was made responsible for the preparation and implementation of the Comprehensive National Land Utilization Plan and the co-ordination of policies concerning land and water resources. The long-sustained problem of land price control has been included as one of the functions of this agency. In this way, the responsibility for overall planning at the national level has been proliferated into the above three agencies, all within the Prime Minister's Office, in which regional development has been identified as the function of the National Land Agency.

A dramatic change in the international scene occurred while this amendment was debated. Oil-exporting countries got together to declare the drastic rise in the cost of the oil in late 1973. Although this was a one-sided declaration by the OPEC member countries, it brought up the problem of the sovereignty of the nations over their national resources, and thus was a dramatic step to open the way to a new international order. This had an exceedingly important implication for Japan, since her economic growth was based on the assumption that she could utilize the world resources in an unlimited manner. As such it was recognized by the Japanese as a critical warning to convert her course of development from a rapid to a slowed-down but stable pace. The energy crisis affected the world economy seriously, and Japan was not an exception. In fact her economic growth rate which continued at a pace of over 10 per cent per annum declined sharply since 1973 and came down to slightly below zero in 1974.

As if to symbolize such a change, Prime Minister Tanaka resigned from his post in December 1974. *Bungei Shunju*, a monthly magazine, took up an elaborated article analysing Tanaka's "financial and personal connections",[11] especially accusing him of scandal related to the transaction of land. This developed into a political issue, and Tanaka voluntarily gave up the premiership to Takeo Miki, another leader of the Conservatives. The National Land Development policy strongly focused on rapid economic growth had really come to a turning point. (Even Prime Minister Miki had to give up his post after two years when the Conservatives suffered a landslide defeat at the election

---

[11]Takashi Tachibana, Tanaka Kakuei Kenkyu: Sono kin-myaku to jin-myaku (Study on Tanaka Kakuei: his financial and personal connections), *Bungei Shunju,* November 1974, pp. 92 - 131 (special issues).

due to their declining reputation as the result of further disclosure of the political scandal of Lockheed Aircraft case over which important Conservative leaders, including Tanaka, were indicted.)

5. THE PERIOD OF POST-INDUSTRIALIZATION (SECOND STAGE): SINCE 1975

5.1. Economic Planning

The pressing problem for Japan was how to reduce quickly the pace of its economic growth without seriously damaging her economic system. Rapid growth was accompanied by such deficiencies as accelerated inflation, environmental disruptions, aggressive expansion of necessary imports and exports, but on the other hand, brought about such benefits as an increase in employment, a rise in living standard, and provision of necessary funds for enlarging social security measures. A critical path had to be found to make a "soft-landing" at a slow but stable level of economic growth by carefully piloting through those conflicting requirements.

This became the key issue in drafting the revision of the National Economic Plan. Some observed that there still remained a potential to keep the growth rate at 7 - 9 per cent. Others argued for less. It was estimated that a 3 per cent growth rate would be the minimum to assure the same living standard to the population still increasing although at a low rate of about 1 per cent per year. The implication of all these alternatives to the Japanese economy was analysed as forecasts. The consensus came to about 5 - 6 per cent. However, the real implication of this figure should further be observed in the light of what will happen in the future.

5.2. Comprehensive National Land Development Planning

The Third Comprehensive National Land Development Plan was deliberated with this background. Since the plan was expected to find a different approach than the economic growth oriented ones in the past, the deliberation had to start from the search for a new paradigm of development which is more concerned about the capacity of the Japanese archipelago. Here I would like to mention some of the salient issues which came out in the process of this deliberation.

The most basic point was the population forecast. In the past, there were two periods when the population in Japan dramatically increased. The first was between the mid-sixteenth century to the early eighteenth century, during which time the population increased threefold from 10 million to 30 million and then became stagnant. This was the time when the feudal system was being established and there was an apparent rise in agricultural productivity as well as the early development of commercial activities. Second was the period of entry into the modern civilization since the late nineteenth century. Until present times, in the matter of one century, the population again increased threefold from 33 million to 110 million. The development in industrialization and urbanization was able to cope with this population increase. This is clear evidence that without new opportunities for employment being opened up, the population level would have to remain stable.

The long-range forecast of the Japanese population was made taking this into consideration. It was estimated to be 137 million by A.D. 2000 and 145 million in A.D. 2025, after which the population will become stable. On the basis of this figure, the future utilization of the Japanese archipelago was considered.

Again the most crucial issue was that of the concentration of population in big urban regions. In 1975 nearly half (45 per cent) of the population lived in three big metropolitan regions[12] which consist of 10.6 per cent of the total national land. If this tendency is allowed to continue, then about half of the 137 million population, namely 65 million, will concentrate in these regions in the year 2000, and there will be a serious problem of accommodating them even from a mere physical point of view (such as water and energy supply). This will be serious especially in the Tokyo Region where about 8 million will be added to the present 27 million within the quarter of a century to come.

At present, however, there is an apparent trend toward the dispersal of the night-time population from central areas to fringe areas in big metropolitan areas in Japan, popularly called the doughnut phenomenon. In accordance with this trend, local administrative and service functions (or daily managerial functions), commercial functions, and research and development functions are found to be locating more and more in the fringe areas with industries being shifted further outwards. In this way there is an apparent trend toward the development of a new regional pattern.

However, the problem is that this new pattern is still strongly constrained by the existence of the central managerial function at the CBD of the metropolis and has resulted in simply expanding urban agglomerations, leaving the hierarchical system basically unchanged. Therefore, if one is to be serious about the decentralization, one should plan to disperse the central managerial function itself by changing the structure of the administrative and managerial system of the country. However, there is no apparent initiation of this—although it has been much talked about—and it is hard to assume that there has already been any effective measure taken to decentralize urban function properly all over Japan.

The Third Comprehensive National Land Development Plan was finally authorized by the Government in November 1977. In essence it was based on the concept of 'permanent settling'. Tazawa, then Minister in charge of the National Land Agency, stated in his introductory note to this plan that "this concept of 'permanent settling' started from the serious quest for what should be done to enable as many Japanese people as possible to find a place to live in satisfaction and to enhance harmonious interaction between themselves and nature toward the long future."[13]

As a means to achieve this, the Plan advocates the establishment of 'permanent settlement spheres' as the basic units of regional development. They are the primary spheres of human living such as river-basins, commuting districts (for jobs as well as for education) or wider livelihood spheres, which are small enough to assure the participation of the people in planning and development. The whole country would consist of about 200-300 of such 'permanent settlement spheres'.

I would like to mention that the concept of such spheres has already been in existence in one way or another under the administration of the local governments. The efforts to develop this into viable units for planning and development has been promoted under the aegis of several ministries of the central government, particularly those of the Ministry

---

[12]For definition, see footnote 4, p. 10.

[13]Yoshiro Tazawa, Minister of State in charge of National Land Agency, "Dai-sanji Zenkoku Sogo Kaihatsu-Keikaku no Sakutej" (Formulation of the Third Comprehensive National Land Development Plan), *Hito to Kokudo* (People and National Land Policy) No. 11, November 1977. p. 10.

of Interior and the Ministry of Construction, which were acting in a competitive manner just like in other cases of regional development.

With growing awareness to the problems of regional development, there has been much effort on the part of the people to consider participatory planning especially at such micro levels. The importance of the Third Comprehensive National Land Development Plan is that the central government identified such a sphere as the basic planning unit for micro level planning on which national plan should be restructured.

6. EPILOGUE

Japan has come into a stage in which her social structure has become quite similar to that of the affluent countries. The average age of the population has become older and the lifetime has become longer. Ratios of urban population in DIDs have been raised to nearly 60 per cent and rural areas have ceased to be the supplier of manpower; most of the people are born, brought up, and will continue to live in urban areas. Educational careers have been further advanced; at present almost all of the middle school graduates go to high school, of which nearly 40 per cent go to universities or colleges. The occupation structure is more and more oriented to white-collar workers; they (administrative, business, and professional occupations) accounted for a quarter of the total labour force in 1970, and this ratio will continue to increase. Blue-collar workers will decrease in ratio; primary industry workers will be reduced to less than 10 per cent by the year 2000 unless some measures are taken to reverse this trend. The economy will be based more on the stock than the flow; marginal utility of the equipment investment will be drastically decreased, since necessary investment will have to accompany demolition of existing facilities. Incentives for new investment will be reduced and the vitality of the Japanese economy will be decreased.

At present there are 3 per cent of the world population living in the Japanese archipelago, the size of which is 0.3 per cent of the world's land area. Since Japan is of steep volcanic landscape, the habitable area is only one-third of the total land area. The density of population per habitable area was 939 person per hectare in 1970 which is about three times higher than most of the affluent countries in north Europe. This means that the national land of Japan is in fact relatively over-utilized. Still, if the world's trend is to intensify national sovereignty over the nation's natural resources, then Japan will be obliged to look seriously into more intensified use of her small land. However, we see that even at present conflicting land uses compete with each other; there is little elbow room to strike out compromises among the conflicting claims. There is a common saying in Japan now: "In principle OK, but in specifics no", meaning matters contrary to established individual interests cannot be accepted.

Of course the other possibility is to look into the means of living together with the world by further enhancing international co-operation. Serious thoughts should be given to keeping pace with the developing world so that the troubles caused by the imbalance in development can be ameliorated. This would mean that Japan should refrain from aggressive international trade policies even at the cost of sacrificing benefits to her economy.

Looking into the future under the constraints of limited national land and resources, and under the forecast of a tapering off of economic growth, we are obliged to seek a deliberate policy for the survival of the Japanese. There is a need to develop a consensus within the nation on a different kind of value system than that which was prevalent at the height of the economic growth period; a philosophy based on reasonable asceticism may be sought. As such, it could not be imposed upon the people, but their wisdom should accept this as a fact if they are serious to see the nation survive. On the other hand, fairness should be assured to all levels and sectors of the nation, so that nobody feels hurt by the sense of unequal sacrifice he or she is obliged to bear under the name of the whole. This should not discourage the people to be creative and forward-looking; they should be made fully aware of the role they have to play within the whole structure of the society in which they can participate by exerting their initiative to the fullest extent. Citizen participation based on sound acknowledgement of such background would be a crucial element in keeping up the morale of the nation. The role of the government would be to service the nation with information on such background as well as to let people feed their initiatives into the body of this information so that a two-way flow would be assured to create a real consensus among the nation as a whole.

In this context I would like to look upon the possible contribution which the governmental set-up for comprehensive planning and development in Japan could make in the future. Through the practice in planning during the post-war years, this has been developed into a multi-level set up, linking different levels and sectors of the government so that co-ordination could be effectuated. In the beginning comprehensive planning was initiated and guided by the central government, while the local governments were placed in the position to work on its sub-programmes and implementation. Through such exercise planning capabilities as well as institutional set-ups grew in the localities. Apparently local governments were in a better position than the central government in dealing directly with the people. Therefore, it has been felt that the wish of the local people is more strongly reflected in the planning of the local government.

I would like to see that the whole set-up thus developed continues to work in an integral manner in order to support the creation of the necessary national consensus. Of course it would be premature to assume that the nature of a bureaucratic set-up once established would be changed overnight. It will not be easy to convert the top - down approach to the down - top approach, in other words, to let local government freely communicate the wishes as well as the initiatives of the local people to the upper tier of the government. Yet I would sincerely hope to see it done, since this is a challenge the Japanese are faced with; for in failing to meet this challenge the future survival of the nation would be seriously jeopardized.

2

THE GROWTH POLE APPROACH TO REGIONAL DEVELOPMENT: A CASE STUDY OF THE MIZUSHIMA INDUSTRIAL COMPLEX, JAPAN*

FU-CHEN LO

INTRODUCTION

The problems of widening regional income disparities, polarized urbanization, and industrial development are currently among the key regional development issues in the less-developed world. In the heart of the problems are two related questions: one asks if regional disparities converge at a later stage of development; the second question deals with whether the primate city is too big. In response to this concern, the growth pole approach has received wide attention in the past two decades or so as a vital policy tool for regional development, as evidenced by the constant reference to it in numerous national planning documents. It has either been applied as a policy of "concentrated decentralization" to cope with the excessive polarization phenomenon of large metropolitan areas or as a strategic public investment policy in the establishment of an industrial core region. In this regard, the growth pole strategy is closely related both to the implementation of the industrial location policy of a national economy and to a strategy of nationwide development.

The purpose of this paper is to study the interregional and intraregional diffusion of development based on a case study of Okayama Prefecture in Japan in which the growth pole approach was adopted under the auspices of the New Industrial City of 1962.

Section 1 deals with a brief description of the Mizushima industrial complex as the core of the growth pole development in Kurashiki - Okayama New Industrial City. Sections 2 and 3 provide an overall assessment of the macro-economic impact on the regional economy of Okayama Prefecture and the spatial pattern of development.

In section 4 interregional dispersions of development are introduced to demonstrate that polarization and decentralization of development are not contradictory phenomena but can be treated as different phases in the development process.

*This paper is a summary of an earlier publication, *The Growth Pole Approach to Regional Development: A Case Study of the Mizushima Industrial Complex, Japan,* UNCRD, Nagoya, Japan, 1975.

1. PLAN FORMULATION AND IMPLEMENTATION OF MIZUSHIMA INDUSTRIAL COMPLEX DEVELOPMENT

1.1. Mizushima Development: An Overview

The Mizushima Industrial Complex is now an integrated part of Kurashiki City in Okayama Prefecture, located 160 km west of Osaka City, comprising an industrial port and its surrounding 42-million-m² industrial complex on the mouth of the Takahashi river. Lying in the heart of Japan's Seto Inland Sea region and situated in western Japan between the Osaka - Kobe metropolitan region and the northern Kyushu industrial region, Mizushima has developed into an industrial magnet in the late 1960s. Before that this area was no more than a fishermen's village with some reclaimed farm land. Post-war industrial development of this area was postponed until the 1950s when the Japanese economy gradually recovered during the Korean War. The pace of industrialization in Mizushima has accelerated since 1960 when an overall regional development plan for Okayama Prefecture was begun to be implemented. Under this master regional plan, working in conjunction with national development plans of the 1960s, a sequence of development programmes were formulated and implemented for Mizushima. By many indicators, the overall economic growth in Mizushima and its hinterland of Okayama Prefecture exceeded planning targets. Thus Mizushima had become one of the success stories of regional industrial development in Japan until the environmental issue quickly emerged as one of the most controversial issues in regional development in Japan from the early 1970s. With the promotion of growth pole approach under the auspices of the Law for the Promotion of New Industrial City Construction in 1962, the Kurashiki - Okayama City area was designated as the Okayama - Kennan (Southern Okayama) New Industrial City with Mizushima as the core industrial area of the growth pole.

By 1970 eighty of Japan's leading firms had established more than ninety branch factories in the Mizushima Industrial District. The major manufacturing industries located here include the iron and steel industry, the petroleum refinery industry, the petro-chemical industry, the automobile manufacturing industry, and the electric power industry.

In the early 1950s Okayama Prefecture was a typical agricultural economy in which *per capita* income was 20 per cent lower than the national average. It was felt that mechanized farming or modernization of the agricultural sector was a promising approach. However, it was a foreseeable fact that this approach could create an excess labour force in the region. Therefore promotion of industrial as well as business activities, in order to increase employment opportunities and to strengthen the regional economic foundation, became a basic strategy for regional development in the minds of planning authorities in Okayama Prefecture. This was in keeping with post-war national policy in Japan which was to promote the development of heavy industries, in particular petrochemical and steel related industries. Since a great proportion of raw materials such as crude oil and iron ore had to be imported, such heavy industrial activities had to be located in the coastal area of Japan equipped with good port facilities for large-size vessels to anchor and a considerable water-front area for industrial location. In this connection, Mizushima, with its supreme potential as an ideal industrial port, was singled out by the Okayama planning authorities as the site for the development of an industrial complex.

1.2. Plan Formulation

Plan formulation for Mizushima's development programme was continuously being revised to accommodate changes in planning goals and economic conditions in the country. As the industrial complex developed, increased demand for industrial land, deeper waterways to accommodate larger tankers, and urban infrastructure was to shift the emphasis of the development programme of Mizushima (Table 1).

TABLE 1.
Changes in Mizushima's development programmes

Year	Plan	Features
1952	Mizushima Coastal Industrial District Development Programme	(1) Dredging a 9-m waterway (2) Development of a port for 10,000-ton vessels (3) Reclaiming 2.2 million m² of land, 1.65 million m² for industrial use (4) The estimated 377 million yen cost to be covered by sale of industrial land
1958	Okayama Prefecture General Advancement Plan I Target Year 1965	(1) Dredging a 13-m-deep waterway for Mizushima and a 5.5-m waterway for Tamashima (2) Reclamation of 7.5 million m² for industrial use in sections A, B, C, D, and E (3) Improvement of Mizushima railroad; construction of Tamashima Harbour railroad
1961	Five-year Development Plan of Mizushima	(1) Development of an iron and steel and petrochemical industrial complex (2) Detailed overall industrial and urban infrastructure development projects (3) Total costs of 154,835 million yen to be financed by national subsidies, bonds, prefectural budget (4) Dredging a 16-m-deep waterway for Mizushima
1965	Okayama Prefecture General Advancement Plan II for 1966-75	(1) Strengthened role of Mizushima (2) Reclamation of additional 2 million m² of industrial land, with 7 million m² of land for other industrial use (3) Expansion of harbours in Mizushima and Tamashima for 100,000 - 150,000-tons class tankers

In 1952, ten years before designation as a New Industrial City, the Mizushima Coastal Industrial District Development Programme was formulated with basic concepts of harbour development which were used in subsequent plans. They were:

(a) Development of Mizushima port; in particular, dredging of waterways and development of a harbour area for tankers and large vessels to facilitate raw material imports for heavy industries into Mizushima.
(b) Use of soil dredged from channels for reclamation of industrial sites.
(c) The financing of the total cost of dredging, reclamation, and improvement of the harbour area by the revenues from the sales of reclaimed land to interested firms.

This unique method of development would permit the development of a port and harbour complex at no cost to the prefectural government. The total costs of dredging the 9-m-deep waterway and reclamation of 2.2 million m² of land (1.65 million m² of industrial land), including compensation to the fishery industry and farm land acquisition, were estimated to be 377 million yen (or 1.42 million dollars). Therefore, the unit cost of an industrial site was estimated to be 755 yen per *tsubo* (or 3.3 m²).

Later in 1958 a ten-year economic development plan for Okayama Prefecture was formulated in accordance with the National Income-doubling Plan of the nation. In this
Okayama Prefecture General Advancement Plan, development of the Mizushima area
into a large-scale industrial district was re-emphasized with some concrete commitment for
implementation. Setting 1965 as the target year, the modified development included the
reclamation of 7,533,900 m² of industrial land with soil obtained from the dredging of a
13-m-deep waterway for Mizushima harbour.

In 1961, with the conclusion of agreements by Mitsubishi Oil, Nippon Mining, and
Kawasaki Steel to locate petroleum refining and steel plants in Mizushima, a five-year
development plan for Mizushima was enacted. In this five-year plan not only the harbour
development and reclamation of industrial land but also urban infrastructure development programmes were included. Using industrial complex analysis, the optimum combination of industrial activities and corresponding levels of industrial production were
determined. From this the labour demand, total tonnage flow and the scale of supporting
tertiary industry were derived, allowing the planning authorities to detail a comprehensive
industrial and urban infrastructure development programme.[1]

In 1962 it was observed that the actual economic growth rates of Okayama Prefecture
had exceeded the planning goals given in the Okayama Prefecture General Advancement
Plan (OPGA Plan) of 1958, as shown in Table 2.

TABLE 2

Growth rates	Planning goals (annual growth rates) (%)	Actual (1960) (%)
Regional products	7	10.8
Per capita income	6	8.7
Manufacturing products	8.3	14.6

The contribution of industrial development in Mizushima was so overwhelming that it
led to an amendment of the OPGA Plan in 1962. After the completion of the OPGA
Plan in 1965, a second OPGA Plan was then formulated to cover the period between 1966
and 1975. In this master plan the role to be played by the Mizushima Industrial District
was strengthened again. The plan included reclamation of an additional 2 million m² of
industrial area together with 7 million m² of land development for other industrial use
and the expansion of harbour facilities in Tamashima and Mizushima harbours for
100,000 - 150,000-ton class tankers.

1.3. Plan Implementation

1.3.1. *Administrative Coordination of Plan Implementation.* As has been observed, the
Mizushima industrial complex development programme was never an independent programme.

Nevertheless, it was rather unusual that in order to implement such a huge project

---

[1]For industrial complex analysis of Mizushima, see E. Kometani, K. Yoshikawa, and K. Ono, Model plan for
a new industrial area through interactivity matrix, *Papers and Proceedings,* First Far East Conference of the
Regional Science Association, Tokyo, 1964, pp. 61-75. Also W. Isard, E. W. Schooler, and T. Vietorize,
Industrial complex analysis and regional development with particular reference to puerto rico, *Papers,*
Regional Science Association, Vol. 1, 1955, and W. Isard, *Methods of Regional Analysis,* MIT Press, 1960.

there was no effort made to create a single local planning authority to be in charge of continuous planning and implementation of the development programmes in Mizushima. Also there was never a single or centralized budgeting and financing system created for these programmes. This was largely due to the special character of the Japanese planning system, with a very strong vertical hierarchy of government organization instead of horizontal coordination of related projects at a regional level. Budgeting and actual implementation of these projects were to be authorized by the appropriate government ministries at the national level. This has been described as "pluralistic planning" by Honjo.[2] It is worth mentioning that the governors of Okayama Prefecture during the past two decades were directly involved in the co-ordination of those regional sectors and played a leading role in seeking assistance from corresponding ministries of the central government and were also deeply devoted to the promotion and establishment in the Mizushima area of branch factories by the leading industrial firms. In this aspect, co-ordination of related projects, budgeting and financing of programme costs, and inducement of industrial activities were all gathered together in the governor's hand.

Figure 1 gives the administrative organizational framework of the co-ordination and implementation scheme for Mizushima development.

The Okayama prefectural government was in charge of overall planning and co-ordination of the development of Mizushima industrial district. The provision of infrastructure facilities, which had to be approved by the appropriate ministry in the central government, was partially financed by the appropriate ministries of the central government and partially by Kurashiki City and other local governments, as well as the private sector, such as the Chugoku Electric Power Co., in the construction of dams and the supply of electric power to the area.

In the development of industrial lands, the Okayama Prefecture Development Corporation was set up by the prefectural government to be in charge of land acquisition. The costs of the reclamation of industrial land and port development programmes were paid out of a special budget account financed by prefectural bonds. In 1960, the Mizushima Port Authority was created under the Civil Engineering Department of the prefectural government to take charge of the development and management of the Mizushima port area and was actively involved with the Civil Engineering Department in the implementation of reclamation programmes.

1.3.2. *Role of public investment and finance.* Before large-scale industrial plants could be physically located in Mizushima, dredging of waterways, redevelopment of harbour areas, and other industrial infrastructure formation had to be far advanced. Direct public investment in Mizushima district by the central, prefectural, and city governments had accumulated to 56.7 billion yen (214 million dollars) between 1953 and 1969.

Up to 1957, public investments were a token 606 million yen, of which 91 per cent was allocated solely for harbour area development and reclamation activities, such as dredging a 9-m-deep waterway and reclaiming 920,000 m² of industrial sites.

The 1958-62 period was a take-off stage of industrialization for Mizushima. The requirements of a 16-m-deep waterway and 2,167,000 m² of industrial land by the leading oil and steel companies led to a greatly accelerated rate of outlays for industrial investment such as railway connections and road development, industrial water supply, dams, and electric power plants, as shown in Table 3. At the same time, public investment in

---

[2]Masahiko Honjo, Trends in development planning in Japan, Chapter 1 in this book.

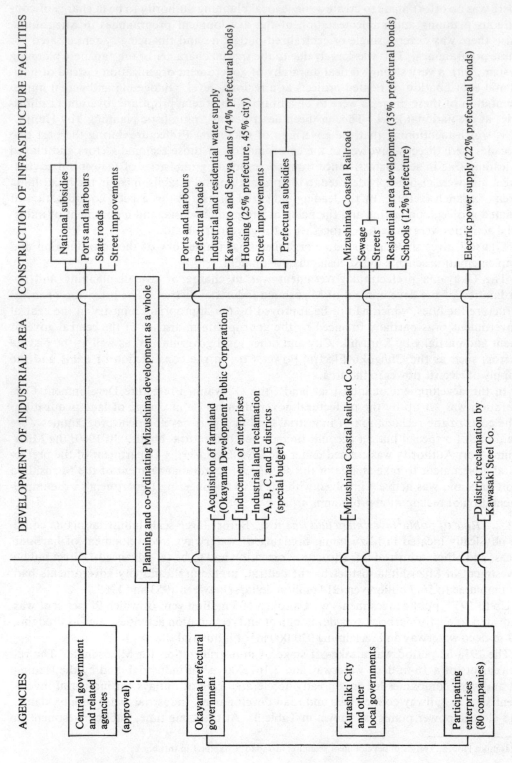

Fig. 1. Organizational framework of Mizushima Development.

urban infrastructure, such as street improvement, schools, parks, and recreation facilities, water and sewage, housing, etc., began to occupy a considerable fraction of total public investment.

In 1963 and 1964 the economic depression of the Japanese economy had adverse effects on the financing of public investment projects in Mizushima, as was reflected in the difficulty the prefectural government experienced in obtaining long-term loans from banks and in the sales of reclaimed land. However, by 1965 financial crisis was averted by the recovery of the national economy, and industries were induced to set up in Mizushima. In this period, though industrial infrastructure investment continued to increase rapidly in absolute terms, it can be noted from Table 9 that urban infrastructure investment began to account for a significantly larger proportion of public investment over time.

TABLE 3.
Public investments in Mizushima

	Up to 1957	1958-62	1963-69
Industrial infrastructure[a]	556 91.7%	13,380 60.6%	20,716 61.1%
Urban infrastructure[b]	50 8.3%	4,200 18.8%	11,109 32.7%
Okayama Development Public Corporation[c]	—	4,552 20.2%	2,102 6.2%
Total	606	22,132	33,927

Source: Okayama Prefectural Government, *Mizushima no Ayumi (The Development Path of Mizushima)*, p. 335.
[a]Includes ports and harbours development reclamation costs, road development, industrial water supply, dams, and electric power plant construction.
[b]Includes street improvement, parks, water and sewage, housing, school facilities, residential district development, etc.
[c]Public corporation dealing mainly with land acquisition and development for both industrial and residential use.

Unlike certain industrial and urban infrastructure investment financed through the usual tax and revenue sources, industrial site reclamation, and waterway dredging costs were financed in accordance with the development concepts outlined earlier. An independent account was created when costs initially incurred in land reclamation and waterway development were financed through the issue of prefecture bonds. These costs were to be recouped from the sales of reclaimed land to induced firms. The balance sheet up to 1972 can be summarized as shown in Table 4.

1.3.3. *Inducement of Big Firms to Mizushima District.* For petrochemical and steel related industries the long-term outlook for market potential and locational advantages of port and factory sites far exceeded the considerations of short-term financial incentives. During the 1960s the expected total investment of an optimum-size petroleum industrial complex was said to be from 25 to 50 billion yen (100 - 200 million dollars). From the very beginning, petroleum and steel industries or "import - export oriented" heavy industries had been the "selected industries" for Mizushima in the minds of the planning authorities.

TABLE 4

(1) *Costs*	11,609.9 million yen	
Prefectural bonds (reclamation costs of A, B, and C districts)		6,308.9
Interest expenditures (up to 1972)		1,984.1
Dredging costs		2,418.6
Fishing rights compensation, land acquisition, etc.		898.3
(2) *Revenues*	11,484.2 million yen	
Sales of A district		623.9
Sales of B district		1,625.0
Sales of C district		7,365.5
Interest revenue		1,869.7
(3) *Balance*	− 125.7 million yen	

In fact from the late 1950s, due to the rapid recovery of the Japanese economy in the post-Korean War period, the leading big firms, stimulated by the National Income-doubling Plan, made plans for a long-term expansion of heavy industries. In particular, petroleum and steel related industries were identified as the basic industries for economic development.

After five years of continuous efforts by the local government, Mitsubishi Oil Co. in 1958 became the first big firm to sign an agreement with Okayama Prefecture and Kura-shiki City. Since Japan is dependent upon imports from other countries for 99 per cent of her crude oil, utilization of larger oil tankers would economize transportation costs. For a 100,000 tons class oil tanker, the draught line is 14 - 15 m deep. Therefore the major concern of Mitsubishi Oil Co. was whether the local government could change the harbour area development plan to extend the depth of the waterway from 9 m to 16 m. In the agreement the local government finally agreed to provide a 16-m-deep waterway by 1961. According to the Law of Special Treatment for the Harbour Facilities of Designated Harbours and Ports, in cases where dredging of a 16-m-deep waterway was necessary, the private firms were asked to share 70 per cent of the total cost, the remaining 30 per cent to be financed equally by the nation and the local governments. However, the prefectural government was forced to bear the firm's share as a result of the agreement with Mitsu-bishi Oil. In 1959 this concession was also included in the inducement agreement with Nippon Mining Co., which is also a leading petroleum- refining firm.

In 1961, for similar reasons, Kawasaki Steel agreed to sign an agreement to locate in Mizushima one of the world's largest iron and steel factories, with more than 10,000 employees and an annual production capacity of 15 million tons of iron. Two years later, Mitsubishi Synthetics (Kasei Mizushima) came to Mizushima, and a pipeline was built linking it to Mitsubishi Oil Factory to transport a direct supply of naphtha to the new petrochemical factory of Mitsubishi Synthetics. In 1964 another petrochemical firm, Asahi Synthetics, established a similar tie with Nippon Mining Co. and was induced to the B district right next to Nippon Mining's site.

With the location of petroleum refinery plants and iron and steel factories in Mizushima, one after another, petrochemical and machinery industries came to the area. By 1972 more than ninety leading firms were located in the Mizushima industrial complex.

2. GROWTH OF THE OKAYAMA REGIONAL ECONOMY AND MULTIPLIER ANALYSIS

The growth of the regional economy showed the typical pattern of an initial heavy wave of public investment in industrial and urban infrastructure followed by private manufacturing investment, generating an increase in the amount of product and employment in Mizushima. The impact on the Okayama regional economy of Mizushima development can be sequentialized as follows. In the first stage the inducement of several key industries to Mizushima generated a cluster of related industries. Subsequent to the growth of the industrial complex, there was significant structural change in the region resulting in an increase in manufacturing product and employment in Okayama Prefecture as a whole. At the same time, growth in the tertiary sector, especially production-oriented service sectors, was induced to serve the manufacturing sector. Further, the increase of production in Mizushima region and Okayama Prefecture as a whole ultimately raised the income and consumption of Okayama Prefecture. This increase of consumption generated a further round of increase in production and employment.

2.1. The Overall Growth of Okayama Prefecture Economy

The development of industrial infrastructure induced a rapid inflow of private manufacturing investment. Private investment in manufacturing started from a very low level in the first half of the 1960s and accelerated at a very high rate in the later half of the 1960s, the majority of this being concentrated in the petrochemical and steel industries.

By 1970 the resulting increase in manufacturing product and employment was remarkable. In Mizushima, where most of the industry was located, manufacturing product increased 10.7 times, while manufacturing employment increased 4 times, or at an average growth rate of 26.7 per cent and 13 per cent per annum respectively. In Okayama Prefecture as a whole, manufacturing product in 1971 was 3.6 times that of 1961, while manufacturing employment increased about 1.5 times, or at an average growth rate of 14 per cent and 3.7 per cent respectively. During this period the manufacturing product of the whole of Japan increased only 2.43 times. Thus the high growth rate of manufacturing product in the whole of Okayama Prefecture during the 1960s could be substantially attributed to the growth of Mizushima industrial complex development (Table 5).

TABLE 5
Manufacturing investment, product, and employment, 1961 - 71

(billion yen (1965))

		Mizushima				Okayama Prefecture			
		Gross product		Employment		Gross product		Employment	
Year	Invetment	Value of shipment	Index	1000	Index	Value of shipment	Index	1000	Index
1961		53.8	100	9.9	100	337.6	100	155.0	100
1966	122.6	196.4	365	20.7	209	607.1	180	195.7	126
1971	539.8	574.5	1069	39.7	400	1212.7	359	225.2	145

The rapid inflow of investment and high growth rates of production and employment had marked effects on the regional economy. Some salient features of such growth in Okayama Prefecture can be seen in Table 6. The first is the increase in the proportion of *per capita* income of Okayama Prefecture compared to that of the national average. Okayama Prefecture enjoyed a higher growth rate of *per capita* income than the nation as a whole during the 1960-70 period. Thus Okayama Prefecture was able to raise its *per capita* income from 0.82 of the national average in 1960 to nearly equal that of the national average in 1970. The second point is the significant change in the economic structure of Okayama Prefecture in this period, marked by the increasing importance of secondary and tertiary industry and a corresponding diminution of the importance of the agricultural sector. In terms of percentage share of net prefectural product the share of primary industry fell from about 18 per cent in 1960 to 6.6 per cent in 1970, while the share of secondary and tertiary industry rose from 36 per cent and 46 per cent in 1960 to 45 per cent and 49 per cent respectively in 1970. In monetary terms, however, the real value of primary industry product remained fairly constant at over 50 billion yen, while the real value of secondary industry and tertiary industry products increased about 4 and 3.6 times respectively from 1960 to 1971.

2.2. Multiplier Analysis with Regional Input - Output Model

By treating the production of the manufacturing sector of Mizushima as exogenously given, the output, income, and employment multipliers have been examined based on Okayama regional input - output table constructed by non-survey techniques.[3]

The results are given in Table 7. Here column 2 refers to the total impact of the manufacturing sectors of Mizushima on the economy of Okayama Prefecture as a whole through the multiplier effect. This in turn can be divided into the impacts given to the secondary sectors (column 3) and tertiary sector (column 4) of Okayama Prefecture.[4]

---

[3]For non-survey techniques see W. A. Schaffer, and Kong Chu, Non-survey techniques for constructing regional interindustry models, *Papers,* Regional Science Association, **23** (1969) 83-101; W. I. Morrison and P. Smith, Non-survey input-output Techniques at the small area level: an evaluation, *Journal of Regional Science* **14** (1974) 1-14.

[4]The calculation method is as follows. Suppose $[B^*_{ij}]$ is the Leontief inverse matrix of the Okayama regional input - output table, and F_j is the vector of the value of production of Mizushima. Here $i, j = 1 \ldots 26$, while $1 \ldots 19$ are secondary sectors, $20 \ldots 26$ are tertiary sectors. Thus:

$$\sum_{i=1}^{21} X_i = \sum_{i=1}^{19} X_i + \sum_{i=20}^{26} X_i$$

$$= \sum_{j=1}^{26} (\sum_{i=1}^{19} b_{ij}^* f_j + \sum_{i=20}^{26} b_{ij}^* f_j)$$

where $\sum^n b^*_{ij}$ is output multiplier of sector j and b^*_{ij} is corresponding $_{ij}$ entry of the Leontief inverse matrix $\sum_{j=1}^{26} \sum_{i=1}^{19} b_{ij}^* f_j$ is the multiplier effects on secondary sectors and $\sum_{j=1}^{26} \sum_{i=20}^{19} b_{ij} f_j$ is the multiplier effects on tertiary sectors.

The income multiplier is defined as the ratio of the direct plus indirect income change to the direct income change resulting from a unit change in production level of any given industry.

Type one income multiplier of sector j is given by $\sum_{i=1}^{n} \frac{b_{ij} a_{hi}}{a_{hj}}$

while a_{hi} is the corresponding i entry of the household sector.

Type two income multiplier takes the induced or consumption effects into account by endogenizing the household sector into the conventional input - output table. Type two income multiplier of sector j is given by

$\frac{b_{hj}^{\Delta}}{a_{hj}}$ while b_{hj}^{Δ} is the j column of the household row of the expanded Leontief inverse matrix.

Employment multiplier is the direct and indirect employment change that is induced by a unit change in level of production of any given industry. If the employment-output ratio π for every industry is known, the employment multiplier of industry j can be defined as
$$\sum_{i=1}^{n} b^*_{ij} \pi_i.$$

See H. W. Richardson, *Input - Output and Regional Economics,* Weidenfeld & Nicolson, London, 1972.

Column 5 shows the ratio of the total impact and the exogenous values that prevailed in Mizushima. We might term this ratio aggregate output (income or employment) multiplier. It is interesting to note the order of the magnitudes of the aggregate output, income, and employment multipliers. The aggregate output impact of Mizushima on the economy of Okayama Prefecture is quite small compared to the aggregative income and employment impacts respectively. This might suggest two facts. Firstly, the basic industries of Mizushima, which are capital intensive, generate more output impacts on the labour intensive sectors than on the capital intensive sectors. Secondly, these labour intensive sectors have

TABLE 6
Per capita income, GDRP and structure of the Okayama Economy

| | *Per capita* income | | | | | | |
Year	Okayama Prefecture (1000 yen) (1)	National average (1000 yen) (2)	National average = 100 (1) + (2)	GDRP (billion yen)	Primary sector (%)	Secondary sector (%)	Tertiary sector (%)
1961	129	154	0.84	249.5	17.1	35.4	47.5
1966	282	308	0.91	520.0	13.3	37.7	47.9
1970	559	571	0.98	1088.3	6.6	45.0	48.3

labour productivities lower than that of the capital intensive sectors. These two facts are understandable if we consider the economic structure of Japan, that is, the petroleum industry and the iron and steel industry, for instance, which rely for their primary inputs from outside the region, and in turn generate the induced demand of machine maintenance, repairing, transporting, etc., from within the region. These induced demands are generally supplied by the so-called subcontract factories which are usually small- to medium-scale firms and have lower labour productivity.

TABLE 7
Multiplier impacts on the Okayama prefecture economy

| Year | Variables | Mizushima industrial complex (1) | Multiplier impacts on the Okayama prefecture economy | | | Multiplier | | |
			Total impacts (2)	Impacts on the secondary sector (3)	Impacts on the tertiary sector (4)	$\frac{(2)}{(1)}$	$\frac{(3)}{(2)} \times 100$	$\frac{(4)}{(2)} \times 100$
1969	Output	469,488.12	968,582.94	845,877.11	122,705.83	2.06	87.33	12.67
	Income	108,688.51	255,543.31	195,477.80	60,065.51	2.35	76.49	23.51
	Employment	30,691	153,153	107,998	45,155	4.99	70.52	29.48
1970	Output	671,572.73	140,088.42	1,221,932.28	178,951.96	2.09	87.23	12.77
	Income	163,028.26	370,760.42	283,149.79	87,610.63	2.27	76.37	23.63
	Employment	35,264	219,290	153,510	65,780	6.22	70.00	30.00
1971	Output	761,830.04	1,552,214.25	1,351,837.48	200,376.77	2.03	87.09	12.91
	Income	144,309.60	406,379.02	308,568.55	97,810.47	2.82	75.93	24.07
	Employment	39,664	238,634	165,560	73,074	6.02	69.38	30.62

The share of net manufacturing products of Mizushima was around 10 per cent of the net prefectural product of Okayama. The income generated by the income multiplier was about one-quarter of the net prefectural product. Furthermore, if we take the multiplicative effect of the consumption through the increase of income into account (type two multiplier), the ultimate effect of the income impact of Mizushima is as high as 40 per cent of the net prefectural product. This might seem unreasonably high at first glance, but if we consider the fact that the manufacturing product of Mizushima was around 45 per cent of that of Okayama Prefecture and, furthermore, the growth of manufacturing sectors has a high inducing effect on the growth of the tertiary industry (as will be shown in the next section), this percentage might be convincing.

Table 8 implies one important fact; that is that Mizushima's share of the net manufacturing product and hence its income impact on the net prefectural product, had its peak in 1970 and was decreasing afterwards. This might suggest that industries in Okayama Prefecture outside Mizushima had started their own growth process, either as a lag response of the impacts generated by Mizushima industrial complex or the spread effect generated outside of the growth pole which is shown in section 3. This is an encouraging fact for the regional economy of Okayama Prefecture.

TABLE 8

Type one and type two income impacts of Mizushima compared to
net prefectural product of Okayama Prefecture (in million yen)

	Net prefectural product (A)	Net manufacturing product of Mizushima (B)	$\frac{B}{A} \times 100$	Type one income multiplier effect (C)	$\frac{C}{A} \times 100$	Type two income multiplier effect (D)	$\frac{D}{A} \times 100$
1968	824,563	80,135	9.72	198,259	24.04	307,668	37.31
1969	1,072,480	108,688	10.13	255,543	23.83	404,831	37.75
1970	1,370,200	163,028	11.90	370,760	27.06	588,045	42.92
1971	1,527,913	144,310	9.44	406,379	26.60	650,755	42.59

3. SPATIAL PATTERN OF DEVELOPMENT

3.1. Regional Redistribution of Population

In the two decades from 1950 to 1970, the spatial distribution of population in Okayama Prefecture has been drastically transformed as shown in Fig. 4. In 1950, with the exception of southern Okayama, the population was fairly evenly distributed. By 1970 the highly populated area with a density of over 1000 people per km² had spread to cover the whole Kurashiki area, which is the location of the Mizushima industrial complex, while in the northern periphery the population had been polarized in a northern arc. It is immediately evident that this population arc coincides with the location of major northern cities connected by a railway (see Fig. 3). This polarization of population both to the Okayama - Kurashiki (OK) growth pole which is located in the south and in the northern cities suggests that strong urbanization forces are at work.

In Okayama Prefecture there are eighty-three municipalities including cities, towns, and villages. In order to trace the pattern of population redistribution all eighty-three municipalities are classified into four groups according to population size and growth

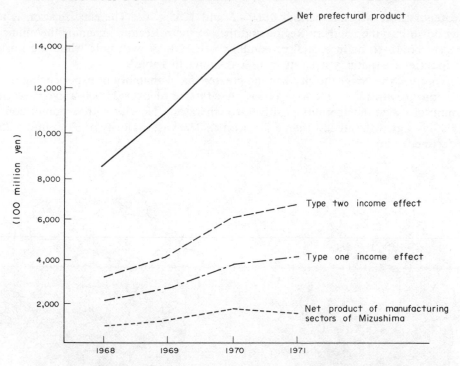

Fig. 2. Type one and Type two income impacts of Mizushima compared to net prefectural product of Okayama Prefecture.

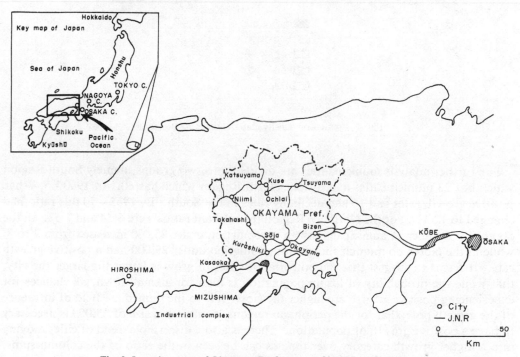

Fig. 3. Location map of Okayama Prefecture and its Urban Centres

rate category for two time periods 1960 - 5 and 1965 - 70. The classification is again
broken down into the Southern Region and the Northern Region, assuming the municipalities in the south to be in spatial proximity to the OK growth pole while the northern
municipalities are spatially separate from it as shown in Table 9.

As expected, the larger the city size the greater the probability of experiencing positive
population growth rates, and vice versa. A city size of over 25,000 appears to be the
minimum city size that permits positive growth rates. No city with a population over
100,000 has a growth rate less than 5.2 per cent. The vast majority of cities under 25,000
have declined.

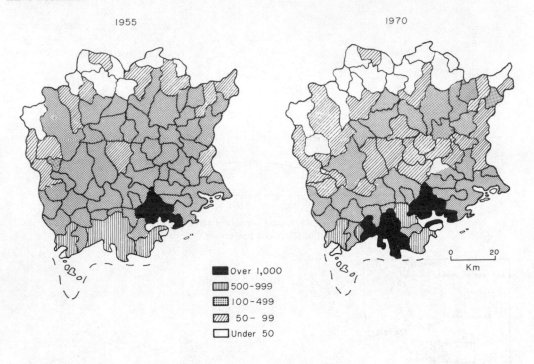

1955   1970

Over 1,000
500-999
100-499
50- 99
Under 50

0   20
Km

Fig. 4. Population density map of Okayama Prefecture.

For further analysis municipalities are divided into two groups, namely South Region
which has 23 municipalities and distant North Region which has 60. In 1960 - 5, 7 had
positive growth rates and 16 had declining rates in the South. By 1965 - 70 this ratio had
changed to 12:11. For the Northern Region the relevant ratios were 6:54 and 7:53. In the
South, the number of municipalities with a population under 25,000 increased from 2 to 8,
while in the North no municipalities with population under 25,000 had a positive growth
rate. It seems to suggest that the potential of cities to grow is larger the larger the city;
that while the probability of losing population is high for a small town, its chances for
experiencing positive growth are higher the closer it is to the immediate field of influence
of the growth pole; that for the peripheral regions, a minimum size of 25,000 is necessary
to have a positive growth of population. There is also a discernible trend of cities moving
into a higher growth category over time as can be seen in the ratio of the column sums,
from 3:10:33:37 to 10:9:33:31.

THE GROWTH POLE APPROACH TO REGIONAL DEVELOPMENT

TABLE 9

Distribution of municipalities by population size and rate of change in Okayama
Prefecture, 1960 - 5 and 1965 - 70

Region	Size of municipality population	% Change of municipality population							
		1960 - 5				1965 - 70			
		R_1	R_2	R_3	R_4	R_1	R_2	R_3	R_4
Okayama Prefecture (83 municipalities)	C_1 (over 100,000)	2	—	—	—	2	—	—	—
	C_2 (50,000 - 100,000)	—	4	—	—	—	4	—	—
	C_3 (25,000 - 50,000)	—	5	—	—	1	4	—	—
	C_4 (under 25,000)	1	1	33	37	7	1	33	31
		3	:10	: 33	:37	10	: 9	: 33	:31
South Okayama Region (23 municipalities)	C_1 (over 100,000)	2	—	—	—	2	—	—	—
	C_2 (50,000 - 100,000)	—	2	—	—	—	2	—	—
	C_3 (25,000 - 50,000)	—	1	—	—	1	—	—	—
	C_4 (under 25,000)	1	1	13	3	6	1	10	1
		7	:	16		12	:	11	
Northern Okayama Region (60 municipalities)	C_1 (over 100,000)	—	—	—	—	—	—	—	—
	C_2 (50,000 - 100,000)	—	2	—	—	—	2	—	—
	C_3 (25,000 - 50,000)	—	4	—	—	—	4	—	—
	C_4 (under 25,000)	—	—	20	34	1	—	23	30
		6	:	54		7	:	53	

Where R_1 = increase over 5.2%; R_2 = increase up to 5.2%; R_3 = decline 10.0% or less; R_4 = decline over 10.0%

3.2. Polarization Effect and Regional Urban Hierarchy

The dynamic aspects of eleven major urban centres in response to the growth pole development deserve attention.

As shown in Fig. 5, the nine major central places outside of the OK growth pole are divided into two groups: (1) those that are located in the southern part of the prefecture with easy access to the OK growth pole and (2) those located in the inland northern part of the prefecture at a grcatcr effective distance from the growth pole.

The growth rate of population of the OK growth pole is positive throughout with a spurt after 1967 that is highest in 1971. This spurt can be readily identified by examining the rate of increase of private investment and manufacturing product accelerating after 1966. The subsequent rapid increase in demand for labour had the effect of polarizing to the OK growth pole from the non-OK regions as well as from outside the prefecture. The resulting increase in the growth rate of the OK growth pole and close cities located in the South was mirrored by corresponding decrease in growth rates of the Northern urban centres.

However, there seems to have been a turning point when "spread effect" began to dominate "polarization effect" which can readily be pinpointed around 1968 - 9. It is significant that this turning point precedes 1971 which was the OK growth pole's period of greatest growth rate of population, suggesting that these non-OK cities had developed sufficient retentive force over their service area population to resist the OK region's polarization force during 1970 and 1971, the peak of OK subregion's growth rate.

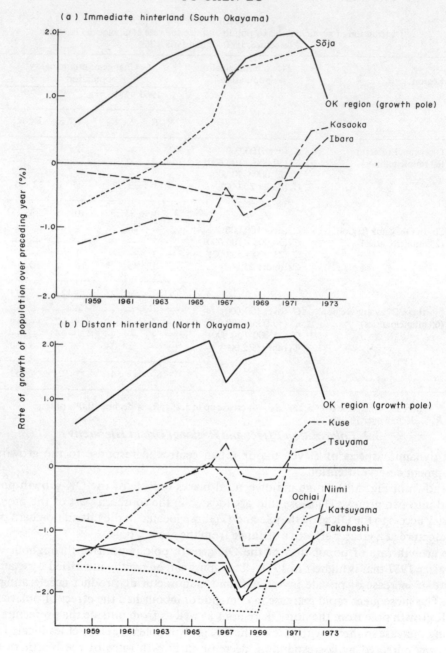

Fig. 5. The rate of population growth of regional urban centres.

A comparison of the growth performance of group 1 and group 2 offers some insights into the growth potential of a city. Group 2 urban centres, that is those spatially distant from the growth pole, most of which have populations under 40,000, experienced negative rates throughout with a drastic drop in rates after 1966 but showing a marked upward trend after 1969.

The group 1 urban centres in the southern part of the prefecture with easy access to the growth pole experienced positive growth rates by 1971. Though their population was subject to polarization to the pole, nevertheless, spatial proximity to the pole accorded them ready access to diffusion of growth impulses from it. Kasaoka had population size (over 70,000) working in its favour, while Ibara had a large automobile industry which predated the Mizushima industrial complex.

The growth-inducing effects of spatial proximity to the growth pole are seen in the case of Soja, which though having a population of less than 40,000 very quickly caught up with the population growth rate of the OK region. The reason for this is the initiation of an automobile industry in Soja that was directly linked to the growth pole.

TABLE 10

Income differential and intra- and interregional migration of major urban centres in Okayama Prefecture 1968

Unit	Intra-prefectural income differential (Prefecture per capital income = 100) (1)	Intraregional migration (%) (2)	Interregional income differential by setting national average = 100 (3)	Interregional migration (%) (4)	Net migration (2) + (4)
Nation	107.5	—	100	—	—
Okayama Prefecture	100.0	—	93.0	-0.05	-0.05
Cities:					
Okayama	134.4	0.47	125.0	0.51	0.98
Kurashiki	125.4	0.87	116.0	1.60	2.47
Tsuyama	85.3	0.13	79.3	-2.00	-1.87
Soja	103.2	0.67	96.0	-0.24	0.43
Takahashi	68.6	-1.23	63.8	-0.76	-1.99
Niimi	78.2	-1.41	72.7	-1.29	-2.70
Kuse	72.3	-0.65	67.2	-2.45	-3.10
Ochiai	59.6	-0.44	55.4	-1.65	-2.09
Katsuyama	69.1	-0.88	64.3	-1.30	-2.18
Kasaoka	80.6	-0.38	74.9	-1.16	-1.54
Ibara	71.9	0.18	66.9	-1.17	-0.99

3.3. Structural Change of the Economies in Urban Centres

The dual functions of an urban centre, i.e. (1) central place service functions and (2) export base manufacturing functions, can be examined through the use of a simple ratio of manufacturing to service employment, called for simplicity the MS ratio. Over fifteen years a constant MS ratio implies no change in the relative size of manufacturing and service employment. A decrease in the MS ratio implies a relative increase in the importance of central place service functions and, conversely, an increase in the ratio suggests the development or growth of export base manufacturing functions. An increase, and subsequent flattening, of the MS ratio would suggest that service employment is called forth by increased manufacturing activity. The absolute size of the MS ratio also reflects the relative importance of manufacturing and service sectors. For the non-OK cities, since we have identified the turning point when "spread effect" took place as being around the 1968 - 9 period, we should expect to see an increase in the MS ratio between 1965 and 1970.

As shown in Fig. 6, this hypothesis is borne out by the accelerated increase in non-OK

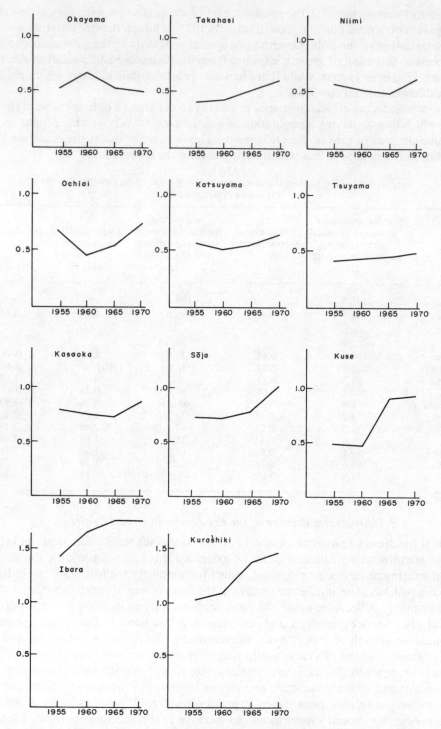

Fig. 6. Ratio of Manufacturing employment to service employment in central cities.
Source: Office of the Prime Minister, *Population Census of Japan.*

urban centres after 1965. When we examine Kurashiki City, the accelerated increase was from 1960 when Mizushima was initiated. However, after 1965 there is a flattening in the slope of the MS ratio which suggests an increase in the service sector called forth by increased manufacturing activity. Kuse and Ibara also have a similar flattening in the MS ratio. Okayama City, on the other hand, shows a marked decrease in the MS ratio, indicating a marked increase in the relative importance of its service sector.

3.4. Summary

There was a substantial polarization of the rural population toward regional urban centres reflecting an urbanization and industrialization process. The widening gap of intersectoral labour productivity was instrumental in shifting labour from rural-oriented agricultural to urban-oriented employment in manufacturing and service sectors. Secondly, interregional and intraregional migration can be traced mainly as responses to income differentials within and between regions. The role of the OK growth pole in this labour reallocative process cannot be overrestimated.

Productivity and income differentials between the growth pole and other central places initially reallocated labour in favour of the growth pole. However, the spread effect of the manufacturing sector began to dominate polarization effects by 1968 - 9 and provide a growth impetus to the other urban centres. This is evidenced in the increasing homo-geneity in the share of manufacturing employment in other central places, which indicates substantial growth of the manufacturing sector outside the growth pole. The develop-ment of high productivity sectors in the growth pole and subsequent diffusion of manu-facturing activities to the other urban centres together provided a strong incentive to movement out of the agricultural sector.

The function of urban centres as service centres to the rural population has been de-clining due to the depopulation of rural areas. However, the function of cities as export-oriented economic bases due to the gradual adoption of manufacturing activities in the entire regional urban hierarchy seems to have enabled the cities to retain their populations against polarization around the pole. The size of city, distance from the growth pole, and historical factors may have determined the potential of cities to resist polarization.

4. INTERREGIONAL DISPERSION OF DEVELOPMENT OF A NATIONAL ECONOMY

The process of spatial development of a national economy has many facets. The main focus here is on an attempt to develop a theoretical framework that may provide some clue to a better understanding of the basic factors associated with the process of polari-zation and decentralization of development in a national economy.

The model to be introduced here is a response to the hypothesis that polarization and decentralization of development are not contradictory phenomena but can be treated as different phases in the development process.[5] Such a development process can be de-

---

[5]Richardson, in reference to Friedmann's core-periphery model, summarized the spatial development pro-cesses of a national economy by classifying them under three hypotheses; namely, (i) the onset of industrialization in a national economy is based upon economic expansion in one, two, or few limited regions, leaving the rest of the economy relatively backward, (ii) subsequent national economic development is associated at some stage with dispersion into other regions, a process which tends to integrate and unify the national economy, (iii) in-dependent of the polarization and subsequent dispersion tendencies interregionally, growth within regions al-ways tends to be spatially concentrated. John Friedmann, *Regional Development Policy: A Case Study of Venezuela,* MIT Press, 1966; H. W. Richardson, *Regional Growth Theory,* Macmillan, 1973.

monstrated by integration of the concepts of agglomeration economies related to urban size and the diffusion process of technology in a neo-classical framework.

4.1. Agglomeration Economies of Urban-Size and Diffusion of Technology[6]

It seems to be a widely accepted theory that the external economies occurring at a certain threshold size of urban centres are a necessity for the inducement of industries to a new location. On the other hand, debate is going on in the literature on the question of the existence of a so-called optimum size of city for particular types of economic activity in which various external diseconomies may result from over-urbanization. Numerous studies pointed in this direction are still groping for more convincing evidence to identify empirically the existence of a U-shape for *per capita* public service expenditures or an upside down U-shape efficiency curve for agglomeration economies related to urban size.[7]

Serious attention should be focused on the point that such efficiency curves may differ by type of economic activity, particularly between manufacturing and tertiary sectors.[8] In this connection, the shape of the efficiency curve of agglomeration economies can partly be explained by the density of urban activities. The writings on urban density functions have indicated that not only does the density of economic activity tend to increase with the size of city, but also that the resulting competition between types of economic activity, in terms of productivity per unit of land, may exclude those extensive land-use activities with low productivity per unit of land due to the high cost of location.[9] In particular, once a city grows to a certain stage, it may become uneconomical for manufacturing activities that require considerable land acreage to be located in an urban centre. The tertiary sector, with high productivity per unit of land, will gradually take its place. Consequently, for the manufacturing sector, efficiency of production will increase initially with city size because of juxtaposition economies till that city reaches a size at which diseconomies of agglomeration, particularly increased land costs, cause a decrease in the efficiency of production.

In considering the comparative advantages of agglomeration economies for industrial location in a system of cities, it is quite conceivable, even in a case in which the growth of a large metropolitan region exceeds the optimum size of a city in terms of a maximum agglomeration economies for a certain type of industry, that decentralization of such industrial activities will not take place if the agglomeration economies of the smaller cities, presumably in less-developed regions, still remain comparatively smaller. El-Shakhs[10] and others have argued that particular types of city-size distributions are related to

---

[6]For a more elaborated discussion of comparative urban efficiency see Fu-chen Lo and Kamal Salih, Growth poles and regional policy in open dualistic economies: Western theory and Asian reality,—Chapter 11 in this volume.

[7]A recent study by Kawashima shows some interesting observations of such efficiency curves estimated for manufacturing sectors in the United States. Tatushiko Kawashima, Urban production functions and economies of urban agglomeration: Optimum urban size and urban-agglomeration-oriented industries, in *Eighteenth North American Meeting, Michigan,* Regional Science Association, 1971.

[8]See Lo and Salih, *op. cit.*

[9]For instance see Edgar M. Hoover, *An Introduction to Regional Economics,* Knopf, New York, 1971.

[10]Salah El-Shakhs, Development, primacy, and systems of cities, *Journal of Developing Areas* 7 (1972) 11-35.

specific stages of development, and he has drawn attention to an interesting observation of high primacy in the urban system of less-developed countries. This observation may help to explain a stronger tendency towards polarization of industrial activities in many capital regions of developing countries due to *relatively higher* agglomeration economies in the already over-congested metropolitan area compared with alternative locations in a much smaller city. Moreover, by the same logic any dispersion of industrialization is likely to trickle down the urban hierarchy to the next largest urban centre and so on.

Another factor which affects comparative regional efficiency of capital is technology. Spatial diffusion of innovation is one of the cornerstones of growth pole theory. Technology, new innovations, information, and/or entrepreneurship take time to spread out from the pole. This may be particularly important in developing countries, where the maintenance of marked spatial differences in technology, educational levels, information, and so on has been a barrier to new investment decentralizing from the developed regions. In some recent studies, an interesting conclusion which deserves special attention is that information diffusion tends to benefit the largest towns most, and the information diffusion process will be diffusion down the urban hierarchy from the large to the small urban centres.[11] At the lower levels diffusion is to lower order centres close by, as further spread is then heavily regulated by the friction of distance.

4.2. Regional Growth and Resource Mobility

Before we proceed to integrate the above-stated urban economic theory with a regional growth model, a brief description of the neo-classical framework may be useful. At any given time the spatial pattern of development in a national economy is largely determined by the spatial distribution of industrial activities. And regional disparities of development are attributed to the existing resource endowment, particularly production capacity of capital stock of the region. However, what is crucial in regional growth is not resource endowment differences in a static situation but the dynamic process of growth. Economic interaction within a system of regions is essentially imperfect competition over space. It is imperfect because of imperfect mobility of goods, resources, information, and the like. In general, the existing factories or infrastructure hardly can be reshuffled to a new location, most likely only new investment has full mobility in response to the equilibratory force of factor price differentials between the regions. In other words where new investment locates will depend upon rates of return to capital among regions in the sense that capital will seek out the most profitable location. By the same token labour will pursue higher wages and, in an imperfect manner, the flow of interregional migration will respond due to interregional disparities in wages or income differentials. Thus, the dynamism of regional growth is basically determined by the direction, magnitude, and speed of resources movement, mainly capital and labour, within a system of regions. When labour is abundant, the relative rate of return to capital among regions plays a fundamental role in determining the spatial allocation of new investment and the growth of regional economy.

[11]P. O. Pedersen, Innovation diffusion in urban systems, *Information Systems for Regional Development—A Seminar (1969), General Papers,* Lund, Royal University, 1971; T. Hagerstrand, Aspects of the spatial structure of social communication and the diffusion of information, *Regional science association papers* 16 (1966), 27-42; B. J. L. Berry, The basis of development filtering and spread in a system of growth centres, in *Growth Centres in Regional Economic Development,* N. Hansen (ed.), pp. 108 - 38, Free Press, New York, 1972; T. Hermansen, A review of the concepts and theories of growth poles and growth centres, Mimeo, United Nations Research Institute for Social Development, 1970.

However, neo-classical theory alone, without properly integrating the theory of urban agglomeration economies introduced earlier, cannot explain the polarization of capital investment in the capital intensive region.

4.3. A Model of Polarization and Decentralization of Development

The dynamic process of regional development patterns in terms of the process of divergence and convergence of *per capita* income can be illustrated in a simple model which integrates the neo-classical growth theory of factor mobility with the concepts of spatial diffusion of technology and optimum size of city.[12]

In order to simplify the model, assume the existence of a two-region economy, where *per capita* income is higher in the developed Region 1 (capital intensive region) compared with the underdeveloped Region 2 with relatively low capital intensity (labour intensive region). It is not unreasonable to assume that the external economy of urban agglomeration and efficiency of technology are also higher in Region 1 relative to Region 2.

For simplicity, let us assume a Cobb - Douglas production function.

$$Q_i = e^{\lambda_i + \theta_i} K_i^\alpha L_i^{1-\alpha} \ (i=1, 2), \tag{1}$$

where Q_i is output of region i $(i=1, 2)$, K_i and L_i are capital and labour respectively, and λ_i and θ_i are technology and agglomeration economies related to urban size. Then regional *per capita* income q_i is

$$q_i = e^{\lambda_i + \theta_i} (k_i)^\alpha \ (i=1, 2) \tag{2}$$

where $q_i = Q_i/L_i$ and $k_i = K_i/L_i$ is the capital labour ratio of region i $(i=1, 2)$[13]

If Region 1 is the developed or capital intensive region, that is $k_1 > k_2$, then the wage rate is higher in Region 1, $w_1 > w_2$. It follows that labour will migrate from the underdeveloped region (Region 2) to the developed region (Region 1). However, whether or not capital investment will move from Region 1 to Region 2 depends upon whether or not the rate of return to capital in Region 2 is higher than that of Region 1, i.e.

$$r_1 \gtrless r_2.$$

From production function (1) then rental ratio between the regions (r_1/r_2) gives

$$\frac{r_1}{r_2} = e^{(\lambda_1 - \lambda_2) + (\theta_1 - \theta_2)} \left(\frac{k_2}{k_1}\right)^\alpha \tag{3}$$

and the ratio of regional *per capita* income between Region 1 and Region 2 gives

$$\frac{q_1}{q_2} = e^{(\lambda_1 - \lambda_2) + (\theta_1 - \theta_2)} \left(\frac{k_1}{k_2}\right)^\alpha \tag{4}$$

---

[12]Robert M. Solow, A contribution to the theory of economic growth, *Quarterly Journal of Economics* **70** (1956) 65-94. Fu-chen Lo, A two-region growth model with imperfect mobility of factors, unpublished PhD dissertation, University of Pennsylvania, 1968.

[13]To complete the model we can further assume that (1) population growth is at a constant rate, (2) the saving ratio is constant, (3) the existing capital stock cannot be reshuffled between regions and only new investment has perfect mobility, and (4) migration of labour (or population) is partially a response to wage (or income) differentials between regional (imperfect mobility of labour).

The *relative* levels of rate of return to capital and regional *per capita* income as given in (3) and (4) are determined by three factors; namely, relative gap of technology $(\lambda_1 - \lambda_2)$, relative efficiency of agglomeration economy $(\theta_1 - \theta_2)$, and relative levels of capital and labour intensity of the regions. Figure 7 illustrates the changes of those relative variables over time.

As shown in Fig. 7a, in the first stage of development, because of capital intensity in

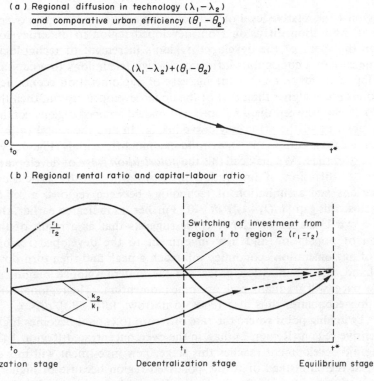

(a) Regional diffusion in technology $(\lambda_1 - \lambda_2)$ and comparative urban efficiency $(\theta_1 - \theta_2)$

$(\lambda_1 - \lambda_2) + (\theta_1 - \theta_2)$

(b) Regional rental ratio and capital–labour ratio

$\dfrac{r_1}{r_2}$

Switching of investment from region 1 to region 2 $(r_1 = r_2)$

$\dfrac{k_2}{k_1}$

Polarization stage	Decentralization stage	Equilibrium stage
$k_1 > k_2$	$k_1 > k_2$	$k_1 = k_2$
$w_1 > w_2$	$w_1 > w_2$	$w_1 = w_2$
$r_1 > r_2$	$r_1 < r_2$	$r_1 = r_2$

(c) Regional per capita income, from divergency to convergency

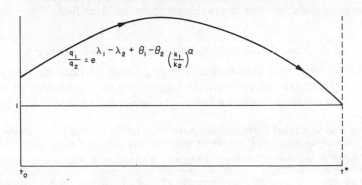

$$\frac{q_1}{q_2} = e^{\lambda_1 - \lambda_2 + \theta_1 - \theta_2} \left(\frac{k_1}{k_2}\right)^{\alpha}$$

Fig. 7.

Region 1, the wage rate (labour productivity) is higher in Region 1 and population will migrate toward the developed region (Region 1). In the meantime, although the capital - labour ratio is higher in Region 1, a relatively higher level of efficiency from technology ($\lambda_1 > \lambda_2$) and agglomeration economies in Region 1 ($\theta_1 > \theta_2$) ensures that the rate of return to capital in Region 1 will be higher than that of Region 2 ($r_1 > r_2$). In other words, both labour (or population) and investment will keep flowing into the developed region (Region 1).

If in Region 1 the relative level of technological efficiency increases over time because the speed of innovation diffusion from developed region to underdeveloped region is slower than the speed of the developed region's increment of technological efficiency (imagine the case of a continuous inflow of foreign technology to a capital region of an underdeveloped country), and/or the increase of agglomeration economies in the developed region is much higher than that of the underdeveloped region, then the gap in rates of return to capital between the developed and underdeveloped regions continues to widen. This is the upswing of the efficiency curve in Fig. 1a and the rental ratio r_1/r_2 curve in Fig. 7b. Under these conditions, *per capita* income differentials (Fig. 7c) will experience a divergence over time. We may call this the *polarization stage* of development.

However, as diffusion of innovation increases with greater efficiency of regional communications and assimilation of technology between regions, a set of forces will operate to close this gap $\langle [d(\lambda_1 - \lambda_2)]/dt \rangle < 0$. Further, as indicated earlier, the existence of an upside down U-shaped efficiency curve suggests that as a result of the continuous polarization of population and new investment to the developed region, productive efficiency of agglomeration economies will reach a peak and then turn downwards. On the other hand, the urbanization process in the underdeveloped region, initially going on at a slow pace, will gradually pick up some momentum. The regional difference in the agglomeration economies thus also tends to narrow $[d(\theta_1 - \theta_2)]/dt) < 0$. Eventually it will reach a switching point where the rate of return to capital becomes higher in the less capital intensive region (Region 2) than in the overconcentrated Region 1 (Fig. 7b at t_1). Once economic development reaches this stage, new investment will move towards the less-developed region instead of to the polarized region because of higher efficiency in capital productivity of Region 2. Sooner or later, relative levels of regional *per capita* income will also switch from divergency to convergency (Fig. 7c).[14]

During the decentralization stage, new investments will continue to flow into Region 2, and the gap of capital intensity between the two regions will diminish over time with the steady convergence of regional *per capita* income. Finally it may reach an equilibrium stage where no regional differences in development can be identified.[15]

4.4. Trend Towards Decentralization: Some Evidence

Concentration of industrial activities in the first stage of post-war industrialization in the 1950s, which apparently enjoyed the agglomeration economies of the Tokaido Megalopolis (Tokyo - Nagoya - Osaka belt), was necessary to maintain high economic

[14]The curve in Fig. 7 may be called a "Williamson curve". See Jeffrey G. Williamson, Regional inequalities and the process of national development, *Economic Development and Cultural Change* 13 (1965) 3 - 45.

[15]As indicated by Meyer, regional difference will become "increasingly smaller and more homogeneous by political and institutional development and by improvement in transportation, communications, and other technologies, with all that these imply for resource mobility". John R. Meyer, Regional economics: a survey, *American Economic Review* 53 (1963) 1954.

growth rates at a time of scarcity of capital. But polarization itself gradually developed into diseconomies of over-concentration for the manufacturing industries which required a decentralization policy to pursue further economic growth in the second stage of industrialization in the 1960s.[16] Thus the new industrial city policy which aimed at decentralization of the industrial activities down to the lower urban hierarchy was a necessary process as industrialization of the Japanese economy proceeded during the 1960s.

One may conclude that decentralization of manufacturing industries in Japan during the 1960s came as the result of diseconomies in the manufacturing industries in the over-urbanized Tokaido Megalopolis reflected in the high costs of land, utility supplies, and transportation and labour costs. Financial incentives and the provision of infrastructure by the public sector only played a role of facilitating the trend of industrial decentralization rather than the other way round.

Decentralization of heavy manufacturing industries from the highly developed Tokaido Megalopolis to the New Industrial Cities, from the theoretical point of view, indicated a switch (although not necessarily a clear-cut one) of investments from the polarized Tokaido belt region to the rest of the country.

In Table 11 the trend of interregional disparities of *per capita* income for selected years are shown by the coefficient of variation (national *per capita* income equals 100). The result is striking that from 1955 to 1963 regional *per capita* income diverged, with the

TABLE 11
Divergence and convergence of regional *per capita* income of Japan, 1955 - 70

Region	1955	1960	1963	1964	1965	1970
Hokkaido	76.0	115.5	171.3	184.4	208.9	473.0
Tohoku	60.4	94.3	145.2	165.1	188.2	410.7
Kanto	90.8	160.8	253.9	283.1	309.0	571.9
Tokai	77.2	141.3	209.5	231.0	250.2	574.0
Hokuriku	72.3	120.0	179.6	199.2	221.2	499.7
Kinki	91.6	156.8	240.4	270.9	298.2	579.3
Chugoku	66.0	107.7	158.9	183.6	203.4	484.6
Shikoku	64.3	102.7	154.7	177.2	199.4	481.5
Kyushu	61.5	96.5	143.6	162.7	187.7	394.3
National *per capita* income	76.6 ($212.7)	130.5 ($362.5)	201.8 ($560.5)	226.9 ($630.3)	251.7 ($699.2)	571.0 ($1581.1)
Regional disparity index[9] (Williamson coefficient) V_w	0.165	0.208	0.223	0.218	0.202	0.152

Sources: Japan Development Bank, *Statistical Analysis of Economic Growth by Region in Japan,* p. 88. Economic Planning Agency, *Chiiki keizai Yoran (Regional Economic Bulletin),* 1973, p. 52.

*The regional disparity index used by Williamson is the weighted coefficient of variation as follows:

$$V_w = \frac{\left[\sum_i^9 (y_i - \bar{y}) \dfrac{f_i}{n} \right]^{1/2}}{\bar{y}},$$

where V_w is Williamson's coefficient of regional disparity, y_i income *per capita* index of the ith region, $\bar{y}$ is the national income *per capita* index, f_i population of the ith region, and n national population (Williamson, *op. cit.*).

[16]See Honjo, *op. cit.*

coefficient of variation increasing from 14.5 to 19.2. From 1963, however, a decreasing trend in the coefficient of variation can be observed. This observation also is a suggestive sign to show a switch from a polarization stage to a decentralization stage. That the timing of this switch coincided with the implementation of the New Industrial City Policy is worth noting. In Table 11, through the entire period of 1955-70 only three regions, namely Kanto (Tokyo), Kinki (Osaka, Kobe, and Kyoto), and Tokai (Nagoya) had exceeded the national average. In any case, decentralization of manufacturing industries seems to have begun operating around the early 1960s; thus, in general, there has been a converging trend in the development gaps between regions since then.

Figure 8 shows a comparison of the growth of national *per capita* income, regional

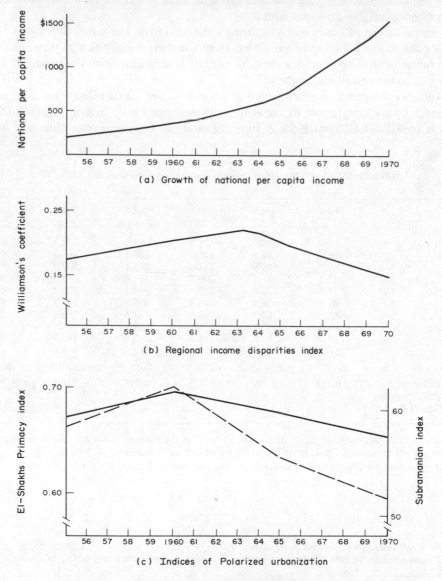

Fig. 8. Japanese experience (1955-1970)

income disparities (coefficient of variation), and urban primacy indices of El-Shakhs and Subramanian.

These findings quite well coincide with the earlier theoretical frame work relating Williamson's study with El-Shakhs' findings.[17]

TABLE 12
Urban primacy indices of Japan, 1950 - 70

Year	El-Sahkhs[a] primacy index	Urban concentration coefficient by Subramanian[a]
1950	0.6580	54.88
1960	0.6974	62.81
1965	0.6813	55.83
1970	0.6607	51.81

[a]Salah El-Shakhs, Development, primacy, and systems of cities, *Journal of Developing Areas* 7 (1972), 11-26; M. Subramanian, An operational measure of urban concentration, *Economic Development and Cultural Change* 20 (1) (1971), 105-16.

[17]Many authors often intuitively mention two related studies. See W. Alonso, Urban and regional imbalance in economic development, *Economic Development and Cultural Change* (2) (1968) 1-14; K. Mera, On the urban agglomeration and economic efficiency, *Economic Development and Cultural Change* 21 (2) (January 1973) 320; B. J. L. Berry, City size and economic development: conceptual synthesis and south and southeast Asia. In L. Jakobson and V. Prakash (ed.), *Urbanization and National Development,* Sage Publication, 1971, p. 138.

3

INDUSTRIALIZATION AND GROWTH POLE DEVELOPMENT IN KOREA: A CASE STUDY OF THE ULSAN INDUSTRIAL COMPLEX*

AN-JAE KIM

INTRODUCTION

In this paper three major topics concerning regional development planning and adoption of the growth pole centre approach in the Republic of Korea are discussed.

The first considers general development policies and processes from 1960 to 1976. Development policies in South Korea reflect the overriding concern with rapid industrialization as the principal strategy in raising aggregate national income. While this basic aim of the development strategy has, by the usual indicators of growth, appeared to have been achieved, a number of problems such as dependency on external sources for food and raw materials and heightened interregional inequalities, have put a slight dent in this success model. In light of these problems, the Korean government in 1972 set forth a new development plan which, while continuing the industrialization strategy, included programmes for rural development and comprehensive land development.

In the second section, with a focus on the southern coastal region, the paper examines the government's industrial location policies and their impacts on decentralization from the Seoul region and the development of the rest of South Korea. The paper suggests that industrial decentralization has been successful to a certain extent, even though polarization of some sectors continue in the Seoul region.

In the third section the paper specifically discusses the structure and expansion of Ulsan City as a growth centre to promote industrial decentralization from Seoul. The paper also attempts to assess the impact of Ulsan City on its rural hinterland.

The paper concludes with an evaluation of the growth pole approach in South Korea and outlines the outstanding problems in the South.

*I should like to acknowledge the able assistance of Yong Hong, Jinichiro Yabuta, and the City of Ulsan in carrying out the research project. The comments from Fu-chen Lo and Kamal Salih on earlier drafts of this paper are also very much appreciated. Responsibility for the contents of this report remain, however, with the author.

1. NATIONAL DEVELOPMENT POLICIES AND PROCESSES

1.1. National Development Policies and Plans, 1950 - 76

During the 1960s the Korean economy experienced a drastic change both in terms of quantity and quality. This change can be attributed to the industrialization strategy and policies laid down in the First Five-year Economic Plan (1962 - 6).

During the 1950s the average annual growth rate of the Korean economy was approximately 4.7 per cent. This growth rate, even allowing for the relative high population growth rate, has proved sufficient in satisfying the basic requirement of relief in the years immediately following the period of hostilities and of rebuilding the economy from the devastation of the three-year Korean War.[1] During this period, manufacturing industries maintained an average annual growth rate of 12.2 per cent, reflecting a sharp increase in industrial demand generated by rehabilitation undertakings in the wake of the Korean War. But the economic structure during this period was a greatly imbalanced one. Firstly, the domestic saving was too low to cover the gross capital formation, which averaged 13.2 per cent. The deficit of national expenditure was covered by a corresponding import surplus financed by foreign aid programmes. Secondly, the manufacturing industries were greatly biased toward consumer goods industries. These industries were almost all engaged in the final processing of raw materials, abundantly supplied by the United States, the United Nations, and other friendly nations and international organizations. The malallocation of investment resources in these final processing industries not only had deprived other sectors of the necessary resources but, due to the slow growth of the domestic market, also resulted in surplus of production and idle capacities in certain fields of consumer goods by the end of the decade. Thirdly, despite the agricultural characteristics of Korean economy, Korea had to import a big part of her food requirement.

Because of the decrease in incoming aid and the disequilibrium of the economy, economic growth of Korea began to slow down from the peak in 1957, eventually declining to 2.3 per cent in 1960 and even further in 1961.

The new government, which came into power in 1961, realized that the ultimate course of the Korean economy lay in industrialization. The basic development strategies laid down in the First Five-year Economic Development Plan are as follows:

(1) During the Plan period, the period of preparation for industrialization, emphasis was to be placed on development of power, coal, and other energy sources. In order to reduce the dependence of the Korean economy on foreign countries and to ameliorate the imbalanced manufacturing structure, gradual expansion of the industrial base into intermediate and capital goods was necessary. During this First Plan period the expansion or creation of such import-substituting industries as cement, chemical fertilizer, and synthetic fibers was an important component of the plan.

(2) To develop the agricultural sector, the sector in which the largest portion of labour was employed, so that self-sufficiency in food-grain could be attained by the target year. This would free the country from its dependence on imported food-grains and at the same time would enhance the welfare of farmers as well as improve the market for domestic products.

---

[1]Summary of the First Five-year Economic Plan, 1962 - 6.

(3) To increase social overhead capital through the mobilization of idle resources. The mobilization of idle resources would not only be effective in providing emergency relief for seasonal or chronic unemployment, but would also help to construct basic facilities required for long-range economic development.

The average annual growth rate during the First Plan period was envisaged to be 7.1 per cent. In order to achieve this target, the ratio of total investment to GDP would have to be increased from that of about 12 per cent in 1960 and 1961 to about 20 per cent in the target year. At the same time, the volume of foreign aid was expected to decrease sharply. Thus to increase domestic savings as well as vigorously expand exports on manufacturing products would not only be necessary to finance Korea's economic growth, but also in the short run to relieve the problem of idle capacity in certain consumer goods industry.

The achievement during the First Plan was very satisfactory. The average annual GDP growth rate during this period was about 10 per cent. Although the agricultural sector had not grown as was expected, this was covered by the exceptionally high growth rate of the manufacturing sector. The implementation of a series of export incentive measures, beginning in 1961 and continuing over the next several years, resulted in such spectacular growth of exports that by 1966 the realized export level was nearly double the target level.[2]

The favourable result of these new policies encouraged the Korean government to pursue the same direction and policy during the Second and Third Five-year Plans (1967 - 71 and 1972 - 6). To keep the economy moving ahead strongly, efficiency has always been the main criteria of decision making. Thus the main questions concerning the industrial structure for the Second, as well as Third Plan were (1) how rapidly exports could be increased, and (2) the timing of building new intermediate and capital goods industries. While continuous expansion of intermediate and capital goods industries were given high priority, limited investable resources would have to be used to capitalize on the rapid growth of exports which emanated mainly from the less capital intensive manufacturing industries. Thus some of the more capital intensive intermediate and capital goods industries would have to be delayed until the growth of demand was sufficient to justify building efficient-sized plants within Korea.[3] Cole and Lyman observed that despite statements at various points in the Second Plan about the importance of building up the machinery sectors, which were designed to appease nationalistic sentiments, the investment tentatively earmarked for them was not very large and much of it was expected to go into electric and mechanical appliances for export and (domestic) consumer markets rather than into the heavier machine-tool industries.[4]

1.2. Economic Development and Structural Changes of Manufacturing Industries

The achievement of Korean economy during the 1960s can be summarized in Figs. 1, 2, and 3.

The GNP of Korea had increased 2.48 times between 1962 and 1972 or an average annual compound growth rate of 9.5 per cent. During the same period, the GNP *per*

[2]Davis C. Cole and Princeton N. Lyman, *Korean Development: The Interplay of Policies and Economics,* Havard University Press, Massachusetts, 1971.

[3]Cole and Lyman, *op. cit.*

[4]Cole and Lyman, *op. cit.*, p. 213.

capita had doubled with an average annual growth rate of 7.4 per cent. As was mentioned, the achievement of the high GNP growth rate was due to the growth rate of secondary industries, especially manufacturing industries. The manufacturing value added had achieved an average annual growth rate of 18.4 per cent during the same period. Thus the share of manufacturing value added in total GNP had been increased from 12.6 per cent in 1963 to 18.7 per cent and 25.2 per cent in 1968 and 1972 respectively.

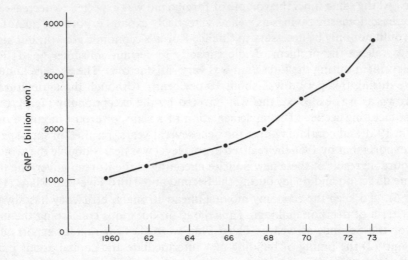

Fig. 1. Growth of GNP.

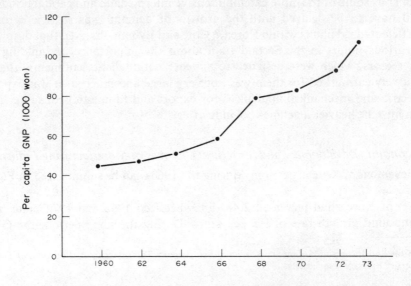

Fig. 2. Growth of *per capita* GNP.

An attempt has been made to distinguish the sources of manufacturing growth in Korea. Four sources of growth can be distinguished (Table 1):[5] (1) the substitution of domestic production for imports; (2) growth in intermediate demand stemming from the more intensive industrial linkage within the economy; (3) growth in final consumption; and (4) growth of exports. The above-mentioned first source can be classified as the change in source of supply, and the other three are classified as change in demand. The significance of each source on the growth of the manufacturing industries of a particular country depend on size, factor endowment, and stage of development of that country.

As was mentioned in the previous section, by the end of the 1950s, although under strict import control, almost all the necessary consumer goods were supplied by domestic industries and limited demand expansion was a severe constraint on the growth of manufacturing of Korea. After the present regime came to power in 1962, the policies to increase domestic demand by increasing the consumption power of the majority, increasing domestic industrial linkages as well as vigorously expanding exports, have been pursued.

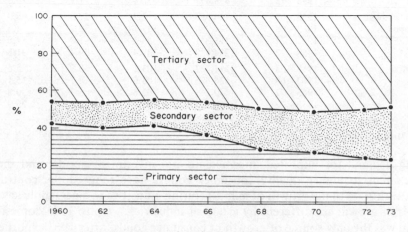

Fig. 3. Proportion of each sector to GNP.

As Table 1 shows, for manufacturing as a whole domestic market expansion (domestic final consumption and intermediate demand) was, and still is, the most important source of manufacturing growth, while export expansion has been increasing its contribution to growth. Although import substitution is going on rapidly in all types of industries, the

---

[5]The table was prepared by applying a technique used by Chenery, Hoffmann, and Tan. The domestic demand is defined as:

$D = X + M - E$, where D, X, M, E are domestic demand, domestic supply, import, and export respectively.   (1)

$$\text{Define } u = \frac{M}{D}, e = \frac{E}{D}, x = \frac{X}{D}$$

$$X_1 - X_0 = D_1(u_0 - u_1) + D_1(e_1 - e_0 - D_1 - D_0)$$ (2)

The logic behind equation (2) is that the growth of output of a certain commodity is attributed to the growth of domestic demand [$x_0(D_1 D_0)$], change in import ratio ($u_0 - u_1$), and change in export ratio ($e_1 - e_0$). H. Chenery, Patterns of industrial growth, *American Economic Review* 50 (4) (1960) and L. Hoffmann and Tan Tew Nee, Pattern of growth and structural change in West Malaysia's manufacturing industry, *Kajian Ekonomi Malaysia* 8 (2) (1971).

TABLE 1
Sources of manufacturing gross output growth

Industry group	Period	Increment of gross output[a]	Contribution coefficient		
			Domestic market expansion (%)	Import substitution (%)	Export expansion (%)
Consumer goods	1958 - 63	107,137	96.2	-1.7	6.0
	1963 - 68	218,107	80.8	-8.7	27.7
	1968 - 72	400,377	72.0	1.6	26.3
	1958 - 72	725,621	73.7	-4.0	30.3
Intermediate goods	1958 - 63	60,348	84.9	8.7	6.4
	1963 - 68	194,008	81.1	10.7	8.1
	1968 - 72	204,541	83.0	1.5	15.5
	1958 - 72	458.897	72.8	11.9	15.3
Investment goods	1953 - 63	44,398	117.7	-23.0	5.0
	1963 - 68	124,780	135.1	-39.2	4.4
	1963 - 72	115,351	43.1	-7.8	64.6
	1958 - 72	284,529	107.4	-39.4	31.8
Total	1958 - 63	211,883	103.1	-8.9	5.6
	1963 - 68	536,895	103.6	-18.7	15.1
	1968 - 72	'70,269	63.6	5.7	30.8
	1958 - 72	1,469,047	85.5	-11.5	25.9

[a]In million won at 1970 constant market price.

increasing demand for imported intermediate and investment goods, and the shift of import content to higher quality consumer goods, have reduced the contribution of import substitution to the growth of manufacturing industries to a negligible level.

Sources of growth are different by group of industries.[6] Up to 1963 domestic market expansion was the only source of growth of consumer goods; after 1963 export expansion began contributing about one-quarter to the growth of this group. Domestic market expansion comprised the main source and has contributed constantly to the growth of intermediate goods industry (continuously contributing more than 80 per cent). As Figs. 4 and 5 show, the import dependency ratio of intermediate goods declined rapidly up to 1968. Since 1968 the ratio of intermediate goods exports to production has increased considerably. These are shown in the shift of sources of growth in the type of industries in Table 1. Domestic market expansion was the only source of growth of investment goods industries up to 1968. Since 1968 the contribution of export expansion to growth of this type of industries has surpassed that of domestic market expansion. As Figs. 4 and 5 show, the import dependency ratio of investment goods had been increasing very rapidly up to 1968 and since then the ratio has been kept constant at the level of 56 - 58 per cent. On the other hand, the ratio of export to production of investment goods has been sharply increased since 1968. Generally speaking, in the past the growth of manu-

[6]Group of industries are defined as follows. *Consumer goods industries:* food, beverage, tobacco, textiles, footwear, wearing apparel and made-up textile goods, furniture and fixtures, paper and paper products, publishing and allied industries, and leather and leather products. *Intermediate goods industries*: wood and cork, rubber products, chemicals and chemical products, petroleum and coal products, clay, glass, and stone products. *Investment goods industries:* basic metal industries, metal products, machinery, electrical machinery, apparatus and appliances, and transport equipment.

facturing could be attributed to the growth of domestic market expansion, but it will be gradually determined by the extent of export expansion. The share of consumer goods exports in total manufacturing exports can be expected to remain more or less constant, while that of investment goods will increase sharply. Due to the increasing processing power in Korea, the export of intermediate goods can be expected to decline in relation to that of investment goods.

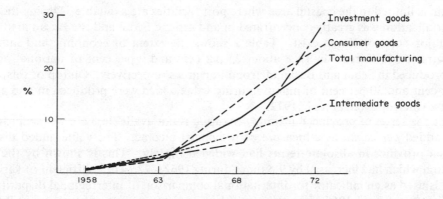

Fig. 4. Rate of export in manufacturing.

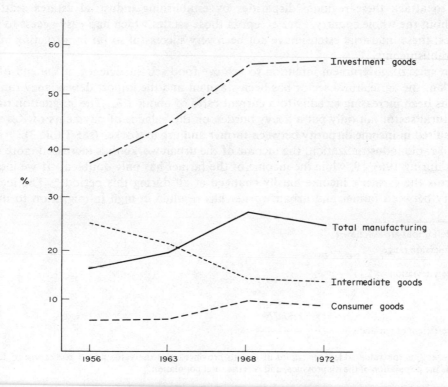

Fig. 5. Rate of manufacturing import dependency.

1.3. The Effect of Rapid Industrialization

The drastic economic growth and structural change achieved by Korea during the last decade has resulted in many serious problems. Some of the most salient points concerning regional development will be mentioned here.

(1) Since Korea has no powerful foreign exchange earning primary export items, vigorous manufacturing export expansion is necessary to finance economic development. Furthermore, almost all the raw materials have to be imported. Thus efficient industrial location is limited to the coastal area where port facilities are available. During the 1960s industrialization was greatly concentrated in and around Seoul and the Busan area where two major ports of Korea exist. Table 2 shows the extent of economic and industrial concentration in Korea. In 1968 about 25 per cent and 9 per cent of national product were produced in Seoul and Busan metropolitan areas respectively. On top of this, about 40 per cent and 30 per cent of manufacturing value added were produced in and around these two metropolitan areas in 1972.

Since the series of provincial income *per capita* is not available, here we use provincial value added *per capita* as a measure of provincial income. The value added disparity between province in absolute terms had widened rapidly. This is shown by the mean deviation which had increased by 9.5 times during 1962 - 72. The coefficient of variation, which is used as an indicator for international comparison of interregional disparity, had been increasing until 1966; even though it decreased afterwards, the value is still higher than in most developed countries.[7] This is shown in Fig. 6. The government has been trying to attack these regional disparities by establishing industrial estates scattered throughout the whole country. But except in those estates which had easy access to port facilities, these industrial estates have not been very successful so far in attracting industrial establishments.

(2) In spite of government intention to achieve food self-sufficiency at the end of the First Plan, the agricultural sector has been stagnant and the import dependency ratio of food has been increasing steadily to a current ratio of about 1:3. The stagnation of the agricultural sector not only put a heavy burden on the balance of payments of Korea, it also resulted in income disparity between farmer and urban worker (see Table 3). As the result of rapid industrialization, the income of the urban worker has increased more than 4 times during 1963 - 9, while the income of the farmer has only doubled. If we look in real terms the farmer's income hardly changed at all during this period.[8] The income disparity between farmer and urban worker has resulted in high in-migration to urban

---

[7] The definitions are as follows:

(a) Dispersion range $= Y_{max} - Y_{min}$.

(b) Mean deviation $= \dfrac{\Sigma_i |Y_i - \bar{Y}| F_i}{\Sigma_i F_i}$

(c) Coefficient of variation $= \dfrac{\sqrt{\Sigma (Y_i - \bar{Y})^2 F_i / N}}{\bar{Y}}$

where Y_i is the value added *per capita* of the ith province, $\bar{Y}$ is the value added *per capita* of Korea, F_i is the population of the ith province, and N is the total population.

[8] Ki-pyok Ch'a, The political implications of industrialization in Korea, paper prepared for ILCORK (International Liaison Committee for Research on Korea) Conference, 23 - 29 August 1971, Seoul, Korea).

TABLE 2
Indices of provincial differences in Korea

Province	(1) Share of national output (1960) (%)	(2) Share of national population (1960) (%)	(3) Share of national output (1968) (%)	(4) Share of national population (1968) (%)	(5) Activity rates (1966)[b] (%)	(6) Activity rates (1966)[b] (%)	(7) Output per worker (1960) (1965 wons)	(8) Output per worker (1968) (1965 wons)	(9) Gross income per capita (1968) (1968 wons)	(10) Rate of population increase (1966 - 70)
Seoul	21.3	9.9	24.7	14.5	21.38	23.22	213,937	250,818	84,775	45.6
Busan	—	4.7	9.1	5.2	21.83	24.20	—	252,379	86,920	31.5
Gyeonggi	11.2	10.9	9.8	10.3	26.41	25.78	87,617	139,036	46,765	8.1
Gangweon	6.3	6.5	5.1	6.1	27.19	25.17	74,693	123,648	42,050	1.9
Chungbuk	4.6	5.5	4.6	5.1	25.21	29.13	75,368	108,303	44,632	-4.4
Chungnam	8.5	10.1	8.6	9.7	27.71	27.59	69,675	114,974	44,054	-1.5
Jeonbuk	7.8	9.6	6.2	8.3	30.77	28.01	64,602	97,876	37,304	-3.5
Jeonnam	10.8	14.2	8.9	13.8	35.10	30.36	50,234	80,815	31,924	-1.1
Gyeongbuk	13.1	15.4	12.6	15.2	27.57	28.70	68,891	101,127	41,050	1.9
Gyeongnam	15.4[a]	12.1	9.3	10.6	28.93	27.73	74,342	117,900	43,661	-1.8
Cheju	1.0	1.1	1.1	1.2	44.10	33.22	49,473	128,677	47,765	8.4

[a]Includes Busan.
[b]Defined here as the ratio of employed population divided by total population and not as working population divided by population of working age.

Source: Bert and M. Renaud, Industrial location and policy in Korea: an analysis of the conflicts between national growth and regional income equality in a rapidly growing economy, paper prepared for ILCORK (International Liaison Committee of Research in Korea) Conference, 22 - 29 August 1971, Seoul, Korea.

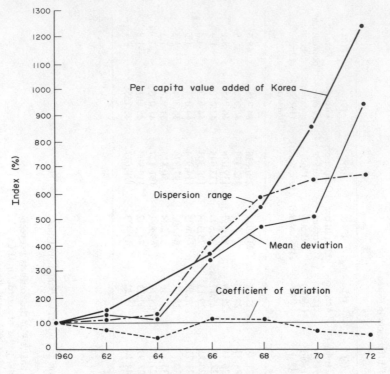

Fig. 6. Degrees of inter-Provincial disparity.

areas. The share of urban population to total population has been increasing from 37.9 per cent in 1960 to 56.2 per cent in 1973. In 1973 the urban population was 196.7 per cent while the rural population was 91.9 per cent compared to that of 1960.

TABLE 3
Income disparity between farmer and urban worker (annual income)

	Farmer	Index	Urban worker	Index	Comparison (urban worker = 100)
1963	93,179	100.0	80,160	100.0	116.2
1966	130,176	139.7	161,520	201.5	80.6
1966	217,874	233.8	353,600	416.2	65.3

Source: *Bank of Korea Monthly Statistical Report,* January 1971.

Note: According to these indices based on per household annual nominal income, the farmer's income was 15 per cent higher than that of the urban worker in 1963 but was 34.7 per cent lower in 1969.

The potential of agricultural growth in Korea is not very high; to increase the farmer's income through raising the price of agricultural products may reduce the competitive power of Korean manufacturing exports which are relatively labour intensive. There have been proposals since the time the Second Five-year Plan was under preparation arguing for continued expansion of exports and of agricultural production but with increasing reliance on a rural-oriented industrial sector to supply the export commodities. This was intended to provide stronger linkages between the urban and rural economic activities and to improve the incomes of the rural inhabitants. The basic strategy of export-led industrial development was generally accepted, but the rural industry emphasis was not, in part out of concern that decentralized, small-scale-producing facilities might be less efficient and therefore impair the competitiveness of Korean exports in world markets.[9]

1.4. Spatial and rural development policies and plans in the 1970s

In the light of the above-mentioned problems, the government of Korea formulated a National Land Development Plan (1972 - 81) and initiated the New Community Development Programme (*Saemaul Undong*) in 1971.

The basic objectives of a comprehensive national land development policy as is specified in the National Land Development Plan is to improve the environment of the national land so that people can enjoy their life in greater security and affluence and to ensure the equitable distribution of industries so as to realize the simultaneous development of agriculture and industry for the balanced growth of urban and rural areas. These basic objectives are broken down into four sub-objectives: the enhancement of efficiency in land use, the expansion of the development foundation, the development of natural resources, the conservation of the natural environment, and the improvement of manmade environments for the quality of life. Under this plan, Korea is divided into four major development regions on the basis of natural resources, especially water resources. These four major regions are further divided into eight intermediate development regions based on the criteria of homogeneity. Those eight regions are finally divided into seventeen subregions, each of which contains at least one polarized city (see Fig. 7). The Korean government has been making regional plans for only the eight intermediate regions. So far, only the Seoul Metropolitan Regional Plan and the Gwangju Regional Plan have been completed by the central government. The Northeastern Regional Plan will be started in 1976.

As mentioned, the New Community Development Programme was initiated in 1971. The objectives are (1) to promote an attitude of self-support and co-operation, (2) to improve the living environment and economic conditions in rural areas through an orientation toward modernization and efficiency and (3) to increase the income level in rural areas by increasing productive employment opportunities.

About 34,000 rural communities are classified into three categories: basic communities which are depressed areas, self-help communities which are developing, and self-sustaining communities which can grow without external support if the basic infrastructures are provided. All programmes of the movement are formulated and implemented according to the characteristics of the community categories. The first stage is to modernize and change the attitudes of the people in the rural communities. The second stage, which is expected to be carried out in the Fourth Five-year Plan (1977 - 81) will emphasize increasing income *per capita* and material well-being in these communities.

The government of Korea is formulating the Fourth Five-year Economic Development Plan emphasizing such basic policies as (1) building up a more independent economic system which will be achievable through the harmonization of continuous economic

[9]Cole and Lyman, *op. cit.*, p. 212.

growth and accelerated development of food, energy, and heavy chemical industry, and
(2) constructing a basis for welfare equalization by social development through the New
Community Development Movement, increase of employment opportunities, manpower
development, population control, education development, housing construction, and
improvement of the labour welfare system.

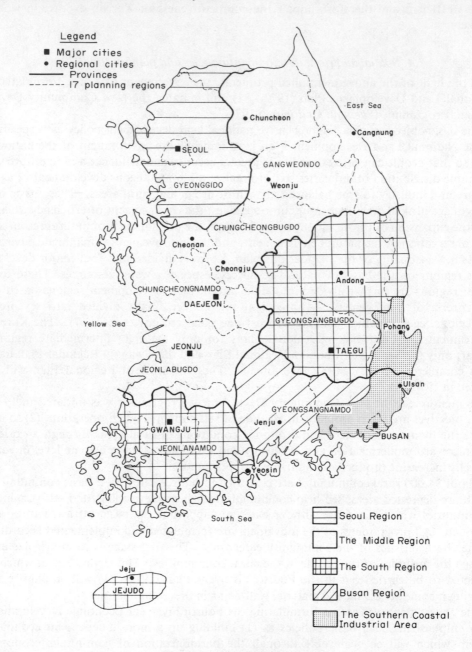

Fig. 7. Major development regions.

These basic objectives can be translated into the following strategies: (1) Develop new regional growth poles around industrial complexes and corridors and reduce concentration of people and economic activities in the largest metropolitan regions. (2) Organize the centre-periphery structure of the country's space economy on the basis of new growth poles and communities to be developed under the Industrial Estates Development Programme and the New Community Development Programme (NCDP). (3) Increase social overhead capital investments in various industrial complexes and major metropolitan regional economies. (4) Develop extensively the four major river basins in order to exploit various domestic resources and to increase agricultural production. (5) Promote intensive programmes linking agriculture and industry in the New Communities and develop service-oriented resources such as tourism. (6) Increase accessibility and efficiency in the transfer of goods, services, and information through development of modern transportation and communication systems consistent with the new spatial structure of the economy.

From the above description the basic strategy of the Korean government in the 1970s to further pursue manufacturing export expansion and industrialization in heavy and chemical industries has not been changed. The necessity to distribute the fruits of economic growth among regions and between rural and urban areas is strongly emphasized. It is the first time that the issues of regional development and rural development have moved into the forefront of the national development plan.

2. REGIONAL DEVELOPMENT IN THE SOUTHERN COASTAL AREA

2.2. Characteristics of the Southern Coastal Area

As is mentioned in the first section, so far the manufacturing activities in Korea are mainly concentrated in the Seoul area and in the Busan area in the southern corner of the Korean Peninsula. Over-congestion in these two cities and income disparity between these two areas and the rest of the country are significant. This stimulated the government to adopt a decentralization policy. Another reason for decentralization that is very important is the necessity to avoid heavy concentration of industrial facilities in the Seoul area and to set up economically self-sustaining regions throughout the country for the purpose of national defence.

Concerning economic activities and relationships, Korea can be divided into two development zones. The first is the Zeoul Zone containing Seoul City and its surrounding five provinces; the other is the Busan Zone containing Busa City and its surrounding four provinces. Each of these two zones can be further divided into two regions; the former into the Seoul Region and the Middle Region, and the latter into the Busan Region and the South Region (see Fig. 6).

Beside this delineation, another special area, the Southern Industrial Area, has been designated. This belt from Pohang City through Ulsan city to Masan city has been chosen as a special industrial area.

The southern coastal area was chosen to be a special industrial area for three reasons. Firstly, the southern coastal area has better conditions for constructing large ports than other coastal areas. As is well known, Korea has few material resources, so importing raw materials and exporting manufacturing goods must be carried out if there is to be continuous growth of the economy. Ports are indispensable for export-oriented industries and

industries with a high import content. Compared to ports, internal transportation costs
are less significant as locational factors, since Korea is a small country with a well-developed
transportation network. Secondly, Busan City, with a large agglomeration of nearly
2 million population, is a potential counterpole to the Seoul area, serving as a central
place for the whole southern region and facilitating industrial location in the whole of

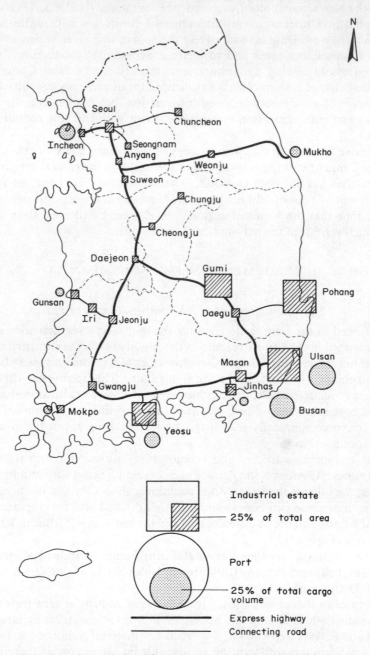

Fig. 8. Locations of industrial estates connected with ports and highways.

the southern coastal area. Thirdly, the southern coastal area enjoys locational advantage because of its high accessibility to Japan, a big market as well as a source of capital.

2.2. Government Policies for Industrial Location

In Korea, the role of government is highly significant in encouraging desirable industrial location. Government policies for industrial location include the development of industrial estates, tax incentives and subsidies, land-price policies, development of infrastructure, such as ports and roads, and various policies to encourage or control urban growth that have indirect effects on industrial location.

The most important tool of the government in controlling industrial location is the construction of industrial estates which occupy 22 per cent of all industrial sites in the country in terms of area as of 1970 (Table 4). There are four kinds of industrial estate:

TABLE 4
Location of Industrial Sites, 1970 (in 1000 m²)

Type of industry	Type of industrial sites	Seoul Region	Middle Region	South Region	Busan Region	Whole country
All industries	All industrial sites	23,793	9,651	8,489	18,900	60,833
	Industrial estate	969	978	3,297	8,162	13,406
	Other	22,824	8,673	5,192	10,738	47,427
Heavy industries	All industrial sites	8,100	1,372	2,923	11,452	23,847
	Industrial estates	428	365	2,090	6,459	9,342
	Other	7,672	1,007	833	4,943	14,505
Light industries	All industrial sites	15,693	8,279	5,566	7,448	36,986
	Industrial estates	541	613	1,198	1,703	4,064
	Other	15,152	7,666	4,368	5,745	32,922
Percentage of heavy industries	All industrial sites	34.0	14.2	34.4	60.6	39.2
	Industrial estates	44.2	37.3	63.4	79.1	69.7
	Other	33.6	11.6	16.0	46.5	30.6
All industries		4.1	10.1	38.9	43.2	22.0
Heavy industries	Percentage of	5.3	26.6	71.5	56.4	39.2
Light industries	industrial estates	3.4	7.4	21.5	22.9	11.0

Source: Ministry of Construction, *Guidelines for Long-range National Land Development*, 1974, p. 337.

coastal industrial estates; inland industrial estates; export industrial estates; which includes free trade zone; and special private industrial estates. In developing industrial estates, the government gives high priority to heavy industries and the southern coastal area. Table 4 shows that 70 per cent of the area of industrial estates is being occupied by heavy industries whereas the proportion of the area for heavy industries accounts for 31 per cent of the industrial areas other than industrial estates developed by the government. The proportions of industrial estates to the total industrial sites are much higher in Busan and the South Region, which are 43 per cent and 39 per cent, respectively. Furthermore, heavy industries occupy 56 per cent and 72 per cent of the area of industrial estates in the Busan Region and the South Region respectively. The same figures for Seoul and the Middle Region are much smaller.

The central government has several policy instruments to enforce industrial estate development. These include the standard price system of real estate, tax exemption and loans to the firms that wish to locate in industrial estates. The purpose of the standard price system of real estate is to fix the land price in the designated areas. This is being applied to all industrial estates. As to tax exemptions, any factory locating in the industrial estates is exempted from property tax. The factories moving from Seoul or Busan cities to these industrial estates are also exempted from other taxes such as income tax, corporation tax, registration tax and acquisition tax. Loans are given by the Korean Industrial Bank with high priority to the firms which are going to establish factories in the industrial estates. On the other hand, high acquisition taxes and registration taxes are levied on any new factory in Seoul to reinforce the decentralization industries. The levy is as high as 5 times the regular one.

Among many infrastructural facilities, the development of transportation facilities including expressway and ports seems to have played a very vital role in determining the spatial distribution of industries. All industrial estates are directly connected with either ports or expressways (see Fig. 13).

2.3. Changes in Socio-Economic Structures

In 1972 the regional distribution of value added of total manufacturing was 45 per cent in the Seoul Region, 29 per cent in the Busan Region, 12 per cent in the South Region, and 14 in the Middle Region. As a whole, industrial activities have been further centralizing in both the Seoul and Busan Regions as reflected in the increase of regional share of value added in these two regions throughout the period from 1958 to 1972.

However, there are clear changes in regional distribution by groups of industries.[10] Consumer goods industries continue to centralize in Seoul Region. Intermediate goods industries rapidly built up in the Busan Region during 1963 - 8, but after 1968 investment in intermediate goods industries gradually shifted to the South Region. Investment goods industries, highly concentrated in the Seoul Region, have been gradually beginning to centralize in the Busan Region after 1968. It seems that the South Region also began to increase its share of value added of investment goods industries after 1968 as the centralization in Busan increased (see Fig. 9).

The decentralization policies of Korea have been successful to a certain extent. As is shown in Fig. 9, in 1958, the Seoul Region occupied about 55 per cent of the total capital formation in manufacturing industries, but it rapidly declined to 35 per cent in 1968 and 1972. The percentage share of employment and value added in the Seoul Region are still showing an increasing trend. After 1963 the percentage share of capital formation of the Seoul Region was much lower than that of employment and value added. This can be said to be the result of increasing concentration of consumer goods industries, which are more labour intensive and higher value added per unit of capital investment, in this region. The percentage share of capital formation in the Busan Region increased during 1958 to 1963, but after 1963 it has been gradually declining. The remarkable increase of capital formation after 1963 is seen in the South Region, though it does not show increase in percentage share of employment and value added. What Fig. 10 implies is that industrial investments were first pushed out from the Seoul Region and then next from the Busan

---

[10]For definition, see footnote 5, page 57.

Region to regions outside the core regions, in particular the South Region which is more favourable for coastal industrial development.

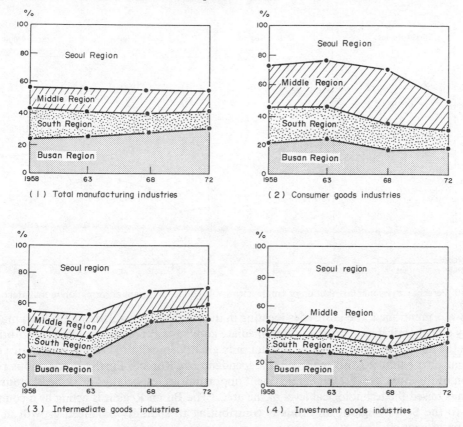

Fig. 9. Changes in regional distribution of manufacturing value added.

The trend of decentralization of manufacturing investment is even more significant at the intraregional level. As is shown in Table 5, the share of Seoul City and Busan City to total Seoul Region and Busan Region, respectively, in manufacturing investment rapidly decreased during 1963 - 72. Busan City even shows a rapid decline in share of manufacturing value added compared to that of the Busan Region. However, the share of manufacturing employment of these two cities to that of their respective regions has not declined to the same extent, and the share of population of these two cities to the total population of the respective regions has even been increasing.

As far as the Busan Region and the South Region are concerned, the growth of manufacturing employment, value added, and capital formation since the 1960s can be attributed to manufacturing development in the southern coastal industrial area which stretches over the eastern coast of these two regions. As was mentioned in the previous section, high priority was given by the government to the development of heavy industries and industrial estates in this southern coastal area. Due to the locational advantage of this area, heavy industries, such as the chemical and steel industries, which are heavily dependent on imported raw materials, located in this area while consumption-oriented goods and tertiary industries were concentrating more and more in the Seoul area.

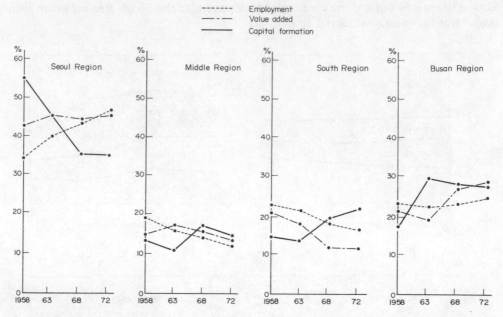

Fig. 10. Percentage regional distribution of employment, value added and capital formation in manufacturing.

As was mentioned, the industries locating in the southern coastal area have been mainly heavy and chemical industries and intermediate goods for export and import substitution. Thus the development of this area has not only greatly contributed to the growth of GNP but has also enhanced the economic independence of Korea. Furthermore, industrialization of this area has created employment opportunities, especially for skilled labourers, and has raised the technological level of the area. The Busan Region is acting as a counterpole to the Seoul Region, and thus is contributing to spatially balanced growth in the country as a whole.

TABLE 5
Percentage share of metropolitan cities in metropolitan areas:
population, employment, value added, and capital formation

Item	Year	% share of Seoul City to Seoul Region	% share of Busan City to Busan Region
Population	1960	47.1	27.8
	1970	62.2	37.6
Manufacturing employment	1963	76.4	76.4
	1972	70.9	68.1
Manufacturing value added	1963	79.1	81.1
	1972	68.5	51.1
Manufacturing capital formation	1963	79.9	88.9
	1972	31.5	38.6

Source: Economic Planning Board, ROK, *Korea Statistical Yearbook*, 1974.
EPB, ROK, *Report on Mining and Manufacturing Census, 1972 and 1966*.

Table 5 implies that the major functions of Seoul City as well as Busan City are gradually changing from manufacturing production to managerial functions and tertiary services. Although the gap between Seoul and Busan is increasing in terms of population size, Busan is a city with nearly 2 million population and has significant agglomeration economies. There is no doubt that Busan City is playing a significant role in promoting industrialization in the southern coastal area. According to the plants locating in Ulsan industrial complex, Busan is indispensable for their activities. It has various parts suppliers which are not available in such a small city as Ulsan. The port in Busan is well equipped with facilities for both export and import of various goods, whereas the port in Ulsan can only deal with import of raw materials and some limited items of exported goods.

3. INDUSTRIALIZATION, GROWTH AND IMPACTS OF ULSAN CITY AS A POLE: CASE STUDY

3.1. Growth and Structural Changes of Ulsan City

Ulsan Town was designated to be a special industrial area in January 1962 and was promoted to city status by enlarging its boundary in June of the same year with a population of 85,082 and an area of 174.32 km². The city was designated an open port in September 1963, and a special industrial region with an area of 1005.72 km², including Ulju County.

During the period 1962 - 74 the average annual population growth rate of Ulsan City was 7.4 per cent (compound growth rate). In 1974 the population of Ulsan City was approximately 200,000. There was a constant flow of migrants into the city.

Figure 11 shows the percentage of in- and out-migrants of Ulsan by origin and destination. Ulsan City is located in Gyeongnam Province. It can be observed that in 1972 most of the in- and out-migration of Ulsan was intra-provincial. However, in 1974, the in-migration from within the province was surpassed, though only slightly, by the in-

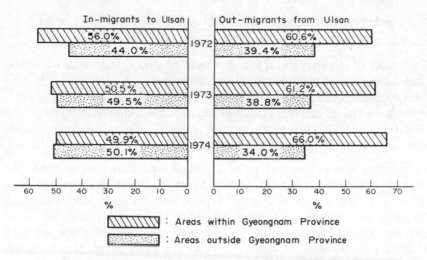

Fig. 11. Proportion of Ulsan's migrants by origin and destination.

migration from outside the province. About 15 per cent of the in-migrants were from Gyeongbuk Province, the adjacent province north of Gyeongnam Province. Next are Busan and Seoul cities, respectively.

During the period of the First Plan (1962 - 7), the total amount of investment in Ulsan was 40,357 million won, corresponding to 6.8 per cent of total national investments. During the periods of the Second and Third Plans (1967 - 72 and 1972 - 6), they were 84,036 and 191,495 million won, or corresponding to 4.6 per cent and 4.0 per cent of total national investments, respectively.

The amounts of products and exports of Ulsan City increased by about 300 times during the eleven years from 1962 to 1973.

Figure 12 indicates the composition in Ulsan by industrial sector since 1962. As is shown, the share of employment in the secondary sector increased very fast while that of the primary sector declined with equal speed.

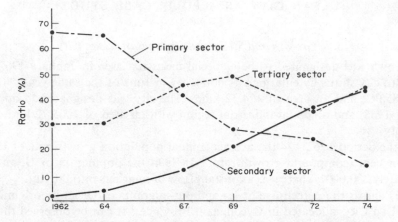

Fig. 12. Composition ratio of employment in Ulsan by industrial sector.

3.2. Formation and Development of Ulsan Industrial Complex

Some advantages of Ulsan for industrial location can be mentioned:

(1) Availability of infrastructural facilities such as a port, industrial water and power.
(2) Availability of cheap and spacious industrial sites.
(3) Good accessibility to major cities including Seoul.
(4) Proximity to an oil refinery plant and the allied petrochemical plants.
(5) Availability of skilled labourers.
(6) Good natural conditions such as rock-based soil.

Since Ulsan city was proclaimed to be a special industrial area in 1962, twenty-two petrochemical plants, fifteen non-petrochemical plants, and three power plants have been located in the industrial complex. Figure 13 shows the process of industrial location indicating the construction period and size of investments for each plant.

The first and largest investment in the Ulsan industrial complex was the construction of a petroleum refinery plant in 1964. Fertilizer and other petrochemical plants started their construction from 1965. Petroleum refinery plants import crude oil from abroad and supply naphtha to the petrochemical plants. Some chemicals that are not available

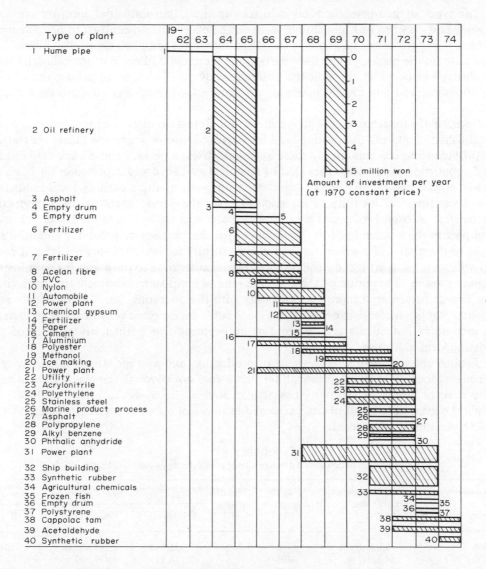

Fig. 13. Industrial location in Ulsan industrial complex, 1962 - 74.

in the industrial complex are imported through the port of Busan. Although there are considerable backward and forward linkages among petrochemical plants in the industrial complex, except for fertilizer all the products of petrochemical plants are intermediate products to be further processed in the big metropolitan areas.

Recently, because of the congestion in Seoul and Busan areas, the intermediate plants which process products from the Ulsan industrial complex are gradually moving into Ulsan or to the adjacent coastal areas. Thus it can be expected that the degree of processing and industrial linkages in the southern coastal area, especially Ulsan, will greatly increase. But the final processing industries—finished goods industries—will still remain in the metropolitan areas in the near future.

The types of non-petrochemical industries in the Ulsan industrial complex are quite diverse and very few linkages among them can be observed. In contrast to petrochemical plants, non-petrochemical plants in the Ulsan industrial complex, especially shipbuilding and automobile plants, gather their parts either from the makers in other industrial areas or through import and assemble the finished products. The scale of production of both shipbuilding and automobile plants is too small to economically support various part makers.

Because of the technological gap, there is still almost no direct linkages between newly established plants and the existing local industries. But now some new plants are starting to provide technical guidance to these local industries, especially those backward linkage and supporting industries. This kind of technical guidance and expected order from the newly established plants should stimulate the growth of these existing local industries. The local financial institutions are also eager for the development of these supporting industries. A branch office of a nationwide bank was set up inside the Ulsan industrial complex in the beginning of its development for the purpose of providing financial services to the plants. However, this office was recently moved down-town so that it could provide services to other industries or individuals rather than to the plants in the industrial complex alone. The reason was that after the initial lump-sum investment, the bank could not expect future expansion if it dealt only with the operating funds of the newly established plants. Increase in deposits and loans could be expected only through an increase in income of individuals and the continuing expansion of both newly established and existing local industries.

Table 6 gives some idea of the scale of production and average labour productivity of the plants located in Ulsan, although this table does not cover all the plants located here. The average labour productivity has almost doubled between the period of 1966 - 74, while the average scale of plants, measured in terms of value of products, has grown by 7.25 times during this period.

TABLE 6
Scale of production and average labour productivity of plants in Ulsan

Division Year	Amount of products (1000 won) (A)	No. of employees (B)	No. of plants (C)	Ratio		
				A/B (won)	A/C (won)	B/C
1966	2,694,808	368	2	7,322,847	1,347,404,000	184
1970	44,635,118	3401	8	13,124,115	5,579,389,750	425
1974	136,835,971	9501	14	14,402,270	9,773,997,928	679

Concerning the employment structure by occupations, as of 1975 the highest proportion of employees to total employees in Ulsan is skilled workers, followed by engineers, unskilled workers, clerical officials, and managerial staff. Regardless of occupation, more than 90 per cent of the employees are living in Ulsan City.

3.3. Change in the Rural Hinterland of Ulsan City

We define the five counties around Ulsan City as its intermediate hinterland. Three of these counties are in Gyeongnam Province, the province of Ulsan City, while the other two are in Gyeongbuk Province (Fig. 14).

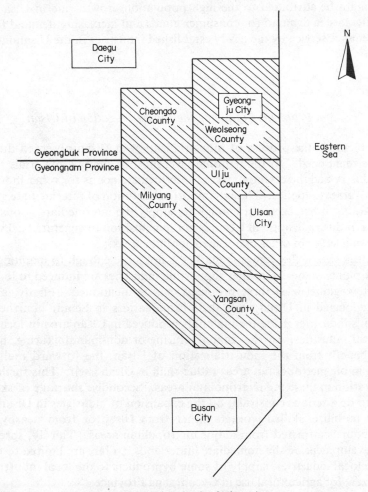

Fig. 14. Rural hinterlands of Ulsan city.

It is very difficult to determine the spread effect from Ulsan City to these counties because Ulsan City is located at the vertex of a triangle, with Daegu and Busan cities (two over-a-million population cities) at the other two vertices. Changes in socioeconomic conditions of these counties might be the result of the spread effect from Busan as well as Daegu, rather than Ulsan alone. Here we will confine ourselves to mention only the following two points.

(1) In contrast with Ulsan City, which has a very high population growth rate during the last fifteen years, the five counties around Ulsan City are rapidly losing their population.

(2) During the period 1966 - 70 the growth rate of manufacturing value added in these five counties was smaller than the average national growth rate; however, industries such as foods and beverages, footwear and personal ornaments, sawing and wood, furniture and equipments, printing and related materials, metal manufacturers, and machinery industries, showed a higher growth rate than that of the national average.

This might be attributed to the high population growth rate in Ulsan City, hence high increase in demand for consumer goods and increasing demand for repair and maintenance service by the newly established industries in the Ulsan industrial complex.

3.4. Problems Following the Industrialization of Ulsan

Some problems in the process of industrialization in Ulsan observed during the case study can be mentioned. At the national level most of the raw materials for the petrochemical industry and the essential part of intermediate goods for other industries are dependent on overseas supplies. Though import substitution of intermediate goods is going on well in Korea, it has been not enough to supply the intermediate goods required for Ulsan. Thus, industrialization in Ulsan is not in a position to generate backward linkages either in Ulsan itself or in other major metropolitan areas.

Secondly, the size of the domestic market is not large enough to maintain the scale of operation of plants to the extent that supporting industries are induced to locate in Ulsan.

At the interregional level three problems can be mentioned. Firstly, almost all the plants being located in Ulsan have their headquarters in Seoul. Furthermore, most finished goods industries using the materials produced in Ulsan are not located in Ulsan. Thus the local industries, whether manufacturing or non-manufacturing, have very few chances to benefit from the industrialization of Ulsan, the forward multiplier effects taking place in big metropolitan areas rather than in Ulsan itself. This further stimulates the concentration in these big metropolitan areas. Secondly, shortage of skilled workers is expected to be a serious constraint on the expansion of industries in Ulsan because it is not easy to mobilize skilled workers either from Ulsan or from nearby rural areas. Required labour is attracted from major metropolitan areas. Thirdly, spread effects of industrial development on the immediate hinterlands, so far, are limited to technical guidance to the local industries, supply of some byproducts to the local industries, and supply of fertilizers for agricultural use in Gyeongsang Province.

Intraregional problems can be summarized as follows. Firstly, infrastructure, power, and water in particular will be insufficient for the expansion of existing facilities in Ulsan. Secondly, Ulsan port is not suitable for the export of products since the port development was intended to serve industries that import raw materials or parts either from abroad or from other coastal areas and export processed materials to the major metropolitan areas. This is justifiable only when the forward linkages are still in major metropolitan areas.

Thirdly, the industrial linkages established within the industrial complex become a constraint on the expansion of plants within the same industrial complex because an industrial plant cannot carry out expansion plans without the expansion of other plants that supply materials. Fourthly, urban development has lagged behind the industrial development itself. The engineers and managerial staff transferred from major metropolitan areas are suffering from lack of urban amenities, welfare facilities, and educational facilities for their children.

Lastly, the industrial complex in Ulsan is not diversified enough to provide various goods, manpower, and information to encourage the location of supporting industries in the industrial complex.

4. CONCLUSION

In many ways the South Korean adoption of the growth pole approach to decentralize industries away from the Seoul Region has been successful, as the development of Ulsan as an industrial complex shows. But there are a number of problems which make it less than a complete success.

In the first instance, the industrial cities and industrial complexes in the southern coastal area do not have close relationships with rural hinterlands in terms of trade or employment and seem to have little impact on rural income distribution. Most of the industrial establishments that are located in the southern coastal area are heavy industries; they are more related to Seoul and foreign countries than to their own hinterlands. Secondly, industrialization of the counterpole areas, at least so far, has not brought about the decentralization of the Seoul population. Population concentration in that capital city continues on. Thirdly, industrialization has reduced agricultural and fishery production in the southern coastal area, and environmental disruption has begun. Finally, the expansion of the local economy has not resulted in much fiscal benefits to the local government.

The South Korean case, where a lagged response in decentralization of population is evident, is suggestive of two possible phases in the growth centre strategy: first, there is an early phase of decentralizing the heavy and semi-heavy industries, after which comes the rather more difficult phase of decentralizing population.[11]

What this implies is that South Korea may soon have to undertake other complementary strategies, as, for instance, she has done with the introduction of the New Community Development Programme, if the objective of a more optimum population and regional income distribution is to be achieved. In the meantime, the growth pole approach has succeeded in effecting some redistribution of industries to meet its other objectives such as maximum industrial growth and security.

---

[11] An explanation of this phenomenon is offered in the Lo - Salih paper (Chapter 11) in this book by using the notion of comparative sectoral efficiencies in urban growth.

4

DECENTRALIZATION POLICY, GROWTH POLE APPROACH, AND RESOURCE FRONTIER DEVELOPMENT: A SYNTHESIS OF THE RESPONSE IN FOUR SOUTHEAST ASIAN COUNTRIES*

KAMAL SALIH, PHISIT PAKKASEM,
Ed. B. PRANTILLA, and SUGIJANTO SOEGIJOKO

INTRODUCTION

The adoption of a growth centre strategy in the four countries of Southeast Asia surveyed in this paper, namely Indonesia, Malaysia, the Philippines, and Thailand, should be seen in two contexts: first, in terms of industrial decentralization to reduce regional development disparities, and, second, in terms of the development of their resource frontier regions. In this case, the Southeast Asian situation, consisting of resource rich countries as major primary exporters, provides an interesting contrast to South and East Asia, which consist of countries which can be classified as relatively resource-poor.

It is, however, not completely accurate to talk of the Southeast Asian experience in the adoption of the growth pole approach. For at this moment the strategy has only entered the language rather than the substance of regional development in each of the four countries. The implementation of regional development planning in general and the growth pole strategy in particular is too recent to permit any meaningful evaluation of the approach. The planning for growth centres, however, appears to be carried out in great earnest, based on increasing knowledge of the problems of uneven development in the respective countries. Whether a growth centre approach is appropriate to the solution of

---

*This paper is a synthesis of four country reports presented to the Seminar on Industrialization Strategies and the Growth Pole Approach to Regional Planning and Development: The Asian Experience, held at the United Nations Centre for Regional Development, Nagoya, Japan, 4-13 November 1975. The four reports are: Kamal Salih *et. al., Industrialization Strategy, Regional Development, and the Growth Centre Approach: Case Study of West Malaysia,* 320 pp.; P. Pakkasem, *Industrialization Strategies and Growth Pole Approach to South Thailand Regional Planning,* 46 pp.; Ed. B. Prantilla, *Industrialization Strategy and Growth Pole Approach to Regional Development Planning: The Philippines Experience,* 106 pp.; and S. Sugijanto, *Growth Centre Development within the Framework of Prevailing Development Policies in Indonesia,* 59 pp. In the process of writing this paper, some new material has, however, been added by the first author.

79

regional problems identified in each country is, of course, another matter, and is yet to be properly determined.

The responses of the four Southeast Asian countries to the problem of unequal spatial development, while no doubt adapted to the particular conditions in each country and integrated uniquely into each country's overall social and economic development policies, nonetheless are couched in terms of decentralization of economic activities, particularly manufacturing, from their central capital regions to the periphery, and in concert with the development of their substantial resource frontiers, they are invariably constituted in some form of growth centre strategy. In the process, some formalization of a regionalization scheme for the country is adopted and within each region growth centres identified. Most of these centres are actually existing towns, and it is not evident yet whether concrete investment expenditure has been directed to those centres. In any case it is obviously too early to determine the likely impact of these decisions. Much of the activity in the four countries have so far concentrated on various regional planning studies, often with the help of foreign consultants. But in a few cases these have been translated into various regional programmes of action. At the very least, these regional planning studies have enabled the central planners and policymakers to better understand the regional structure and spatial organization of their economies.

In examining the growth centre approach in Southeast Asia it is much better to see it in the context of an understanding of what regional development problems occupy the attention of Southeast Asian planners and thus help to determine its proper place in the overall regional and national development policy of each country. This is the aim of this paper through first considering the regional structure and problems of each of the four countries, the policies that are formulated, and the programmes and instruments introduced to solve them, and then finally to conclude with a discussion of the problems of the growth pole approach in relation to the broad range of appropriate regional policies for Southeast Asian countries.

1. REGIONAL STRUCTURE AND UNEVEN ECONOMIC DEVELOPMENT IN SOUTHEAST ASIA

The four Southeast Asian countries share a common concern over extreme regional inequalities in their economic growth. It is obvious that this problem is not new, arising mainly from the particular orientation of their economic policy towards industrialization and the expansion of their primary export sector to finance it and other social development projects. The recognition of the importance of this issue has coincided with the emergence of two factors: one, the shift which is occurring throughout the Third World in thinking on development goals associated with the UN Second Development Decade from an exclusive concern for economic growth to the lingering problems of poverty, inequality, and unemployment; and two, the increasing apprehension on the part of central governments and central planners concerning the political untenability of continued regional socioeconomic inequalities, especially as a result of pressure from—but more perhaps from the security threat in—peripheral areas.

In the four Southeast Asian countries examined in this paper, regional disparities appear to be quite severe. This can be judged from the Williamson coefficients of variation of *per capita* income calculated for the four countries; namely, 0.522 for Indonesia (in 1972), 0.556 for the Philippines (in 1957, which may have increased since), and 0.377 for West Malaysia (in 1968), all above the cross-national average of 0.30 found by Williamson.[1] The spatial manifestation of these disparities is found in the core-periphery structure of these four countries, perhaps less obvious in Malaysia's case, centred on their capital regions, namely Jakarta, Manila, Bangkok, and Kuala Lumpur. The concentration of major economic activities, especially manufacturing, in these primate cities is now well known, and exacerbates the structure of their regional economies. But the dimensions reflecting the gap between the core regions and the lagging areas in the national periphery are not in terms of economic indicators only but social and physical infrastructure as well. A survey of the main features of their regional economic structures would therefore be useful to show the nature and severity of the problem of regional disparities in Southeast Asia. This in turn will emphasize the importance of decentralization policy in each of these countries.

1.1. Indonesia

As the world's largest island country, Indonesia's (regional) development faces some unique issues due to its regional dissimilarities.

The country, which extends to some 5110 km (3400 miles) from the northwestern tip of north Sumatra to the eastern border of Irian Jaya (West Irian) with a land area of approximately 2 million km^2 or some 750,000 $miles^2$ consists of 3000 islands (see Fig. 1). One major difficulty in the country's regional development is therefore the wide variety of physical and agronomic characteristics of the islands and their accessibility structure. In this sense, Indonesia shares characteristics similar to those of the Philippines.

Another problem is the uneven population distribution: about two-thirds of the 120 million population or some 70 million are in the island of Java, which possesses a mere 6.64 per cent of the total area of Indonesia. This made Java the most densely populated area, estimated to be about 565 persons per km^2. On the other extreme, Kalimantan, as the largest island (its area is 27.17 per cent of the whole country), has only a population of approximately 5.1 million or only 4.32 per cent of the Indonesian total population. Irian Jaya with a total population of 923,000 and an area of 412.718 km^2 has the lowest density, i.e. 2 persons per km^2.

A third problem is the imbalanced development between Java and the rest of the country. Throughout history, Java has always been the seat of the central government, before as well as after independence. Development in Indonesia had always been focused on Java. The other bigger islands, endowed with more potential natural resources, have been left more or less "untouched" until recently. Development in the period up to independence has always been aimed at socio-political stability in the well-populated areas—in this case Java—and exploitation of the economy in the islands outside Java. In other words, Java has always enjoyed the major share of productive and infrastructure investment, while the "outer islands" have received the bare minimum, adequate only to exploit the resources.

Although after independence, the Indonesian government has made conscious efforts to cope with this imbalance, the impact of the earlier policies can still be felt. Among others it is apparent in the inequalities of the national economy, in the total as well as *per*

[1]J. G. Williamson, Regional inequality and the process of national development: a description of the patterns, *Economic Development and Cultural Change* 13 (1965) 3 - 45. The Indonesian figure was calculated by H. Esmara, Regional income disparity in indonesia, Joint JERC - CAMS Seminar on Income Distribution, Employment and Economic Development in Southeast and East Asia, 16-20 December, 1974, Tokyo, and the Malaysian case by L. L. Lim, *Some Aspects of Income Differentials in West Malaysia,* K. Lumbur, 1971, p. 45.

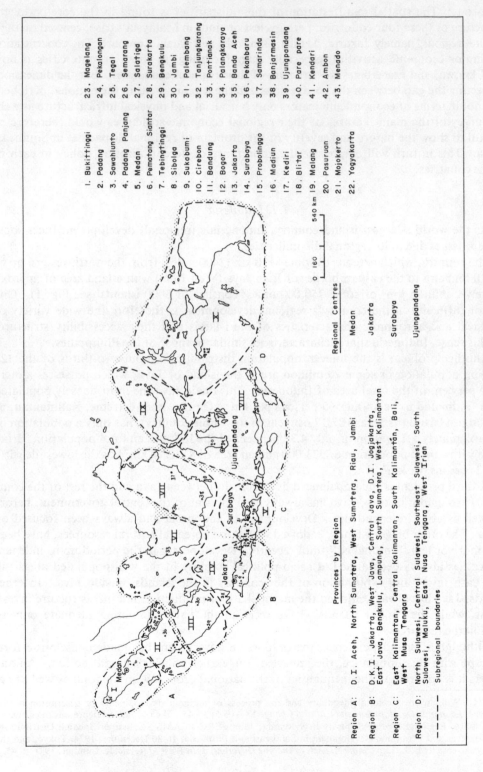

1. Bukittinggi
2. Padang
3. Sawahlunto
4. Padang Panjang
5. Medan
6. Pematang Siantar
7. Tebingtinggi
8. Sibolga
9. Sukabumi
10. Cirebon
11. Bandung
12. Bogor
13. Jakarta
14. Surabaya
15. Probolinggo
16. Madiun
17. Kediri
18. Blitar
19. Malang
20. Pasuruan
21. Mojokerto
22. Yogyakarta
23. Magelang
24. Pekalongan
25. Tegal
26. Semarang
27. Salatiga
28. Surakarta
29. Bengkulu
30. Jambi
31. Palembang
32. Tanjungkarang
33. Pontianak
34. Palangkaraya
35. Banda Aceh
36. Pekanbaru
37. Samarinda
38. Banjarmasin
39. Ujungpandang
40. Pare pare
41. Kendari
42. Ambon
43. Menado

540 km
0   160

Regional Centres

Medan

Jakarta

Surabaya

Ujungpandang

Provinces by Region

Region A: D.I. Aceh, North Sumatera, West Sumatera, Riau, Jambi

Region B: D.K.I. Jakarta, West Java, Central Java, D.I. Jogjakarta,
           East Java, Bengkulu, Lampung, South Sumatera, West Kalimantan

Region C: East Kalimantan, Central Kalimantan, South Kalimantan, Bali,
           West Nusa Tenggara

Region D: North Sulawesi, Central Sulawesi, Southeast Sulawesi, South
           Sulawesi, Maluku, East Nusa Tenggara, West Irian

- - - - - Subregional boundaries

Fig. 1. Designated growth centres and planning/development regions: Indonesia.

capita income (Table 1). Slightly more than half of Indonesia's Gross Regional Domestic Product (including oil) originated from Java (nearly 60 per cent if oil was excluded). Sumatra—especially the Province of Riau which produced 80 per cent of Indonesia's crude oil—contributed most of the crude oil income, but Sumatra's overall share of GDP was only half that of Java. Java and Sumatra together contributed nearly 83 per cent of Indonesia's GRDP. Although Java alone contributes 60 per cent of Indonesia's GDP because of the concentration of population on the island, its position in *per capita* terms, however, is somewhat depressed. As has been discussed by many writers, disguised unemployment occurs to a great extent in the agricultural sector while considerable underemployment can be found in the informal sector of Jakarta.[2] In addition, daily wages paid to various categories of workers on public works projects are lower than in any other

TABLE 1

Gross domestic and *per capita* regional product for twenty-six provinces (in rupiah)

	GRDP[a]	%	*Per capita* income[b]	% of national average
1. Aceh	66,128.3	2.1	37,887.37	112.4
2. North Sumatra	222,078.5	7.1	43,668.58	129.6
3. West Sumatra	70,514.5	2.2	28,338.37	84.1
4. Riau	100,285.5	3.2	87,880,95	260.8
5. Jambi	35,557.3	1.1	43,327.00	128.6
6. South Sumatra	110,028.4	3.5	44,268.81	131.4
7. Bengkulu	14,565.8	0.5	32,744.54	97.2
8. Lampung	73,468.9	2.3	30,974.32	91.9
9. DKI Jakarta Raya	190,168.9	6.0	54,568.38	161.9
10. West Java	451,455.1	14.3	26,542.24	78.8
11. Central Java	446,351.5	14.2	25,389.43	75.3
12. Yogyakarta	44,296.5	1.4	23,529.60	69.8
13. East Java	687,791.5	21.9	36,425.78	108.1
14. Bali	54,362.6	1.7	29,663.99	88.0
15. West Nusa Tenggara	32,454.3	1.0	17,980.10	53.4
16. East Nusa Tenggara	33,814.1	1.1	19,559.22	58.0
17. West Kalimantan	46,673.9	1.5	23,360.68	69.3
18. Central Kalimantan	39,927.1	1.3	63,392.32	188.1
19. South Kalimantan	52,580.9	1.7	36,017.06	106.9
20. East Kalimantan	119,153.1	3.8	221,546.36	657.5
21. North Sulawesi	37,367.7	1.2	24,951.27	74.0
22. Central Sulawesi	20,112.2	0.6	24,745.50	73.4
23. South Sulawesi	111,095.8	3.5	23,803.00	70.6
24. Southeast Sulawesi	15,058.4	0.5	27,754.10	82.4
25. Maluku	35,796.9	1.1	41,128.38	122.1
26. Irian Jaya	30,676.8	1.0	37,020.94	109.9
27. Central Government	4,470.0	0.1	—	—
Total: Indonesia	3,146,234.6	100.0	33,695.81	100.0

Source: Regional income study group, University of Indonesia, 1974: tables 2.3.2 (p. 29) and 2.5.2 (p. 30a).

[a]Gross regional domestic product at 1969 price in millions of rupiah in 1972.

[b]*Per capita* income at current market price in rupiah in 1972.

---

[2]See, for instance, C. Geertz, *Agricultural Involution,* Berkeley, 1963, and S. V. Sethuraman, *Jakarta's Informal Sector,* International Labour Organization, Geneva, 1972.

TABLE 2

Indonesia: per cent distribution of gross regional domestic product at current market prices by industrial origin, by region and by province, 1972

Region and province	Agriculture %	Agriculture R	Mining %	Mining R	Manufacturing %	Manufacturing R	Construction %	Construction R	Electricity and gas %	Electricity and gas R	Transportation and communication %	Transportation and communication R	Trade %	Trade R	Banking and finance %	Banking and finance R	Ownership of dwelling %	Ownership of dwelling R	Public administration and defense %	Public administration and defense R	Services %	Services R	Total
Region 1																							
1. Aceh	63.3	140.0	—	—	6.3	61.8	1.6	41.0	0.1	20.0	2.3	51.1	14.8	72.2	0.5	38.5	2.9	131.8	5.7	87.7	2.5	52.1	100.0
2. North Sumatra	47.2	104.4	—	—	9.5	93.1	3.9	100.0	0.3	60.0	3.7	82.2	24.1	117.6	0.9	69.2	2.8	127.3	4.6	70.7	3.0	62.5	100.0
Region 2																							
1. West Sumatra	54.3	120.1	0.3	75.0	5.8	56.7	4.6	117.9	0.2	40.0	3.9	86.7	13.7	66.8	0.7	53.8	3.1	140.9	8.1	124.6	5.3	110.4	100.0
2. Riau	23.7	52.4	1.7	425.0	2.5	24.5	1.8	46.2	0.1	20.0	16.6	368.9	47.2	230.2	0.3	23.1	1.9	86.4	2.5	38.5	1.7	35.4	100.0
Region 3																							
1. Jambi	56.0	123.9	—	—	7.2	70.6	1.9	48.7	0.2	40.0	3.8	84.4	19.0	92.7	0.9	69.2	4.1	186.4	4.3	66.2	2.6	54.2	100.0
2. South Sumatra	37.5	83.0	0.7	1750.0	5.9	57.8	4.6	117.9	0.3	60.0	14.8	328.9	19.8	96.6	0.6	46.2	2.7	122.7	3.9	60.0	2.9	60.4	100.0
3. Bengkulu	62.6	138.5	—	—	5.2	51.0	2.1	53.8	0.5	100.0	3.0	66.7	13.1	63.9	0.2	15.4	4.5	204.5	6.2	95.4	2.6	54.2	100.0
Region 4																							
1. Lampung	57.9	128.1	—	—	6.5	63.7	2.3	59.0	0.2	40.0	2.7	60.0	19.0	92.7	0.9	69.2	2.8	127.3	4.4	67.7	3.3	68.8	100.0
2. Jakarta Raya	14.2	31.4	—	—	9.1	89.2	11.3	289.7	2.3	460.0	11.5	255.6	15.8	77.1	11.7	900.0	2.6	118.2	12.8	196.9	8.7	181.2	100.0
3. West Java	40.2	88.9	0.1	25.0	14.7	144.1	5.3	135.9	0.6	120.0	3.2	71.1	21.1	102.9	0.7	53.8	2.2	100.0	6.4	98.5	5.5	114.6	100.0
4. Central Java	44.3	98.0	—	—	14.0	137.3	2.7	69.3	0.3	60.0	2.5	55.6	20.4	99.5	0.6	46.2	1.8	81.8	7.1	109.2	6.3	131.2	100.0
5. Yogjakarta	45.6	100.9	—	—	10.7	104.9	3.9	100.0	0.4	80.0	2.9	64.4	15.9	77.6	0.6	46.2	2.9	131.8	9.2	141.5	7.9	164.6	100.0
Region 5																							
1. East Java	45.6	100.9	—	—	14.4	141.2	2.6	66.7	0.4	80.0	2.9	64.4	22.0	107.3	0.5	38.5	1.4	63.6	5.5	84.6	4.7	97.9	100.0
2. Bali	60.7	134.3	—	—	4.0	39.2	4.5	115.4	0.2	40.0	5.5	122.2	12.8	62.4	0.4	30.8	2.6	118.2	4.8	73.8	4.5	93.8	100.0
Region 6																							
1. West Kalimantan	57.0	126.1	—	—	5.0	49.0	2.1	53.8	0.3	60.0	2.2	48.9	21.4	104.4	1.7	130.8	3.3	150.0	4.5	69.2	2.5	52.1	100.0
Region 7																							
1. Central Kalimantan	72.7	160.8	—		1.5	14.7	1.0	25.6	—	—	0.7	15.6	17.5	85.4	0.2	15.4	1.3	59.1	3.5		1.6	33.3	100.0
2. South Kalimantan	50.8	112.4	—	—	6.4	62.7	2.4	61.5	0.1	20.0	3.4	75.6	20.1	98.0	1.1	84.6	3.5	159.1	7.5	115.4	4.7	97.9	100.0
3. East Kalimantan	74.8	165.5	—	—	0.5	4.9	1.4	35.9	0.1	20.0	1.8	40.0	18.3	39.3	0.3	23.1	0.6	27.3	1.1	16.9	1.1	22.9	100.0
Region 8																							
1. West Nusa Tenggara	53.5	118.4	—	—	5.7	55.9	5.7	146.2	0.1	20.0	3.0	66.7	13.6	66.3	0.4	30.8	3.9	177.3	8.0	123.1	6.1	127.1	100.0
2. East Nusa Tenggara	59.6	131.9	—	—	3.0	29.4	3.4	87.2	0.1	20.0	1.7	37.8	10.1	49.3	0.1	7.7	5.7	259.1	10.3	158.5	6.0	125.0	100.0
3. South Sulawesi	53.4	118.1	—	—	5.8	56.7	2.7	69.2	0.3	60.0	4.6	102.2	13.9	67.8	0.8	61.5	2.4	109.1	11.8	181.5	4.3	89.6	100.0
4. Southeast Sulawesi	47.7	105.5	20.8	5200.0	3.2	31.4	1.8	46.2	0.0	—	2.3	51.1	12.0	58.5	0.1	7.7	2.6	118.2	7.3	112.3	2.2	45.8	100.0
Region 9																							
1. North Sulawesi	42.2	93.4	—	—	4.4	43.1	5.9	151.3	0.7	140.0	8.8	195.6	12.4	60.5	2.6	200.0	3.6	163.6	11.4	175.4	8.0	166.7	100.0
2. Central Sulawesi	63.1	139.6	—	—	3.8	37.3	2.4	61.5	0.0	—	3.0	66.7	11.4	55.6	1.1	84.6	2.7	122.7	6.9	106.2	5.6	116.7	100.0
Region 10																							
1. Maluku	65.3	144.5	—	—	1.7	16.7	2.0	51.3	0.1	20.0	2.2	48.9	16.7	81.5	0.4	30.8	2.7	122.7	5.5	84.6	3.4	70.8	100.0
2. Irian Jaya	37.4	82.7	—	—	2.6	25.5	25.5	653.8	0.4	30.0	4.7	104.4	8.3	40.5	1.0	76.9	3.0	136.4	7.4	113.8	9.7	202.1	100.0
Indonesia	45.2	100.0	0.4	100.0	10.2	100.0	3.9	100.0	0.5	100.0	4.5	100.0	20.5	100.0	1.3	100.0	2.2	100.0	6.5	100.0	4.8	100.0	100.0

Note: $R = \dfrac{\%\,\text{share of the province}}{\%\,\text{share of Indonesia}} \times 100$.

Source: The figure was calculated by H. Esmara, Regional income disparity in Indonesia, Joint JERC-CAMS Seminar on Income Distribution, Employment and Economic Development in Southeast and East Asia, 16-20 December 1974, Tokyo.

place.[3] In outer Java there has existed a shortage of manpower with the result of higher daily wages especially in East Kalimantan.

Another impact can be felt in the structural disparity of the economic sectors between Java and the outer islands (Table 2). Most of the economic activities outside Java depend upon primary industries such as agricultural and extractive industries. Inter-industry economic relations are, however, non-existent. On the other hand, Java has a relatively advanced industrial sector. Nearly 75 per cent of the large and medium establishments are located in Java, especially in textiles and food industries (Table 3). This pattern is also re-

TABLE 3

Large and medium manufacturing establishments, employment, and value added by major regions, 1971 (percentage distribution)

Item	Regional groups					
	Java	Sumatra	Kali- mantan	Sulawesi	Other islands	Total
1971 population	63.8	17.5	4.3	7.2	7.2	100.0
Establishments:						
Large	82.7	12.6	1.4	1.5	1.8	100.0
Medium	71.9	16.0	3.7	5.9	2.5	100.0
Total	74.8	14.5	3.0	5.4	2.3	100.0
Food and tobacco	71.4	13.5	3.8	8.5	2.8	100.0
Textiles	95.6	2.6	0.1	0.5	1.2	100.0
Wood, etc.	42.1	45.2	6.9	3.2	2.6	100.0
Rubber, etc.	67.6	24.8	5.6	0.8	1.2	100.0
Others	74.8	15.5	1.7	5.5	2.5	100.0
Workers:						
Large	87.3	10.0	1.0	0.7	1.0	100.0
Medium	78.5	12.2	3.0	3.8	2.5	100.0
Total	85.1	10.6	1.4	1.5	1.4	100.0
Food and tobacco	89.6	7.0	0.6	1.4	1.4	100.0
Textiles	94.2	3.2	0.1	0.6	1.9	100.0
Wood, etc.	41.6	33.0	15.7	2.6	7.1	100.0
Rubber, etc.	72.2	23.5	3.2	1.0	0.1	100.0
Others	82.7	10.6	0.6	4.8	1.3	100.0
Value added:						
Food and tobacco	86.1	11.6	0.3	1.0	1.0	100.0
Textiles	95.2	3.1	—	0.3	1.4	100.0
Wood, etc.	42.4	33.3	16.2	2.5	5.6	100.0
Rubber, etc.	60.3	35.7	3.8	0.2	—	100.0
Others	84.7	11.0	0.4	3.6	0.3	100.0
Total	80.3	16.6	1.3	1.0	0.8	100.0

Source: Statistik Industri, 1971; also in Esmara, op. cit.

Note: The large establishments are defined as those engaging 100 or more persons without the use of power, or engaging 50 or more persons when power is used. The "medium" establishments are defined to include all those engaging 10 - 99 persons without the use of power or 5 - 49 persons with the use of power. Vide Central Bureau of Statistics, Survey of Manufacturing Industries 1971, Jakarta, 1973, p. iv.

flected in employment and value-added terms. Furthermore, with some 60 per cent of the population of Indonesia living in Java, the bulk of the country's economic activity—investment generation of income, trade, and commerce—naturally takes place in this

---

[3]H. W. Arndt, Regional wage differentials, Bulletin of Indonesia Economic Studies **8** (1) (March 1972) 90-91, as cited in Hendra Esmara, ibid., p. 7.

island. The concentration of population in a limited space affords certain economies in
the use of economic infrastructure such as roads and irrigation. On the other hand, the
lack of manpower and infrastructure facilities, coupled with enclave extractive industries,
has hampered the development of the outer islands.

In further support of these indicators on regional disparities, data on the pattern of
regional investments as shown in Table 4 indicate much the same tendency to concentrate
in Java. As much as 73 per cent of total project investment by mid-1973 was located in
development region B (which comprised of Java, South Sumatra, and West Kalimantan[4]),
Java's share alone being some 64 per cent.

TABLE 4
Approved investment by region, Indonesia

Region[a]	% total approved by domestic investment law April 1973	% total approved by foreign investment law, March 1973	Total investment equivalent (billion rupiah)	Share (%)
A	10.5	6.4	138.7	8.2
B	72.5	41.8	952.7	56.4
C	9.6	18.4	243.3	14.4
D	7.4	33.4	354.3	21.0
Total[b]	100.0	100.0	1,689.0	100.0

[a]Provinces by region:
  A: DI Aceh, N. Sumatera, W. Sumatera, Raui, Jambi.
  B: DKI Jakarta, W. Java, Central Java, DI Jogjakarta, E. Java, Bengkulu, Lampung,
    S. Sumatera, W. Kalimantan.
  C: E. Kalimantan, Central Kalimantan, S. Kalimantan, Bali, W. Nusa Tenggara.
  D: N. Sulawesi, Central Sulawesi, Southeast Sulawesi, S. Sulawesi, Maluku, E. Nusa
    Tenggara, W. Irian.
[b]Total excludes "other" investments totalling 32.6 billion rupiah.
  Source: Based on Domestic Foreign Investment Board, unpublished figures.

The last point underlines the severity of Indonesia's pattern of regional inequality, and
indications are that these disparities have increased in spite of government efforts, maybe
even because of it, at least up to the beginning of REPELITA II (Second Five-year Plan,
1974/5 - 1978/9).[5]

1.2. Malaysia

One of the major problems of regional development in Malaysia is the significant disparities in the welfare of the states in the federation. These inequalities were inherited
from the colonial period of resource exploitation, mainly of tin and rubber. This history
of colonial development is reflected in the penetration lines of the major rail and road
transport emanating from the west coast of Peninsula Malaysia and the neglect of the

---

[4]See below on Indonesia's regionalization scheme (Fig. 1).

[5]Majid Ibrahim, Some problems of regional development in Indonesia, Program Perencanaan Nasional,
FEUI-BAPPENAS, *Regional Development Seminar,* Jakarta, August 1973, p. 5, and Esmara, *op. cit.,* p. 53.

east coast states of Kelantan, Trengganu, and Pahang.[6] In this context, Sabah and Sarawak (comprising the eastern part of Malaysia) consist of a vast resource frontier which became incorporated into the Federation in 1963.

The pattern of regional disparities is shown in Table 5 displaying various indicators of income *per capita*, population distribution, and racial composition for Peninsula Malaysia by states. It shows that Selangor, Penang, and Perak in 1970 are the three most developed states in terms of GDP *per capita,* each having these values above the Peninsula Malaysia average. On the other hand, the four poorest states consist of Perlis, Kedah, Trengganu and Kelantan (the latter two in the east coast of Peninsula Malaysia), about 50 per cent points below the national average. The biggest extreme is evidently that between Selangor and Kelantan, the former's GDP *per capita* being more than 3.5 times that of the former. The gap between Selangor and the rest of the states is also very clear, being about 67 per cent above the Peninsula Malaysia average in 1970, its dominant position, and from columns 2 - 4 of Table 5 appears to have increased between 1963 to 1970. On the other hand, Kelantan as the poorest state showed little change over the same period, and, in fact, declined somewhat.

TABLE 5

Indicators of income *per capita,* population, and racial composition, Malaysia

	GDP *per capita* 1970 ($)	*Per capita* GDP as ratio of Peninsular Malaysia mean			Shares of GDP and population—1970			Malays as percentage of 1970 population
		Mean 1963 - 5	Mean 1966 - 70	1970	GDP share (%)	Popula-tion	Popula-tion (%)	
Selangor	1520	1.57	1.64	1.67	30.8	1,699,435	18.5	34.6
Penang	939	0.98	1.02	1.03	9.1	808,122	8.5	30.7
Perak	911	1.03	1.01	1.00	17.8	1,635,295	17.8	43.1
Negri Sembilan	907	1.09	1.03	0.99	5.4	501,784	5.4	45.4
Pahang	855	1.00	0.95	0.94	5.4	526,180	5.7	61.2
Johor	835	0.94	0.91	0.92	13.3	1,330,789	14.5	53.4
Malacca	761	0.94	0.88	0.83	3.8	421,168	4.6	51.8
Kedah/Perlis	605	0.69	0.68	0.66	8.1	1,121,078	12.2	55.7
Trengganu	536	0.63	0.59	0.59	2.7	422,631	4.6	93.9
Kelantan	420	0.49	0.44	0.46	3.6	715,190	7.8	92.8
Peninsula Malaysia Mean	912	1.0	1.0	1.0	100.0	9,181,672	100.0	54.0

Source: Economic Planning Unit, 1974.

Thus, even though the period 1963 - 70 is too short to determine properly the trend in disparities and that overall disparities have not changed significantly, the gap between the richest and the poorest states appear to be increasing (from 1.57 to 1.67 in 1970 for Selangor, and from 0.49 to 0.46 in the same year for Kelantan).

[6]Y. K. Khoo, The East - West Highway Project: analysis of the potential impacts of transportation investments on regional development, MA thesis submitted to the Universiti Sains Malaysia, 1975, pp. 46-53.

TABLE 6

Malaysia: gross domestic product by sector of origin and state, 1975 ($ million in 1970 prices)

Sector	Johor	Kedah[a]/Perlis	Kelantan	Malacca	Negri Sembilan	Pahang	Penang	Perak	Sabah	Sarawak	Selango[b]	Trengganu	Malaysia
Agriculture, forestry, fishing, etc.	786.6	518.0	174.9	148.7	280.3	328.7	171.2	588.7	554.0	339.0	508.6	164.1	4563
Mining and quarrying	20.0	8.0	0.7	0.6	3.0	21.0	1.0	248.4	5.0	169.0	130.1	5.0	612
Manufacturing	332.7	87.3	35.4	51.0	128.6	93.5	229.0	248.7	42.0	127.0	780.8	40.6	2197
Construction	46.1	49.4	27.0	20.8	44.5	24.9	69.2	56.6	73.0	63.0	224.4	11.7	711
Utilities	45.1	13.9	8.0	17.5	22.6	11.5	49.2	79.2	15.0	18.0	117.9	3.3	401
Transport, storage, and communications	115.4	51.2	35.2	29.7	52.1	37.2	110.6	109.3	69.0	98.0	372.3	17.6	1098
Wholesale and retail trade	196.1	80.9	56.6	104.3	77.5	65.6	273.7	251.5	145.0	150.0	653.4	31.5	2086
Ownership of dwellings, banking, insurance and real estate	109.9	72.7	39.0	43.0	52.3	54.6	103.6	134.9	79.0	90.0	295.0	34.9	1109
Public administration and defence	134.5	69.3	42.7	55.6	65.0	69.3	51.5	124.8	67.0	65.0	422.6	31.9	1199
Other services	120.5	80.6	46.8	50.7	56.3	49.1	122.4	147.5	107.0	126.0	300.9	29.1	1237
Statistical discrepancy	—	—	—	—	—	—	—	—	—	—	—	—	+102
Gross domestic product (GDP)	1906.9	1031.3	466.3	521.9	782.2	755.4	1181.4	1989.6	1156.0	1245.0	3806.0	369.7	15,315[c]
Population (000)	1511	1245	792	472	566	631	893	1807	751	1113	1985	483	12,249
Per capita GDP ($)	1262.0	828.4	588.8	1105.7	1382.0	1197.2	1323.0	1101.1	1539.3	1118.6	1917.4	765.4	1250.3
Ratio to Malaysian average	1.01	0.66	0.47	0.88	1.11	0.96	1.06	0.88	1.23	0.90	1.53	0.61	1.00
Population growth rate, 1971 - 5	2.7	2.2	2.2	2.4	2.5	3.8	2.1	2.1	2.8	2.7	3.2	2.8	2.6

[a]Kedah and Perlis are two distinct states but are shown together here because much of the available statistical data for the two states are combined.
[b]Includes the Federal Territory of Kuala Lumpur.
[c]The GDP for individual states do not add up to the total for Malaysia because of the statistical discrepancy of $102 million.

Source: Reproduced from table 10-1, p. 201, *Third Malaysia Plan, 1976 - 80*, Kuala Lumpur.

TABLE 7
GDP *per capita,* sectoral shares of GDP and urbanization by state, 1970

	GDP *per capita*		Sectoral shares[a] of GDP (%)			urban share[b] of population (%)
	($)	Index	A	I	S	
Selangor	1520	167	14	38	48	45
Penang/PW	939	103	18	22	60	51
Perak	911	100	29	35	36	28
Negri Sembilan	907	99	37	25	38	21
Pahang	855	94	42	23	35	19
Johor	835	92	40	21	39	26
Malacca	761	83	31	10	59	25
Kedah/Perlis	605	66	58	12	30	13
Trengganu	536	59	38	22	40	27
Kelantan	420	46	43	12	45	15
Peninsula Malaysia	912	100	29	28	43	29

[a]Sectors: A: Agriculture, forestry, fishing.
        I: Mining, manufacturing, construction, utilities.
        S: Transport, commerce, government, other services.
[b]Minimum urban concentration: 10,000 persons.
Sources: Statistics Department, Population Census, 1970. Economic Planning Unit, GDP by state. Calculations were performed by D. J. Blake, whose permission to reproduce it here is gratefully acknowledged.

The economic structure of the states are also worth examining to illustrate further the regional disparities present. Table 6 shows this structure of the different states in detail, which highlights further the importance of Selangor as the core region of the economy. Overall, as Table 7 summarizes, the richer states appear to have higher shares in the modern sector of the economy (I), especially manufacturing, whereas the reverse is true in the poorer states, where agriculture tends to dominate. Services (S) form a large component of all states, and reflects the state of the economy as a whole. Also, there appears to be a relationship between sectoral diversity, reflected by a more or less equal distribution of the sectors for each state and the level of GDP *per capita.*

The disparities among the various states in the Federation, however, extend beyond measures of income. Table 8 shows the pattern for different social indicators on standards of living for 1975, which not only tends to confirm the basic disparities in income, but indicates the deeper socioeconomic problems of unequal development.

A comparison of the last columns of Tables 5, 7, and 8, namely referring to the percentage share of Malays (the dominant ethnic group in Malaysia) in the state population, the percentage urban share of the population, and the level of poverty in the state respectively, shows significant correlations which make the Malaysian case unique when compared with the other Southeast Asian countries.

The incidence of poverty varies inversely with differences in average *per capita* income. For example, Kelantan has 65 per cent of its households living in poverty, whereas Selangor has only 19 per cent. The four poorest states together have percentages of households in poverty ranging from 59 per cent to 65 per cent. Penang, incidentally, has about 30 per cent of its households below the $25 line. There is also some ethnic correlations to the incidence of poverty (and distribution of income) by states shown by a close

TABLE 8

Malaysia: Social indicators on standards of living, 1975

State	*Per capita* value added of selected services sectors ($)				Persons per living quarters[a]	Persons per doctor	Students per teacher	Persons per acute hospital bed	Rural population per health centre or sub-centre	Rural population per clinic or midwives clinic	Private cars per 100 persons	Motor cycles per 100 persons	Percentage of households in poverty[a]
	Utilities	Transport	Commerce	Other services sectors[a]									
Johor	29.8	76.4	129.4	79.7	6.1	6716	30.5	608	19,338	3686	3.2	6.9	45.7
Kedah/Perlis	11.2	41.1	65.0	64.7	5.3	9222	29.6	907	26,085	4767	1.8	6.1	64.5
Kelantan	10.1	44.4	71.5	59.1	4.7	11647	32.0	934	20,045	4334	1.5	3.4	76.1
Malacca	37.1	62.9	221.0	107.4	6.1	5021	29.9	587	20,353	4219	3.9	6.3	44.9
Negri Sembilan	39.9	92.0	136.9	99.5	5.4	4717	27.2	398	21,581	3942	4.2	7.5	44.8
Pahang	18.2	58.9	104.0	77.8	5.0	6573	29.3	572	13,813	2290	2.5	6.4	43.2
Penang	55.1	123.9	306.5	137.1	6.5	3986	32.0	638	31,170	5870	5.1	10.0	43.7
Perak	43.8	60.5	139.2	81.6	5.9	5944	31.3	648	22,152	5367	3.1	6.8	48.6
Sabah	20.0	91.9	193.1	142.5	7.2[b]	9159	26.2	549	n.a.	n.a.	4.57[c]	0.6	n.a.
Sarawak	16.2	88.1	134.8	113.2	7.8[b]	8904	32.5	702	n.a.	n.a.	2.4	2.9	n.a.
Selangor	59.4	187.6	329.2	151.6	6.1	2327	32.4	542	26,195	5701	7.4	8.7	29.2
Trengganu	6.8	36.4	65.2	60.2	4.6	10063	32.1	694	18,724	3585	1.2	3.1	68.9
Malaysia	32.7	89.6	170.3	101.0	5.5	4344	30.8	627	21,641[d]	4312[d]	3.8	6.9	49.3[d]

[a]For 1970 only.
[b]For major towns and townships only.
[c]Includes private cars, taxis and hired cars.
[d]Peninsular Malaysia only.

Source: Reproduced from table 10-2, p. 202, *Third Malaysia Plan, 1976 - 80*, Kuala Lumpur.

inverse relationship between the percentage of Malays in the population and GDP *per capita* by states. Furthermore, the poorer states tend also to be the least urbanized. It is these correlations which are highlighted in the New Economic Policy, and which makes regional development planning so critical in the Malaysian context. In some instances of regional planning, these correlates in development policy tended to be overdrawn, as when frontier zone development (e.g. the Pahang Tenggara project) is seen as the major outlet for Malay rural dwellers on low productivity and uneconomic-sized farms in Kelantan and Trengganu. Many of these questions are only now being more critically examined than when the strategy was first formulated.

In terms of urbanization and the distribution of population, Malaysia also is somewhat distinct from the other three countries where in the latter countries urban primacy appears to be a dominant concern of the decentralization policy. In Malaysia, the historical urbanization process, coupled with the country's rural development policy, has not given rise to the problems of urban concentration in the capital region to the same degree as is the case in Bangkok, Manila, and Jakarta.

In spite of this, however, the decentralization question is not considered any less serious. The pattern of regional economic interaction which is basically similar to any situation derived from an open dualistic system belies the apparent rank-size structure of Malaysia's urbanization. The results of a canonical correlation analysis of commodity flows in Peninsula Malaysia, shown in Table 9, confirm this. The first variate alone, resulting from the maximally derived interflows of resource-based industrial commodities and processing manufacturing products and assembled goods based on imported raw materials or parts, clearly suggests the dominance of Kuala Lumpur with respect to other urban nodes in the country and points to the regional importance of Penang. Other dominant dyads on this dimension include the flows between Kuantan and Kuala Lumpur, the Johore Baru and Kuala Lumpur, and Singapore and Kuala Lumpur.[7] In this fashion, the pattern of interaction is able to accurately demonstrate the upper circuit of commodity flows which form the basic locational matrix for building of a system of growth centres in the process of industrial decentralization. On this score it is of interest to note that the largest amount of interaction occurs within the Klang Valley itself, which is the core region of the Peninsula Malaysia economy. It is important to note also that this pattern of commodity inflow - outflow is between the two basic commodity systems under alternative possibilities for choice of industrialization strategy, namely import substitution as against export substitution.

Further interpretation of the other variates, which together show the pattern of regional interactions based on dominant interflows of goods, identifies a hierarchy of urban nodes appearing to interact more with each other than with their respective hinterlands. This is an obvious character of the spatial structure of dualistic economies, which adds substantially to the pattern of regional economic disparities described earlier. When one examines further the process and pattern of population redistribution in West Malaysia in which the dominance of Kuala Lumpur is also obvious, one is persuaded to conclude that the rank-size structure of the Peninsula Malaysia city system (and the presumed optimality of this statistical distribution) is more apparent than real, and belies the seriousness of open dualistic economic development in the spatial context.

These issues of unequal development seem to preoccupy Malaysia's central planners and policymakers, and have persuaded them to view regional development as one strategy

[7]See Fig. 2 for location of these cities.

to achieve a fairer sharing of economic development. It may be concluded, however, that unlike the other three countries, except perhaps the case of Muslim Mindanao, the ethnic issue, namely the question of imbalanced economic shares between the different ethnic groups (particularly between Malays and the non-Malays), appears to have dominated their thinking among other things in the direction of redistribution of economic benefits to the less developed states.

TABLE 9

Regional interaction: Commodity flows in Malaysia matrix of correlations and redundancy measures, canonical component structure

	Canonical variates				
	I	II	III	IV	
Outflows					
G.I	-0.20	-0.99[a]	0.13	0.05	
G.II	-0.99[a]	0.15	0.07	-0.06	
G.III	-0.05	0.05	-0.34	0.16	
G.IV	-0.10	0.10	-0.99[a]	0.28	
G.V	-0.07	-0.12	-0.04	0.44[a]	
G.VI	-0.01	-0.08	-0.16	-0.93[a]	
Variance extracted	0.17	0.18	0.20	0.19	
Contribution to redundancy	0.15	0.12	0.04	0.02	Total redundancy of first set given to second set = 0.33
Inflows					
G.I	-0.10	-0.93[a]	0.28	-0.15	
G.II	-0.26	0.03	-0.89[a]	-0.28	
G.III	-0.91[a]	0.13	0.43[a]	-0.09	
G.IV	-0.02	-0.24	-0.23	0.88[a]	
G.V	0.02	-0.05	0.01	0.03	
G.VI	-0.11	-0.36	-0.31	0.20	
Variance extracted	0.15	0.18	0.20	0.16	
Contribution to redundancy	0.13	0.12	0.04	0.016	Total redundancy of second set given to first set = 0.306

[a]Correlations above 0.40.

Source: Kamal Salih, *et al.*, *Industrialization Strategy, Regional Development, and the Growth Centre Approach: A Case Study of West Malaysia*, Appendix VII.

Notes: Group I: Manufactured consumer non-durables (14 commodities).
Group II: Resource-based industries (including construction material, plywood/veneer, rubber, palm oil).
Group III: Manufacturing assembly based on imported raw materials or parts (machines, petrol, textiles).
Group IV: Bulky manufactured products (fertilizer, salt, beverages).
Group V: Very bulky resource-based products (including bricks, logs, coconuts).
Group VI: Grain and grain products including animal feed.

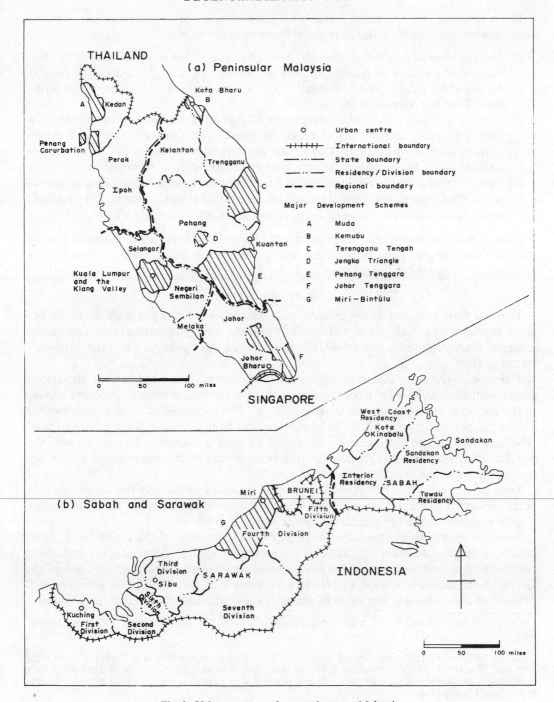

Fig. 2. Urban centres and economic areas: Malaysia.

To summarize the empirical bases which determine the formulation of regional development policy in Malaysia, one can offer three problem areas:

(1) The problem of regional disparities, which become highly political due to the coincidence of the bulk of bumiputra (Malay) population, a high incidence of poverty among them (ethnically and spatially), and a disarticulation of the economic structure of the less-developed states.

(2) The problem of uneven urban development—not so much in terms of city size, but more the spatial distribution of urban functions (an absence of large and a denser pattern of cities in the East Coast, the less-developed states)—and an ethnic imbalance in the demographic and occupational composition of urban areas.

(3) The problem of industrial location, which reflects in the concentration of industries in the Klang Valley (the capital region) and to a lesser extent in Penang (the northern region), and spatial unevenness in the provision of off-farm employment.

It is clear from the above that the problems of regional development in Malaysia are not just the problem of uneven development in a spatial context but are highly related to the problem of unequal development in its entire economic, social, and political contexts.

1.3. Philippines

The first solid evidence of the existing wide income gaps among regions in the Philippines appeared in a study made by Gerardo P. Sicat.[8] Using an implied *per capita* gross product, Sicat reported a gap of 1973 pesos between the "poorest" and the "richest" region in 1966.

The most significant aspect of Sicat's study, however, is his report that all regions except Metropolitan Manila[9] have lower implied gross *per capita* regional products relative to the national implied gross *per capita* product. The estimates of Sicat also show that during the period between 1948 - 66, the percentage contribution of each region to total GNP has not changed significantly. Metropolitan Manila maintains its position with the province of Rizal gaining in prominence (this province at present is considered by some as part of Metropolitan Manila).

Most recent estimates of regional economic structure supported the conclusions of Sicat's study. The breakdown available with the recent estimate enables us to grasp more significantly the degree of regional income disparity.[10]

Table 10 shows the comparative rankings and the structure of the regions (Fig. 3) by industrial origin. As expected, Region IV (Southern Tagalog[11] dominates the rest of the regions with a contribution of 12.9 billion pesos, representing about 47 per cent of the GNP. A far second is Region VI (Western Visayas) with 2.4 billion pesos gross regional product and the lowest is Region II (Cagayan Valley) with only 664 million pesos output.

---

[8]Gerardo P. Sicat, Dimensions of regional economic growth in the Philippines, *Annals of Regional Science,* June 1970.

[9]Before 1972 the Philippines was divided into ten regions with Metropolitan Manila as Region I. In the latest Four-year Plan (1978 - 81), which was not published at the time of writing this paper, the Philippines has been reorganized into twelve regions, with Metro Manila constituted as a separate region instead of being included in Southern Tagalog (Region IV) (see Fig. 3).

[10]In the regional income estimates, the Philippines is divided into eleven regions using the framework defined by the Integrated Reorganization Plan of the Philippines, March 1972.

[11]Here includes Metropolitan Manila.

TABLE 10

Gross regional product by industrial origin (in million pesos) by region, Philippines, 1967

Industry group	Region											Philippines
	I	II	III	IV	V	VI	VII	VIII	IX	X	XI	
Agriculture, fishery and forestry	594 7.43	325 4.07	839 10.50	1413 17.68	456 5.71	849 10.62	478 5.98	452 5.66	489 6.12	1084 13.57	1012 12.66	7991 100.00
Mining and quarrying	170 37.30	4 0.87	30 6.56	31 6.77	25 5.46	42 9.09	104 22.84	34 7.42	4 0.87	6 1.39	7 1.52	457 100.00
Manufacturing	93 1.54	94 1.56	377 6.26	808 63.20	85 1.41	541 8.98	183 3.04	61 1.01	30 0.50	439 7.29	314 5.21	6025 100.00
Construction	44 4.85	26 2.82	109 11.87	273 29.88	63 6.87	102 11.14	84 9.19	36 3.91	24 2.61	60 6.58	94 10.28	915 100.00
Transportation, communication, storage and utilities	13 0.86	7 0.44	54 3.51	1166 75.23	21 1.37	79 5.10	108 6.94	10 0.67	7 0.44	26 1.71	58 3.73	549 100.00
Commerce	203 4.06	84 1.69	216 4.32	3203 64.14	206 4.12	251 5.04	242 4.85	102 2.05	54 1.09	192 3.85	239 4.79	4992 100.00
Services	287 5.04	124 2.19	408 7.18	3056 53.72	214 3.76	377 6.63	376 6.62	153 2.69	171 3.00	260 4.56	262 4.61	5688 100.00
Total	1404 5.08	664 2.41	2033 7.36	12,950 46.89	1070 3.87	2241 8.12	1575 5.70	848 3.07	719 2.82	2067 7.49	1986 7.19	27,617 100.00

Source: Regional Income Account Project, Preliminary Report, NEDA, 1974.

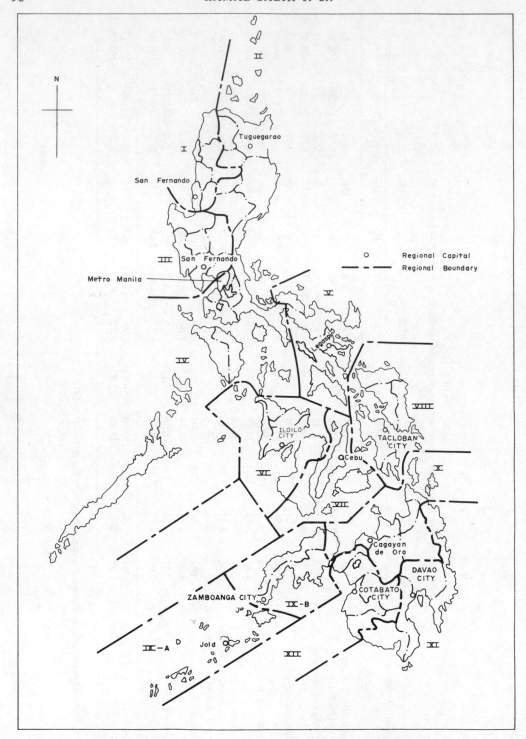

Fig. 3. Regional centres and economic development regions: Philippines.

On a *per capita* basis, the highest is also exhibited by Region IV with 1752 pesos or more than twice the national average of 821 pesos for the same year. Far behind are Regions X (Northern Mindanao) and XI (Southern Mindanao) with 759 and 736 pesos respectively. The depressed regions, however, are Region VIII (Eastern Visayas) with 372 pesos, Region V (Bicol) with 385 pesos, and Region II (Cagayan Valley) with 432 pesos, all exhibiting *per capita* gross regional product around 50 per cent of the national average.

With the exception of Region IV, almost all regions of the Philippines are dependent on the "primary" industries for at least 40 per cent of their regional product. The highest dependency on agriculture is exhibited by Region IX with 63 per cent. Exceptions, of course, are Region IV whose "secondary" and "tertiary" industries contribute about 89 per cent to its total regional output; and Central and Western Visayas whose "primary" industries contribute only around 38 and 30 per cent respectively to their gross output.

The extent to which Region IV influences the overall economy can be seen from the contribution of its various sectors. On the average, Region IV accounts for 75.2 per cent gross output of the transportation - communication - storage - utilities sector of the country, 63.2 per cent of total manufacturing output, 64.1 per cent of commerce sector, 53.7 per cent of the services sector, and 29.9 per cent of the construction sector. Surprisingly, Region IV's contribution of 17.7 per cent to total agriculture sector output is the highest among the eleven regions surpassing Regions X and XI by more than 4 per cent.

About 60 per cent of the total income from mining and quarrying for the whole country comes from the aggregate output of Region I (Ilocos/Mt. Province) whose contribution amounts to 37.3 per cent and Region VII (Central Visayas) with 22.8 per cent. This could be explained by the fact that the largest mines in the country (Benguet gold mines and the Toledo copper mines) are located in these regions.

Intraregionally, the manufacturing sector of Region IV accounts for 29.41 per cent of its gross regional product, followed by commerce and service sectors, with 24.73 and 23.60 per cent respectively. This almost parallel development of manufacturing, commerce, and service sectors are followed by other regions with few exceptions. The contrast is exhibited by Region IX.

With manufacturing contributing only 3.85 per cent to its gross regional product, Region IX is the least industrialized of all eleven regions. Nevertheless, Region IX has a relatively large service sector contribution (21.95 per cent), second only to agriculture. Surprisingly, the transportation - communication - storage - utilities sector of Region IX contributes less than 1 per cent to its gross regional product. This, however, illustrates vividly the highly heterogenous characteristics of most regions. Region IX, though less developed, has within its territory Zamboanga City—one of the prime tourist spots of the Philippines.

Except for two commodity groups, namely: (1) the production of leather and leather and fur products except footwear and other wearing apparel, and (2) production of wood, cane, and cork, except furniture, the superiority of Region IV in the manufacturing sector is straightforward. To mention a few, Region IV accounts for 96.3 per cent of the total gross income of manufactured tobacco; 94.28 per cent of electrical machinery, apparatus, appliances, and supplies output; 94.4 per cent of the total value added in printing, publishing, and allied products; 88.56 per cent of the total value added in the manufacture of rubber products; 86.52 per cent of total value added in the manufacture of metal products, except machinery and transport equipment, and about 73 per cent of the total value added in the manufacture of machinery (except electrical machinery).

The other extreme is provided by Region IX (Western Mindanao), which contributes less than one-half of 1 per cent to the total value added in manufacturing of the country. Region IX exhibits a situation where negligible "secondary" activity occurs. The same can also be said of Region VIII (Eastern Visayas), Region V (Bicol), Region I (Ilocos/Mt. Province), and Region II (Cagayan Valley).

It can be noted, however, that even though these regions have generally an agro-based economy, significant food processing can only be found in Regions IV and VI (Western Visayas).

An examination of the transport - communication - storage - utilities sector and the commerce and services sectors further reinforce the previous conclusion. Region IV accounts for over three-quarters of the total value added in the country's transportation - communication - storage - utilities sector. This is broken down into the following: 71.64 per cent of the total output of gas, electricity, and water; 76.67 per cent of the total value added in transportation and 68.91 per cent of the communication and storage sector. Region IV also contributes 71.23 per cent of the total value added in wholesale and retail trade; 63.3 per cent of the finance, banking and non-banking institutions income; and 52.61 per cent of the country's real estate income.

Alternatively, 39.11 per cent of the country's gross value added in government services sector comes from Region IV. The almost taken-for-granted conclusion that the best education is found in Metro Manila is supported by the fact that 48.15 per cent of the total value added due to educational services is accounted for by Region IV.

Surprisingly, even the agriculture sector is dominated by Region IV. Southern Tagalog's contribution of 13.17 per cent of the gross value added in agricultural crops; 19.16 per cent in livestock; 27.82 per cent in poultry; and 59.75 per cent in fishery is significantly larger than those of other regions. It is only in forestry gross income that Region X (Northern Mindanao) and Region XI (Southern Mindanao) command a considerable lead.

Within the mining and quarrying sector where the resource endowments and its developments play a considerable role, regional dominance vary. Because of the Benguet gold mines in Region I, 90.3 per cent of the country's total income in gold mining comes from the Ilocos/Mt. Province Region. Region I also excels in iron-ore mining with a 30.63 per cent contribution, and in other metals with 33.1 per cent. Chromium ore mining in the country, however, is concentrated in Region III (Central Luzon), whose contribution of 98.97 per cent of the total value added in this activity is almost the country's total output.

From the foregoing on regional income structure it can be attested that policies and the concentration of social overhead capital in Metro Manila had resulted in the agglomeration of industries in Region IV. The dominance of this core region of the Philippines, in much the same manner as the other three Southeast Asian countries, can be further confirmed by examination of Table 11. Region IV (Manila/Rizal) exhibited an average family income almost twice the national average, had grown the fastest among the regions in the post-war period (between 1948 and 1966), less than half its household below 5000 pesos per year compared to the other areas and on other indicators perform relatively much better.

1.4. Thailand

It is known that the Thai economy is highly centralized. While centralization is not necessarily undesirable from the point of view of Thailand as a whole especially during the

TABLE 11

Selected regional socioeconomic indicators for the Philippines

Region	Average family[a] income, (pesos) 1971		GRP growth[b] coefficients 1948 - 66	% families with[c] incomes below 5000 pesos per year, 1971	Average daily *per*[d] *capita* intake of calories, 1958 - 67	Infant mortality[e] rate per 1000 1973
Manila and Suburbs (Rizal)	7285	(194.5)[f]	3.90	48.6	1727.0	51.21
Ilocos/Mt. Province	3299	(88.7)	0.97	83.0	1972.0	67.45
Cagayan Valley and Batanes	2390	(63.8)	0.84	91.8	1809.0	88.03
Central Luzon	4127	(110.2)	0.89	83.9	—	52.55
Southern Luzon and Islands	4332	(115.6)	1.00	73.6	1705.0	64.97
Bicol	2784	(74.3)	0.81	87.3	—	53.78
W. Visayas	3206	(85.6)	0.79	84.7	1661.0	65.51
E. Visayas	2548	(68.0)	0.85	86.5	1503.0	72.53
Northern Mindanao	3062	(81.7)	1.27[g]	86.2	1743.0[g]	85.44
Southern Mindanao and Sulu	3577	(95.5)	1.40[h]	79.8	1607.0[h]	74.22
Philippines	3746	(100.0)	—	—	—	67.57

[a]*NEDA Statistical Yearbook 1974,* table 13.1.
[b]G. P. Sicat, *Economic Policy and Philippines Development,* Univ. of Philippines Press, Manila, 1972, table 15.1, p. 352.
[c]*NEDA Statistical Yearbook 1974,* table 13.4.
[d]M. Mangahas (ed.), *Measuring Philippines Development,* Development Academy of Philippines, 1976, table 2/19, p. 81.
[e]*Ibid.,* table 2/2, p. 68.
[f]Figures in brackets are calculated as percentage of Philippines average income.
[g]Northeastern Mindanao.
[h]Southwestern Mindanao.

first decade of national development efforts in the 1960s which aimed at national growth, there is a general agreement now that benefits will be derived from counteracting the pull of Bangkok by encouraging industrial growth in other regions. There has been no real effort as yet to sponsor industrial development in the regions, especially the South, as compared with the metropolitan region of Bangkok. This is understandable, since Thailand's industrialization has been of relatively short duration and it is unreasonable to expect the government to have intervened in a way which might conceivably have weakened the industrialization impetus.

Table 12 clearly shows the basic pattern of the Thai economy: the complete dominance of the Central Region, which includes Bangkok as the primate city. In terms of regional GDP the Central Region has captured more than half of the total national product, and from 1960 to 1976 has managed to increase this from 52.2 per cent to close to 60 per cent of total Thai output. This, as can be seen from Table 13, has been at the expense of all the other regions in the country, which have shown relatively declining shares over the same period by as much as three percentage points (the Northeast). Of course this is due to the higher growth rates of the Central Region compared to the others. During the Third Five-year Plan (1971 - 6) the Central Region's economy grew at an annual average of 7.1 per cent compared to the national average of 6.2 per cent.

It has also been found that during the Third Plan period there is an intensification of the degree of economic concentration in the Bangkok metropolitan area.[12] By 1976 the Bangkok area accounted for about 50 per cent of the GDP of the Central Region and about 30 per cent of national production. Government planners asserted that this pheno-

TABLE 12

Trends in income distribution and regional share of national production, 1960 - 76
(million baht)

	North	Northeast	Central	South	Whole kingdom
Regional GDP					
1960[a]	8900	10,100	29,200	7,900	56,000
1971[b]	18,653	19,935	74,117	16,912	129,617
1976	23,097	25,851	104,523	21,395	174,866
Aug. annual growth rate, 1960 - 76					
Third Plan (1971 - 6)	4.5	5.4	7.1	4.8	6.2
Regional share of GDP (%)					
1960	15.9	18.0	52.2	13.8	100.0
1971	14.4	15.4	57.2	13.0	100.0
1976	13.2	14.8	59.8	12.2	100.0

[a]P. Pakkasem, *Thailand's Northeast Economic Development planning*, NESDB/DED 1973-No. 1, Bangkok, table 2.4, p. 36.
[b]*Fourth Five Year Plan, 1977-81,* NESDB , Bangkok, table 4.1, p. 139.

menal growth of Bangkok in effect had pushed up the growth rate of the Central Region as a whole and must be considered a main factor responsible for the increasing income disparities in Thailand.[13] The dominance of Bangkok in this respect can also be seen from

TABLE 13

Factories located in Bangkok and elsewhere by level of capital investment (million baht)

	Level of capital investment			
	Less than 1 million baht	1 - 10 million baht	More than 10 million baht	Total
Bangkok	14,300	817	114	15,321 (30.6%)
Other of which	48,613	1128	256	49,907
South Thailand	7,571	104	4	7,679
Total	62,913	1,945	370	65,228

Source: Ministry of Industry, NESDB, RPS: reproduced from Pakkasem, *op. cit.*, p. 10.

---

[12]Government of Thailand, *Fourth Five Year Plan, 1976 - 81*, Bangkok, NESDB, 1976, p. 138.

[13]*ibid.*, p. 138.

Table 13, which shows the concentration in the area of a substantial share of capital investments in all categories; over 30 per cent of total investment, in fact.

The sectoral breakdown of the regional economies, seen in detail in Table 14, shows that the basic factor in the disparities between the Central Region and the rest of the economy is the fact that the latter are dominated by agriculture. In 1960 about half of the Northern and Northeastern regions' GDP is in this sector, whereas it accounted for only 27 per cent of the Central Region's GDP. Even in 1972, when the North and the Northeast had managed to reduce the share of agriculture in the regions' GDP, it is still substantial. But here the Central Region itself exhibited an increase in its agricultural share to some 30 per cent of the total agricultural product for the whole kingdom. The importance of the Central Plains in agriculture, and of the Bangkok-centred region in manufacturing underlies the basic decentralization issue in Bangkok, as severe as that of Metropolitan Manila and Java.

TABLE 14

Sectoral breakdown of gross domestic regional product in Thailand, 1976 (million baht in constant prices)

Sectors	Whole kingdom		Northeast		North		South		Central	
	Amount	%	Amount	%	Amount	%	Amount	%	Amount	%
Agriculture	97,135	100.0	21,728	22.4	26,607	27.4	15,372	15.8	32,852	33.8
	(29.9)		(45.6)		(53.1)		(39.9)		(32.3)	
Mining and quarrying	3,964	100.0	219	5.5	733	18.5	1.673	42.2	1,339	33.8
	(1.2)		(0.5)		(1.5)		(4.3)		(1.3)	
Manufacturing	59,529	100.0	3,852	6.5	3,423	5.8	3,000	5.0	29,199	49.0
	(18.3)		(3.1)		(6.8)		(7.8)		(28.7)	
Construction	13,791	100.0	2,218	16.1	2,371	17.2	1,448	10.5	3,249	23.6
	(4.2)		(4.7)		(4.7)		(3.7)		(3.2)	
Electricity and water supply	3,499	100.0	258	7.4	611	17.5	156	4.5	1,603	4.6
	(1.1)		(0.5)		(1.2)		(0.4)		(1.6)	
Transport and communication	20,689	100.0	2,350	11.4	2,489	12.0	2,311	11.2	3,439	16.6
	(6.4)		(4.9)		(5.0)		(6.0)		(3.4)	
Wholesale and retail trade	58,797	100.0	7,297	12.4	7,796	13.3	2,778	14.9	15,558	26.5
	(18.1)		(15.3)		(15.6)		(22.8)		(15.3)	
Banking, insurance, real estate and ownership of dwellings	22,365	100.0	1,786	8.0	1,282	5.7	1,219	5.5	3,540	15.8
	(6.9)		(3.7)		(2.6)		(3.2)		(3.5)	
Public Administration and defense	14,255	100.0	2,679	18.8	1,979	13.9	1,424	10.0	3,501	24.6
	(4.4)		(5.6)		(4.0)		(3.7)		(3.4)	
Services	31,088	100.0	5,316	17.1	2,777	8.9	3,149	10.1	7,464	24.0
	(9.5)		(11.1)		(5.5)		(8.2)		(7.3)	
Gross regional product	325,112	100.0	47,703	14.7	50,068	15.4	38,530	11.6	101,744	31.3
	(100.0)		(100.0)		(100.0)		(100.0)		(100.0)	

Source: NESDB, Bangkok, 1976.

There is also concern that the benefits from regional production, showed as it were to the Bangkok region, have tended to accrue mainly to higher income groups. As shown in Table 15, most of those households earning the top annual income of more than 30,000 baht are located in the Bangkok Metropolitan area. On the other hand, the Northeast

TABLE 15

Income distribution among household groups in different
regions, using income categories of 1973

Income class Regions	Under 6000 baht	From 6000 to 30,000 baht	Over 30,000 baht	Total
North	25.5	70.1	4.4	100.0
Northeast	41.1	49.6	9.3	100.0
South	15.2	74.3	10.5	100.0
Central[a]	4.1	78.5	17.4	100.0
Bangkok	0.7	54.8	44.5	100.0
Whole kingdom	22.2	64.6	13.2	100.0

[a]Not including the Bangkok Metropolitan area.

consist of the largest proportion of poor households, that is 41.1 per cent, taking as definition of the poverty line on annual income of 6000 bahts. This is followed by the North (25.5 per cent of its households) and the South (15.2) per cent; the least, of course, in Bangkok and the Central Region.

Another perspective on household income inequality on a regional basis is given in Table 16, where the regions are further broken down into urban and rural areas. In terms of average household total income, the table merely confirms the superiority of the Bangkok-centred region for both rural and urban incomes. It is also evident that *per capita* rural - urban income disparities are least in the Central Region than in the other areas, the most severe being in the northeast. The marked contrast for the whole kingdom between urban and rural areas is rather clear, urban incomes (in *per capita* terms) being as much as 2.5 times rural incomes; further, urban incomes in all the four regions are above the national average, with only the Central Region, including Bangkok/Chonburi, having a better than average rural performance. In terms of the Gini coefficient, the Central Region appears to be less worse off than the other regions in terms of urban incomes, but performed relatively poorer in terms of rural incomes. It turns out also that rural areas in Thailand have a relatively more equal distribution of household income than the urban areas.

Two reasons have been given for the increasing interregional economic disparities, in particular between the Central region and the rest of the country and the concentration in the Bangkok Metropolitan Area. First, the production structure of the Central Region is more diversified, including a large manufacturing sector, whereas the other regions, especially the Northeast and South, are narrowly based on certain agricultural products. Second, the higher growth rates of all sectors, agricultural as well as manufacturing, in the Central Region, and in Bangkok particularly for the industrial groups, when compared to the slow expansion of the other regions. Having a narrower resource base in those peripheral areas as compared to Indonesia and the Philippines as well as Malaysia, the problems of industrial decentralization from the Bangkok region becomes a critical issue in Thailand.

TABLE 16
Thailand: income distribution by regions

	Northeast	North	Center/East	South	Bangkok/Chon Buri	Whole kingdom	Average
(A) Average household total income (cash and kind) by region and location, 1968/9							
Average household total income (baht/year)							
Towns	26,161	23,182	26,216	26,172	33,800	29,403	13,198
Villages	9,079	10,331	15,699	9,244	24,290	11,214	2,288
Household total income/person (baht/year)							
Towns	4,641	4,630	4,751	4,698	5,403	5,026	
Villages	1,484	1,836	2,807	1,749	3,774	1,947	
(B) Average household total income relative to the whole kingdom average							
Average household total income (%)							
Towns	221	176	199	198	256	223	100
Villages	69	78	119	70	184	85	
Household total income/person (%)							
Towns	203	202	208	205	236	220	100
Villages	65	80	123	76	165	85	
(C) Gini coefficients of household total income							
Towns	0.4495	0.4404	0.3996	0.4501	0.4085	0.4290	0.4289
Villages	0.3473	0.3450	0.3917	0.3249	0.3928	0.3813	

Source: Data from Tables 3.3.1a – 3.3.1c of Oey Astra Meesook's *Income Distribution in Thailand,* Compiled from data tapes of the *Socio-Economic Survey 1968/69,* National Statistical Office, Bangkok.

2. POLICY RESPONSES TOWARD REGIONAL DEVELOPMENT
IN SOUTHEAST ASIA

The involvement of the Southeast Asian countries in regional development marks a new dimension in their national development planning effort. This is mainly in response to increasing regional disparities after the sustained economic growth of the post-war period. In addition, the opening of resource frontier zones in order to support further economic expansion had induced their interest in regional development. Some of these latter developments were in fact initiated by the interests of foreign investment.

The previous orientation of the Southeast Asian countries, however, was towards a broader consideration of development issues, from a national point of view, rather than toward specifically defined regional questions. The development goals have been focused on economic growth, industrialization, and aspects of socioeconomic modernization such as rural development, security, etc., the planning of which has been carried out mainly in sectoral terms. In examining the recent policy responses toward the problems of disparities. The new regional dimension, which has been introduced into the national planning effort of these countries, cannot be seen as separate from the earlier concerns, but in fact should be seen as their extension to the treatment of these issues in a spatially integrated fashion aimed at decentralized development. The Southeast Asian governments' understanding of regional development, and some of its concepts such as the growth pole approach, cannot thus be understood in terms of single-purpose one-dimensional strategies for decentralized development without reference to the broader policy issues.

In this sense the responses of the Southeast Asian countries toward regional development should be seen essentially as policy instruments in achieving the broad goals of national development. The immediate reaction seems to be in acceptance of the notion of regional planning itself, and the administrative reorganization which it engendered. This initial experience has enabled the Southeast Asian planners and policymakers to continually improve the formulation of regional development policy in their countries. The growth pole approach as adopted in the Southeast Asian context should therefore be seen as a part of this learning experience. These items will now be considered in turn below.

2.1. Regional Development Planning and Administrative Reorganization

Most policymakers and central planners in the four Southeast Asian countries examined in this paper seem to recognize the seriousness of the problem of regional inequalities, and that these disparities are increasing. In general, their concern for regional development policy had emerged largely from increasing knowledge of the structure of their regional economies, which was made possible by numerous planning studies conducted in separate parts of the four countries. These studies were commissioned mainly to provide baseline data for the severely underdeveloped areas as well as the frontier regions in order to expand their primary export bases.

Some of the areas have been selected by the central governments for concentrated development effort, such as South Thailand, Mindanao (Philippines), Pahang Tenggara (Malaysia), and South Sumatra (Indonesia).

Considerable international technical aid was involved in many of these studies, and no doubt contributed to the diffusion of regional development planning ideas developed in North America and western Europe and applied at an earlier stage to some Latin American countries, notably Venezuela and Chile. It is certain also that the studies conducted in some areas, especially the border areas, arose out of concern for national security, and in some as a response to growing dissatisfaction and political pressure from the peripheral areas themselves against the unequal sharing of development with the national core regions. This is the case perhaps of the East Coast States in Peninsula Malaysia, the Northeast and South in Thailand, Muslim Mindanao in the Philippines, and Sumatra in Indonesia. Provincialism, no doubt exacerbated by physical factors such as in Indonesia and the Philippines, also contributed to these regional planning studies.

Whatever the reason which first motivated the four Southeast Asian governments to take a definite, and one may add healthy, stand on regional development policy, the concern for regional disparities, and the economic welfare of the largely rural populations in their national peripheries, appears to be genuine. The regional planning studies, which made available many of the data, especially on regional income accounts, used in the section above, have enabled the central planners to formulate a more definite regional development policy than previously was possible. Earlier, these were couched, if at all, in general terms related to broad development objectives. The definition of clear regional policies, however broad, is nonetheless a very recent phenomenon, and is reflected in the latest five-year plans of the four countries. This is the case in Thailand's Fourth Five-year Plan (1977 - 81), Malaysia's Third Five-year Plan (1976 - 80), where a whole chapter in each is devoted to their respective regional development policy and related objects. The Philippines adopted a more integrated approach, and in their Four-year Development Plan (1974 - 77) a special supplement was added for their regional development projects.[14] In Indonesia, REPELITA II (1974/5 - 1978/9) is clearly conscious of regional development goals, and their regional planning bodies are currently actively translating these into concrete regional development plans.

It would be difficult, however, to assess these planning efforts at such an early stage. The real test must be in the implementation of these plans and their likely success. The regional plans, to the extent that they are available and incorporated into the overall regional development policy, and more importantly translated into actual development projects, have been carried out at varying degrees of sophistication. In this connection, however, it is legitimate to consider the extent to which these regional plans are fitted together into a consistent national plan for regional development.

As noted earlier, most of the regional planning studies were carried out by separate and independent teams with sometimes rather different terms of reference. This is certainly the case in Malaysia, Thailand, and Indonesia. The task of integration of these separate planning studies into a consistent, if not optimum, national plan is, of course, the function of the central planning agencies in each country, and must reflect the actual constraints at both regional and national levels. This is not entirely evident in the various national five-year plans currently being implemented. However, a detailed outline of the aggregation of the regional plans cannot be expected in broad terms at the conceptual and policy level.

In reality, planning at the regional level in these Southeast Asian countries is hampered by the general lack of skilled manpower and expertise. This is particularly felt at the level of identification of projects. As a consequence, the formulation of a national policy of regional development, as in the case of Malaysia and Thailand, is less the result of an aggregation of regional plans as the perception of central planners regarding the regional allocation of development projects, i.e., as a partial disaggregation of the national plan.

---

[14]A draft of a yet-to-be-published Perspective Plan for the Philippines (1978 - 2000) includes a chapter on the development of regions to the year 2000.

The planning function, however, is increasingly being decentralized in all four countries. This has been carried out simultaneously with the identification of planning regions, especially in Indonesia, the Philippines, and Thailand (Figs. 1, 3, and 4, respectively). In Indonesia, the BAPEDAs (the provincial planning boards) are actively being assisted by local universities in drawing up regional plans for submission to the central planning agency in Jakarta, BAPPENAS, in order to obtain central government funds for regional development. In the Philippines and Thailand similar planning boards have been created for the planning regions identified, each responsible to their respective central planning agencies, the National Economic and Development Authority (NEDA) in the Philippines, and the National Economic and Social Development Board (NESDB) in Thailand. In Malaysia, which has a federal structure since the beginning, and where the central planning is carried out mainly by the Economic Planning Unit (EPU), the decentralization of the planning function is achieved through the creation of a State Planning Unit (SPU) in each of the states of the Federation (Fig. 2).

Whether this administrative response, namely the decentralization of the planning function, will lead to actual decentralization of development and more importantly to the reduction of regional inequalities, is another matter. One factor in this regard is the extent to which the regional authorities (state, provincial, etc.) have the fiscal capacity to undertake the implementation of their plans. As mentioned earlier, this however depends to a considerable extent on central government transfers through their current or development budgets. Another factor is the degree of discretionary authority which have been allocated to the newly created institutions (the regional authorities, the regional development boards, etc.). The distribution of power, between different levels of government and different authorities at the regional level, is an important aspect to consider in order to determine the pattern and likely success of the regional planning response in Southeast Asian countries. The approach and the experience of each country in this regard can be expected to vary.

These administrative responses to the regional development question are an important part of regional policy in Southeast Asia. The regionalization exercise carried out in Indonesia, the Philippines, and Thailand should be seen in the first instance as a conceptualization and in the second as an actualization of each country's spatial organization for regional development, and constitutes as much instrumental value as the allocation of development projects themselves. In the three countries mentioned, the regionalization and creation of regional authorities represent a reordering of the space economy in order to rationalize the allocation of development expenditure which would not be the case under the pre-existing administrative structure.[15] In Malaysia the state boundaries are retained, but a number of new regional authorities have been created by the Federal government to implement a number of regional plans, such as the Pahang Tenggara Authority and the Johore Tenggara Authority. This has created interesting federal - state - regional relationships which could in the final analysis determine the success of such regional development efforts.[16] Thailand also had undertaken a number of admini-

[15]In the Philippines case, see R. P. de Guzman and A. G. Pacho, *Administration for Regional Development: The Philippine Experience,* Manila, November 1972, mimeo., p. 83; and Interagency Committee on Administrative Regional Areas, *Preliminary Report on Administrative Regional Areas,* Manila, December 1971, 66 pp and appendices.

[16]See Kamal Salih, Administrative structures, allocative efficiency, and regional development: the case of West Malaysia, *Proceedings of Xth World Congress,* International Political Science Association, Edinburgh, August 1976.

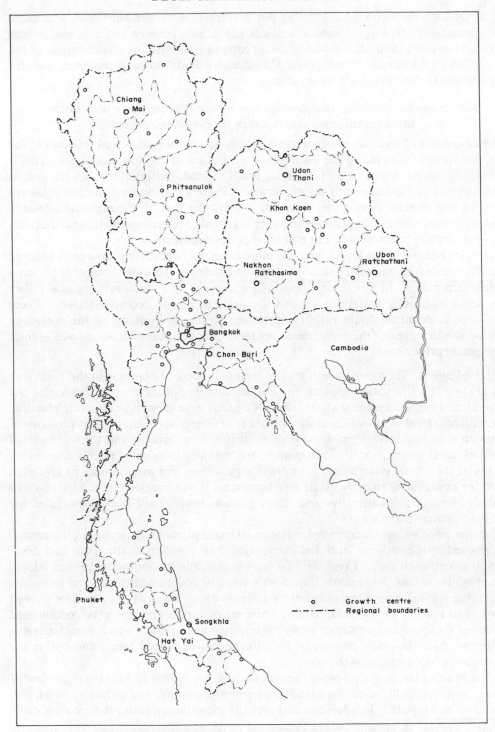

Fig. 4. Designated growth centres and development regions: Thailand.

strative reforms throughout its history, but the creation of the Northeast Economic Development (NEED) Project marked a significant turning point in Thai regional policy. Indonesia's experiment in this respect began as early as 1963 with the establishment of the BAKOPDA (the Regional Development Coordinative Body) in each province, but this has given way to the current ten region scheme.

2.2. Southeast Asian regional development policy: The common orientation to decentralization and resource frontier development

The emergence of regional development policy in Southeast Asia is well reflected in the latest five (four in the case of the Philippines) year plans of the four countries. This is most clearly evident in the case of Malaysia and Thailand, but relatively less obvious in the Philippines and Indonesia. They all, however, share a common orientation to decentralization and resource frontier development, in particular that of dispersion of industries to the peripheral regions. In general the policy is geared to reduction of regional inequalities as one strategy to achieving a fairer sharing of development.

However, because of the broad front, or more accurately multifront, approach adopted by the four countries, regional policy is usually embedded in the wider context of national development policy. In this regard the configurations of each country's regional policy show some interesting variations around the basic theme of decentralization. These differences in detail no doubt reflect adaptations to or conditioning by the prevailing situation in each country, the constraints they face, their political realities, as well as their development priorities.

2.2.1. *Philippines.* The move toward greater regionalization of planning in the Four-year Plan (1974 - 7) reflects their concern for a wider distribution of growth dividends. As we mentioned earlier, Regional Development Councils were created to integrate planning at the regional level so as to harmonize a number of objectives: employment promotion, maximum economic growth, more equitable distribution of income and wealth, regional industrial development, social development, and stability in prices. In this connection the role of the central government is to provide guidelines and programmes to give each region the opportunity to mobilize its own resources. Twelve regions (plus Metropolitan Manila), based on administrative and ethnic considerations, have been demarcated for local development planning.

With the emphasis on comprehensive integrated regional planning, sectoral programmes are designed at the national level and disaggregated to conform to the needs and development potential of various regions. To achieve this, the Philippines approach adopts clear priorities among the regions. Based on a series of government social and economic studies, the regions have been assigned to a hierarchy of levels of development ranked according to Leading Development Areas, where major investments are to be concentrated at appropriate levels and locations, explicitly rejecting an approach which would disperse investments over the entire country or even to the less-developed areas, and opting for the creation of economic growth poles.

In the fourth plan, a special place appears to have been given to Mindanao in view of the vast potential in the southern island in agriculture, mining, and industry, which still remains to be tapped.[17] In addition, and perhaps more importantly, the growing dissi-

---

[17]NEDA, *Regional Development Projects* (Supplement to the Four-year Development Plan, (1974 - 7), Manila 1973, p. 4. See also *Reconstruction and Development Program: Muslim Mindanao,* Vols. I and II, Presidential Task Force on the Reconstruction and Development of Mindanao, DMS Control No. 08-73-1, 1973.

dence among the Muslims in the south is cited as underlining the need for "wider and more intensive implementation of regional dispersal policies.[18] Overall, four general types of investments are identified including agricultural, tourism, mining, and industrial. Allocations of expenditure for infrastructure, public works programmes, and fiscal policies combine to give incentives for the decentralization of economic activity from the present areas of concentration around Metropolitan Manila.

The Philippine integrated regional development approach, as enunciated in the Four-year Plan 1974 - 7, should be elaborated on as this appears to be the basic model of regional policy among the four countries, of which the growth pole approach (explicitly or implicitly) is a subcomponent. The basic idea, as is well known, is that the location and organization of investments to meet development goals and to reconcile between the supposedly conflicting goals of efficiency versus welfare should be achieved through a strategy of functional and geographic integration of the various development elements using space as the plan frame.[19] Hence, the importance of a regionalization or delineation of regions. Within this spatial frame a "Physical Planning Strategy for the Philippines" was formulated as an integral part of the national (sectoral) plan framework.

The justification for this approach, which shows how the Philippines (and it can be said of the other Southeast Asian countries as well) have conceptualized their regional policy, is that integrated (regional) planning within the framework of national development policy is "a tool for classifying and defining the spatial structure of the country, indicating the appropriate functions and interrelationships of its growth centres and other geographical areas to meet varying mixes of objectives . . [aiding] in setting sectoral and regional priorities, and provides a rational basis for the identification of interrelated investment projects on a package basis . . . [and] effecting the much needed coordination of national and local development plans".[20]

Implementation of this approach in the Philippines is reflected in the Regional Development Projects supplement of the Four-year Development Plan 1974 - 7 cited earlier. Two priority areas preoccupy the regional development strategy: (i) the Manila Bay Metropolitan Strategic Plan, aimed at guiding the orderly and efficient development of the metro region (a concern equally applicable in the other three Southeast Asian countries), and (ii) Mindanao regional development, which has already been mentioned. In addition to these a number of area-based development projects are under consideration, e.g. the Bicol River Basin Development, the Cagayan Land Reform Infrastructure Package, schemes which are similar to the Kemubu and Muda Regional projects in Peninsula Malaysia (see below). In addition to this is the Regional Capital Development Programme that forms the main thrust of the growth-centre approach in the Philippines, which we shall consider in the following section. Finally, all the physical infrastructure projects (roads, water resources, power, irrigation, etc.) are organized by regional categories under the National Physical Planning Strategy framework.

2.2.2. *Thailand.* The Fourth Five-year Plan (1977 - 81 aims at providing social justice by reducing internal disparities. Two important structural problems have been identified as being at the root of regional and social inequalities: (1) lack of diversification of

---

[18]*Four Year Development Plan, 1974 - 7*, Government of the Philippines, Manila, 1973, p. 21.

[19]*Regional Development Project, loc. cit.*, p. 3.

[20]*Ibid.*, p. 4.

economic activities, and dependence upon a few agricultural crops for income in outer regions; (2) concentration of production gains in both agriculture and industry in the Central Region. Thus while industrial activity expanded, greater regional inequalities were generated as agriculture in peripheral regions made slow advances. The strategy of regional development adopted by Thai planners is to reduce inequalities in income distribution by improving the economic structure of lagging regions. The objective of reducing interpersonal income inequality underlies policies for reducing interregional inequalities.

Thailand's regional development policies are aimed at correcting regional differences in production structures, unequal patterns of ownership of production factors, and the over-emphasis on growth over distribution. Four approaches are combined to carry out the regional development strategy. First are policies directed toward income redistribution and poverty eradication. The poorest and most economically backward rural areas and peripheral urban areas with high unemployment have been identified as recipient areas under these policies which include direct development assistance to the poorer groups.

The second policy category seeks to improve regional and community production structures by diversifying and increasing production in agriculture. Irrigation, land-use intensification, land reform (especially in the Central Region), and comprehensive package programmes for increasing linkages between agriculture and urban production are envisaged. Also included is the recognition of the need to develop local resources such as mineral deposits.

Third is the designation of specific areas characterized by social and political instability as areas in need of special attention. Specific areas have been identified within each of the four regions, and policies attempt to tailor development to these areas, among which are areas with little arable land, minority groups, increasing underemployment due to in-migration, uncontrolled resource use (deforestation), low levels of public services and infrastructural development, and problems of land tenure.

The fourth policy area focuses on the promotion of employment outside of the Bangkok Metropolis. The rapidly increasing labour force and the limited ability of the capital city to absorb migrants in search of work provides the logic for policies to stimulate local construction work and the cultivation of cash crops, to invest in agro-industries and services in rural areas, to expand credit facilities, and to develop medium-size communities in different regions to serve as main agricultural centres.

A number of guidelines for the development of specific areas in each of the major regions have also been included in the Fourth Plan. In the Northern Region the relative underdevelopment of the upper part due to shortage of arable land and lack of irrigation facilities, and of the status of minority groups in the highland areas, have been identified. The plan is to reduce the disparity between the upper part and the lower part of the region which has to absorb more labour (note that the Plan's migration policy is to encourage more intraregional than interregional migration). In the Northeast, where there are large pockets of poverty, man - land ratios are very high, and considerable out-migration exists, the Plan envisages the increase of comprehensive rural development package programmes. In the Southern Region, where the cultural/religious differences are recognized, a broad programme of social and economic, as well as infrastructure programmes, are planned. Special attention is to be given to major pockets of poverty. Land reform on the other land is the principal concern in the Central Region.

The Thai policy of decentralization is given considerable weight, naturally, in the

Fourth Plan. Three chapters, on a decentralized urbanization strategy, decentralization of basic infrastructure, and of social services, are included in the Plan document. The substance of this decentralization strategy in Thailand will be discussed in the next section.

2.2.3. *Malaysia.* The introduction of the New Economic Policy in 1970, together with the launching of the Second Malaysia Plan (1971 - 5), mark the real beginning of regional development policy in the country. Up to 1970, in the previous two Malaya plans as well as the First Malaysia Plan (1965 - 9), the concern was for rural - urban disparities and the focus of national development toward rural and agricultural (primary export) development.

The New Economic Policy (NEP) seeks the eradication of poverty regardless of race, and a restructuring of Malaysian society so as to reduce the identification of employment with race and location within the context of an expanding economy. This programme is to take place within a twenty-year Perspective Plan, by which time it is expected that the bumiputra population, hitherto economically underrepresented in relation to their population strength, will own about 30 per cent of the wealth in the country, and the foreign component substantially reduced from its present dominant position in some of the major sectors of the economy. The strategy of the NEP also envisages a restructuring of the employment structure by inducing greater bumiputra participation in industrial and commercial activities. A major implication of this strategy is a deliberate policy of Malay urbanization, where previously they were largely rural and engaged mainly in agricultural activities.

The NEP, however, gave a major impetus to the formulation and adoption of regional development as a strategy of national economic development. As part of this exercise, many regional planning studies for various parts of the country had been conducted during the 1970 - 5 period. In the meantime several State Development Corporations (SEDCs) were created to undertake the development of each of the states; and an Urban Development Authority was established to implement programmes for increased participation of bumiputras in urban areas. The regional masterplanning studies added considerably to the understanding of Malaysia's regional structure. By the Mid-term Review of the Second Malaysia Plan, the problems of regional disparities and other structural imbalances as described in the first section of this paper have been clearly outlined.

It was, however, still not possible to formulate a consistent national regional development policy on the basis of these regional studies. They were conducted at different times, used dissimilar methodologies, are formulated according to different terms of reference, and most importantly are not ordered on a clear system of priorities so as to facilitate implementation given the limited financial resources available to meet all developmental requirements. A similar situation may have also occurred in Indonesia, and, to a lesser extent, in Thailand. It is possible that some of the targets and strategies outlined in each plan may be in conflict with each other if not modified. Yet such modifications require a prior national regional development policy which could form the basis of either a regionalization of the national plan or an aggregation of the several regional plans.

While this overall policy may not be forthcoming from these studies, the creation of regional development authorities such as for Pahang Tenggara, Johore Tenggara, and Trengganu Tengah for the development of Peninsula Malaysia frontier areas (see Fig. 2), shows that regional development in this Second Malaysia Plan period is seen as merely a land development strategy, and an extension of the Jengka - FELDA model. On the other hand, the Klang Valley Plan, while it may not have been adopted in total, appears to be guiding the growth of Malaysia's premier development corridor. An active industrial estates programme is also being implemented, distributed all over the peninsula, and supported by a newly introduced Locational Incentive Act. New towns are being built, not only in the frontier zones of Pahang Tenggara, but also by the SEDCs in the various states. In addition, a *de facto* growth pole approach is being implemented, with development in Kuantan, Penang, Johore Bharu, and, at a lower level, Ipoh, Malacca, Seremban, each reinforced by industrial estates around it. These towns have shown remarkable growth over the past five years or so.

In spite of these, or rather because of these programmes, one can conjecture that these projects have tended to aggravate the uneven spatial development by reinforcing the already developed areas. The lack of a clear regional development policy which aims at reducing disparities, and thus focusing more on the less-developed states, is obvious in the first five years of the emergent regional policy. Like the dilemma facing national economic planners regarding overall development policy, the regional policy in the Second Malaysia Plan similarly lacks a definite sense of purpose.

The shift in regional development policy to the less-developed states is, however, evident in the Third Malaysia Plan (1976 - 80), just as in terms of overall policy it directs greater attention on the poverty eradication prong of the NEP. In light of the entrenched condition of uneven development, this shift is obviously important, even though the effectiveness of the programmes of implementation remains to be seen as it is too early to say. The place of regional policy in this plan and the coming ones, however, is clearly illustrated with the incorporation of a chapter devoted to it in the Third Malaysia Plan.

The outline of regional strategy in the Third Malaysia Plan is quite straightforward, and as a package the programmes offer a consistent line of action, given the constraints it must operate under. The main objective is to reduce regional gaps in incomes and other welfare indicators between the less-developed states and the rest of the country. This is to be achieved in several ways. The main focus of regional development is through new land development—a continuation of previous plan strategies. There are two types: the first involves opening of available land in the poor states themselves, especially Trengganu and Kelantan, the two poorest states. The second involves the frontier zones of Pahang and Johore. An out-migration of landless farmers from the poor states to Pahang and Johore Tenggara, and other land schemes in the resource frontier zone, is envisaged. In the poor states themselves agricultural development projects—especially of the integrated type—are planned, aimed at increasing productivity through the improvement of access to inputs and marketing outlets. To induce industrial development and dispersion into the less-developed states, as well as for the whole country, a system of growth centres and corridor development are being planned as well as to rationalize the settlement structure through a denser pattern of urban development in the east coast of Peninsula Malaysia. It is hoped that this will not only enhance bumiputra participation in urban activities but also will induce a modernization of the rural sector in the poor states.

We may classify the projects in the Third Malaysian Plan into three sets roughly coincident with a three-region scheme for the country. First, a core region development, which programme comprises the Klang Valley, Penang/Butterworth Region, and the Johore Baru/SouthJohore Region. These areas will be undertaking the major task of export-oriented industrialization. A dispersion of industry from Kuala Lumpur is implemented through incentives for the outlier subsystems, and a disincentive structure for the Klang

Valley. These areas form the highest order growth centres for the national system. Second, a less-developed states programme, consisting of land development in Kelantan, the North Malaysia Region (Kedah/Perlis), Trengganu, Negri Sembilan Timor, and the Trans-Perak scheme (the latter still under study). This also includes a regionalized agriculture programme, with improved access to inputs and outlets in the major irrigation areas such as Kemubu and Muda. Target group strategy is adopted which identifies the various poverty groups. And, finally, a resource utilization area programme, which consists of the Pahang Tenggara, Johore Tenggara, and North Perak projects. These development programmes are based on primary export crops and timber resource exploitation. Kuantan is seen as the eastern regional growth centre. The entire programme is supported by major transport investments. In this last set, the whole of Sabah and Sarawak comprising East Malaysia, may be also seen as a programme of development of a large resource frontier region, quite autonomous in terms of its second-tier federal relationship with the rest of Malaysia. A major land development scheme in Sarawak is the Miri/Bintulu project.

In this regional development framework we should include the planning of growth centres for the entire nation. A hierarchy of such centres have been identified in the Third Plan. Together with this system of growth centres one should also include the programme of rural industrialization based on the small towns, even though there is as yet no active smalltowns policy.

2.2.4. *Indonesia.* The pattern of emergence of regional development policy in Indonesia is almost the same as with its Southeast Asian neighbours. With the attainment of political and economic stability during the first REPELITA, a new range of issues is emerging in Indonesia. A new concern about problems arising from the wide disparities in social and economic conditions that exist in the various parts of the country and the realization that sectoral planning alone is likely to increase rather than decrease these problems, compelled the government to review the previous policies and plans. The case for formulation of a regional development policy during the REPELITA II (1974/75 - 1978/79) rests primarily on the fact that given the existing diversities in Indonesia, an equal welfare distribution and social justice will not necessarily flow from national and sectoral plans that emphasize rapid and efficient growth. Hence, bearing in mind the fundamental problem of regional disparities in social and economic progress, regional and provincial development constitutes a principal thrust of the REPELITA II.

The principal objectives of Indonesian regional development were formulated in a series of directives by the country's Peoples Assembly: first is to achieve balance between regional and sectoral development. Regional consideration is to be included in sectoral planning. Second is to reduce inequalities in the rate of development between provinces. During the first five-year planning period it was found that strictly sectoral planning produced the greatest growth in provinces already well endowed with infrastructure and large-scale developments. This is to be countered by distributing development activities to the poorest provinces. The third concern is to help the provincial governments solve large scale provincial problems. This involves the balancing of sectoral priorities with provincial development priorities. And lastly, Indonesian planners are directed to improve the planning, development and taxing capacities of the provinces. This involves both efforts to increase provincial planning capabilities and the attempt to improve developmental management capacities and resources.

The above directives have since been translated by BAPPENAS into a number of policy guidelines to assist the provincial planning bodies in formulating strategy plans for their regions. In this regard, the issue of reducing regional disparities was primal, including the strategy of containment of the Jakarta Metropolitan area. BAPPENAS is also concerned to reap the highest possible benefits from the potentials of the different regions, both from the national development point of view and from that of the individual region. This goal includes transmigration, which was one of the first examples of an explicitly national settlement policy aimed at resettlement of people from Java in new unexploited land in the outer islands such as Sumatra and Kalimantan. It was considered that the programme was too small in scale to make any effective impact on the concentration of population in Java island, that a more comprehensive regional development would be necessary. A second regional policy concern in BAPPENAS is how to develop mutually profitable economic links between the provinces in the context of unified national economy. The creation of regional groups of provinces with respect to urban manufacturing growth centres is an associated objective. The regionalization of Indonesia into ten planning regions, and further into four development regions (Fig. 1) is to be seen in this context. Finally, as in Thailand and the Philippines a number of what are called "backward", "critical", and/or "border" areas have been identified for special attention.

In addition to these designation strategies, the enhancement of regional planning capacities in the provinces (which perhaps have raised the possibility of regional demands to a higher level), Indonesia has been involved in the preparation of laws governing the financial balance between central and provincial governments so as to strengthen their fiscal capacity to undertake regional development projects. The Kabupaten subsidy programme and the village subsidy scheme are examples of this arrangement. Discussions on the appropriate revenue sharing schemes are being undertaken so as to prevent the possibility of current inequalities from being further aggravated. The ADO compensation scheme, in which the transfer of central government revenues is to be calculated on the basis of the export revenue, for instance, will benefit the major resource frontier areas such as North Sumatra. It is in this regard that the various planning, fiscal, and administrative relationships between provincial, regional bodies, and BAPPENAS become critical in order to achieve the proper balance between regional and national needs.

Regional policy in Indonesia will be more concretely defined once the planning studies at the provincial level are completed. It is then that the relative claims for priority of infrastructure development in the resource frontier areas, the spatial organization of nation wide system of growth centres, and decentralization of industry and population, need to be rationalized within the overall frame of national development.

In general, then, the regional policies in the four Southeast Asian countries, which are at various degrees of completeness in terms of detail, all emphasize balance between regional and national needs. Their common orientation to reduction of regional disparities— one of the basic rationale for any regional development policy—and of decentralization or dispersion from the national core regions, seem to be quite obvious, and understandable if seen in the context of the changing paradigm of development occurring among underdeveloped countries. Also evident from the above description is the broad range of issues in regional development which confronts the development planners in Southeast Asia, as elsewhere in the underdeveloped countries. The growth pole approach in Southeast Asia incorporated as one strategy into their national regional development plans, if it is not their basic foundation, should be examined in this light.

3. GROWTH POLE APPROACH IN SOUTHEAST ASIA

The growth pole approach is quite explicitly incorporated into the latest national plans of the four countries examined. Essentially the approach as adopted by these countries is aimed at dispersal of new manufacturing activity to the outer regions by various supporting infrastructure and fiscal policies, and generally to prevent further concentration in the capital regions. Usually, this strategy of industrial decentralization is also coupled with the aim of achieving a better balance in urban growth among the regions. In addition, it is evident that the development of such growth centres is planned so as to utilize the resource potential of the peripheral regions where available, and, through this expansion of their economic base, contribute to the reduction of regional disparities.

In the Philippines, the decision to channel resources to strategic leading growth points, which have developed economic base and potentials, was made on the basis of an explicit attempt to balance in the classic sense of growth pole theory, equity, and efficiency considerations in short-run spatial allocation of investments.[21] A similar philosophy is implied in Indonesia in the identification of regional centres which would serve a larger grouping of provinces than the political situation demands.[22]

In Thailand the policies and programmes for product diversification, income generation, and the decentralization of industries and employment are to be based on regional urban centres to be established in each region. The promotion of regional growth centres is here also seen as a strategy to check migration into the Bangkok Metropolitan area.[23] The Regional Capital Development programme in the Philippines should also be seen in this context.[24] The policy to decentralize new manufacturing activity away from the established areas, especially the Klang Valley, is no less obvious in the case of Malaysia. Together with physical infrastructure development, including industrial estates and fiscal incentives, Malaysia's growth centre strategy seeks a spatially balanced distribution of urban development especially in the east coast of Peninsula Malaysia.[25]

It is difficult to find fault in the conception of the growth pole approach in Southeast Asia, for its adoption appears to be made on rational grounds and true to the prescriptions of theory. Political considerations seemed to be minimal, which might be explained in terms of the strength of the central governments, in the fiscal sense if not politically, to decide on the identification and promotion of growth centres in their respective countries. In this connection also one should remember that the growth pole approach was adopted at the time when the four Southeast Asian countries were just beginning to be aware of the seriousness of the problem of internal disparities, and of the importance of the regional or spatial dimension in national development planning. This was also the time when the approach was in current vogue, and was actively being promoted throughout the underdeveloped world. The growth pole approach was therefore readily accepted by the Southeast Asian planners.

However, in examining it in the Southeast Asian context, a clear distinction must be made between growth poles in theory and growth poles in fact. At issue is not that what is conceived, in the five-year plans or elsewhere, by the planners is consistent with what has been written and advocated in the literature, but whether the proposed strategy will

---

[21]*Four Year Development Plan, 1974 - 77, loc. cit.*, p. 3.
[22]Majid Ibrahim, *op. cit.*, p. 7.
[23]*Fourth Five Year Plan, 1977 - 81*, p. 64.
[24]*Four Year Plan, 1974 - 77*, p. 6.
[25]*Third Malaysia Five Year Plan, 1976 - 80*, p. 212.

actually achieve the goals set for it. For the problems it is supposed to solve are wide ranging and certainly difficult. In addition to this, regardless of what the achievements of the Venezuelan or Chilean experience are, the efficacy and ability of growth centres to generate positive impact on their regional hinterlands are in too many instances being questioned. It is likely that, given the present stage, and the context, of Southeast Asian economic development, and considering the many problems which each country has to solve, the growth pole strategy will not be able to solve their distributional goals, at least in the short run. Nonetheless, the growth pole strategy is here to stay and will continue to be promoted in Southeast Asia. The task for each country is therefore to ensure that the complementary strategies (such as integrated rural development) would be able to take up the slack in regional development in these countries. In other words, the growth pole approach is only one policy instrument in a whole range of programmes in the strategy of nationwide regional development which the Sotheast Asian countries have incorporated into their national development planning.

In the meantime, the four countries have proceeded to plan for the development of growth centres in their respective regions. The procedure appears to have been in each case a natural extension of the organization of the entire nation into a number of planning or development regions. As evident in Figs. 1, 2, 3, and 4 above, the regionalization essentially either accepted the basic subnational administrative units, as in Malaysia where the states are used, or undertook some regrouping of the subnational units (provinces) into larger regions. The regionalization also took into account, in some cases the physical and economic structure of the provinces, as was done in the Philippines and Indonesia, and to some extent in Thailand. On the basis of this regionalization, an urban centre or a system of urban centres in each region are identified for active promotion as growth centres. Invariably, these centres are existing cities which have shown some potential for development in relation to the region in which it is located, and fitted into the entire urban system. In all instances the major regional centres are to serve as counterpoles to the dominance of the national metropolitan city.

In the Philippines, such a system of growth centres have been identified in its recently completed 1978 - 2000 Perspective Plan, and planned for implementation in the first phase of this period in the latest five-year plan (1978 - 82). Two countermagnet areas outside of the Manila Metropolitan Area (MMA) have been selected, namely, the Cebu - Mandane - Lapu - Lapu Area and the Davao - Tagum Area. At the next level a number of primary and secondary centres are then chosen in each region; twelve are located in Luzon which is to serve as the primary thrust of regional industrialization; in the Visayas Metro Cebu is the major centre supported by four other peripheral growth centres; in Mindanao, in order to mobilize its agricultural resource potential and to counteract the concentration of industrial activity in Luzon, eight cities are classified as primary centres outside of Davao, including Zamboanga City and Cotabato. Each of these centres are to be planned as self-sufficient and attractive centres in order to capture new industrial and commercial establishments that would otherwise go to the MMA, and in so doing achieve a more rational distribution of the expected urban population growth and to absorb the additional non-agricultural labour force up to the year 2000.

Growth centre planning in Malaysia is also closely related to a concern for balanced urban growth. An emphasis on the East Coast States of Peninsula Malaysia is evident, where a denser pattern of cities than at present and as found in the West Coast is to be promoted. In this connection the principal objective is the creation of an integrated system of cities with Kuantan as the regional growth pole. Its centrality in the region and potential relations to the resource frontier development in Pahang Tenggara make it a logical choice, and with active infrastructure and industrial estate promotion its population is expected to grow to 200,000 by the year 1990 from less than 50,000 in 1970. In the central region of the West Coast, with Kuala Lumpur and the Klang Valley as the national and regional centre, the aim is to decentralize urban and manufacturing growth to the outlying towns, such as Tanjung Malium/Ulu Bernam, Klang/Port Klang, and Seremban. In the Northern region, a dense urban system already exists, focused on Georgetown (Penang) and Ipoh. The Georgetown - Butterworth - Prai - Bukit Mertajam (so-called Penang Cornubation), which by the year 2000 could reach a population of over a million, is planned as the major counterpole to the Klang Valley. To a lesser extent, Johore Bharu in the south is similarly identified, but more to serve the resource frontier project in Johore Tenggara, and perhaps to capture some of the economic spin-offs of Singapore. In the east Malaysian states of Sabah and Sarawak, similar systems may develop with the growth of the state capitals Kota Kinabalu and Kucing respectively.

The basic preoccupation of growth centre planning in Thailand is how to counter the development of the Bangkok Metropolitan Area. The development of the outer and resource frontier regions through regional urban growth, of course, complements this strategy. The development of regional urban growth centres are focused on the upgrading of the intermediate size cities in each region. In the northeast Khon Kaen, Udon Thani, Nakhon Ratchasima, and Ubon Ratchathani have been identified; in the northern region Chingmai and Phitsanulok; in the south Songkhla - Hat Yai and Phuket. The immediate industrial decentralization from the Bangkok Metropolitan area, however, would be mostly toward Chonburi in the Eastern Region which forms a development corridor in much the same way as Kuala Lumpur and Klang/Port Klang in Malaysia. Masterplans for these cities are being prepared as well as for the physical development of Bangkok.

Indonesia's approach can be clearly seen from Fig. 1. In each of the four major development regions a primary growth centre has been identified: Jakarta, of course, in region B, Medan in region A, Surabaya in region C, and Ujongpadang in region D. As in Thailand and the Philippines, the idea here is to decentralize manufacturing activities from Jakarta, especially to Medan and Ujongpadang. The next tier of growth centres is located in the intermediate size cities in the subregions, for example Padang in subregion II, Bandung in subregion IV, Malang in subregion V, and Menado in subregion IX. Most of these cities are based on resource exploitation projects. The co-ordinated planning of these centres are expected to be further expanded in the coming REPELITA.

While it is evident from the above that all four countries have seriously incorporated the growth pole approach into their overall regional development strategy, one needs to ask the question of whether the four countries can sustain the implementation of such a system of growth centres as they have planned. This question is quite apart from the equally important issue of the appropriateness of the strategy in the context of overall economic development in Southeast Asia. It is, however, an important problem which must be resolved in view of the many competing claims on the allocation of resources in each country.

One of the important constraints to be considered is the fiscal capacity of the national and regional authorities to undertake the programmes and projects to support the strategy. Another is whether the inducing instruments, such as industrial estates and other physical infrastructure programmes, the tax incentive system, the provision of amenities, utility pricing, etc., will be sufficiently powerful to overcome the dominant locational advantages of the existing centres of concentrated development, namely the capital regions. Also important in this connection is the availability of skilled manpower, not only to participate in the decentralized industries themselves but to provide the expertise and know-how for planning and implementing the strategy at the local level.

While the different countries will solve these problems according to their available resources and in terms of their own priorities, the role of government is going to be critical to the success of the growth pole approach and the overall development policy. In this regard the financial and administrative relationships will have to be appropriately geared toward greater decentralization if self-reliance in regional development (and hopefully this will lead to a reduction of disparities) is to be possible. The role of government is even more important with respect to influencing the private sector in the direction of decentralization of development. The promotion of growth centres is aimed, after all, at influencing the locational decisions of industrialists, as well as their other production decisions, and that leaving development entirely to market forces will in fact lead to aggravation of regional disparities. How much governments can influence and intervene in the market process is therefore one of the critical binding factors in growth centre development and the reduction of regional disparities. Even more serious in this is when foreign capital is involved, especially in the large-scale industrial and resource exploitation projects. The success of decentralization policies will depend on the convergence of interests of private capital and government policy. When government policy and market calculations coincide, such as in the case of resource exploitation which requires foreign technology, capital, and expertise, the likelihood of achieving decentralization objectives will be enhanced. Projects in Sumatra, Mindanao, South Thailand, and Sabah or Pahang fall into this category.

It is, however, in achieving the equity goals of reducing interregional and intraregional inequalities (in income, employment, poverty, and so on) that the growth centre strategy by itself will pose problems no matter how it is stated and incorporated into the South east Asian national plans. All the four countries have recognized the important problem of labour absorption in the non-agricultural sector to cope with the expected high population increase in the coming generation, the problem of an underdeveloped agriculture which at this moment is incapable of reducing the considerable under-employment of the rural labour force, and of their rapid immigration into the capital cities. If growth pole development is based entirely on natural resource exploitation rather than on human resources, using imported capital-intensive technology rather than labour-intensive, then it is not likely that growth centres will enable a decentralization of industries and population with improved income distribution as well as other development benefits derived from it. This is why the emphasis on small-scale or medium-scale industries, agro-based and oriented to the home market, and appropriate government measures to rectify the distorted incentive structure (subsidies, pricing, agricultural inputs, etc.), will be critical in complementing the growth pole approach.

In this broad sense, then, the growth pole approach in Southeast Asia can only be properly examined if located in the overall context of other regional development strategies adopted by the four countries as part of their national development effort. From this survey of the regional development policy in the Southeast Asian countries, where the growth pole approach is but one of many regional strategies, it is evident that central planners of the four countries have themselves accepted this fact.

4. CONCLUSION

In this paper, regional policy in Southeast Asia has been examined in terms of the adoption of the growth pole approach as a strategy to decentralize industries from capital regions and to develop the vast resource frontier in order to reduce regional disparities. It is obvious in this respect that the growth pole concept is one of the first to be adopted by Southeast Asian central planners, almost simultaneously with their increasing awareness of the regional problems in their countries. Given the constraints of resources in order to develop the peripheral regions, and the need to expand the national economic base, the attractiveness of the short-run spatially discriminatory strategy of growth centre development is understandable.

But, as we found in this paper, the list of problems of development faced by the four countries is long and requires the proper balance between national sectoral and regional needs. How the growth pole strategy will contribute to regional and national development in these countries, to balance urban and rural development, reduce unemployment, eliminate poverty, and to improve household income distribution, is the critical question. Of course, growth poles as a conditional strategy of accelerated industrialization may not be meant to do this. If so, then we need to know how the growth pole approach fits into the overall regional development strategy and what complementary programmes are required.

In any case, the growth pole approach will continue to be pursued in Southeast Asia. What impact it will have on the regional development of these countries is another matter. Judging from some of the findings in other countries which have implemented some form of this approach, the results are not too encouraging. However, in Southeast Asia it still may be too early to say one way or the other, and this depends on what criteria of success will be used to evaluate it later. Whatever it is, the choice of appropriate and effective complementary strategies is the crucial factor in achieving the goals of regional development in Southeast Asia.

5

THE PROBLEM OF REGIONAL DISPARITIES: AN ANALYSIS OF INDIAN POLICIES AND PROGRAMMES

O. P. MATHUR

1. NATURE OF THE PROBLEM

1.1 General Context

By the year 2000 India's population is expected to exceed 900 million. Of this total, approximately 180 million people will be living in regions of extreme low levels of economic development and another 225 million in areas only a shade better than the former group. At the current rates of regional income growth, disparities between poor *and* relatively better-off states will rise at least to 5.5:1 from the present level to 2.6:1. Further concentrations of industry are anticipated in Gujarat, Maharashtra, Tamil Nadu, and West Bengal; some estimates suggest that by that year these states will produce 70 - 75 per cent of the country's total industrial production, leaving 25 - 30 per cent to be manufactured in the rest of the country. These are guess estimates but sufficient to suggest what the scale of the regional problem will be and what additional crises will be faced in India in the year 2000 if some of these dimensions are not adequately recognized.

In the past few years, India, like most countries in the world, has become increasingly concerned with the problem of regional disparities.[1] Enough evidence appears to have been accumulated to show that the growth which took place in the country during the past two decades or so was confined to selected areas and had little or no impact on many regions which remained underdeveloped, stagnant, and marginal. With this has come the realization that the pattern of unequal regional growth exemplified by the existence within the country of large depressed areas is inconsistent with the concept of national development, and that such inequalities should be minimized for attaining the goals of a just and egalitarian society. This evolution in attitudes has neither been easy nor continuous, but the emergence of this view has had several important consequences within the country. It has, firstly, called upon the Indian planners and academic community

---

[1]Regional problems have been the principal theme of at least two recent conferences held under the aegis of IEA and of the research programme on regional development at the UNRISD and UNCRD. See, E.A.G. Robinson, *Backward areas in Advanced Countries,* proceedings of a conference held at Varenna, MacMillan, 1969; and Ranis Gustav, *The Gap Between Rich and Poor Nations,* proceedings of a conference held at Bled, Macmillan, 1972.

to examine the nature of regional development problems and policies more vigorously. For instance, the utility of using global approaches and aggregative indicators for identifying regional development problems has been seriously doubted. It is stated in this connection that in India and most developing economies which are characterized by sectoral lags and imbalanced development, it is hardly advisable to rely on indicators such as the *per capita* incomes, the activity rates, or unemployment. These are neither representative nor adequate, and what is perhaps needed for purposes of evolving regional development strategies is the knowledge about the *nature* and *structure* of regional - local economies rather than a mere assessment of their levels of development. This thinking has added new dimensions in the recent work and studies of the professional community in India.[2]

The second consequence emanates directly from the first. Following the proposition that the nature and structure of regional economies are important elements in evolving appropriate development strategies, it has become evident that the regional problems arising out of the diversity of resources and endowment should be distinguished and looked at separately from those whose locale lies in investment or economic development decisions. Thus, the erstwhile tendency to treat all kinds of poverty or backward areas as one single problem has been replaced by more rational and differentiated policies in this respect.

A third consequence of this awareness has been that reliance on isolated and unrelated investment decisions—a kind of cathedral in the desert policy for stimulating regional growth—has been on the decline. There is a clear emphasis on the fact that the regional problem is much wider in scope and requires a greater degree of change in economic structures, production technology, and inevitably a fuller understanding into the problems, potentialities, and resources of regional economies. All these mean much more scientific study and research.

A fourth consequence which is by far the most important in the Indian context is the realization that a regional development policy is not something which must invariably spring or be promoted from above. What seems to be emerging is that in addition to a *national view* of regional development, there is also a *regional view* of regional development and that attention should be given to procedures and mechanisms which would bring about greater rationality in decision making at this level. This development is of critical significance in a country of India's size and diversity. Besides dampening the debate on whether regional plans are the disaggregation of national plans, or the National Plan is an aggregation of regional plans, it has focused attention on reorganization of traditional procedures and the creation of new ones in order that the regional dimension of the economy may be more clearly exposed.[3]

1.2. The Indian Scenario

The regional problem in India is not the typical north - south problem like the one observed in most developed and many developing countries. Here, the north - south prob-

---

[2]This is reflected in the preliminary work done by the Multilevel Planning Section, Planning Commission for the Committee on Backward Areas, set up under the chairmanship of Professor S. Chakravarty, Member Planning Commission.

[3]The setting up of Planning Boards in states, i.e. apex bodies on the lines of the National Planning Commission, is certainly a beginning, a modest one though, in the direction of restructuring of planning procedures at the state levels.

lem is interspersed throughout the country in a very unsymmetrical fashion, extending the task of Indian planners enormously, particularly in the area of evolving appropriate and objective mechanisms for selecting areas and regions for special attention.[4] From a methodological angle, and from several other points of view, this phase of inquiry is truly complicated.

Secondly, the problem here cannot be explained in terms of poor or rich endowment of resources. There are regions which are rich because of their raw material endowment; there are regions which are rich despite their poor raw material resources; there are regions which are poor despite their rich raw material resources; and, finally, of course, there are regions which are poor because of their poor resources. Thus there is little consistent relationship between the availability of resources and the levels of regional development, and the former, though a welcome ingredient, neither ensures growth nor explains the differences in regional growth rates.

Thirdly, the regional problem in India is not unduly overshadowed by the existence of a few primate cities and vast underdeveloped regions around them. While there are, so to speak, a few large cities which have developed at the expense of their hinterland, the growth of cities in general has followed such a chequered course of history and conditions that it would be hopeless to enumerate cases and examples to group them into specified categories.[5]

And, lastly, it is not a problem of regional unemployment or low *per capita* regional incomes. Indeed, it would seem somewhat easier to tackle such uni-dimensional problems than those which are characterized by several kinds of poverty traps, a version similar to Friedmann's "syndrome of collective poverty".[6]

The Indian federation, where planning—an extremely loose form of mechanism without any force of legal enactment—is the concurrent responsibility of the Central and State governments, cannot be expected to be free of regional problems.[7] The roots of the problems lie in the interplay of several factors. For one thing the country has diverse resources and a complex geography. There are vast arid and desert areas, on the one hand, and hills and mountains, on the other. These require a different planning technology and strategy which, despite all the rich background of the Indian planners, is in a very underdeveloped state in the country.[8] Superimposed on this is a spatial system which India has inherited from the past. This system had been created to serve external interests

---

[4]The non-symmetrical distribution of poverty areas is clearly borne out in Mitra's study, see A. Mitra, *Levels of Regional Development in India,* Census of India, 1961, Part 1-A(1), Manager of Publications, Delhi, 1965.

[5]See *City Survey Reports* published under the auspices of the erstwhile Research Programmes Committee, Planning Commission, New Delhi. Also, K. V. Sundaram, Million cities of India—Delhi, a paper presented at the *First Asian Symposium on Regional Planning and Development,* held at the Institute of Development Studies, Mysore, July 1974.

[6]John Friedmann, Poor regions and poor nations; perspectives on the problem of Appalachia, *Southern Economic Journal,* 32, April 1966.

[7]For an elaborate description and analysis of planning process in India, see S. Chakravarty, The planning process in India: an appraisal and a framework, Planning Commission, New Delhi, mimeo., 1972. Also, Planning Commission, *The Planning Process,* Manager of Publications, New Delhi, 1975.

[8]Work on developing methodologies for planning of drought-prone areas, hill regions, etc., is still continuing in the Planning Commission. One of the latest in the series is the report of a task force appointed to suggest ways and measures for tackling drought-prone areas. See, Planning Commission, *Integrated Agricultural Development in Drought-prone Areas,* Report by the Task Force on Integrated Rural Development, June 1973.

rather than the cause of regional and national integration. In today's context when the objectives of development have been redefined, this pattern has become an absolute anachronism; at the same time, altering this spatial pattern for reducing imbalances is proving to be an immensely difficult task for the Indian planners. Further, certain post-1951 decisions, particularly in respect of investment locations, have further perpetuated regional disparities. The result is that today we have a pattern which is grossly uneven and unbalanced. It is this historical background which must be constantly kept in view while looking at the facts and statistics concerning this problem.

1.3. Regional Income Differentials

Estimates of states *per capita* net domestic product, the percentage share of individual states and its comparison with population shares are shown in Table 1. There are several observations which can be made from this table. The first one is that in 1969 - 70 as many as twelve states, comprising 54.9 per cent of the total population, had less than the national average *per capita* net domestic product. These states held 46 per cent of the country's total net domestic product.[9] The most striking feature

TABLE 1

State net domestic product at current prices

State	Net domestic product 1969 - 70		% share of individual states in total popu- lation, 1971	*Per capita* net domestic product	
	Million rupees	% share		1960 - 1	1969 - 70
Andhra Pradesh	23,390	7.6	7.9	314	554
Assam, including Meghalaya	8,453	2.7	2.9	349	554
Bihar	22,117	7.2	10.3	216	404
Gujarat	18,002	5.9	4.9	380	701
Haryana	8,819	2.9	1.8	350	921
Himachal Pradesh	2,028	0.7	0.6	—	610
Jammu and Kashmir	2,037	0.7	0.8	267	451
Karnataka	16,738	5.5	5.3	292	591
Kerala	12,491	4.0	3.9	278	607
Madhya Pradesh	19,107	6.2	.7.6	274	476
Maharashtra	34,953	11.4	9.2	419	720
Manipur	432	0.1	0.2	—	423
Nagaland	204	0.1	0.1	—	416
Orissa	10.903	3.6	4.0	226	514
Punjab	12,988	4.2	2.5	383	992
Rajasthan	11,544	3.8	4.7	271	456
Tamil Nadu	23,596	7.7	7.5	344	591
Tripura	734	0.2	0.3	—	493
Uttar Pradesh	42,619	13.9	16.1	244	495
West Bengal	29,370	9.6	8.1	386	685
All India	300,525	97.9	98.7	307	579

Note: This does not include union territories. Estimates pertain to the boundaries as existing in the reference years.

[9]Estimates of state income do not include the income of the defence personnel and officers abroad, and business outside of India.

of this domestic product distribution is that Punjab's *per capita* was 171 per cent of the national average while for Bihar it was 70 per cent. Secondly, the time-series data on net domestic product would show that the income differentials between states are not only wide but widening; differences in *per capita* net domestic product increased to 2.6:1 in 1969 - 70, from 1.9:1 in 1960 - 1. While there does not appear to be any close relationship between the rate of growth and the state's *per capita* net domestic product, on very close examination it would seem that the rate of growth is low in low-income states and high in high-income states. Clear examples are Orissa and Rajasthan in the low-income categories and Punjab and Haryana in the high-income groups. This evidence would seem to confirm Williamson's hypothesis that "in the initial stages of national development regional inequality is likely to increase all the more sharply due to a number of disequilibrating effects".[10] These trends have been of considerable concern to the Indian planners, and the question that they have continually faced in this respect is this: In what manner should the rate of growth in the *per capita* GNP of the low-income states should be stepped up without slowing down the rates of growth in the high-income states?

1.4. Imbalances in Urban and Industrial Sectors

Table 2 shows that as of 1971 only 19.9 per cent of the country's population lived in urban areas.[11] This percentage displayed sharp variations from one state to another. The lowest urbanized states in the country were Himachal Pradesh and Orissa with only 7 and 8.4 per cent of their population living in urban areas. In contrast were Maharashtra and Tamil Nadu with over 30 per cent of their populations living in cities and towns.

The distribution of urban population by size of urban centres is grossly uneven in the country. As may be seen in Table 3, 55.8 per cent of the total urban population was concentrated in cities of more than 100,000. As compared to this, the share of medium-sized cities (those between 20,000 - 100,000 in the total urban population) was only 27.64 per cent indicating a weak middle base to sustain the urban structure of the country.

Table 3 also shows that 100,000 + cities registered the highest growth rate in population between 1961 - 71. The growth rate declines with the size group of urban centre, indicating a positive correlation between these two variables. This tendency observed during the most intensive period of development has far-reaching implications for the spatial policy of the country to which we shall revert in subsequent parts of the Country Report.

Analysis of state data on the percentage distribution of urban population as given in Table 2 confirms the picture which is obtained at the national level. For instance, the percentage or urban population living in 100,000 + cities exceeds that in the 20,000 - 100,000 size category in all but three states, namely, Assam, Haryana, and Kerala. The urban economy of the smaller states stands on even weaker foundations. Manipur, Meghalaya, and Tripura, for instance, have no urban place of medium size, and their entire urban base consists of a large town and a few very small ones.

---

[10]See J. G. Williamson, Regional inequality and the process of national development: a description of the patterns, *Economic Development and Cultural Change,* **13**, (1965). The author has reservations about the inevitability of this phenomenon. Having been under the influence that development effort should be concentrated in the early stages, most nations perpetuate the process of inequality.

[11]Urban area is defined as (a) all places with a municipality, corporation, or a notified area committee; (b) fulfilling the following conditions: (i) a minimum of 5000 population, (ii) at least 75 per cent of male working population in non-agricultural occupations, (iii) a density of 400 persons/km^2.

TABLE 2

Urban - industrial and rural - agriculture statistics

State	Percentage of urban to total population	Percentage of urban population in different sizes of urban centres						% of workers in manufacturing population, 1971	'increase' in manufacturing working force, 1961-71	Total manufacturing working force	Total value added 1968	% of rural population living in villages of less than 2000 habitants, 1971	% of agricultural workers to total working population 1971	Per capita net sown area, 1970-71 hectares	Crop intensity 1970 - 1	% of gross irrigated area to (gross) area 1970-71
		100,000	50,000 - 100,000	20,000 - 50,000	10,000 - 20,000	5,000 - 10,000	Less than 5000									
1	2	3	4	5	6	7	8	9	10	11	12	13	14	15	16	17
Andhra Pradesh	19.3	48.4	13.4	20.9	13.4	3.8	0.2	4.2	58.8	7.1	3.7	43.1	37.9	0.93	13.7	31.6
Assam	8.8	15.5	24.4	20.8	24.8	12.5	2.0	2.8	14.3	1.1	1.0	83.7	9.9	0.83	24.6	20.6
Bihar	10.0	45.4	11.1	23.9	14.4	4.8	0.5	2.6	6.7	4.2	5.9	63.9	38.9	0.59	30.4	24.8
Gujarat	28.1	49.0	15.4	15.7	12.8	6.8	0.3	9.3	44.8	7.2	8.8	60.6	22.5	1.71	6.5	13.0
Haryana	17.7	17.7	39.8	26.1	12.5	7.8	1.0	6.7	63.0	1.7	2.2	52.2	16.2	2.06	39.0	45.0
Himachal Pradesh	7.0	—	22.9	8.8	27.2	19.6	21.5	1.6	44.8	0.2	0.1	95.6	4.2	0.57	67.5	17.1
Jammu and Kashmir	18.6	68.5		9.5	5.3	11.0	5.7	2.8	12.9	0.4	0.2	81.7	3.1	0.76	22.7	38.1
Karnataka	24.3	51.1	8.2	15.4	19.4	4.7	1.2	5.9	42.9	5.6	5.0	65.8	26.7	1.51	6.2	13.2
Kerala	16.2	42.3	13.4	31.8	10.1	2.2	0.3	11.5	34.5	6.6	5.0	0.2	30.7	0.72	35.0	25.5
Madhya Pradesh	16.3	45.1	10.3	19.8	14.4	10.1	0.4	3.0	38.1	4.3	3.7	87.9	26.6	1.51	12.0	7.4
Maharashtra	31.2	70.8	6.9	11.1	8.1	2.8	0.3	10.0	40.0	17.1	26.2	61.9	29.3	1.53	5.4	8.6
Manipur	13.2	70.9				22.2	6.9	1.7	425.5	neg.		69.5	3.7	0.68	5.0	39.9
Meghalaya	14.5	83.4			10.5	6.1		1.3	35.1	neg.		97.6	9.9	0.46	19.6	19.0
Nagaland	10.0	—		41.9	58.1			0.8	253.3	neg.		88.6	1.4	0.48	2.0	11.8
Orissa	8.4	38.3	3.9	29.2	15.5	12.7	0.5	2.3	82.5	1.5	1.6	88.1	28.3	1.15	37.0	19.2
Punjab	23.7	40.6	15.7	21.7	13.8	7.0	1.2	8.1	36.6	3.0	2.6	69.5	20.1	1.65	40.9	74.7
Rajasthan	17.6	41.9	10.8	20.5	19.8	6.8	0.4	3.2	49.7	2.4	1.7	73.7	9.3	2.54	10.2	14.7
Tamil Nadu	30.3	57.7	14.2	15.1	9.9	2.8	0.3	8.8	53.5	12.2	9.4	34.4	30.5	0.68	19.7	46.2
Tripura	10.4	61.8			32.5	5.8	0.2	2.1	-15.3	neg.		86.2	20.2	0.75	43.8	7.0
Uttar Pradesh	14.0	57.1	10.8	16.7	10.4	4.7	0.2	3.6	23.6	9.2	6.7	74.6	20.0	0.82	34.1	34.2
West Bengal	24.7	71.0	11.9	9.6	5.0	2.4	0.1	11.4	6.6	13.1	15.7	60.7	26.5	0.77	28.0	21.7
All India	19.9	55.8	11.3	16.3	11.3	4.7	0.5	5.9	34.4	96.9	99.5	63.6	26.3	1.12	18.6	23.0

TABLE 3

Size of urban centre	% of total urban population	% growth rate, 1961 - 71
100,000 +	55.8	59.5
50,000 - 100,000	11.3	31.5
20,000 - 50,000	16.3	21.6
10,000 - 20,000	11.3	20.1
5,000 - 10,000	4.7	-9.8
Less than 5000	0.5	-25.2
Total	100.0	38.2

The distribution of urban population *within* the state boundaries is also very uneven. In order to find out whether this unevenness is more pronounced in low-urbanized states or high-urbanized states, we have worked out the coefficient of variations by using the urban population of the districts as the principal base figures. These are given in Table 4.

TABLE 4

High-urbanized states	Coefficient of variation	Low-urbanized states	Coefficient of variation
Gujarat	69.8874	Andhra Pradesh	67.0030
Karnataka	44.2990	Assam	33.5313
Maharashtra	78.1960	Bihar	86.8810
Punjab	28.0510	Haryana	35.7027
Tamil Nadu	68.1432	Jammu and Kashmir	99.9158
West Bengal	109.7476	Kerala	47.0563
		Madhya Pradesh	81.6241
		Nagaland	79.8965
		Orissa	62.9920
		Rajasthan	68.3132
		Uttar Pradesh	85.7582
		Himachal Pradesh	115.6879
		Manipur	132.7852
		Tripura	84.7206
		Meghalaya	70.2072

These figures indicate that disparities in urban growth within the states are noticeably high. However, these disparities are no greater in low-income states in comparison with high-income states. As may be seen from Table 4, among the high income states only the coefficient of variation for West Bengal is higher than the average of the country as a whole, which is 90.1744. Among the low-income states, the coefficient of variation is higher for three states, namely Jammu and Kashmir, Himachal Pradesh, and Manipur.

Disparities in the industrial sector are shown in Table 2. A number of observations are possible to be made from this table. Firstly, the percentage of workers in manufacturing (excluding household industry) is extremely low for India; it was only 5.9 per cent in the year 1971. Further, there are only seven states whose manufacturing base is larger than the average for the country, these being Gujarat (9.3), Haryana (6.7), Kerala (11.5),

Maharashtra (10.0), Punjab (8.1), Tamil Nadu (8.8), and West Bengal (3.6). The point
to be noted in respect of these states is that all of them, excepting West Bengal, registered
a higher than average rate of growth in manufacturing working force during the period
1961 - 71. There is an indication in this evidence that the states which have attained some
level of manufacturing threshold show a greater pull to attract more and more industries.
The redeeming feature in these sets of figures, however, is that Andhra Pradesh, Madhya
Pradesh, Orissa, Rajasthan, and a few smaller states registered a growth rate in manufacturing working force which was higher than the national average. These are the states
whose percentage of manufacturing working force is less than the national average of
5.9 per cent.

The second observation from Table 2 relates to the process of industrial concentration.
It would be seen from the table that 49.4 per cent of the total manufacturing working
force were concentrated in the four relatively industrialized States of Gujarat, Maharashtra,
Tamil Nadu, and West Bengal. Furthermore, their share in total value added was as high
as 60.1 per cent, suggesting not only that these four states had the "industrial monopoly"
in the country but also that the industrial productivity was higher than that of the industrial sector elsewhere in the country. In terms of population, the share of these states was
only 29.7 per cent. These figures have been arranged in a consolidated form (Table 5)
just to indicate how sharp these variations are in this respect in the country.

TABLE 5

	Share in		
States	Population	Manufacturing working force	Value added
Industrialized states	29.7	49.6	60.1
Rest of the country	70.3	50.4	39.9

Even more disturbing is the fact that within these four industrialized states who command a major interest in the industrial development of the country there are sharp disparities in the distribution of manufacturing employment. We have computed the coefficient
of variation using the district data on manufacturing employment to show these disparities.
For these four states, the coefficients of variation are as follows:

Gujarat	82.0631
Maharashtra	124.6882
Tamil Nadu	60.1512
West Bengal	111.5024

These coefficients show that there is greater polarization in Maharashtra and West
Bengal in respect of industrial sector. On the other hand, the spatial distribution of industry is far more even in Tamil Nadu. Coefficients of variation are also very high in Bihar
(97.7339), Madhya Pradesh (126.1233), and Orissa (111.4140)—the three less industrialized
States where new industrial towns were established with a view to generating industrial
dispersal.

1.5. Disparities in Agriculture and Rural Sector

Relevant facts in respect of agriculture and rural sector were given in Table 2. It must, however, be stated in the beginning that these facts are hardly inadequate to bring out the real nature of the regional - spatial problems of this sector. There are a number of qualitative and exogeneous factors (nature, endowment, traditions, and culture) which impinge on the development of this sector, thereby obscuring the real nature of regional problems.

Table 2 shows three kinds of problems concerning this sector. The first problem of this sector is the non-viability of its settlement pattern. As can be seen, 37.9 per cent of the total rural population in the country live in villages whose population is less than 1000, and another 25.8 per cent live in villages of 1000 - 2000. In many states, the percentage of rural population living in villages of less than 2000 size is much higher: Assam (83.7), Madhya Pradesh (87.9), Orissa (88.1), Rajasthan (73.7), and Uttar Pradesh (74.6). This kind of settlement pattern can hardly support any system of communal services and facilities, and poses some hard choice issues for the planners.

The second problem of this sector is that there are some states which have a disproportionately high percentage of agricultural workers—a marginal and non-viable section of the rural community. Regional distribution of this class—given in Table 2—shows that this problem is particularly severe in Andhra Pradesh, Bihar, Kerala, Maharashtra, Orissa, and Tamil Nadu.

The third problem of the agricultural sector is shown by the combined figures of *per capita* net sown area, crop intensity, and use of irrigation waters. *Per capita* net sown area varies sharply from one state to another: in Bihar, for instance, *per capita* net sown area is 0.59 hectares compared to 2.54 hectares in Rajasthan. Crop intensity is the highest for Punjab[12] and lowest in Maharashtra. Use of irrigated waters also varies sharply from one state to another. These differences raise the basic issue whether it is possible to bring about some kind of an equity in the sphere of agricultural sector.

1.6. Inter-sectoral Correlations and Disparities

Appendix II presents the results of multiple correlations worked out between several indicators of development. These show whether correlations between *per capita* net domestic product and other development indicators are significant or not. The results of this exercise are interesting. *Per capita* net domestic product is significantly correlated with the following indicators:

(1) Percentage of urban to total population (+ 0.5036).
(2) Percentage of scheduled caste population to total population (+ 0.4602).
(3) Percentage of agricultural workers to total working force (-0.5608).
(4) Percentage of gross irrigated area to gross cropped area (+ 0.4980).
(5) Net sown area per agricultural worker (+ 0.4562).
(6) *Per capita* bank deposits (+ 0.6985).
(7) *Per capita* bank advances (+ 0.4758).
(8) Number of workers in registered factories per 100,000 of population (+ 0.6331).

While these relationships are expected, what is conspicuous is the absence of significant

---

[12]While the crop intensity is highest in Himachal Pradesh, we have preferred not to mention this in the text because this state has a totally different physico-geographic character.

correlations between *per capita* net domestic product and literacy, road, networks, and industrial value added. Similarly, this matrix does not reveal any positive correlation between the two most expected indicators of development, i.e. urbanization and industrial value added. Again, some significant correlations in this matrix would seem to be aberrations rather than a reflection of any consistent behavior. For instance, it is shown in the matrix that there is a medium - high positive correlation between crop intensity (Table 2), Col. 9) and per industrial worker value added (col. 15)—one of the most unexpected correlations.

The main points emerging from this discussion are as follows:

(1) The nature of the regional problem in India is different from the regional problem obtaining in most developed and many developing countries. It is neither a typical north - south problem nor can it be explained exclusively in terms of the availability of natural resources. The phenomenon of primate cities exists in this country in a very limited form. Further, it is not a uni-dimensional problem, and perhaps can be understood better with the help of several factors rather than by *per capita* incomes or unemployment rates.

(2) As generalizations, it can be said that the roots of the regional problem in India lie in (i) diverse resources and complex geography, (ii) highly imbalanced spatial pattern inherited from its colonial past, and (iii) post-1957 locational policies which perpetuated regional disparities.

(3) Regional disparities in *per capita* net domestic product are not only wide but widening. Between 1960 - 1 and 1969 - 70 disparities in *per capita* net domestic product increased to 2.6:1 from 1.9:1. This would seem to confirm the hypothesis that disparities have a tendency to grow in the initial stages of economic development.

(4) There is enough evidence that *per capita* net domestic product (NDP) is not a representative indicator to be used for determining the levels of development. For instance, it would normally be surmised that *per capita* NDP is higher in states that have high literacy, high value added per industrial worker, and better transport network; this is, however, not borne out by the facts presented in this section. Similarly, *per capita* NDP does not bear any relationship, negative or positive, with the percentage of landless, agricultural labour class, or crop intensity.

(5) The urban structure of the country is highly imbalanced. It is shown by the fact that only 27.6 per cent of the total urban population live in medium-sized cities (20,000 - 100,000) in comparison with 55.8 per cent in cities of 100,000+ size. The 100,000+ group has also registered a growth rate of population which is significantly higher than any other size group.

(6) The distribution of urban population *within* the state boundaries is also very uneven.

(7) There is a significantly large concentration of industry in Gujarat, Maharashtra, Tamil Nadu, and West Bengal. These states have command over 60 per cent of the total industrial value added and nearly 50 per cent of the total manufacturing working force. The industrial base of the country is, therefore, highly imbalanced.

(8) The agricultural sector is beset with problems of a highly imbalanced settlement pattern and a large landless, agricultural working class. Over 60 per cent of the total rural population live in villages of less than 2000 population. In many states this percentage is as high as 88.1 per cent. Landless labour constitutes 26.3 per cent of the total working population. No significant correlation exists between crop intensity, use of irrigated waters, and net sown area per agricultural worker.

2. PLANNING FRAMEWORK, POLICIES, AND PROGRAMMES

A conscious regional development policy has been in existence in India for barely four Five-year Plan periods. By almost any standards this period is too short to have either solved the problem of regional disparities or even to have made any noticeable impact on the same. What is important, however, is to see whether the regional approach, which has been developed in the country during this period, reflects the necessary awareness and perception of the problem and takes into account its basic nature and dimension— the kinds of which we discussed in section 1 of this paper.[13]

2.1. Planning Framework

While the purpose here is to explain that part of the framework that deals with regional perspectives, at least one opening statement in respect of the overall planning model would seem pertinent. This is that the Indian planning exercises are essentially aggregative and sectoral in character. These rely on a macro-economic model which provides information on the macro-economic projections for gross domestic product which is consistent with a desired average compound rate over the plan period as a whole. Regional considerations and perspectives do not enter into the macro-economic growth models; neither are the regional implications of the planning decisions worked out in the sense of breaking up sectoral targets on a state basis.

The macro-economic character of Indian planning has led many to believe that the Indian five-year plans do not have any regional dimension, and that the national policy for regional development is at best, a charter of intentions. Such a view lacks a proper perspective of the planning process in India which, even through macro, permits entry of regional - spatial dimension through several forms of direct and indirect intervention.

The Indian planning framework concerning regional development has been built around the principles of factor mobility, social equity and decentralized decision making. The principle of factor mobility is that in an imperfect economic system disequilibrium between regions can be corrected only by a deliberate policy of mobility of labour, or of capital, or both. Leaving the economy to the forces of market may well lead to the clustering of activities in regions which yield above-average returns, the result of which may be further accentuation of regional imbalances in the country.[14] The framework, therefore, is such that it can manipulate capital and labour markets to achieve the regional objectives.

The second element of the planning framework concerning regional development is based on the principle of social equity. The underlying tenet here is that labour and capital become mobile (in favour of depressed areas) when there is a certain degree of spatial

---

[13]The exercises follow an input - output model of a Leontief type with provisions made for endogeneous estimates of import requirements. A special consumption model has been developed for the Fifth Plan, 1974 - 9, through which the redistribution of consumption against different sections of the population is directly linked with the model. See, Government of India, Planning Commission, *Draft Fifth Five Year Plan, 1974-79,* Vol. 1, New Delhi, 1973; also *id., A Technical Note.*

[14]Extremists in the country argue that in a long-range perspective the competitive forces of the market do create an optimum distribution of economic activity over space, and if certain areas continue to remain depressed it would clearly signal that the country has, in both absolute and relative terms, a declining need for those parts of country's space. They see that this phenomenon would strengthen rather than weaken the country's economy. See, Om Prakash Mathur, The regional problem in India: some reflections on a viable strategy, in *Anvesak, Journal of the Sardar Patel Institute of Economic and Social Research,* Ahmedabad, June-December 1973.

equity in the provision of social services and facilities. This form of social equity in space—whose justification rests as much on economic considerations as on social grounds —constitutes yet another element in the Indian planning framework through which regional disparities are sought to be redressed.[15]

The third element of the planning framework draws its essential features from the principle of decentralized decision making under which the centre, states, districts, and blocks share the planning responsibilities. There is, thus, a built-in provision in the Indian planning framework for regionalized decision making.[16]

It is within this framework that policies concerning regional development have been evolved in India.

2.2 Policy for Regional Development

Prior to the beginning of the Third Five-year Plan regional development policy in India existed mainly as a shadow of industrial policy and, to some extent, as a fallout of urban growth. There is little evidence that till this time the objectives of regional policy were thought of in any comprehensive manner.

2.2.1. *Third Plan, 1961 - 6.* From the Third Plan onwards it is possible to see the main points of a strategy emerging and the policy measures adapted accordingly. The Third Plan strategy, 1961 - 6, followed three lines of action. Firstly, it was recognized that the problem of uneven development was so varied in this country that a global solution could hardly be expected to be effective. This is evident from the Third Five-year Plan which suggested that: "in each region the nature of the problem and the impediments to rapid development in particular fields should be carefully studied and appropriate measures be devised for accelerated development. The essential object should be to secure the fullest possible utilization of the resources of each region so that it can contribute its best to the national pool and take its due share from the benefits accruing from national development."[17] This marks the beginning of the regional approach to regional development in the country.

Secondly, regional policy came increasingly to be based on the development of selected backward regions through the creation of *industrial growth poles.* The Third Plan suggested that every major project should be regarded as a nucleus for integrated development of the region as a whole, and indicated that such possibilities of development existed in all regions where new resources were proposed to be developed.[18] Establishment of *new towns* was also proposed as a solution to the regulation of the growth of metropolitan cities such as Calcutta, Bombay, Delhi, and others.

The third line of action was aimed at evolving appropriate measures which would help in the integration of regions with the national economy. This had wider implications,

[15]Equity in the provision of items of social consumption (as opposed to private consumption) is one of the main planks of the Fifth-plan Strategy in India. See Government of India, Planning Commission, *Draft Fifth Five Year Plan, 1974 - 9,* chapters 2 and 8.

[16]A regionalized decision-making system has the advantage of being economical. This point has been forcefully brought out by S. Chakravarty in his paper, A note on the structure of multilevel planning for India, planning Commission, New Delhi, 1972.

[17]*Ibid.,* chapter IX, p. 143.

[18]*Ibid.,* pp. 149 - 50.

but the most important was that it dispelled the common apprehension that national and regional development objectives were on different axis and a conflict between the two was inevitable.

A strategy of regional development thus began to be emerged along these lines during the Third-plan period. However, no specific programmes to support these lines of action were undertaken during this period.

2.2.2. *Fourth Plan, 1969 - 74.* The Fourth Plan, 1969 - 74, saw the first signs of integration of regional policy into the national planning framework and the adoption of a comprehensive view of various regional problems.[19] The statement of regional policy in the Plan was influenced by a great amount of preparatory work which had been done in related fields. The first was the publication of the comparable estimates of state net domestic product which showed that income disparities between states were growing. The second piece of evidence on regional disparities came through the work of the two committees which showed that nine out of seventeen states were industrially backward and needed particular attention.[20] Experience gained during the Third Plan also served as a valuable source of information for devising the regional policy for the Fourth-plan period. Of critical significance was the experience that there should be greater local initiative in the selection of projects and programmes for achieving better implementation, and that the tendency to impose priorities from above should be replaced by regional and local decision making.

The effect of these influences can be seen in the Fourth-plan approach to the problems of regional disparities. This approach consisted of four principal elements which were as follows:

(i) change the criteria of allocation of central assistance to states in a way that it would take into account the relative backwardness of the states;

(ii) change the procedures and policies of the national financial and other institutions in such a way that investments would be attracted to industrially backward regions and areas;

(iii) identify areas for special attention particularly those which have either unfavourable physico-geographic conditions or are inhabited by tribal population and other marginal groups;

(iv) continue the industrial location policies which were embodied in the Industrial Policy Resolution, 1956.[21]

A fifth element of the Fourth-plan policy was to encourage the state to take up the preparation of district plans and integrated plans for local areas.

The Fourth Five-year Plan was aimed at the reduction of interregional (interstate) income differentials, on the one hand, and the development of different categories of special-problem areas and backward areas on the other hand. We shall explain in the next subsection the nature of programmes taken up in these areas.

---

[19]Government of India, Planning Commission, *Fourth Five Year Plan, 1969 - 74,* Manager of Publications, Delhi, 1970.

[20]Government of India, Planning Commission, *Identification of Backward Areas,* Report by the Working Group, 1969; and Government of India, Ministry of Industrial Development, *Fiscal and Financial Incentives for Starting Industries in Backward Areas,* April 1969.

[21]See Appendix B on Extracts from the Industrial Policy Resolution, 1956, paragraph 10 in particular.

2.2.3. *Fifth Plan, 1974 - 9.* The policy for the Fifth Plan, 1974 - 9, with regard to the development of backward areas has been formulated on the basis of the following considerations:

(i) that the problem of backwardness is a long-term problem which can be tackled only over a long period of time;

(ii) that allocation of adequate financial resources is only one of the many steps necessary for the accelerated development of these areas: other essential measures being the evolution of locally oriented integrated strategies and the development of suitable programmes with appropriate norms, procedures, and technologies;

(iii) the states would have to bear the main responsibility for the development of their backward areas; the central government would, however, actively participate in this task by (a) continuing and further extending the liberal patterns of central assistance, and (b) providing special incentives for the flow of private investments to identified backward areas;

(iv) providing technical support in respect of planning as well as programme development.

The most significant development in the Fifth Five-year Plan in respect of reduction of regional disparities was the launching of the National Programme of Minimum Needs under which action has been proposed to take care of marked deficiencies of social consumption in backward areas by extending facilities of elementary education, rural health and water supply, nutrition, rural roads, and rural electrification. This programme will enable the disadvantaged areas to achieve parity in the items of social consumption.

This is the regional policy network in India. Beginning with a very *ad hoc* concern for disparities in the context of the growth of cities, today the policy network encompasses a much wider sphere ranging from attention to specific problem areas, to the reduction of interregional disparities. In this process of evolution, much greater significance has emerged for local regional initiative for purposes of optimization in resource utilization.

We shall now review the specific programmes and schemes which have been taken up to reduce regional disparities and develop backward areas.

2.3. Programmes for Regional Development

We have seen in section 1 that the regional policy network in India is extraordinarily varied. Representing the conditions of a large laboratory a wide variety of programmes are on trial here, some moving toward the goal, others away from it. This section explains these programmes and instruments; their impact on the problem of regional disparities is discussed in Section 3. For purposes of some order, these have been discussed under two headings: (1) integrated area approach and local planning, and (2) industrial location and regional development.

Allocation of central assistance to states for development purposes is an important instrument for reducing regional disparities. Criteria evolved for the allocation of assistance comprised the following elements: (i) population, 60 per cent, (ii) *per capita* income for states below the national average, 10 per cent, (iii) tax effort in relation to *per capita* income, 10 per cent, (iv) special problems of the state such as floods, unemployment, metropolitan development, 10 per cent, and (v) outlays required for major power and irrigation projects costing 200 million rupees, 10 per cent.

2.3.1. *Integrated Area Approach and Local Planning.* One of the important measures for reducing regional disparities in India, currently on experiment, relates to the preparation of integrated plans for selected areas and to the formulation of district plans. The case for such locally oriented plans is argued on two main grounds. Firstly, the natural environment within each country is interregionally differentiated, and these differences which are manifest in climate, topography, vegetation, and mineral resources have important implications for economic and social planning. The underlying premise in this argument is that even though the natural environment can be radically altered, the social and individual costs involved are so high that these may not permit the adoption of a deterministic doctrine of natural environment. Secondly, there is non-uniformity in the stages of economic and social development, and, therefore, an identical treatment of districts in matters of planning and development will result in distortions in the determination of priorities and production relationships.[22]

Based on these arguments, the preparation of integrated plans for hill areas, drought-prone areas, tribal areas, and areas with concentration of marginal and small farmers has begun. In all these plans, the focus of attention is on evolving a pattern and strategy of development which will take into account the local resources and problems of the area. Methodologies have been prepared to serve as guidelines for the states who have the basic responsibility for the preparation of these plans.[23] Many states have taken up the preparation of district plans on systematic lines.

A significant development in the Fifth Plan has been to launch a National Programme of Minimum Needs. This is a norm-oriented and location-specific programme and, therefore, calls for detailed local planning. The objective of this programme is to provide a minimum of social services and services to all areas, subject to their satisfying the locational norms.

2.3.2. *Industrial Location and Regional Development.* Location of industries is by far the most important instrument currently being used in India for achieving balanced regional development. Four kinds of programmes and schemes have been taken up in the country to encourage the location of industry in backward areas. These are:

(1) Concessional finance and investment subsidy schemes to attract industry in identified backward areas;
(2) creation of industrial infrastructure, particularly in industrial estates;
(3) establishment of public sector industrial undertakings in backward regions (parallel to industrial growth poles);
(4) preference to backward areas in the licensing of industries, subject to techno-economic viability considerations.

2.3.3. *Concessional Finance Scheme.* Under the scheme of concessional finance, 230 backward districts and areas identified on the basis of criteria given by the centre are eligible for concessional finance from the national financial institutions, namely the Industrial Development Bank of India (IDBI), Industrial Finance Corporation of India (IFCI),

---

[22]For a discussion on the analytical problems being faced in the preparation of district plans, see Om Prakash Mathur, Planning for districts: some problems in developing a conceptual framework, *PRAJNAN, Journal of the NIBM,* Bombay, 1973.

[23]See, Ministry of Home Affairs, Government of India, *Tribal Development in the Fifth Plan,* Vol. 1, 1975, for the guidelines prepared by the Planning Commission on the preparation of subplans for tribal regions; also, Planning Commission, *Guidelines for the Preparation of District Plans,* 1969.

and Industrial Credit and Investment Corporation of India (ICICI). Concessions extended by these institutions relate to (i) lower rate of interest, (ii) longer amortization period, (iii) longer initial moratorium in the repayment of loans, (iv) participation in the share of capital to a greater extent, and (v) reduction in the underwriting commissions.[24]

2.3.4. *Investment Subsidy Scheme.* This scheme has been extended to ninety-seven industrially backward districts and areas in the country. Under this scheme the central government has undertaken to provide an outright grant or subsidy amounting to 15 per cent of the total fixed capital investment in the case of new industrial units, or additional fixed capital investment in the case of existing units undergoing substantial expansion. The maximum amount of the subsidy is fixed at 1.5 million rupees. The total subsidy distributed up to the end of 1974 was 45.60 million rupees.

2.3.5. *Creation of Industrial Infrastructure Particularly Industrial Estates.* Industrial estates are an important tool for achieving regional development. These have been used in the country to (i) promote decentralization by preventing excessive concentration of industrial enterprizes in large metropolitan areas; (ii) encourage industries in depressed and backward regions, and (iii) develop and strengthen the base of small towns and rural areas. Over 440 industrial estates have been functioning in the country in 1973 of which 98 were "rural industrial estates", 138 "semi-urban", and 208 "urban estates". Estimates are that approximately 500 million rupees had been spent in their construction facilities.[25]

2.3.6. *Establishment of Public Sector Industrial Undertakings in Backward Regions.* Establishment of public sector industrial undertakings is one of the important ways in which the objective of balanced regional development is sought in the country. A clear enunciation of this policy came into being during the Third Five-year Plan which observed "the broad objective must be to secure balanced development between rural and urban areas". While this is by no means easy to realize, the main ingredients of development policy are:

(i) as far as possible, new industries should be established away from large and congested cities;
(ii) in the planning of large industries, the concept of region should be adopted: in each case, planning should extend beyond the immediate environs to a larger area for whose development the new industry would serve as a major focal point.

In pursuance of this broad policy, preference has been given to backward areas in the location of public sector industrial enterprizes. As of March 1974, over 60 per cent of the

---

[24]Criteria proposed by the central government for the identification of industrially backward areas are:

Per capita foodgrains - commercial crops production;
rates of population to agricultural workers;
Per capita gross industrial output;
Number of factory employees per 100,000 population or, alternatively, number of persons engaged in secondary and tertiary activities per 100,000 population;
Per capita consumption of electricity;
length of surfaced roads or rail mileage in relation to population.

Excepting four states, others have made variations in this set of criteria for identifying their industrially backward areas.

[25]See Ministry of Industrial Development, Government of India, *Industrial Estates in India,* half yearly progress report for the period ending September 1973, 1974.

total central investments in such undertakings had been made in the six backward states of Bihar, Kerala, Madhya Pradesh, Orissa, Rajasthan, and Uttar Pradesh.

Table 6 shows the distribution on a state basis. It shows that a major share (51.6 per cent) of central investments has been channeled to three most backward states of the country, namely Bihar, Madhya Pradesh, and Orissa. These investments have been made in building up capital intensive complexes of iron and steel, aluminium, heavy engineering, and fertilizers.

TABLE 6
Share of individual states in central investments in industrial
and mining projects (%)

States	March 1963	March 1973	March 1974
Andhra Pradesh	0.8	3.5	3.8
Assam	1.5	3.2	3.0
Bihar	15.9	26.9	27.8
Gujarat	Neg	4.7	4.7
Haryana	—	0.2	0.2
Himachal Pradesh	Neg	Neg	Neg
Jammu and Kashmir	—	0.1	0.1
Kerala	0.2	3.2	3.3
Madhya Pradesh	23.7	14.0	13.8
Maharashtra	2.0	3.9	3.9
Mysore (Karnataka)	3.6	2.8	3.0
Orissa	21.4	11.0	10.0
Punjab	2.8	0.8	0.8
Rajasthan	0.2	1.8	2.2
Tamil Nadu	8.3	7.5	6.9
Uttar Pradesh	0.2	3.9	4.1
West Bengal	19.4	12.5	12.3
All India (actuals) (million rupees)	1118.8	4701.1	5285.0

Source: Adapted from the Report on Public Sector Undertakings, 1974, Bureau of Public Enterprises, New Delhi.

2.3.7. *Preference to Backward Areas in the Licensing of Industries.* Licensing of industries is yet another instrument for directing new investments towards backward areas and regions. The claims of such areas are kept in view while considering the applications for licenses and, other things being equal, location in backward areas is preferred. The extent of utilization of the licensing procedures for achieving balanced development is limited partly by technical considerations (non-viability of projects in certain locations), and partly by its negative nature. Thus, while the government can refuse to give a licence for a particular industry on grounds of location, it has no powers to compel any industrial entrepreneur to set up an industry in any particular place.

Data available on the number of licences on a state basis are out-dated. Between 1952 - 67 a total of 11,268 licences had been issued of which about 60 per cent were issued to the four most industrialized states of the country.

2.3.8. *Pricing Policy for Balanced Development.* One of the other instruments for promoting regional development in India concerns the pricing of critical industrial raw materials such as steel and cement. Through a system of freight equalization, indigeneous

steel and cement are delivered at the same price either at the railheads (steel), or in all locations (cement) throughout the country. The system of freight equalization has been
designed to benefit the more distant consumers. It seeks to provide an incentive to areas
distantly located from the centres of production in the matter of development of industries
based on steel.

It is through a mix of these direct and indirect measures that balanced regional development is sought to be achieved in this country.

This section has described the policy-planning framework and the programmes which
have been taken up in the country for accomplishing balanced regional development. The
salient features of these are recapitulated below.

(1) Even though Indian planning is essentially macro and aggregative, its framework
is such that it permits entry of regional - spatial aspects through a variety of direct and
indirect policies and programmes. Justification for regional aspects in the Indian planning
framework is drawn from the principles of equity, decentralized decision making, and
the mobility of factors of production, in particular capital and labour.

(2) With successive Five-year Plans, there is a larger measure of policy commitment
to balanced regional development. Prior to the Third Plan, attention to the problem of
regional disparities was *ad hoc* and an adjunct of Industrial Policy Resolution. It is possible to see a wider policy towards regional development emerging from the Third Plan—
1961 onwards.

(3) During the Fourth Five-year Plan the problems of regional disparities came to be
looked upon from at least three points of view. It was seen, firstly, as a problem of reduction of interregional differences in incomes; secondly, of development of resource -
frontier regions; and local planning. The policy framework centred round these problems.

(4) The Fifth Plan, 1974 - 9, continues this policy framework. An additional input
during this period relates to the provision of social services and facilities on a norm-
oriented and location - specific basis.

(5) Within this policy framework, a number of programmes and instruments have been
taken up to reduce regional disparities in the country. These are related to the (i) criteria
for interregional allocation of central assistance, (ii) integrated area approach and local
planning, and (iii) industrial location. As a part of industrial location policies, incentives
and subsidies are being provided to the industrially backward areas; public sector industrial undertakings have been set up as industrial growth poles in backward resource
regions; industrial infrastructure, and, in particular, industrial estates have been set up
to promote decentralization and regional development; and licensing procedures have
been modified so as to favour backward regions.

(6) Emphasis has been placed on the preparation of integrated plans for areas which
are different on physico-geographic or ethnic grounds.

The next part is devoted to the impact of these programmes on these problems and to
future directions.

3. EXPECTATIONS, IMPACT, AND FUTURE DIRECTIONS

What are our expectations from the various policies and programmes taken up in the
country for reducing regional disparities is an extremely difficult question to answer with
any degree of precision. In order, however, to keep the analysis of the impact of the

policies programmes as objective as possible, some statements in regard to what we *do not* expect from these policies would be relevant. Firstly, we are not expecting a *zero-disparity* situation or model to emerge from these policies and programmes. That some disparities will persist is quite an acceptable proposition in the Indian situation though there is no clarity about the spheres where such disparities will be acceptable. Secondly, we are not expecting that the structure and pattern of development will be identical in all regions. Structural differences are inherent in the Indian economy which will continue to play an important part in determining the region's development profiles. Thirdly, the development and planning norms expressed in terms of size and distance (school for 1000 population, or within a radius of 1.5 km) will not be the same throughout the country. These will differ according to settlement patterns, topography, etc.

At the level of programmes and operational instruments, while it is comparatively easier to fix the expectations, other kinds of difficulties arise in assessing their effectiveness. For one thing, the time frame involved in regional policy is necessarily long, and it is too early to expect any substantial reversal of trends of widening regional disparities. Difficulties also arise on account of the changes and shifts that have taken place in the content of regional policies within a short period. A further complication, of course, is to make any definite suggestion that improvement in a region's situation took place as a result of a particular regional planning programme.

Within these constraints, let us look into the results of some of the programmes and instruments which were discussed in section 2. One of the important innovations made during the Fourth Plan to bridge the gap between relatively advanced and backward states was related to the principles of interregional allocation of central assistance. The principles were designed to strike a balance between equity and efficiency considerations. The states to benefit from equity considerations were Bihar, Kerala, Madhya, Pradesh, Orissa, Rajasthan, and Uttar Pradesh; it was expected that the *per capita* central assistance to these states, which had remained below the national average, will be stepped up under the revised formula.

Results of the allocations of central assistance to states during the Fourth Plan and the preceding plan periods are shown in Table 7.[26]

It will be seen from the table that among the low-income states the *per capita* central assistance continued to be below the national average of 63 rupees for Bihar and Uttar Pradesh during the Fourth Plan. The revisions made in the allocation criteria did not help these two states in raising their *per capita* central assistance.

The second important measure taken to influence the development of backward regions was related to the industrial location policies and variants thereof. There were four specific programmes and schemes in this regard, namely (i) schemes of concessional finance and investment subsidy, (ii) creation of industrial infrastructure through the establishment of industrial estates, (iii) location of public sector industrial undertakings, and (iv) licensing procedures. All these programmes were related to the theory of transfer of capital to backward areas either through direct public investments or indirect measures. Central to this theory was the fact that private capital movements were extremely sensitive to market phenomena which operated strictly on the principle of seeking highest profits. As long as

---

[26]Adapted from Anand Sarup, Preparation of state plans: an appraisal of the 4th plan experience and issues for the Fifth Plan, a paper presented in the *Seminar on Growth and Social Justice,* National Academy of Administration, Mussoorie, 1972.

TABLE 7

High-income states (rupees)			Low-income states (rupees)		
	1951 - 69	1969 - 74		1951 - 69	1969 - 75
Andhra Pradesh	144	54	Bihar	107	57
Assam	189	134			
Gujarat	126	57	Kerala	155	80
Haryana	50	75	Madhya Pradesh	155	62
Maharastra	97	47			
Mysore	156	57	Orissa	203	72
Punjab	343	66	Rajasthan	190	81
Tamil Nadu	120	50	Uttar Pradesh	106	56
West Bengal	130	48			
Average	141	63			

the profitability advantage rested with the advanced regions, private capital will not move into the backward areas.

The main expectation from the schemes of concessional finance and investment subsidies was that these would be able to offset the diseconomies of the backward areas, and private capital would move into them in response to these concessions and incentives. In Table 8 are given some facts which provide information on the extent of subsidies given to various areas - states as a part of the scheme of investment subsidy.

It would be seen from the table that 62.1 per cent of the total investment subsidy distributed up to the end of 1974 went to high-income states and 34.7 per cent to low-income states. [27]

The point to note here is that the main beneficiaries of this scheme were Maharashtra, Tamil Nadu, Karnataka, and Kerala, who accounted for over 50 per cent of the total subsidy and only 25.9 per cent of the country's population. Among the low-income states, Andhra Pradesh took the maximum advantage of the scheme by claiming 13 per cent of the total investment subsidy. These facts clearly suggest that either the quantum of investment subsidy (15 per cent of fixed capital) is inadequate to offset the locational disadvantages of the backward areas or that industries to grow require other conditions to be fulfilled.

Facts in respect of the industrial estate programme which was aimed at dispersal and regional development are no different from the above. Table 9 gives the locational distribution of industrial estates in different sizes of cities for two reference dates.

It is observed from Table 9 that as of September 1973, 43 per cent of the total industrial estates in the country were located in 100,000 + cities as compared to 37.6 per cent in cities of 20,000 - 100,000 sizes. What is important to note is the trend between 1963 - 73 when, it seems, a decision was taken to reverse the location policy of industrial estates in favour of larger cities. This would tend to suggest that medium-sized towns are not wholly viable for industrial growth and development.

The third instrument, i.e. of location of public sector industrial undertakings presents evidence of a different kind. We saw in Table 6 that up to the end of March 1974, 51.6 per

[27] The division of states into high income and low income is based on the latest data on *per capita* state net domestic product.

cent of the total central investments in industrial and mining projects were made in the three low-income states of Bihar, Madhya Pradesh, and Orissa. Their share in 1963 was 61 per cent. In absolute terms, too, these were substantial investments.

There have been no specific studies of assessing the impact of these investments on the growth and development of these three and other backward states. Indirect evidence is,

TABLE 8

Regional distribution of financial assistance under
central subsidy scheme, 1971

States	Financial assistance up to 1974		% share of individual states in total population
	Total rupees (million)	% share of individual states	
Low-income states			
Andhra Pradesh	6.15	13.05	7.9
Assam	1.09	2.32	2.7
Bihar	1.27	2.70	10.3
Jammu and Kashmir	nil	—	0.8
Madhya Pradesh	1.28	2.71	7.6
Manipur	0.01	0.04	0.2
Meghalaya	nil	—	0.2
Nagaland	0.38	0.80	0.1
Orissa	0.88	1.88	4.0
Rajasthan	2.43	5.16	4.7
Tripura	nil	—	0.3
Uttar Pradesh	2.84	6.03	16.1
Sub-total	16.33	34.69	54.9
High-income states			
Gujarat	1.69	3.59	4.9
Haryana	nil	—	1.8
Himachal Pradesh	2.37	5.02	0.6
Karnataka	2.86	6.07	5.3
Kerala	2.98	6.33	3.9
Maharashtra	13.12	27.84	9.2
Punjab	1.17	2.48	2.5
Tamil Nadu	4.92	10.45	7.5
West Bengal	0.16	0.34	8.1
Sub-total	29.27	62.12	43.8

Note: sub-totals do not include union territories.

however, available from a report prepared by the Town and Country Planning Organization which has revealed that the expected spill-over effects of these investments have not been generated in the region of the locations of public sector undertakings.[28] Further, these locations have become small islands of development bearing little or no relationship with the regional economy. The *per capita* incomes of the recipient states persist to be lower than the national average. This evidence is of basic policy significance and calls for a re-examination of the expectations from the location of public sector undertakings in backward regions.

[28]Government of India, Ministry of Works, Housing and Supply, *Report of the Committee on Coordination of Industrial Development and Location with Urban and Regional Planning,* New Delhi (undated).

TABLE 9
Locational distribution of industrial estates
in different sizes of cities

City sizes	Percentage distribution	
	December 1963	September 1973
100,000+	25.64	43.06
50,000 - 100,000	15.79	17.34
20,000 - 50,000	22.77	20.23
10,000 - 20,000	10.88	7.80
5,000 - 10,000	7.69	1.45
Less than 5000	16.00	10.12[a]
Villages	1.23	
Total	100.00	100.00

[a]Locations could not be identified at the time of the preparation of this table.
Source: Industrial Estates in India, Ministry of Industrial Development, New Delhi.

Two observations must be made to put this evidence in the correct perspective. The first observation is that the investment structure of these central industrial projects was such that the "disposable" income of the population of the region did not show any appreciable increase notwithstanding large quantum of investments. Investments were of a capital-intensive nature and had little employment component. Any expectations of substantial regional gains were, therefore, unwarranted. The second observation is that with another national policy of equalization of prices of critical industrial goods where, incidentally, central investments had taken place, the locational advantages of these producing centres were almost wholly nullified, and the expected ancillary development did not take place. On the other side, there was no attempt to provide any link, functional and physical, between the public sector undertakings and the regional economy. An observation from the previously quoted Report (footnote 28) is pertinent in this respect: it says that one of the problems that has arisen around the public sector industrial townships relates to "imbalanced or lop-sided development within the influence region of the project due to absence of a regional plan to maximize and spread the overall benefits of the project and its multiplier effect over wider areas".

Almost identical conclusions follow from the very scanty facts which are available from the spatial distribution of industrial licences. Of all the licences issued between 1952 and 1967, Maharashtra, West Bengal, Tamil Nadu, and Gujarat accounted for almost 60 per cent; the remaining 40 per cent were dispersed in other states.[29] In recent years, however, the less-developed states have secured a larger share of new undertakings while the traditionally industrialized states continue to dominate in obtaining licences for substantial expansions.

As regards the use of the third principal instrument, i.e. integrated areas development and local planning for redressing imbalances between regions, any comment at this stage

[29]See Indian Institute of Public Administration, Industrial licensing policy in relation to regional development, a background paper presented at the *Seminar on Regional Imbalances: The Problems and Policies*, New Delhi, 1972.

would be premature. The thrust to local - area planning efforts has come in the last 4 - 5 years. During these years many states have taken up the preparation of integrated local plans. Several problems of conceptual, analytical, and statistical type have come to notice, and there is considerable ambiguity about their scope and feasibility. At the same time, principles are being innovated so as to make these exercises meaningful and realistic. [30]

Where have matters gone wrong in respect of these programmes? While a cause-and-effect analysis is a complex business to attempt in any branch of planning, it has been possible to develop some hypotheses as to why these regional development programmes did not yield the desired level of impact. The first hypothesis relates to the concept of backwardness. There has been a general impression that in India and in most developing countries, backwardness is largely composite and collective, meaning thereby that an area which is agriculturally stagnant is stagnant in other respects too. As opposed to this, the delimitation of backward areas in this country has been done on sectoral basis .

In order to test whether the backward areas identified on the basis of sectoral deficiencies (industrial backwardness), or on grounds of special problems (drought-prone) were also backward in other spheres, we worked out the T-values by treating drought-prone districts and industrially backward districts as individual groups, and the remaining districts as another distinct group. In conducting the test of significance, indicators other than those which were used in the identification of drought-prone and industrial backward areas were used. [31] Results of this showed that these areas were backward in respect of several other indicators which were used for computing the T-values. This provides an important policy conclusion. If the industrially backward areas and drought-prone areas are backward in other respects as well, it would seem that preferences and incentives should be extended to other sectors as well, and be available for an integrated attack on the problem of these backward areas. The circumscribed approach currently being followed may perhaps explain the reasons for low degree of impact of the incentives policy in India.

The second hypothesis is that the scope of generalized and universal solutions is severely limited in India. The instance of the scheme of investment subsidy may again be cited. This scheme, which provides for 15 per cent subsidy to entrepreneurs in industrially backward areas, implies that (i) this will offset the diseconomies of the areas, and (ii) the amount of the subsidy sufficient to attract private investment is the same in all the regions. Because of these implied assumptions the scheme has become standardized and inflexible. On the other hand, what level and quantum of subsidy will be required to attract industrial investment is an entirely local - regional assessment. The hypothesis here is that the success of incentive-subsidy scheme is vitally linked with the area's potentiality and levels of development, and that unless the quantum of subsidy can be varied on the basis of local situation, its impact would hardly be consistent.

The third hypothesis is that the development of an area is dependent not so much on the volume of investment but on its structure. Further, structure is essentially a function of local - regional economy and can be determined only on the basis of an assessment of problems, possibilities, and potentialities.

It is around these hypotheses that the Indian regional policies and programmes will

---

[30]See State Government of Maharashtra, *Draft Fifth Five Year Plan, 1974 - 9,* 1973.

[31]See Om Prakash Mathur, National policy for backward area development: a structural analysis, *Indian Journal of Regional Science* (New Delhi) 1 (1974).

have to be further tested and strengthened. Already certain measures are on the horizon which indicate growing interest in the economics of local - regional areas. The future of the Indian policies would seem to lie not in keeping the interregional balance as the focus of attention but on fuller utilization of the regional resources and altering the national consumption patterns to fall in line with these resource possibilities.

Historically, development in the pluralistic societies has been like an oasis in the desert. Its benefits have accrued to the élite areas such as the port towns, selected metropolitan areas, and a few agriculturally rich regions. Even now, the pattern of development priorities is such that the situation tends to perpetuate itself. The time has come to re-examine the policies and their possible impact on regional imbalances.

Appendix I. Indicators of economic development

State	Per capita net domestic product (at current prices), 1969-70	Urban population to total population	Scheduled cases to total population	Scheduled tribes to total population	Literates to total population	Agricultural workers to total working force	Agricultural labourers to total working force	Gross irrigated area to gross cropped area, 1970-1	Gross cropped area to net sown area 1970-1	Net sown area per agricultural worker, 1970-1	Surfaced roads: Kms per (as on 31 March 1972) 100 km² of area	Surfaced roads: Kms per (as on 31 March 1972) 100,000 population	Per capita deposits of scheduled commercial banks (rupees)	Per capita advances of scheduled commercial banks (rupees)	Value added per industrial labourer, 1970 (rupees)	Fixed capital per industrial labourer, 1970 (rupees)	Number of factory workers per 100,000 population
1	2	3	4	5	6	7	8	9	10	11	12	13	14	15	16	17	18
1. Andhra Pradesh	554	19.31	13.27	3.81	24.57	70.10	37.92	31.60	113.73	0.93	15.11	96.13	63	54	3,341	14,866	748.32
2. Assam	554	8.82[a]	6.24[a]	10.99[a]	23.15[a]	65.78[a]	9.92[a]	20.63[a]	124.57[a]	0.83[a]	6.64	44.18	37	17	4,864	20,484	601.16
3. Bihar	404	10.00	14.11	8.75	19.94	82.25	38.92	24.78	130.42	0.59	16.41	50.63	67	14	6,590	27,006	467.62
4. Gujarat	701	28.07	6.84	13.99	35.79	65.60	22.48	13.01	106.54	1.71	11.32	33.07	226	123	6,073	12,125	1774.70
5. Haryana	921	17.66	18.89	—	26.89	65.29	16.21	44.98	139.05	2.06	29.93	132.10	110	55	6,781	21,438	1022.25
6. Himachal Pradesh	610	6.99	22.24	4.35	31.96	74.81	4.17	17.12	167.46	0.57	5.11	82.36	106	12	51,224	11,764	449.80
7. Jammu and Kashmir	459	18.59	8.26	—	18.58	67.83	3.05	38.11	122.66	0.76	2.50	120.52	108	25	1,562	24,453	363.66
8. Karnataka	591	24.31	13.14	0.79	31.52	66.70	26.70	13.21	106.23	1.51	28.62	187.39	125	108	7,310	16,730	837.31
9. Kerala	607	16.24	8.30	1.26	60.42	48.49	30.69	20.49	135.03	0.72	111.84	203.60	104	69	4,514	9,617	937.31
10. Madhya Pradesh	476	16.29	13.08	20.4	22.14	79.41	26.56	7.40	112.04	1.04	8.00	85.07	38	21	5,502	26,138	487.55
11. Maharashtra	720	31.17	6.00	5.86	39.18	64.87	29.33	8.58	105.46	1.53	15.08	92.11	353	305	8,414	13,725	1989.72
12. Manipur	423	—	1.53	31.18	32.91	70.64	3.65	39.89	105.02	0.69	5.46	113.82	17	11	1,691	1,578	82.68
13. Meghalaya	—	14.55	0.38	80.48	29.49	79.02	9.88	18.98	119.63	0.46	3.81	84.71	150	16	—	—	—
14. Nagaland	416	9.95	—	88.61	27.40	79.02	1.45	11.79	102.00	0.48	5.62	179.69	37	8	—	—	—
15. Orissa	514	8.41	15.09	23.11	26.18	77.44	28.28	19.24	136.98	1.15	6.95	49.34	25	11	6,658	46,316	407.09
16. Punjab	992	23.73	24.71	—	33.67	62.66	20.11	74.73	140.09	1.65	29.45	109.44	267	76	5,108	19,192	1026.37
17. Rajasthan	465	17.63	15.82	12.13	19.07	74.22	9.31	14.66	110.21	2.54	6.88	91.43	54	29	5,929	26,796	434.40
18. Tamil Nadu	591	30.26	17.76	0.76	39.46	61.71	30.46	46.18	119.70	0.68	40.47	127.78	110	128	5,433	16,105	1383.94
19. Tripura	493	10.43	12.39	28.95	30.98	74.37	19.96	6.97	143.79	0.75	10.00	67.34	76	8	1,637	1,376	172.71
20. Uttar Pradesh	495	14.02	21.00	0.22	21.70	77.38	19.95	34.17	134.11	0.82	12.38	41.25	70	29	5,318	24,760	443.82
21. West Bengal	685	24.75	19.90	5.72	33.20	58.42	26.45	21.73	127.97	0.77	22.96	45.51	230	182	5,060	12,386	1911.07
All India	579	19.91	14.60	6.94	29.45	69.66	26.33	23.03	118.59	1.12	14.38	86.14	137	98	6,158	16,833	953.41

[a] Assam as it is now (excluding Mizoram).
Columns 2 - 10 have been expressed in percentage. Data for cols. 2 - 8 relate to the year 1971, while for cols. 14 - 15, it relates to June 1972.

Appendix II. Correlation Matrix (corresponding to Appendix I)

	2	3	4	5	6	7	8	9	10	11	12	13	14	15	16	17
1	0.503[a]	0.460[a]	-0.434	0.350	-0.560[a]	0.147	0.498[a]	0.276	0.456[a]	0.293	0.109	0.698[a]	0.475[a]	0.126	-0.009	0.633[a]
2		0.087	-0.399	0.328	-0.561	0.373	0.201	-0.437	0.390	0.232	0.220	0.749[a]	0.834[a]	-0.239	-0.106	0.830[a]
3			-0.538[a]	-0.149	-0.012	0.257	0.422	0.652	0.215	0.066	0.317	0.177	-0.002	0.400	0.405	0.176
4				-0.125	0.443	-0.406	-0.354	-0.340	-0.255	-0.307	0.183	-0.357	-0.311	-0.221	-0.378	-0.460[a]
5					-0.779[a]	0.235	-0.000	0.079	-0.164	0.807[a]	0.482*	0.385	0.440	0.060	-0.450	0.458[a]
6						-0.172	-0.278	0.015	-0.058	-0.736[a]	-0.413	-0.505[a]	-0.530[a]	0.124	0.273	-0.633[a]
7							-0.045	-0.035	0.034	0.402	-0.116	0.244	0.398	-0.204	-0.276	0.467[a]
8								0.230	0.023	0.153	0.077	0.140	-0.070	-0.125	0.105	0.049
9									-0.233	0.154	-0.283	-0.036	-0.303	0.596[a]	0.166	-0.141
10										-0.065	0.038	0.283	0.227	-0.108	0.342	0.285
11											0.568[a]	0.156	0.209	-0.106	-0.155	0.295
12												0.004	0.061	-0.128	-0.401	-0.041
13													0.860[a]	0.073	-0.158	0.837[a]
14														-0.056	-0.151	0.900[a]
15															-0.007	-0.008
16																-0.043

[a]Significant at 5% level; all values above 0.4438 are significant.

6

RURAL INDUSTRIALIZATION IN CHINA: APPROACHES AND RESULTS*

JON SIGURDSON

The existence of a rapidly growing rural industrial sector which consists of a large number of small and medium-sized enterprises is characteristic of the present development strategy in China. The systematic and integrated development of this sector has hardly any parallel in other developing countries, even if many similarities can be found in other countries, particularly in India.[1]

1. RURAL INDUSTRIALIZATION AND INDUSTRIAL DECENTRALIZATION

Most developing countries, particularly those in Asia with a dominant part of the population in rural villages, used to have very substantial numbers of artisans. Those are now quickly disappearing due to changing demands and inefficiency of operation. On the other hand, modernization and industrialization are, and apparently have to be, to a considerable extent, based on modern large-scale enterprises located in the cities. Consequently, employment opportunities are disappearing from rural areas proper, and activities which would otherwise serve as catalysts of modernization are being monopolized in a few major cities.

The development is different in China, where rural industries span a considerable part of the industrial spectrum between traditional village crafts and modern large-scale industry. Rural industrialization should here be seen as part of a systematic attempt to decentralize industrial activity and promote regional development.

Many developing nations are today faced with the problem that they cannot provide

---

*This article is based on research carried out at the Science Policy Research Unit at the University of Sussex and on two field visits to China in 1971 and 1973. A full presentation is found in Rural Industrialization in China, published in the monograph series of the East Asian Research Centre, Harvard University, 1977. The research has been generously supported by the Bank of Sweden Tercentenary Fund, The Swedish Board for Technical Development and the Ford Foundation.

[1] It should be noted that the Indian government in the early 1960s launched a massive programme of rural industrialization. The aim of the programme was to transform the existing lop-sided agricultural economy into a balanced "agro-industrial" economy. And it was also stressed that rural industrialization was to be based primarily on local resources and local needs (see, e.g., P. M. Mathai, Rural industrialization and the maximization of employment opportunities in India, *Small Industry Bulletin for Asia and the Far East*, No. 9 (1972).

147

enough employment opportunities in rural areas for people reaching working age, which in most countries has led to an undesirable migration into cities. Agriculture is in many developing countries in the process of being modernized through the use of new high-yielding varieties, more fertilizer and improved irrigation and drainage—increasing *land* productivity. But agriculture is also in the process of being mechanized—increasing *labour* productivity—which is likely to have a considerable effect on the labour supply/demand situation. The labour force is at the same time increasing through the natural population increase. In the long run, a very large number of people will be released from agriculture, of which it is likely that the modern industrial sector can absorb only a small percentage. Consequently, it is essential to find planning mechanisms by which the released manpower from agriculture can be gainfully employed.

Almost every person in rural areas in China is a member of a people's commune, which provides him with basic security. Agricultural mechanization is, in principle, controlled and people are hindered from migrating into the cities. However, there can be no doubt that it will be impossible for China to mechanize agriculture as well as to keep a majority of an increasing labour force in agriculture, so China has to come to grips with the problem of releasing manpower from agriculture. It certainly appears that different forms of rural industry—small-scale industry in areas dominated by agricultural or stock-farming activities—will play an important role. However, during the first stages of rural industrial development, employment is not primarily created in industrial production, but in repair and maintenance, in production of industrial raw materials, in transportation and in other services and in an increasingly diversified agriculture. At the same time, industrial structures are created outside the big cities. With the simultaneous expansion of national and local enterprises in rural areas, the former can increasingly draw on the manufacturing potential of a large number of small enterprises. Before continuing the discussion, however, it is necessary to make a clear distinction between rural industrialization and industrial decentralization.

To explain the difference, it is necessary to classify population centres according to size.[2] Communities may usefully be categorized in four size ranges:

(1) Rural communities with up to 10,000 - 20,000 inhabitants (market towns).
(2) Small urban centres with up to about 200,000 inhabitants.
(3) Secondary urban centres with up to about 1,000,000 inhabitants.
(4) Metropolitan centres with over 1,000,000 inhabitants.

The population marks are only approximate. The basic distinguishing feature is the economic base of the community. Small urban centres are defined as those whose existence is based mainly on the services they furnish to the surrounding rural areas. In secondary urban centres other activities take precedence over agro-related activities, and agriculture in the surrounding countryside is based mainly on the demand for food created by the urban centre. Metropolitan areas are the one or few largest population centres in almost any country, in which most industry, government and commerce are concentrated.

Industrial decentralization is a generic name for moving industry out of the metropolis to any other community. The chief aim of an industrial decentralization policy is usually

---

[2]The discussion is partly based on Rural industrialization in Mexico: a case study, prepared for the UN Expert Group Meeting on Rural Industrialization in Bucharest, 24 - 28 September 1973, Document ESA/SD/AC.5/9, 27 February 1973.

to achieve a shift of future industrial growth from a metropolitan area to secondary urban centres. In most countries only a minority of the new industries—mostly those which process natural resources—are decentralized down to smaller urban centres, and, to a much smaller extent, to rural communities. It is suggested that such industries be termed *regional industries*. This pattern of industrial decentralization and the place of rural industry are shown in Fig. 1.

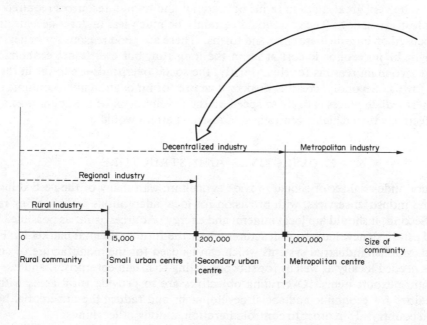

Fig. 1. The relation between rural industrialization and industrial decentralization.

Industrial concentration in one or a couple of centres is commonly found in countries in the early stages of industrialization. The spreading of industrialization to secondary urban centres is found in industrially more advanced developing countries like Pakistan and India. The further spreading of industry to rural communities is found in mature industrial countries. The hypothesis has been advanced that the above order of industrial development is the optimal one. However, the experience in Japan and more recently in China indicates that an entirely different pattern involving rural communities at an early stage of development is feasible—even if the circumstances and necessary conditions are not yet fully known.

It is certainly desirable to bring industrial employment and income, and the indirect employment and income generated by industry, closer to the majority of the population living in the villages. But it does not follow that the best way to do this is to seek to locate a considerable proportion of manufacturing industry directly in the villages or even in the small urban centres (market towns). In order to achieve the objectives mentioned it is likely to be more effective to focus on the industrial development of selected towns and cities which are intermediate between villages on the one hand and secondary urban and metropolitan centres on the other hand, with a considerable emphasis on upgrading traditional village crafts serving agriculture. This would then take advantage of reasonably low costs for industrial facilities like power and transportation, and provide important external economies associated with urban locations. It would still bring industry and related services substantially closer to the majority of the population, who still live in villages.

The social and political benefits of decentralization are worth some economic cost. If decentralization were taken to mean pushing industry directly into villages, which was partly the case in China during the initial stage of the Great Leap Forward in 1958, the cost would be very great, both in terms of material and human resources required and in terms of lost efficiency. The cost would certainly be much less under a decentralization policy focused on intermediate cities and towns. There are good reasons for believing that there might be no economic cost at all in the long run, but even a net economic gain. There are two main reasons for this. Firstly, the social overheads are lower in the intermediate towns. Secondly, creating dispersed centres of innovation and economic change in the intermediate places is likely to speed up the development of the country as a whole more effectively than a highly centralized industrial pattern would do.

2. OBJECTIVES AND STRUCTURE

The rural industrial sector should provide agriculture with many of the needed industrial inputs and industrial services, with provision for local adaptations and changing requirements. Second, it should tap local mineral and energy resources as far as possible. Third, it should establish new industrial structures where the future potential market is. Fourth, it should establish industrial systems which can be used for the manufacture of complex products needed locally as well as for subcontracting to urban enterprises, and lately also manufacture export items. Overriding objectives are to provide rural areas with more opportunities for economic and social development and reduce the differential between cities and countryside in order to control migration, among other things.

The rural industrial sector in China consists of enterprises which vary greatly in size and in degree of technological sophistication. The total number of enterprises is very high. The largest category consists of the very small brigade-level repair and manufacture shops, of which there may be several hundred thousands. The second largest category is likely to be the small mines—or mining spots—of which there are likely to be considerably more than 100,000. There are also 50,000 small hydroelectric stations. A large number of the 50,000 communes are likely to have their own workshops for grain-milling, oil-pressing and other food processing plants, wood-working shops etc. which are usually organized in multipurpose units. Rural heavy industry—small iron and steel plants, cement plants, chemical fertilizer plants and other chemical plants—may amount to between 5000 and 10,000 units. The number of country-run machinery plants may amount to more than 3000 units. Then there is also a large number of light (consumer) industry enterprises in counties, communes and brigades and these may amount to more than 100,000 units. So, the total number of industrial units—within the rural industrial sector—is likely to be in the region of 500,000 or more.

However, total rural industrial employment is still limited and total employment is estimated to be in the region of 10 - 17 million—which may still correspond to approximately 50 per cent of total employment in manufacturing and mining. A couple of provinces have since the summer of 1973 clearly indicated that—based on local conditions and relevant instructions from higher authorities—the number of workers used by industries at county, commune and brigade levels should not exceed 5 per cent of the labour force in a county. And all other available information indicates that this may be the upper limit today.[3]

China has not released any national figures for employment in county-, commune- and brigade-level enterprises. There can be no doubt that employment in various parts of the country differs widely. Rural areas which are under the administration of big industrial cities have 20 per cent or more of the labour force in industry. Remote places in the interior of the county may hardly have any industrial activity at all. Information from a number of relatively—in terms of rural industrialization—well developed regions in Hopei Province indicates that less than 5 per cent of China's total labour force is engaged in rural industries. The labour force is estimated to be approximately 350 million which is about 70 per cent of the population between the ages of 15 and 64.

Rural industry is distributed within a county at brigade-, commune- and county-level, with the heavy industry and larger enterprises located in the county capitals. The larger county capitals would usually not have a population exceeding 20,000. Most of the rural industrial enterprises are relatively small, rarely exceeding a few hundred employed. When discussing rural industry in China it is essential to realize that many of them are not small by international classification and that many of them are located in small urban centres—county seats with a population of up to 20,000—which are not considered rural areas according to international classification.

Rural industry in this article is not defined on the basis of size but as any local industry run by county, commune or brigade. The enterprise may be collectively owned, jointly financed by the state and collective units, or wholly owned by the state but under local management. Rural industry also includes units attached to middle schools, hospitals and health clinics.

Rural industry in China forms one part of the small-scale industrial sector which is basically made up of two different parts, of which the other is the urban small-scale industrial sector. The latter is not discussed in this article. The sophistication and scope of industrial activities are dependent on the level of education, economic development, natural resource endowment, nearness to ideas and new information. Consequently, it is realistic to differentiate between *rural industry in city-near locations* and *rural industry in rural areas proper*. The former seems to have much more in common with urban-based small-scale industry than is the case for the rest of rural industry.

The development of industries in rural areas around Shanghai, Peking and Tientsin—with a substantial amount of subcontracting—may indicate the long-term prospects for rural industry in the rest of the country. The formation of technical and organizational skills is only in the early stages of development in most parts of rural China. This and the still low level of mechanization explains why the industrial level is still comparatively low compared with more favoured rural areas around the big cities.

3. THE INTEGRATED APPROACH

Rural industrialization is a function of both demand and availability of local resources, where it is generally easier to influence the former than the latter. Rural industry in China can—with reference to the model for the rural industry system in Fig. 2—be categorized in

---

[3]The industrial employment in rural areas is seasonally adjusted and may vary considerably to accommodate the changes in demand for agricultural manpower and some enterprises may even be closed during the busy harvest seasons. This is particularly true for many of the commune- and brigade-level enterprises which are generally much less capital intensive than the larger and more complex county-level enterprises.

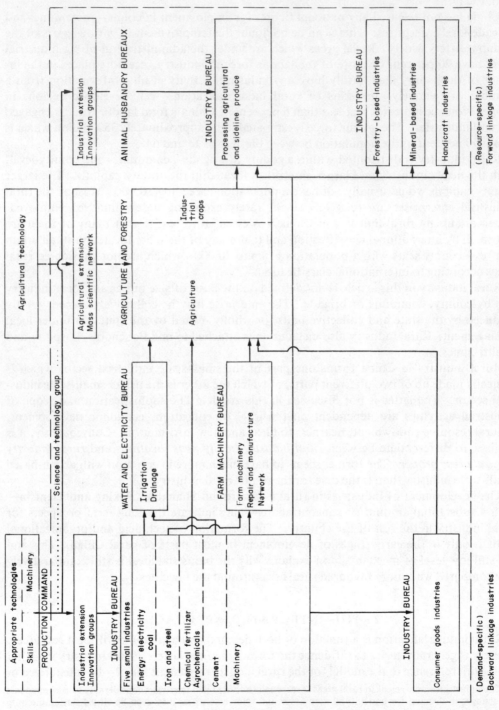

Fig. 2. Model of a rural industrial system in China.

backward-linkage industries meeting a demand for agricultural inputs, and consumer goods, and *forward-linkage industries* being mainly based on locally available physical and human resources. The backward-linkage industries of course require local human resources but are initially very dependent on external technological and financial resources.

Rural industries with backward linkages to agriculture usually cannot be introduced until changes in agricultural technology create the demand for industrial inputs. And forward-linkage industries are often dependent on supplies arising from increased agricultural production. Furthermore, the demand for many industrial products will be limited until there is a general increase in the purchasing power of the locality. This is in most places, at least initially, almost totally dependent on increases in agricultural productivity. In sum, rural industrialization can progress only gradually and must be closely integrated with the over-all planning of the localities.

Figure 2 illustrates the flow chart for a county or a locality which is well endowed with natural resources including coal, iron ore and limestone. In such a locality the industrial activities can be divided into five different components. The first is the heavy small-scale industry which includes what the Chinese often term "five small industries". These supply energy, cement, chemical fertilizer, iron and steel and machinery, which directly or indirectly provide agriculture with the inputs necessary to raise productivity. These plants are usually run by the county.

The second component is various resource-specific industries which may provide raw materials such as coal, iron ore, limestone and other minerals to the "five small industries" or to larger national enterprises. It is evident that the resource base—location, size and quality—decides to what extent small-scale heavy industries can be set up. Economies of scale and the development of the transportation system are other important factors.

The third and fourth components of industrial activity in a county both belong to light industry. The main responsibility of this sector is to process agricultural and sideline produce and to provide the locality with some of the needed consumer goods. This may include flour-milling, oil-pressing, cotton-ginning, etc., as well as manufacture of textiles and shoes, household goods of porcelain and metal, canned fruit, and so on. Light industrial enterprises are found at county, commune and brigade levels.

The fifth component, the farm machinery repair and manufacture network, produces simple farm implements, tools, and also heavier equipment. The repair and maintenance of farm implements and machinery in order to sustain a high rate of machinery utilization is of primary importance. The repair and manufacture network has as a rule a three-tier structure, with each brigade and each commune within a county maintaining its own unit. Naturally, the smallest units are run by the brigades, medium-sized ones by the communes and the relatively large units by the county. The goal is to develop a clear division of labour among units at different levels: the brigade units should engage in simple repairs and manufacturing; the commune units should be able to carry out more complex repairs, and also manufacture heavier equipment; the county stations should be able to carry out the repairs of any complex farm machinery being used within the county, and also manufacture heavy equipment to be used in agriculture or in the units of the repair and manufacture network.

The Chinese planners have attempted to use the demand arising from a modernizing agriculture to create backward linkages, in a rural context, for almost all the important inputs required by agriculture. Some of the backward-linkage industries, like cement and chemical fertilizer, are justified because of the existence of local raw material resources. However, their development has not been triggered because of existing local resources, but from a demand caused mainly by changes in agricultural technology, and they lack justification without local demand.

Mechanical inputs are manufactured in county-, commune- and brigade-level units, with the activity at brigade level usually consisting only of a couple of metalworkers using a few pieces of relatively simple machinery. Chemical inputs are usually produced in county-level enterprises even if mixing and simple phosphate fertilizer production may be found in commune-level enterprises. The manufacture of consumer goods is carried out at all three levels, but more complex products, e.g., moulded plastic sandals, only in county-level units. Processing of agricultural and sideline produce is mainly carried out by brigades and communes. Forestry-based and mineral-based industry is generally undertaken by brigades and communes, depending on the resource base, the manpower situation and the technology utilized. Handicraft industry is found at commune, brigade and household level. All this relates to industry in rural areas proper, and the situation may be quite different in city-near locations.

Rural industries generally serve a small market, the size of which varies with the level—brigade, commune, county or region—where the enterprise is found. Through choice of enterprise size and manufacturing technology it has been possible in many industrial sectors to transfer industry into rural areas and manufacture economically to meet a local demand, if all externalities are considered. Further, size of enterprise and technology is closely related to the control-initiative level, and many localities—communes and counties—are already being drawn into subcontracting and manufacturing export items, thus also meeting an external demand. This is particularly true for rural industry in city-near locations.

It appears that the Chinese planners are now guided by a conviction that most of the facilities for economic and social activities in rural areas can be provided most effectively and economically when they are clustered in space so as to take advantage of interdependence in their functions and use.

To fully understand the financial implications of an integrated approach to agricultural development and rural industrialization it may be advantageous once more to look at the diagram (Fig. 2), which shows the commodity flow between industrial components and agriculture. The figure also shows which economic units at county level control the various parts of the economic system. The county agricultural-industrial system should here be seen as one functional organization with a number of subdivisions. All the different units must not necessarily operate with a surplus. The farm machinery repair and manufacture network usually operates with little or no surplus.

The command or control of the operations of the enterprises does not lie within the single units but is vested in the *production command* of the county (left top of the figure). Under its direct control are the various economic bureaux—industry bureau, farm machinery bureau, agriculture and forestry bureau, water and electricity bureau, etc. The over-all productivity of the system depends, aside from capital accumulation, on technology improvements in agriculture and industry. So it is natural to find that both industrial and agricultural extension are under the science and technology group, which is a sub-group of the production command.

The Chinese news media have in the past few years published information on a substantial number of localities where there has existed a conflict between the development of agriculture and industry. In Tayeh County in Hupeh,[4] which may exemplify this, it was reported that efforts were made before the Cultural Revolution to change the backward features of the county's industry. However, emphasis on industry led to contention between industry and agriculture for manpower and funds with the result that agriculture was brushed aside, according to the report. In 1970 the new administration decided on a plan covering both industrial and agricultural production. It then worked out plans for the use of manpower, funds, and materials for both industrial and agricultural production and construction in order to strictly control the scope and rate of growth of the local industry within the limits permitted by agricultural production. Now the county has in the past few years spent 80 per cent of local financial expenditures for agricultural production, including investments in those local industries which serve agricultural production.

4. TECHNOLOGY DIFFUSION

Technology is an essential aspect of modernization knowledge in a developing country. If we now limit our discussion to the rural sector, it is obvious that there is almost everywhere need for new knowledge which must be transferred into effective demand. And it is most unlikely that technology resources will be forthcoming until the demand has been articulated through the development of a technology capability in the locality.

The justification for the locality to have its own technology capability can be summarized in the following three points. First, conditions are rapidly changing outside and inside the locality. Secondly, relevant knowledge is often not immediately available, and consequently local search (or research) must be initiated. Thirdly, there is a need to gradually train technical forces and build up a problem-solving capability for the future.

A local technology system[5] would have the following main components:

(1) *Mass scientific network.* This is basically an extension network covering agriculture and related activities, public health and industry.
(2) *Local problem-solving capability.* Formalized groups within rural industries and other production units: (a) to articulate its demand for additional inputs; (b) to establish outward linkages into the national S & T system; (c) to extend inward linkages into the extension network serving the locality.
(3) *Local research institutes.*

The Chinese leadership has on several occasions, at least for short periods, repudiated the structural features of modernity as we know them in already industrialized countries. The Chinese seem to reason that complex mechanization and automation place increasingly rigid technical constraints on the contribution that purely practical knowledge can make to further the modernization of the country. And the Chinese leadership views mass participation as a method of incorporating distinctively native elements into the creation of a modern state.

[4]New China News Agency, as reported in BBC Summary of World Broadcasts, *Weekly Economic Report,* FE/W713 (28 February 1973).

[5]It was recently reported that over 10 million people now take part in scientific experiments in rural areas, which approximately corresponds to 1.25 per cent of the country's population. And there are also experimental stations and groups in most rural people's communes and production brigades. (China develops science and technology independently and self-reliantly, *Peking Review,* No. 46 (1974) 14.) For a fuller discussion of local technology systems in China, see Jon Sigurdson, China's autonomous development of technology and science. Seminar Paper, OECD Seminar on Science, Technology and Development in a Changing World, Paris, April 1975.

China has used ideological education to make strong and consistent efforts to redistribute opportunities of generating technological and cultural change. This redistribution leads to a downplaying of the role of professional elites and foreign technology, and may be particularly relevant within the traditional and rural sectors. The integration of innovation and production on one hand, and of technology and labour on the other, presents an obvious contrast to the development process in modern industrial societies. Modern technological activity outside China is based upon formal scientific training, highly specialized, and carried out in specific institutions which are almost exclusively geared to technological innovation. The Chinese approach may be highly successful as sectorial technological policy—particularly in sectors where development is relatively less science-based. But China has on two occasions tried to implement this different approach as a global technological policy—and has apparently failed.

What makes the rural sector such a challenging problem in terms of technology in developing countries is the fact that the need for new knowledge must be changed into an effective demand. This can be done in a number of ways. One is the raising of the educational level through expanded primary education, adult education, literacy campaigns, building of local technology institutions, etc., which is a slow and tedious process. In China this has at times been strongly supported by political campaigns such as those of the Great Leap Forward and the Cultural Revolution. The notion of the earlier campaign was that the peasants could master any industrial technology and that their demand for technology resources should be met without reservation from the modern sector.

No doubt, the demand exercised from the rural sector in 1958 - 60 was effective: some would say too effective. There are still many conflicting interpretations of the mistakes made during the Great Leap Forward. However, in terms of technology, it is true to state that the technology demand was not an articulated one. The same may partly be true during a short period of the Cultural Revolution. Economic feasibility was sometimes neglected, technical feasibility sometimes, and, on occasions, both.

A primary requirement for (rural) development in the localities is compatibility between technology and delivery system on the one hand, and potential demand on the other. This leads to the following two, secondary, requirements: first, the locality must have an efficient system for introduction/delivery of technology; secondly, there must be a good match between the costs of goods and services on one hand, and the purchasing power of the locality on the other.

Rural development and rural industrialization has required technology of two different kinds. In the early stages transfer of technology was needed to initiate any development. It is now in a consolidation stage where it is necessary to develop a local technical capacity, i.e., problem-solving capability.

Technology utilized in rural areas can be transferred in three different ways. First, part of it comes capital-embodied, i.e. incorporated in equipment and intermediate goods. This approach has been important for all of the more complex small-scale process industries in rural areas. Second, another part is human-embodied, i.e., incorporated as knowledge and experience of human resources. This approach has been very important in the initial stage of rural industrialization. Finally, another part is disembodied technology, such as handbooks, product and process specifications, etc. The latter approach is becoming increasingly important as the localities have built up a capability to demand and utilize this kind of knowledge.

However, due to unfamiliarity with industrial technology and lack of ability to interpret printed technical descriptions, it has been necessary to rely extensively on personal contacts to transmit technical knowledge. Industrial knowledge may be carried by two categories of persons. Technicians, engineers and managers from more advanced plants travel to the sites of small rural plants to assist in all stages from planning to production and distribution. At the same time people from the localities are sent for shorter or longer training periods to advanced industrial units and are given posts of responsibility for technical or managerial matters when they return. Further, people are transferred more or less permanently to work in rural areas. This formation of production and organizational skills in rural areas may be schematized as follows:

(1) *Training of personnel*
  (a) City-based, old factories train workers recruited to rural factories.
  (b) Rural factories undertake training of new workers.
(2) *Transfer of personnel*
  (a) Technical personnel are transferred from old to new factories.
  (b) Newly graduated students are allocated to new, rural factories.

A heavy reliance on person-to-person contacts in solving industrial problems indicates that the Chinese have found this to be the most effective method of technology transfer and that the problem-solving activities cannot be successfully carried out without personal contacts in the field involving responsibilities for both parties involved. Technology transfer can be initiated within the enterprise or within the local administration with responsibility for the enterprise in question. Both ways are common.

Rural industry provides a further downward transfer of technology. Agricultural workers from teams and brigades are trained in local industries, e.g., to repair pumps, electric motors and other necessary equipment for the irrigation networks. In addition, other people are trained to repair farm tools and farm machinery, and in the technique involved in the use of fertilizer. Further, most of the rural industries send repair and instruction teams to assist in relevant tasks within the agricultural units. Thus, the rural industrial system serves as an important training ground for local technicians. This method of technology transfer is illustrated in the following schema, showing the activities used to build up repair and maintenance skills in a region in Honan Province.

(1) *Formal factory training*
  Short-term courses are arranged in commune-level enterprises during slack farming seasons.
  Principles, structure, operation and maintenance of machines are being taught.
(2) *Informal factory training*
  Production teams send on their own initiative members to factories for 'learning by doing'.
(3) *Delivery training*
  Commune-level enterprises send technicians to buying units at the time of delivery.
(4) *Mobile repair and maintenance teams training*
  People are trained on the spot at the time when repair or maintenance is required.
(5) *Factory repair training*
  Team members accompany machinery to the repair unit.

Source: Anyang Region Industrial Bureau (Honan), July 1973.

5. CONCLUSIONS

The encouragement of small-scale industries in rural areas in China is today an essential element of regional development programmes which focus on agricultural development and diversification, local raw material utilization, resource mobilization and long-term employment impact.

However, rural industry in China is not a homogeneous concept, as it is the consequence of two different strategy approaches. First, it is the logical outcome of *sector strategy* involving technology choices in a number of industrial sectors, most of which were initiated during the Great Leap Forward. This has required the *scaling down* of modern large-scale technology through a product and/or quality choice combined with design changes in the manufacturing process.[6] Second, rural industry is part of an *integrated rural development* strategy where a number of activities are integrated within or closely related to the commune system. They are then often rooted in the traditional sector of the economy and have often been preceded by a long tradition of village crafts. Such industries are often based on the *scaling up* of village crafts. The scaling up of cottage industries in China is not based on improvement of technology alone, but the cottage industries have been converted into modern small-scale industries through cooperativization, electrification and access to low-cost simple machinery. The assumption for both categories is that, in the main, they should be using local resources and be meeting a local demand for producer goods and industrial services.

Industrialization in rural areas proper appears to have been successful only when the local character has been stressed. In other words, those activities, which have high coefficients for backward linkages to agriculture and for forward linkages to final users in the localities have been successful. A distinct difference between rural industrialization in the late fifties and since the Cultural Revolution is that the latter approach appears to have much higher coefficients for forward and backward linkages in the locality.

It seems that the greatest merit of small enterprises as experienced in China lies not in the superiority of their capital—labour or capital—output ratios, but, in the over-all savings in resources they make possible.[7]

The diseconomies of small-scale production are such for certain process industries that local enterprises can only operate under very favourable conditions, or for limited periods until economic development removes constraints such as transportation bottlenecks, foreign exchange limitations, etc.

Rural industry is also part of a communication network where an important task is to spread innovations as quickly as possible within a local technology system. New things and ideas often look complicated to an outsider and therefore people have to be able to ask questions, test things and try ideas, and to get a feeling for them in order fully to

---

[6]The best-known examples are small-scale production of nitrogen, chemical fertilizer, cement and iron, all of which are discussed at length in Jon Sigurdson, ibid. For a theoretical discussion of the issues involved, see Shigeru Ishikawa, A note on the choice of technology in China, *The Journal of Development Studies*, (1) (1972) 161 - 86.

[7]Watanabe argues that "small enterprises seem to contribute most to the economic development of countries with surplus labour and shortage of capital (which applies to China at her present stage of development) under the following conditions:

(1) Where they can be set up without heavy overhead capital expenditure on buildings, land and infrastructure;
(2) where the diseconomies of small enterprises are compensated by the use of idle capital, labour and raw materials;
(3) where division of labour between enterprises in different size groups, e.g., in the form of subcontracting, enhances the over-all efficiency of the industry." Susum Watanabe, Reflections on current policies for promoting small enterprises and subcontracting, *International Labour Review*, **110** (5) November 1974.

understand and accept them. A tightly meshed network is then a consequence of the fact that the links of personal communications are heavily restricted by distance for most individuals. And it is a fact that personal communication between pairs of individuals and direct observation are still the basic instruments for the diffusion of innovations.

Further, small-scale industries serve as an important training ground for peasants who are learning manufacturing skills and adapting to an industrial environment and thus to conditions found in larger enterprises. This training is part of a general process of breaking down the barriers to a transition from a traditional to a modern economy. Consequently, rural industrialization has positive implications for the social development of the country. This is one of the major reasons why the leadership has attempted to make rural industries reach almost every corner of the country, and thus contribute to the local formation of technical and organization skills.

Even if rural industrialization has a limited impact on the employment pattern, in relative terms, it must not be forgotten that the sector engages approximately 3 per cent of the total number of people of working age. Another 2 per cent are engaged in the mass scientific network in rural areas. Consequently, altogether 5 per cent of the working age population are in rural areas, actively engaged in activities, which are likely to have a strong impact not only on productivity but also on the mental outlook in rural areas.

However, China's rural industrialization programmes have in the past undergone sharp oscillations between acceptance and rejection of major portions of a development strategy. These oscillations reflect a political struggle and changing internal and external conditions. The struggle involves contention over the most fundamental questions of social-economic goals and it affects every aspect of economic policy.

It has taken time to develop the necessary institutions and attitudes towards a development strategy which emphasizes the use of large numbers of small-scale industries in rural areas. In the meantime, a slower pace of industrial development has sometimes been accepted so that social and political objectives can be furthered first.

The encouragement of efficient and productive small-scale industries in rural as well as in urban areas has never been presented as an alternative to the development of medium- and large-scale enterprises, but they have always been seen as complementary elements in the industrialization processes. The experience of already developed countries suggests that a balanced industrial structure requires a considerable scale span of enterprises. The provision of a strong and viable development basis in China for small-scale industries is then likely to have significant long-term economic as well as social advantages.

REFERENCES

Larsen, Kjeld, China's regional industry (Danish), Institute of Development Research, Copenhagen 1975.

Mathai, P. M., Rural industrialization in India: a case study, prepared for the Expert Group Meeting on Rural Industrialization, Bucharest, 24 - 28 September 1973.

Neilson, Alexander and the UN Secretariat, Rural industrialization in developing countries, prepared for the Expert Group meeting on Rural Industrialization, Bucharest, 24 - 28 September 1973.

Report of the Expert Group Meeting on Rural Industrialization, Bucharest, 24 - 28 September 1973, *Rural Industrialization,* Department of Economic and Social Affairs (New York; United Nations, 1974).

Riskin, Carl, *Local Industry and the Choice of Techniques in the Planning of Industrial Development in Mainland China: Planning for Advanced Skills and Technologies,* UNIDO Industrial Planning and Programming Series No. 3 (New York: United Nations, 1969) pp. 171 - 80.

_____, Small industry and the Chinese model of development, *The China Quarterly* No. 46 (1971) 245 - 73.

Wong, Y. Lang, Establishment of industrial estates in a rural setting, in *Industrial Estates in Asia and the Far East,* United Nations, New York (1962).

PART II

Alternative Approaches to Regional Development in Asia

7

AGROPOLITAN DEVELOPMENT: TOWARDS A NEW STRATEGY FOR REGIONAL PLANNING IN ASIA

JOHN FRIEDMANN AND MIKE DOUGLASS

The last few years have seen a reaching out for new paradigms of planning for development. The old paradigm is no longer compelling in its logic. The underlying idea was that human happiness and sense of well-being would flow, more or less spontaneously, from the relentless pursuit of economic growth; that economic growth would most readily result from rapid industrialization; that rapid industrialization would be accommodated most efficiently in a few metropolitan centers from where its benefits would "spread" to the rest of the national territory; that planning for growth, industrialization, and urbanization could be accomplished only through coordinated central planning; and that coordinated central planning was a technical task that would be solved through complex econometric modeling joined to sophisticated administrative technique.

Spatial planners tried to find a place for themselves within this scheme. Their principal contribution to developmental planning was the notion of growth poles and growth centers (Kuklinski, 1972; Kuklinski and Petrella, 1972). They argued that investments had to be considered in a spatial dimension; that although the efficiency of investments might be maximized by concentrating them initially in large urban places, equity considerations called for a policy of concentrated decentralization, and that, in order to incorporate a spatial dimension into planning for national economic growth, planning would have to encompass at least three levels of spatial aggregation: urban, regional, and national. In this way, they claimed, the spatial integration of the national economy would be achieved (Lefeber and Datta-Chaudhuri, 1971; Misra *et al.,* 1974).

In both its nonspatial and spatial dimensions, however, this paradigm has come under fire. On the one hand, it is argued that the paradigm has failed to bring about the results expected from it (Faber and Seers, 1972). On the other hand, the last few years seem to be signaling the transition of the international economy to a new state of affairs which suggests that the unmodified pursuit of the old paradigm would be, to put it bluntly, suicidal (Mesarovic and Pestel, 1974).

As a consequence of this double criticism, the contours of a possible new paradigm are beginning to emerge. Its primary objective is no longer economic growth but social development, with focus on specific human needs (Seers, 1970; Ul Haq, 1972). According to this paradigm, development must be fitted to ecological constraints; priority attention (in agrarian economies) must be given to rural development; and planning for rural development must be decentralized, participatory, and deeply immersed in the particulars of local settings. Planning, therefore, will have to be based on qualitative judgments as much as on quantitative techniques, and its style will have to be transactive (Friedmann, 1973a).

Our intention here is to propose a spatial policy for the emerging paradigm. The discussion is divided into two main parts. In the first, we assess the results of the strategy of accelerated industrialization in six Asian countries: India, Indonesia, West Malaysia, the Philippines, Republic of Korea, and Thailand. Two major conclusions are reached. The traditional paradigm, we argue, has generated contradictions of crisis proportions in the structure of national development. These contradictions of "dualistic dependency" are intensified by the present transition of the world capitalist economy from an era of high sustained growth to one of structural imbalance and stagnation. A strategy of accelerated rural development is seen as the most appropriate response to the emerging conditions.

The question of a spatial policy for implementing the new strategy is considered in Section 2.[1] After stating some of the structural characteristics of a policies framework which aims at fusing urban and rural conditions of living, the relevant experience in the six countries is reviewed. We conclude that current efforts are inadequate to meet the needs of the new strategy. The urgency of the present situation calls for heightened political commitment to an inward-looking and rurally based strategy of national development. In this way the contradictions of dualistic dependency may be overcome and national economies protected against the shock waves engendered by the structural changes inherent in the current world transition.

1. A CRITIQUE OF DEVELOPMENT STRATEGY UNDER CONDITIONS OF DUALISTIC DEPENDENCY

1.1. The Failures of the Industrialization Paradigm

Since gaining their independence, the six countries which are the subject of this study have chosen to follow a strategy of accelerated industrialization as the high road to economic growth and national prosperity. For simplicity's sake, we shall refer to this as Strategy I. In accordance with this strategy, the rapid expansion of a large-scale, corporate manufacturing sector was expected to bring bountiful benefits to the nation: a basis for further growth and rapid capital accumulation, full employment, higher levels of living for the entire population, increased national autonomy, a breakthrough into "modernity".

The strategy relied on four principal sources of financing. Three of them tied the country's development path to the world capitalist system: primary materials exports, private foreign investments, and international aid; the fourth relied on the country's internal capacity for savings primarily from within the agricultural sector. Public investments were to be used chiefly for building up the social infrastructure in support of private activity in the industrial sector. Where necessary, government might join with private capital in new industrial ventures; on the whole, however, these ventures were to remain in private hands.

Initially, Strategy I was oriented towards the substitution of manufactured imports, but the installation of only a few industries quickly saturated domestic markets. As a result of market limitations (and the difficulties experienced in achieving a vertical integration of

---

[1]For an earlier formulation of a spatial policy for rural development, see Friedmann (1974).

industries), many countries began to shift to a policy of encouraging the export of manufactured products overseas.

Whereas the earlier policy of import-substitution had resulted in high-cost and relatively inefficient production, the change to export orientation made it imperative to cut costs to competitive international levels. In both cases, however, technology had to be imported from abroad. The chief competitive advantage of Asian countries was, therefore, their abundant supply of low-cost labor. By applying low-cost labor to a capital-intensive technology and by maintaining high production standards, Asian countries could attempt to supply Western markets at a competitive advantage. In addition, countries such as India began to promote the export of labor-intensive products such as textiles, electronics, and traditional handicrafts.

Unfortunately, the results of Strategy I were not at all what had been hoped for. By the mid-1970s it had become clear that, far from being the high road to national development, the strategy of accelerated industrialization had generated, and was continuing to generate and reinforce, a homologous set of economic, social, and spatial structures that confounded the rhetoric of national objectives. We shall call them the structures of dualistic dependency (Paauw and Fei, 1973).

In the "vertical" dimension, dualistic dependency displays a set of opposing structures. The corporate sector exercises dominance over the traditional household sector of the economy. An urban-based elite dominates the growing proletariat and subproletariat in cities no less effectively than it does the masses of peasants and landless laborers in the countryside. A capital-intensive imported technology successfully competes against a labor-intensive indigenous technology.

In their "horizontal", or spatial dimension, dualistic dependency structures find expression in one or, at best, a small number of highly urbanized "core regions" which, in turn, control the development path of regional economies in their periphery.

Dualistic dependency, however, is more than a set of dichotomous relationships in contradiction. It is, as well, a particular mode of integrating a national economy into the system of world capitalism (Wallerstein, 1974). The vertical components of corporate production, urban elites, and capital-intensive technology are, for the most part, concentrated in the core areas of their respective countries. These areas fulfill a double role, however. On the one hand, they function as nodal points in the periphery of the world capitalist system; on the other hand, they dominate (and exploit) their own peripheries in much the same way as they, in turn, are dominated (and exploited) by the world core regions of Western Europe, the northeastern part of the United States, and central Japan.

The emergence of dualistic dependency structures has had profound consequences for national development. Space does not allow for a careful tracing through of causal effects, but the major trends may be noted.

1.1.1. *Hyperurbanization and rural densities.* The concept of hyper-urbanization refers to the concentration of populations in dense urban settlements at a rate that, except on a basis of inequality and exploitation, renders their integration into the emerging social order impossible. The resulting "crisis of inclusion" forces governments to adopt policies that either undermine the basic premises of Strategy I by shifting resources to pacify social demands or lead to political repression.

In an earlier study, Friedmann suggested a doubling period for urban population growth of less than 20 years as a more or less arbitrary standard for identifying the existence of hyperurbanization (Friedmann, 1973b). Translated into rates of growth, this is equivalent to a decennial increase in urban population of at least 41 percent. The actual rates for our sample of six countries are shown in Table 1.

TABLE 1
Total population and urban growth, six Asian countries, 1960 - 70

| | Change, 1960 - 70 | | | per cent |
	Total population	Urban population	(2) ÷ (1)	Urban
	(1)	(2)	(3)	(4)
India	26	41	1.58	20 (1973)
Thailand	37	62	1.68	15 (1970)
Philippines	34	59	1.74	32 (1970)
West Malaysia	36	72	2.00	17 (1970)
Indonesia (Java)	23	52	2.26	18 (1971)
Republic of Korea	29	74	2.55	56 (1973)

Sources: Cols. (1) and (4) from respective government official statistics. Col. (2) from *UN Statistical Yearbook for Asia and the Far East*, 1972, Table 20. Among countries, the measure of "urban" is not strictly comparable.

Several conclusions may be drawn from these data. First, all countries had doubling rates equal to or in excess of the 20-year threshold of hyper-urbanization. Second, urban growth in every country was greater than the growth of total population, reflecting large-scale rural - urban migration (Intermet, 1973). Third, the populations in the six countries were still predominantly rural at the end of the decade.[2] The high level of urbanization in Korea may be more apparent than real; labor statistics show that 55 percent of the work force in 1970 was agricultural (United Nations, 1974).

A corollary of these conclusions may be stated at this juncture: between 1960 and 1970 *the bulk of the population increase had to be absorbed in rural areas* (Table 2). This was especially true for India, Indonesia, and Thailand where around two-thirds of the demographic increase was so accommodated. In India, at least, this densification of rural population led to an eight percent decline in physical productivity per male worker (Hayami and Ruttan, 1971, table 4-2). Unless a major policy reversal occurs, rural densities will continue to rise throughout the region with results for labor productivity that are at best uncertain (United Nations, 1973c).

1.1.2. *Spatial concentration of population and "modern" activity.* Planners typically reside in cities. They therefore tend to see a country's development through the distorting prism of city life. But the fact is that what passes for "modern" development is highly concentrated in only a few urban centers, while the rest of the country is relatively isolated from the social and economic changes that so preoccupy the planners' attention.

To illustrate: the top four cities in five out of the six countries accounted for between

---

[2]The definition of "urban" finds little consistency from nation to nation. The Korean definition exaggerates urban population size by using township boundaries which are much broader than actual built-up areas. Over 50 percent of the population in the smaller "cities" is in agricultural employment (United Nations, 1973a). A definition, such as the one adopted in India, which requires both a minimum density and specified non-agricultural employment levels, seems most appropriate under current conditions of urbanization in Asia. For a full discussion of the problem of urban definitions in Asia, see Bose (1971).

TABLE 2

Population absorption in rural areas and increases in rural
population densities, 1960 - 70

	Rural population absorption[a] (%)	Rural population densities[c]		
		1960	1970	1960 - 70
		(per hectare)		(%)
Thailand	76	2.04	2.70	32.3
India	75	2.32	2.71	16.8
Indonesia (Java)	70[b]	5.83	7.27	24.7
West Malaysia	62[b]	n.a.	1.80	n.a.
Philippines	55	2.49	2.81	12.9
Republic of Korea	30	7.78	8.52	9.6

[a]*UN Statistical Yearbook for Asia and the Far East,* 1972, Table 20.
[b]From official government publications.
[c]India, Republic of Korea: *UN Statistical Yearbook,* 1972. Indonesia:
Tjondronegoro, 1972, p. 2. W. Malaysia: UN, 1973d, table 39. Philippines: ILO, UNDP, 1973. Thailand: Government of Thailand, *Population Growth in Thailand,* 1972.

one-third and two-thirds of total urban population in 1970. Moreover, there was a pronounced tendency for larger cities to grow more rapidly than smaller ones, and for the
degree of urban primacy to increase over the preceding decade. By 1970, the largest city in
four out of the six countries was between 1.2 and 9.0 times the size of the next three largest
cities (Table 3).

TABLE 3

Urban primacy and urban population changes by city size, 1960 - 70

	Proportion of urban population in four largest cities, 1970 (%)	Urban population increase, 1960 - 70		Four city primacy index	
		<100,000 (%)	>100,000 (%)	1960	1970
Republic of Korea	63	5.0	6.2	1.09	1.45
Philippines	56	3.4	4.7	4.27	4.56
Thailand	61	3.5	5.2	n.a.	9.00[a]
Indonesia	39	3.4	4.7	1.13	1.20
West Malaysia	31	5.1	7.5	n.a.	0.93
India	18	2.2	3.5	0.72	0.68

Source: Davis, 1969, table G.
[a]Davis's index was changed by combining the adjacent cities of Bangkok and Thonburi.

Data pertaining to the spatial distribution of manufacturing are not readily available.
Korean experience, however, may be illustrative of the more general case. As one proceeds from all manufacturing to the elite industries of the corporate sector, the concentration in the primate city increases in steady progression. In 1968, 81 percent of corporate
employment was located in Seoul (Table 4).

1.1.3. *Unemployment and underemployment.* Policies under Strategy I aim at accelerating
investment and production in the corporate sector of cities—particularly in large-scale

manufacturing and supporting infrastructure and services—as well as at expanding commercial agriculture. What consequences has this strategy had for employment?

In the preceding sections we have shown how Strategy I promoted the rapid transfer of rural people to cities; nevertheless, a large proportion of the population had to be "absorbed" in agriculture, contributing to a sharp rise in rural densities.

The urban economy, however, was by no means ready to provide full, productive employment to everyone. A significant part of the labor force remained unemployed. Oshima (1971), for example, estimates the general level of open unemployment in Asian cities at 10 percent, and the ratio of unemployed has been projected to rise to within 15 percent by 1980 (United Nations, 1973a). Individual cities have already reached or exceeded that level.

TABLE 4
Republic of Korea: concentration of manufacturing employment in Seoul, 1968 (percent)

Total population	Total manufacturing establishments	Total manufacturing workers	Total "regularly" employed	Total corporations	Total corporate employees
14	25	35	37	57	81

Source: *Korea Statistical Yearbook,* 1972, p. 173.

These are orders of magnitude only; precise measurements of open unemployment do not exist and, in any event, are greatly dependent on the formal definitions used. In Korea, for example, a person is counted as employed even if he or she worked only one hour per week.

The concept of underemployment is widely used in conjunction with open unemployment to provide a more complete picture of how labor is actually being used in the project of national construction. But the reliability of figures here is no greater than in the case of unemployment. Table 5 is an attempt to overcome some of these difficulties and to suggest the consequences of Strategy I for the employment structure of five Asian countries. Studying this table, we note:

(1) The dominant role which agriculture still plays as a labor-absorbing sector of the economy and the correspondingly small contribution of manufacturing to total employment.

(2) The large proportion of wage employment in agriculture, reflecting the high ratio of landless laborers in all countries, excepting Thailand and Korea.[3] Yet rural wages are typically only a fraction of what comparable wage levels are in cities.

(3) The large share of manufacturing employment accounted for by the non-wage sector, most of which represents employment in individual and small-scale family enterprises.

(4) The size of the trades and services sector which, in some cases, is beginning to rival agriculture as a source of employment (Malaysia, Korea).

(5) The exceptionally large proportion of the trades and services sector which is represented by non-wage employment and which, together with the non-wage sector of manufacturing, constitutes the so-called informal sector of the urban economy.

[3] In Indonesia and India, landless laborers account for 30 percent of the agricultural worker force (IBRD, 1970).

TABLE 5
Agricultural and non-agricultural employment, by wage and non-wage sectors (percent)

	India 1971[b]	Indonesia 1971	West Malaysia 1967	Thailand 1970	Republic of Korea 1972
Agriculture					
Wage	49	23	44	4	14
Non-wage[a]	51	77	56	96	86
Percent agriculture of					
total employment	71	62	50	75	49
Non-agriculture					
A. Manufacturing					
Wage	19	12	15	18	21
Non-wage	19	9	8	6	9
Manufacturing as					
percent of total					
employment	10	7	3	4	13
B. Trades and services					
Wage	39	39	52	47	42
Non-wage	23	40	25	29	28
Trades and services					
as percent of total					
employment	16	26	31	13	30
Total non-agriculture					
(A + B)[c]					
Wage	58	51	67	65	63
Non-wage	42	49	33	35	37

Source: ILO, *Labour Statistics Yearbook,* 1974.
[a]"Non-wage" includes self-employed and family workers.
[b]Data are subject to extreme bias in that 70 percent of the labor force was "status unknown"
and could not be included in the calculations.
[c]Mining and construction are not included.

In general, non-wage employment displays a level of productivity (reflected in remuneration) which is very much lower than that in the wage economy as a whole. This may be illustrated with data from the Philippines where small manufacturing enterprises (much of whose employment was unpaid family labor) not only declined under the "involutionary" pressures of growth in the labor force (McGee, 1974), but was only three percent of the productivity in the corporate sector of manufacturing (Table 6). This would seem to be the rule rather than the exception, and Friedmann and Sullivan (1974) have argued that consumption levels in the informal sector of the urban economy (including the unemployed) tend, as a result of poverty-sharing among kin and fictive kin, to be reduced to mere subsistence. This appears inevitable under conditions where the rise in output from manufacturing is from two to four times the rate of increase in manufacturing employment (de Haan, 1974).

Government responses to the employment problem are themselves caught up in the contradictions of Strategy I. The recent shift from import-substitution to a greater emphasis on manufactured exports has led to a number of serious problems that had not been anticipated.

(a) Employment in many of the new industries responds violently to even small changes in external demand. In Malaysia, for example, saw mills began working at half shift in

1974, and loggers in Sabah and the East Coast of the Peninsula had to cut their labor force by 19,000 workers over 1973 (Malaysia, 1975). The same effect was felt by labor-intensive industries, such as textiles, throughout the Asian region.

Estate agriculture, which is a primary source of wage employment in rural areas, suffers a similar fate. During 1974 depressed auto sales in the United States translated into a steep decline in the demand for rubber, one of the major export commodities of Thailand, Malaysia, and Indonesia.

(b) Productivity increases under Strategy I are being achieved at the expense of employment. As an extreme example, rubber production in Malaysia rose by nearly 50 percent during the 1960s, *but employment dropped by 10 percent.* Rather than upgrading skill levels on a national scale, governments imported modern machinery and new technologies in agriculture that displaced both current and future members of the labor force toward low-income occupations in the informal sector (United Nations, 1973a).

(c) National plans tend rather simplistically to tie employment creation to GNP growth rates despite the lack of consistent empirical support for such association (United Nations, 1973a; Ariff, 1973; India, 1972; Malaysia, 1973). The fallacy becomes evident when it is seen that the only sector growing significantly more than the labor force is manufacturing which employs only a small proportion of worker and displays a strong tendency for productivity to outpace employment.[4]

TABLE 6
Employment and productivity in informally organized and corporate
manufacturing sectors, Philippines, 1956 and 1966

	Informally organized sector (less than five workers)		Corporate sector (twenty or more workers)	
	Labor force in manufacturing (%)	Productivity per worker (1955 pesos)	Labor force in manufacturing (%)	Productivity per worker (1955 pesos)
1956	79	485	15	6135
1966	73	247	22	7246

Source: Government of Philippines, *Annual Survey of Manufactures and Statistical Reporter* and *BCHHS Labor Force Survey,* as reported by Bautista, 1974, tables 1 and 2.

To summarize: Strategy I was reasonably effective in raising GNP (see Table 10); it failed in expanding economic opportunities at a rate sufficient for a rapidly growing population. Rural areas suffered the most from policy neglect, from densification, from expansion of the corporate sector, and from massive income transfers to urban areas. The latter performed little better in providing means of livelihood. The majority of workers came to be absorbed into low-level trades and services. At the same time, open unemployment was gaining, and underemployment came to affect as many as 40 percent of the existing work force. As a result of what McGee (1971, 1974) calls involution, productivity in the small-scale, informal sector of the urban economy declined.

---

[4]Thus Malaysia uses an annual manufacturing growth rate projection of 12.3 percent over the next 20 years. This, in turn, predicts a manufacturing employment growth rate of 7.5 percent, but the low base level of manufacturing elasticity, implying no increases in labor productivity, renders the projected relationship exceedingly doubtful.

1.1.4. *Income inequality and poverty.* It is symptomatic of Strategy I that inequalities in levels of living and actual poverty conditions are measured in monetary income. If we accept this standard, rather than more appropriate physical measures, it comes as no surprise when we find that existing incomes in the six countries are highly unequally distributed.

Social increases in income disparity are generally displayed in terms of a decrease in the percentage of income received by the rural poor who make up the vast majority of those in poverty (Adelman, 1975). In both the Philippines and Thailand the income position of this group deteriorated during the 1960s, although for poverty groups in urban areas the trend seems to be reversed (Table 7).[5]

TABLE 7
Income distribution in India, West Malaysia, the Philippines, and Thailand

A. India (mid-sixties)
    Lowest 40 percent of population—20 percent of income
    Middle 40 percent of population—38 percent of income
    Highest 20 percent of population—42 percent of income
B. West Malaysia (1970)
    Lowest 20 percent of population—4 percent of income
    Middle 60 percent of population—41 percent of income
    Highest 20 percent of population—55 percent of income
    Gini coefficient—0.499
C. Philippines

	Percent of income					
	Total		Rural		Urban	
	1961	1971	1961	1971	1961	1971
Lowest 20 percent of population	4.2	3.8	5.9	4.4	3.8	4.6
Next 20 percent of population	7.9	8.1	11.8	8.9	7.5	9.4
Next 20 percent of population	12.1	13.2	13.5	13.9	12.5	13.4
Next 20 percent of population	19.3	21.1	21.9	21.8	19.5	21.9
Highest 20 percent of population	56.4	53.9	46.9	51.0	57.1	50.7
Gini coefficient	0.50	0.49	0.40	0.46	0.52	0.45

D. Thailand

	Percent of income			
	Rural		Urban	
	1962	1970	1962	1970
Lowest 20 percent of population	6.0	5.5	3.5	6.5
Next 20 percent of population	9.0	8.5	9.5	10.5
Next 20 percent of population	13.5	14.0	14.5	15.0
Next 20 percent of population	20.5	21.0	22.5	22.5
Highest 20 percent of population	51.0	51.0	50.0	45.5
Gini coefficient	0.50[a]			

Sources: India (1972), Malaysia (1975), Marzouk (for Thailand) (1972), ILO (1974).
[a]Oshima (1970).

Income statistics do not support the hypothesis that the rich are getting richer. But such a conclusion must be treated with caution. The incomes of the wealthy are suspect of being

[5]In India the official poverty level of 40.6 rupees per month (in 1972 prices) yields a forecast that about 30 per cent of the population will be living in poverty at the end of the current planning period (1986). But this projection does not take inflation into account (India, 1972).

grossly underreported and, in any event, do not reflect accumulations of wealth (see Table 12). In India, for example, 70 percent of personal wealth in cities is held in the form of residential property, and 80 percent of urban property may be held by as few as 5 percent of the people (United Nations, 1974).

With these qualifications in mind, it is revealing that close to half the incomes in countries for which data are available flows into the hands of the richest 20 percent of the population and that, at least in Malaysia and the Philippines, *the top 10 percent of the population receive as much as 40 percent of all incomes!* (The concentration of incomes for the same decile in Thailand, on the other hand, is reported to be "only" 29 percent for urban and 35 percent for rural populations. See Kerdpibule, 1975.)

Spatial comparisons of income distribution show more marked disparities. In every documented case, *rural incomes declined relative to urban incomes* (Table 8). Furthermore, except for the Republic of Korea, rural incomes are only a fraction of urban income levels. In Malaysia, for example, rural people receive only one-third of the income of urban residents, and 87 percent of the poverty households in the country are reported to be in rural areas—a ratio that is significantly higher than the proportion of the rural population in the country as a whole (Malaysia, 1975). In India, rural poverty increased dramatically during the sixties. In Korea, *per capita* income for Seoul was twice the national average in 1968 (Republic of Korea, 1972). And Indonesian data similarly reveal enormous rural-urban income disparities (Esmara, 1975).

TABLE 8
Rural incomes as a percentage of urban incomes

India	Indonesia	West Malaysia	Philippines	Republic of Korea	Thailand
56.8 (1961)	75.2 (1964)	40.0[b] (1960)	40.0 (1965)	88.1 (1965)	42.5 (1962)
38.9[a] (1970)	62.0 (1967)	33.0[b] (1970)	n.a.	80.2 (1973)	40.7 (1970)

Sources: United Nations, 1973c, table I-9.
For Republic of Korea, calculations are based on Economic Planning Board, *Urban Household Survey Report, 1961 - 73,* and on Ministry of Agriculture and Forestry, *Farm Household Economic Survey Report, 1961 - 73.*
[a]Daily wage rate of agricultural workers as a percentage of daily wage rate of manufacturing workers. This ratio is therefore not strictly comparable to the rural - urban income ratio for 1961.
[b]Gross value per worker in small holder agriculture as a percentage of gross value per worker in the rest of the economy.

Returning briefly to the question of employment, the dualism suggested previously relates directly and most importantly to the distribution of income. The generation of low-productivity work for an increasing number of people, the denial of access to "modern" employment and its commensurate higher wages, and the low returns to agriculture outside the corporate sector, all of which are associated with Strategy I, display themselves in terms of marked income inequalities. The highest incidence of poverty is among the self-employed and landless laborers. In Malaysia, this group constituted 55 percent of those living in poverty (Malaysia, 1975).

1.1.5. *Persistent food shortages.* The almost singular interest of Strategy I in promoting development of the corporate sector has resulted in a substantial neglect of domestic food production. Moreover, the emphasis on exports has led farmers to allocate their labor and land away from food to the production of so-called cash-crops. Although all six nations have repeatedly aimed at self-sufficiency, Thailand is the only country in Asia which is still able to meet its own requirements for rice (between 1968 and 1970, Thailand's ratio of production to food imports was 119 percent compared to a low of 68 percent for West Malaysia. Cf. Table 9). During the 1960s *per capita* food production declined in both India and Indonesia, remained stable in the Philippines, and increased in the remaining countries. Four out of the six countries are obliged to spend large sums for the importation of basic foods: for the period 1969 - 71, India and Malaysia led with 21 percent of their total import bill, followed by Korea (16 percent) and Indonesia (13 percent). In more recent years, these percentages have risen still further (Table 9).

Statistical measures of food shortages obscure the widespread prevalence of malnutrition and hunger. Although each nation claims close to a sufficiency in grain supplies, inclusive of imports, undernourishment is reported in many regions (most strikingly in India) and, according to an estimate for 1966, at least one-fifth of the population in poor countries was calorie-deficient, while about one-third suffered from a lack of protein (United Nations, 1973b).[6] Of critical concern, then, are both supply and distribution.

Dealing first with supply, Asia will have to increase cereal production by 40 percent during the present decade simply to maintain current (and mostly insufficient) consumption levels (United Nations, 1973b). Given that arable land is relatively fixed, and that Strategy I is reluctant to convert land in cash crops to cereal production, much faith has been put into the new technologies of the Green Revolution.[7]

The Green Revolution brings the issue of supply and distribution together and illustrates the contradictions inherent in current structural relationships. Three points summarize the effects of adopting the new technologies without changing the patterns of dualistic dependency. First, the Green Revolution has given a temporary respite from, but has not ended, endemic food shortages (United Nations, 1973b). Second, increased output can result in loss of income to those farmers who are institutionally denied access to the new techniques for increasing production on their land (Dorner, 1972). Third, the net effect is that, over the long run, the Green Revolution may fail to keep pace with increasing demand and, over the short run, will serve to benefit only the relatively few farmers who have sufficiently large land holdings and resources to take advantage of the new technologies.[8] The FAO has concluded darkly that rural poverty for small farmers, sharecroppers, and landless laborers, i.e., for the majority of people in Asia, excluding China, is likely to increase. The portent is one of increased malnutrition and hunger in both relative and absolute terms (United Nations, 1973b).

---

[6]Using a *per capita* nutritional adequacy standard of 2250 calories, 40 percent of rural and 50 percent of urban populations were receiving less than satisfactory nutrition in India in 1971 (Dandekar and Rath, 1971). In Indonesia over one-half of the rural families are short on calorie and protein intake (*Far Eastern Economic Review,* Sept. 5, 1975).

[7]The question of arable land is a complex one, involving such issues as the availability of water for irrigation, resettlement, and long-distance migration. For Korea and Java the physical limit of crop land appears to have been reached already. Elsewhere, there exists at least a theoretical possibility for expanding agricultural land.

[8]It is a matter of dispute whether the Green Revolution has actually pushed small and poor farmers off their land and into the cities. In any event, the Green Revolution introduces capitalist practices into a traditional rural economy and thus encourages the formation of rural wage labor.

TABLE 9
Food production and supply

		India	Indonesia	West Malaysia	Philippines	Republic of Korea	Thailand
Agricultural productivity indices[a] (1963 = 100)	Total	109	114	130	106	122	111
	1968	118	128	150	118	139	123
	1970						
	Food	110	116	124	115	120	115
	1968	121	128	142	127	136	127
	1970						
Annual growth rate[b]	Agric. Food	2.2	2.1	5.7	3.2	4.5	5.2
	1960 - 70						
	Food	2.2	2.2	5.5	3.2	4.0	5.2
	1960 - 70						
	Food *per capita*	-0.2	-0.3	2.4	0.0	1.3	2.5
	1960 - 70						
Percentage change in *per capita* food production from previous year[b]	1968	4.1	6.7	4.9	-3.1	-4.2	4.1
	1969	1.0	-2.1	5.5	7.5	12.2	4.8
	1970	2.9	5.3	3.7	-2.0	-3.1	0.8
	1971	-	1.0	5.7	1.0	-	0.8
Ratio of production to food imports[c]	1968 - 70	96	94	64	94	78	119
US $ *per capita* food imports[c]	1969 - 71	0.8	0.9	18.5	1.5	10.3	1.5
Food as percentage of total imports	1969 - 71	21	13	21	4	16	4
Grain imports in 1974 as percentage of total imports, 1970 - 72[d]		28	n.a.	n.a.	13	25	n.a.

[a]United Nations, *Statistical Yearbook for Asia and the Far East, 1972.*
[b]FAO, *A Review of Agricultural Development in the ECAFE Region in 1971,* Tables 2, 4, and 5.
[c]United Nations, *World Economic Survey, 1973,* tables 39 - 41.
[d]*OECD Observer,* 74, March - April, 1975.

1.1.6. *Deteriorating material conditions of farm population.* The decline of rural (relative to urban) incomes has already been noted (Table 8). But this is not the only source of impoverization which the faithful pursuit of Strategy I has imposed on rural people. Another, and far more serious consequence of dualistic dependency, is the adverse terms of trade that peasant farmers have to accept in their dealings with metropolitan economies. Data supporting this proposition are unavailable for the six countries, but theoretical grounds for accepting it are strong and deserve to be explored.

The argument can be divided into two parts. According to the first, inflationary pressures are generated in core regions and are then "exported" to the rural periphery. As a result, the prices of commodities bought by farmers, such as farm implements, irrigation pumps, fertilizers, insecticides, textiles, shoes, bicycles, etc., are tending to rise faster than the prices they receive for their own produce. The second line of reasoning suggests that the price of agricultural staples (primarily rice) is frequently "stabilized" by governments to the advantage of the growing masses of urban workers whose interests are more "visible" to politicians than those of a peasantry that is not only physically remote but is also less readily mobilized for political ends (hence, their characterization as "peripheral and dependent"). With steadily rising prices for manufactured products and the relatively stable prices received by farmers, the "terms of trade" of at least the food-producing sector will obviously be adverse and declining. This is especially true at a time when world commodity prices (and the prices of essential raw materials that have to be imported, such as oil) are advancing at annual rates greater than 10 percent.

More generally, it can be claimed that the material conditions of the poor are nowhere in the world greatly improving. Under conditions of dualistic dependency, they may, in fact, deteriorate.

As we have already noted, poverty in Asia is most pervasive in rural areas. To come to grips with this phenomenon, the term "peasant farmer" must be subjected to a series of refinements. For example, cash-crop farming must be separated from food production; estate farming (which, in Malaysia, is 60 percent foreign-controlled) must be separated from non-corporate types of farming; tenants and owners must be compared; and farm sizes must be assigned to their relevant population size groups. In other words, terms of trade for a land-holding elite must be distinguished from those for the majority of peasant farmers. Some examples will help to illustrate this point.

Given present rural densities (see Table 2), average farm sizes in the six countries are not only small but getting smaller. On Java, for instance, farms are scarcely more than garden plots, or half a hectare in size (50 by 50 m); the situation is only slightly better in Thailand, where the typical farm measures 3.5 hectares. Other countries fall between these two extremes (see Table 12). As for tenancy relations, their incidence in Asian countries is extremely high and rising. Over a period of only six years, for example, tenancy rates in Thailand increased from 29 percent in 1963 to 40 percent in 1969 (Baldwin, 1974). And tenant farmers are typically obliged to pay from one-third to one-half their crop value to owners (Horii, 1972; Marzouk, 1972).

Neither the declining size of farm holdings nor the increases in tenure (and consequently absentee landlordism which underlies the process of income transfer from the periphery to the core) are conducive to rural savings and to their eventual reinvestment in land and farm technology. Average-size holdings in Thailand and Malaysia actually showed dissavings in recent years. For all these reasons, then, many farmers in Asia are too poor to join the Green Revolution.

1.1.7. *External dependency.* Countries pursuing a strategy that succeeds only in saturating domestic markets, which pay for this "development" primarily through exports and which enlarge their corporate sector through the importation of foreign capital, become increasingly dependent upon their presumptive benefactor. They gravitate in the outer periphery of an economic system that is dominated by the advanced industrial nations of world capitalism.

Poor and dependent, they supply essential raw materials to these nations, provide an opportunity for profit-making investments from abroad, and present a valuable market for core - region exports. In all these ways they help sustain high growth rates in the world economy and, above all, a level of affluence in the industrialized countries that stands in stark contrast to their own poverty.

Dependency relations can take many forms. Among the most important is the dependency of peripheral economies on export markets. Its consequences may be illustrated with the example of Malaysia, 44 percent of whose GNP in 1970 was concentrated in export production (Malaysia, 1975). Between 1960 and 1970, Malaysia's rubber production increased 50 percent; yet a fall in the international price for rubber reduced this otherwise remarkable expansion of physical output to a *negative* growth of 1.5 percent in value added.

Elsewhere the story is similar.[9] Although the international system is able to absorb price fluctuations of single commodities without much notice, such changes can have dramatic effects on subregional economies that specialize in the production of the commodity in question.

The "solution" offered is typically one of diversifying the country's (or the region's) exports. Thus Malaysia adds palm oil to its list of exports to ease the shock of a drop in the price of rubber, and the Philippines emphasizes its "top ten exports" to do the same. But the results of this solution are, at best, ephemeral. At worst, they leave the economy more vulnerable than before.

A policy of "export substitution" may be tried for the same reason. According to present practice the products of light manufacturing—electronics, plastics, textiles, and the like—are aggressively pushed onto international markets. For the most part, however, their number remains small, competitive advantages favor foreign-controlled investments, and dependency on international markets becomes more entrenched.

Dependency mediated through trade relationships, of which export-dependency is a part, will thus have adverse consequences for the peripheral economy. In the most general case it will create and reinforce dualistic structures whose most immediate consequences have already been described:

(a) Hyper-urbanization, which tends to set the direction and emphasis for the nation's development process;

(b) the replication, on a *national* scale, of a worldwide core - periphery structure leading to a growing concentration of population and "modern" economic activities in a small number of metropolitan areas and their immediate surroundings;

(c) formation of national elites, which control a large and growing part of the nation's income and wealth and become coopted by their more powerful international counterparts whose life styles they emulate;

---

[9]Export stagnation in Thailand has been attributed to three external relationships: (1) international price fluctuations, (2) decline in US military spending, and (3) a decline in foreign investments (Thailand, 1972).

(d) rising urban unemployment and underemployment, which in a class perspective takes the form of an impoverished subproletariat that may encompass as much as 40 percent of the urban labor force but which, in an economic perspective, may be seen as a massive reservoir of cheap labor that helps to guarantee, by its mere presence, continuance of the incredibly high living standards that have become a way of life in world core regions (Emmanuel, 1972);

(e) progressive pauperization of the rural masses;

(f) growing food shortages, which deepen dependency relations to world core regions that, at least for the present, are still able to meet these deficits.

When understood in this light, the price that a nation is forced to pay for being externally dependent is, indeed, steep. A vicious cycle is set in motion that, by deepening dependency relations, renders the peripheral economy more vulnerable to exogenous change and reinforces its commitment to Strategy I which appears increasingly as the only path to national salvation. Foreign investments must be encouraged for reasons of becoming competitive in international markets but also because less and less can be squeezed out of a rural sector that is already close to subsistence. Foreign, capital-intensive technology must be imported for the same reason. Both policies tend significantly to raise the bill of imports, a trend which is intensified because of severe and growing shortages of food. The more specialized the economy becomes in the international division of labor, the more it is subject to periodic and violent fluctuations which are met, not with appropriate countervailing measures, but with policies that prescribe more of the same medicine. As inflation is imported, income differences become more pronounced, and the process of pauperization is speeded up.

Finally, political dependency, which follows in the footsteps of economic dependency, appears as almost a natural consequence, a way of life. The policies of peripheral development are being shaped by the interests of world core region elites that have little, if anything, to do with the true interests of the rural populations in whose name they are promulgated. Rising social unrest, which is the ineluctable consequence of contradictions inherent in the world periphery under conditions of dualistic dependency, is met by repression. The growing number of authoritarian regimes and military dictatorships throughout Asia attests to this trend with tragic regularity.

1.2. Dualistic Dependency and the World Economic Transition

The internal contradictions of Strategy I are often accepted with equanimity because, whatever else may follow, the strategy is believed to permit the achievement of high internal rates of growth in production. The empirical basis for this claim is not established unambiguously. But, except for India and Indonesia, our sample of six countries has, in fact, performed reasonably well over the recent period (Table 10).

It would be committing a gross error, however, to assume that Strategy I was, by itself, chiefly responsible for the achievement of high growth rates. During the sixties and early seventies, peripheral countries benefited directly from the benign economic climate that followed World War II and the perverse opportunities created by wars in Korea and Vietnam. World core areas led the way with the sustained expansion of their economies. Demand was high, production costs were low, and West European economies actually experienced a prolonged period of overemployment. During the past several years, however, it has become clear that this era of economic euphoria has come to an end. World capitalism is in the midst of a major transition whose probable repercussions on its periphery cast doubt on the realism of the high growth rates that are still being projected by Asian planners (Table 10).[10] If these "planned" production rates are not, in fact, achieved, the internal contradictions created by dualistic dependency structures will be so intensified as to raise serious questions about the continued viability of Strategy I itself.

TABLE 10

Gross national product and population growth rates since 1960 - 72

	GNP/cap US$ 1972	GNP growth rate			Population growth rate, 1960 - 72	GNP/cap growth rate,	
		1960 - 70[a]	1974[b]	Projected, 1970 - 80[a]		1960 - 72	1965 - 72
India	110	3.8	n.a.	5.5 - 6.5	2.3	1.1	1.4
Indonesia	90	3.3	7.0	n.a.	2.0	2.1	4.3
West Malaysia	430	6.3	6.3	6.5	2.9	3.1	2.9
Philippines	220	5.7	n.a.	6.0 - 7.0	3.0	2.2	2.4
Republic of Korea	310	9.2	8.2[c]	8.0 - 10.0	2.2	6.8	8.5
Thailand	220	7.9	n.a.	8.0 - 8.5	3.1	4.6	4.2

Source: IBRD, *World Bank Atlas,* 1974.

[a]Tabulated from *UN Economic Survey of Asia and the Far East,* 1971, table II-I-2.

[b]From respective government official publications.

[c]*Far Eastern Economic Review,* July 1975, states that the GNP will grow at about 7 percent in 1975, below expected 9 percent.

What we refer to as the world economic transition is reflected in two major tendencies that directly affect the production possibilities and, hence, living conditions, in the world periphery: first, steep increases in world commodity prices, and, second, restricted expansion of export markets. A few pertinent observations are in order.

1.2.1. *Commodity price inflation.* This may be broken down into the major components of petroleum, other raw materials, food, and manufactures (Table 11).

(a) *Petroleum.* Known world reserves of oil are expected to last for only another two to four decades (Mesarovic and Pestel, 1974). In the light of these projections, major national producers have begun to raise the price of petroleum. Because international de-

---

[10]Reasons for doubting current planned GNP growth rates are reflected in the sober thinking of World Bank economists, as shown in the following table:

Income levels, 1970 - 80, for developed and developing countries[a]
(in 1970 $)

	1975 pop. (millions)	GNP *per capita*			Annual rate
		1970	1980	Difference	
1. Low-income countries (Under 200 p.c.)	1000	105	108	3	0.2
2. Middle-income countries (Over $200 p.c.)	725	410	540	130	2.8
3. OECD countries	675	3100	4000	900	2.6

Source: Robert S. McNamara, Address to the Board of Governors, World Bank, September 1, 1975, p. 7.

[a]Excludes centrally planned economies and OPEC. Growth rates assume no increase in international capital flows in real terms.

TABLE 11

Forecast indices of primary and international commodity prices (1973 = 100)

	Petrol	Minerals and metals	Food	Manufactures
1970		80	71	-
1971	60	68	68	-
1972		68	74	-
1973	100	100	100	100
1974	362	140	156	122
1975	387	130	155	133
1980	563	194	177	197
1985	790	289	259	276
1976 - 80[a]	7.5	7.2	4.8	7.5
1980 - 5[b]	7.0	8.3	7.7	7.0

Source: World Bank, *Forecasts of Primary Products,* July 1974. Manufactures were tabulated from World Bank, International Economy Division, Economic Analysis and Projections Department data (April 2, 1975) and includes developed countries' exports of manufactures SITC 5-8 categories (chemicals, manufactured goods classified chiefly by materials, machinery and transport equipment, and miscellaneous manufactured articles).

[a] Average annual percentage change.
[b] Annual rate of growth.

mand for petroleum is relatively inelastic, these increases have come to be directly translated into the trade balances of countries whose economies are dependent on the continued supply of this vital energy source and industrial raw material.

This trend is not likely to be reversed. The IBRD expects the average price of crude oil to jump from $10.46 per barrel at the end of 1973 to twice this amount by the mid-eighties.

Present and prospective oil-producing countries, such as Indonesia, Malaysia, and Thailand, may derive substantial benefit from this situation. But this advantage may be more apparent than real, as higher costs are paid to buy back the same products processed and refined in industrialized nations. Non-producers—among them India, Korea, and the Philippines—have no advantage at all.

Petroleum is an input to general production, from power generation to food processing, fertilizers, insecticides, plastics, petrochemicals, and transportation services. Continuing price inflation of petroleum and its derivatives will thus be diffused throughout the entire domestic economy, raising prices across the board.

(b) *Other raw materials.* Critical raw materials, other than petroleum, can also be expected to undergo dramatic price increases. World Bank estimates for 1985 put the world price index for minerals at nearly three times the level for 1973. A tin exporter, such as Thailand, is likely to see an increase of this magnitude as a gain. But tin-importing countries, e.g., Korea, may find it difficult to compensate for these increases with corresponding export earnings. In general, countries that control a significant share of world markets will be able to raise prices almost at will, though limits may be set by the possibility of synthetic substitutes, on the one hand, and the rate of resource exhaustion, on the other. In any event, resource-poor countries will be faced with import bills that are steadily gaining relative to the value of their exports.[11]

[11] Increases in foreign aid from OPEC, DAC, and communist countries have failed to keep pace with the combination of inflation and import price increases. In the food sector alone, requirements outweigh aid (OECD Observer 74, March - April 1975).

(c) *Food.* The story is similar with respect to staple foods. Recent events and projections reveal the stark magnitude of the crisis. The world is no longer merely a composite of independent units; a world system has come into being which makes American wheat sales to the Soviet Union impact profoundly upon people in areas of persistent food shortage in Asia and elsewhere (Mesarovic and Pestel, 1974). In sum, world food surpluses are being exhausted almost the instant they are produced, leaving nothing for nations suffering from crop failures and other disasters.[12]

The situation will become more severe during the present decade. By 1985 food prices are projected to rise 2.6 times above the level for 1973. This forecast must be evaluated against the persisting and rising food shortages in the six country areas which we have documented in Table 9.

By the middle of the next decade world demand and surplus are expected to come momentarily into balance, after which demand will exceed supply. With growing inequities in distribution, however, and under conditions where demand begins to exceed the available supply on a regular basis, heavy food purchases will only accentuate the division between poor and rich.[13]

(d) *Manufactures.* Finally, there is the expected long-term price inflation for manufactured commodities. This may be attributed to rising fuel and raw material costs no less than to wage pressures generated by worldwide, secular inflation. What is likely to happen, however, is that export commodities from poor, peripheral economies will increase less in price than the products they must import, with the losses being absorbed by indigenous workers who are not only less well organized than their counterparts in world core regions but are also available in practically unlimited quantities. The terms of trade of developing countries have taken a sharp downward turn. During 1974 the prices of their imports rose by 40 percent, but their export prices increased only 27 percent. This year (1975), inflation is expected to add at least another 6 percent to the cost of their imports, but very little to the price of their exports (McNamara, 1975).[14]

1.2.2. *Restricted market expansion.* The world economic transition is changing as well the prospects for manufactured exports from the periphery. The sustained growth rates of the past two decades are no more. Growing unemployment, rising commodity prices, problems of environmental pollution, and impending zero population growth all contribute to a slowdown in the already industrialized countries. Pressure from organized labor in these countries, as well as a general trend towards self-sufficiency in large economic "blocks" such as the United States and western Europe, are beginning to lead to a reassessment of the time-honored free trade doctrine of economic liberalism. In many cases, this will preclude the underselling of domestic products by equivalent imports from the periphery, whose major selling point is its ability to absorb tariff increases in the form of lower wages. The limit here, of course, is bare subsistence, or about US$1.00 per day.

---

[12]In cognizance of this problem, the United States recently proposed a comprehensive international cooperative approach to providing food security by establishing an international system of nationally held grain reserves. See speech by the US Secretary of State to the United Nations, September 1, 1975.

[13]One permutation of coupling contradictions was seen in 1972 when natural calamities in Indonesia and the Philippines increased demand for Thai rice. Prices in Thailand began to rise, leading the government to reimpose a rice premium which had previously been blamed for lowering production levels (United Nations, 1973c).

[14]A concrete example from one of our six countries may help to emphasize this point. During 1973 and 1974, Korea's terms of trade deteriorated drastically. The unit price of imports rose by 116 percent while that of exports rose by only 57 percent. As a result, the terms of trade declined by 24 percent over 1972. The single largest reason for this increase in the price of imports may be attributed to the change in oil prices.

This evolving situation has the further and vicious consequence of putting poor countries in direct conflict with each other as each tries desperately to outbid the others in essentially the same range of manufactured commodities, attempting to gain a tiny foothold in
world export markets. Constant product innovation on the Japanese model would, in
principle, be able to counteract this steady movement towards the restriction of export
markets. The only other area of "opportunity" would be in heavily polluting industries
that, foreclosed from further expansion in the industrial centers of the West and in Japan,
may seek a more "receptive" climate in the poor countries of the world periphery.

1.3. Conclusion

In the light of these trends, continued adherence to Strategy I may become untenable.
If this strategy created glaring social contradictions during the relatively "friendly" sixties,
when growth rates in excess of 5 percent were not unusual, the contradictions will be intensified to the point of general crisis if a mere 5 percent growth rate should become no longer
the rule but the exception.[15]

Rising import prices, declining export markets, and deteriorating terms of trade combine to make Strategy I inoperative as a guide to the future. We can look forward to a
period when starvation will become general and endemic; when subsistence and below-
subsistence survival in the countryside will no longer be overshadowed by relatively better
living conditions in the city; when, even there in the metropolis, the economic environment starts to deteriorate.

For all these reasons, then, a case can be made for a thorough-going reassessment of
national development strategies. The following policy elements would seem to be included
on the agenda:

(1) *Limited and specific human needs should replace unlimited, generalized wants as
    the fundamental criterion of successful national development.* The old GNP stan-
    dard, based on the idea that a sustained and rapid growth in income and production
    is the appropriate measure of development, would thus give way to new forms of
    social accounting that take as their starting point *guaranteed national minimum
    standards* across a wide spectrum of biological, familial, and communal needs.
    Although GNP accounts would be retained, they would require revision—to reflect
    the social costs of production; refinement—to reflect the social valuation of speci-
    fic production sectors (one dollar's worth of food does not equal one dollar's worth
    of automobile); and expansion—to reflect the costs of production in terms of scarce
    energy units. Revised GNP accounts would be supplemented by social indicators
    showing progress made towards the attainment of specific national minima, such
    as protein intake and access to sanitary water supply.

(2) *Agriculture should be regarded as a leading or "propulsive" sector of the economy.*
    The social efficiency of investments in agriculture is thus assumed to be high (parti-
    cularly with regard to the productivity of land) and capable of generating signifi-
    cant multipliers in agro-industries, commerce, transportation, and construction.

(3) *Attaining self-sufficiency in domestic food production should be regarded as a
    high priority objective.* An adequate supply of domestically produced food is a
    basic condition for meaningful participation in the world economy. Participation

---

[15]According to rough estimates by de Haan (1974) for the present decade, sustained annual growth rates of
9 ± 1 in GDP would be required fully to absorb into non-agricultural occupations the net increase of labor force.
Failure to achieve such growth rates would imply both increased rural densities (and growing poverty) and
increased absorption into the individual and unemployed sectors of the economy of Asian cities.

would be on a highly selective basis, however, and guided by national requirements.

(4) *Existing inequalities in income and living conditions between social classes and between urban and rural areas should be reduced.* The problem of distribution should not, however, be separated, either conceptually or in practice, from that of growth. Regional policy should be seen, not so much in terms of reducing disparities but of increasing generative growth through a full development of natural resources and human skills (Richardson, 1973, pp. 86 - 88). A concept of dynamic efficiency (Leibenstein, 1966), would replace the traditional criterion of allocative efficiency in capital allocation.

(5) *Facilitative measures to increase production of wage goods for domestic consumption should be given high priority.* This will become possible to the extent that agricultural and, more generally, rural incomes are improved. A national policy of encouraging the wage - goods sector, emphasizing small-scale production and labor-intensive methods, should help materially in the decentralization of manufacturing processes and in experimenting with new organizational settings.

(6) *A policy of planned industrial dualism should be adopted whereby small-scale production for the domestic market is protected against competition from large-scale capital intensive enterprise.* The latter should be oriented primarily to export and/or to the production of basic materials and intermediate products. At the same time, the small-scale industry might be linked to corporate production through expanded systems of subcontracting.

We shall call a strategy which incorporates these elements a *strategy of accelerated rural development* or, in abbreviated form, Strategy II.

2. TOWARDS A SPATIAL POLICY OF AGROPOLITAN DEVELOPMENT

2.1. Criteria for Spatial Development Policy

Just as growth center policies correspond to Strategy I (Hansen, 1975), so a strategy of accelerated rural development (Strategy II) requires an appropriate spatial framework for planning and development (Friedmann, 1975). This must be designed to be suitable under Asian condit.ons, including the prevailing low levels of urbanization (less than 20 percent), the high and steadily rising levels of rural density (in excess of 200 per km²), a settlement pattern of clustered villages and towns, and conditions of extreme poverty and physical deprivation.

Commitment to Strategy II will confront policy planners with a series of practical problems that must be resolved if the strategy is to be made operational: how to engage in the development process the millions of rural households dispersed throughout the countryside, each a residential and production unit simultaneously; how to coordinate "sectoral" development in rural areas to achieve the broad purposes of the strategy; how to define, as a basis for accelerated rural development, spatial units larger than a single village; and how to organize on a territorial basis the new planning and development functions. A spatial policies framework for Strategy II will have to respond to these questions. In addition, it will have to be made consistent with a series of criteria that translate Strategy II into programs for implementation. Since none of the six countries under study have as yet committed themselves to the strategy of accelerated rural development, policy criteria will have to be invented in a vacuum of relevant experience.[16] Eventually, they will have to be refined in practice.

What would a strategy of accelerated rural development hope to achieve? This is simply another way of asking how we may determine its success or failure. The following statements are a first attempt to translate the idea of Strategy II into operational language.

(1) To transform the countryside by introducing and adapting elements of urbanism to specific rural settings. This means: instead of encouraging the drift of rural people to cities by investing in cities, encouraging them to remain where they are by investing in rural districts, and so transmute existing settlements into a hybrid form we call *agropolis* or city-in-the-fields.[17] In agropolitan development the age-old conflict between town and countryside can be transcended (Stuckey, 1975).[18]

(2) To extend the network of social interaction in rural areas beyond the single village, creating a larger socioeconomic and political space or *agropolitan district*. (Agropolitan districts can also be adapted to become the basic settlement units for large cities or metrocenters, especially along their growing edge.)

(3) To reduce social dislocation in the course of development, preserving the integrity of the family, strengthening psychological security, and providing for both individual and social fulfillment in the construction of a new order of community.

(4) To stabilize both rural and urban incomes and to reduce differences between them by diversifying opportunities for productive work and, more specifically, by joining agricultural to non-agricultural activities within the same territorial community.

(5) To use available labor more effectively by directing it towards a greatly intensified development of the natural resource base of each agropolitan district, including improvements in agricultural production, major conservation and water control projects, rural public works, expanded rural services, and agriculturally oriented industries.[19]

(6) To link agropolitan districts into regional networks by building up and improving physical channels of communication among agropolitan districts and to larger towns, and by regionalizing certain higher-order services and support activities that require a larger population base than is available within a single district.[20]

[16]There is, of course, the overwhelming example of China's successful rural development effort (Gurley, 1975).

[17]An evocative image of agropolis is found in a Sung Dynasty painting reproduced in Mumford (1961), plate 64.

[18]This is not as crazy as it sounds. Under a capitalist framework, it has already been achieved in countries such as Switzerland and Germany, where the contrast between rural and urban has virtually disappeared. Rural, or rather "agropolitan" life there has become simply another "life style".

[19]Location economists have long argued the case for agglomeration economies. But not a single study exists which has succeeded in measuring them (Richardson, 1973). Actual locations, particularly in Germany, seem to belie the theoretical speculations of economists. Thousands of small- and medium-scale industries in Germany are scattered throughout rural areas even at a considerable distance from larger cities. But even if significant agglomeration economies existed for certain industries, they would be measured only in terms of their returns to private capital. A social cost-accounting might show a very different result.

[20]In line with an explicit policy of industrial dualism (see p. 182), Strategy II would be complemented by a policy of selective industrialization primarily for export and for basic materials supportive of Strategy II. The character of these industries, most of them of highly sophisticated and advanced design in line with international standards, is such that they frequently gain in productive efficiency by locating in close proximity to one another, forming industrial complexes or "growth poles". These "poles" would constitute regional enclave economies at major ports or in other suitable locations and would not necessarily be spatially integrated with agropolitan development. As a result of secondary urbanization effects, however, they would be expected to exert some influence on surrounding populated regions by providing both income and employment opportunities. For a detailed analysis of the regional effects of such a complex, see Kim (1975).

184　　　　JOHN FRIEDMANN AND MIKE DOUGLASS

(7) To devise a system of governance and planning that is ecologically specific and gives substantial control over development priorities and program implementation to district populations. What is envisioned here is a system of governance in which effective power for decisions is devolved to agropolitan districts to enable them to take advantage of ecological opportunities where they exist (while being mindful of ecological constraints), to harness the richly personal, embodied learning of local inhabitants to the more formal, abstract knowledge of specialists and others experienced in agropolitan development, and to encourage a growing sense of identification of local people with the enlarged communal space of the agropolis.

(8) To provide adequate financing for agropolitan development by (a) ensuring the reinvestment of a large part of local savings in the district, (b) instituting a system of work-in-lieu-of-taxes for every adult member of the community,[21] (c) transferring development funds from metrocenters and specialized industrial areas to agropolitan development, and (d) reversing the adverse terms of trade between peasantry and city populations.[22]

2.2. The Agropolitan District

The concept of an agropolitan district may now be given greater substance. Like the traditional city, it corresponds to a certain size/density function, to the presence of services and conveniences that are appropriate at this scale and adjusted to prevailing levels of cultural and economic development, to the existence of substantial off-farm employment, and to the principle of self-governance.[23] In this sense, then, agropolitan districts may truly be called cities-in-the-fields whose population would place them in the middle range of a national size-distribution of cities.

---

[21]Work-in-lieu-of-taxes may be regarded as a major source of capital formation under Strategy II as well as a form of building personal commitments to the tasks of national development. The basic concept is, in fact, quite simple, even though its execution will present considerable practical problems that will have to be worked out. Every ablebodied adult, from the Prime Minister on down to the lowliest street sweeper, would be liable for a fixed number of hours each year devoted to "service in national development". Time would be credited to public works projects or essential services, such as health or education. Skilled as well as unskilled labor would thus be equally valued.

[22]The Japanese economist Koichi Mera has raised the question whether, in fact, rural development and, in particular, small farmers, are not already being "subsidized" by the urban corporate sector (personal communication). This is a crucial issue that must ultimately be resolved on empirical grounds. In the absence of conclusive evidence, however, certain qualitative judgments may be ventured. (1) It would appear that in most Asian countries public investments are treated as positive externalities by private firms and are not reflected in the cost structure of private production. (2) Both transport rates and service charges for public utilities tend to favor large-scale corporate production and so contribute to the high degree of spatial concentration of "modern" activities. (3) Tax and other fiscal advantages abound in the corporate sector so that, in the typical case, complete amortization of the initial investment is accomplished in ònly a few years. (4) In many countries the private banking system serves primarily as a channel for mobilizing rural savings and for transferring them to the primate city of the country, where they become available for urban investments principally in the construction of offices and luxury apartments as well as for real estate speculation. (5) Regional terms of trade are generally against agriculture, particularly in the staple food-producing subsector, as governments tend to control the price of basic foodstuffs in the interest of a politically alert urban proletariat, while inflation in the manufactured goods sector is "exported" to rural populations. All told, the thesis that cities not only finance their own economic expansion but actually transfer resources to help in rural development is, at least in the case of developing Asian economies, an exceedingly dubious one (Harvey, 1973).

[23]Throughout Asia, many so-called cities of up to 100,000 population may have a large proportion of their population classified as agricultural.

In purely formal terms, agropolitan districts might be defined as rural areas that have an effective population density of at least 200 per km^2 (for prevailing densities, see Table 2).[24] A town of between 10,000 - 25,000 inhabitants would normally be found within the district, and district boundaries would be defined by a "commuting"radius of between 5 and 10 km (or approximately one hour's travel time by bicycle).[25] Such dimensions would yield an overall size of population ranging from 50,000 to 150,000 of whom a majority would be initially engaged in farming (Friedmann, 1974).

This is the abstract geometry of agropolitan units. Their actual definition in geographic space would, of course, be far more flexible than is suggested here, and would take account of existing patterns of social and economic relations, linguistic and religious boundaries, ecological complementarities, effective population densities, the distribution of traditional market towns, etc.

In addition, agropolitan districts may also be formed within the perimeter of large and growing cities (metrocenters). For just as agropolitan development attempts to bring the city to the countryside, so the countryside can be brought to the city ("fields in the city"). In other words, a modified agropolitan model can be introduced to help restructure the form of existing large cities by opening the built-up areas of the city to fields and urban farming. In this connection it may be noted that most Asian cities will more than double their populations in the next 20 years. The possibilities for restructuring their physical form as well as form of governance would thus appear to be quite considerable.

Although agropolitan districts may have both a town center and a dispersed village population, the key to successful agropolitan development is the treatment of each district as a *single, integrated, and self-governing unit*. Correlative with this idea of agropolitan development is the requirement that each unit has sufficient autonomy and economic resources to plan and carry out its own development.[26] In this scheme the tasks of central

---

[24]According to common practice in the United States, an area is considered "urbanized" when it lies adjacent to a city of at least 50,000 people and has a minimum settlement density of 100 housing units per square mile. Using the 1970 average size of household 3.17, this translates into a population density of 120 persons per km^2. At the older ratio of 4.0 persons per household, the density would be 152 per km^2.

[25]For an equivalent definition of "urban fields" in the United States based on travel distance by automobile, see Friedmann and Miller (1965).

[26]To render the idea of agropolitan development a bit more clearly, a sample of specific developmental actions is listed below:

  (a) Intensive development of land, water, forestry, and fishery resources for sustained yield; land reclamation schemes; conservation practices; development of small livestock.

  (b) Agropolitan electrification; water supply system.

  (c) Construction of all-weather roads and bicycle paths (capillary penetration). Inter-agropolitan transport systems as well as good transport connections to major trunk roads and to larger cities.

  (d) Improvements in agropolitan communications: microwave telephone and radio; bus services; postal offices.

  (e) Provision of basic agropolitan social services: primary, secondary, and technical schools, child care centers, training and research centers, libraries, cultural and recreational facilities, health services, and family planning centers.

  (f) Construction of weather- and vermin-proof storage facilities for agricultural products (to reduce crop losses and stabilize supply) and of distribution centers for agricultural implements, pesticides, fertilizers, etc.

  (g) Implementation of environmental sanitation programs.

  (h) Formation of cooperative marketing services. Credit facilities.

  (i) Introduction of light, labor-intensive industries oriented primarily towards the domestic market and producing wage goods, farm implements, processed agricultural materials, and subcontracted parts for final assembly in large-scale, export-oriented industry (Sigurdson, 1975).

government would be to support locally initiated developments with financial, material, and technical resources to undertake projects of national significance, to ensure inter-regional equity in the allocation of development funds, and to maintain system-wide balances in the major macro-economic parameters. In addition the central government would monitor the achievement of the guaranteed national minima and assist with accelerating progress in areas of marked shortfalls from the established standards.

2.3. Problems of Implementation: An Evaluation of the Asian Experience

Assuming a political commitment to Strategy II, a thoroughgoing land reform appears as the first and quintessential step in a practical program of implementation. The relation of agropolitan development to land reform is summarized in the following imperatives:

(1) Local autonomy, resource management, and a sense of personal involvement must be engendered to sustain development. This cannot be accomplished unless landed and other wealth is returned to the control of members of each agropolitan district. The question of how much land should remain in individual ownership will have to be determined on a case-by-case basis. It may be noted, however, that unless a substantial share of the total farm land comes under effective communal control, the old inequalities will sooner or later reassert themselves, cancelling the initial effort at redistribution.

(2) Minimum and maximum limits of size holdings must be established in order to permit more rational and productive use of land resources. Fragmented land holdings must be reassembled for efficient production, preferably on a communal basis.

(3) Greater reinvestment of profits from local activity into agropolitan development must be made to raise productivity and to create environments conducive to sustained economic growth. To do this, the flow of resources to large cities, especially in the form of rental payments to absentee landlords, must be reversed.

The extent to which present patterns of land distribution inhibit accelerated rural development is suggested by Table 12. Except for Thailand, average farm sizes are near or below minimum levels for productive farming.[27]

Tenancy rates, which translate into a loss of from 30 to 50 percent of crop values for the farmer, range from 27 to 50 percent in the six nations. And the richest 5 percent of the rural population in countries for which data are available control from one-fifth to over one-third of total farm land.

Arguments for land reform have been widely accepted in theory and intention. Every non-communist nation in Asia has legislation which grants government the right to expropriate land (United Nations, 1973d), and all six nations in our sample have, at one time or another, expressed land redistribution as a goal.

Performance, however, has been poor. Land redistribution schemes are not proceeding either widely or effectively. The much-heralded programs carried out in the Republic of Korea in the early 1950s have not been continued; shrinking farm sizes are re-emerging as a problem in agricultural development (IBRD, 1974). Thailand and Indonesia have opted for reliance on new, Green Revolution technologies requiring large-scale mechanized

---

[27]Though such minimums vary according to local situations, in Malaysia the suggested level has been set by one author at 3 - 4 hectares (Kedhra, 1972); in Indonesia, 1 hectare has been considered as a minimum to allow all year-round rice consumption for a farm family (Tjondrenegoro, 1972); in the Philippines the minimum size has been set at 3 hectares (Philippines, 1972).

cultivation. In lieu of land reform, such reliance will most likely increase, rather than decrease, rural inequalities by giving cumulative advantage to owners of large farms who represent only a small portion of the rural population.

Malaysia has been able to avoid land redistribution policies by opening up remaining areas of virgin land for the rural poor from already developed areas. India and the Philippines are the only two nations that currently stress land reform as a central planning issue. Indian progress, however, is mired in its bureaucracy, and rents and tenancy insecurity are increasing (IBRD, 1974). The Philippines promulgated a national policy of land reform in 1972. Some two million hectares are to be transferred to one million farmers. Minimum and maximum sizes have been set. Although assessment of the Philippine policies of land reform cannot be made at this time, the approach is in the desired direction.

TABLE 12

Farm size, tenancy, and concentration of ownership

	Average farm size[a] (hectares)	Farms in tenancy[b] (percent)	Farmland in tenancy[b] (percent)	Percentage of land held by top 5% income group[c]
India	1.1 (1969)	27.3	n.a.	36 (1960)
Indonesia (Java)	0.5 (1969)	35.9	25.9	31 (1963)
West Malaysia	2.7 (1972)	31.2	15.7	
Philippines	2.7 (1970)	54.3	40.4	
Republic of Korea	2.1 (1961)	n.a.	n.a.	
Thailand	3.5 (1970)	40.0 (1969)	n.a.	20 (1969)

[a]United Nations, *World Economic Survey, 1973.*
[b]IBRD (1974), tables 5 and 10. Figures are from latest available dates in 1960s. Data refer to all Indonesia and all Malaysia.
[c]United Nations (1973c) p. 29.

Despite the low priority assigned to land reform in five of the six nations, all countries are pursuing policies which, in one form or another, seem related to agropolitan development. They are briefly described below.

India. Under the Fourth Five-year Plan (1969 - 1974) a pilot program for rural growth centers with an accent on rural - urban integration was initiated. This beginning effort was to be buttressed by a "minimum needs program" focused on educational, water and health facilities, home sites for landless laborers, rural roads, and rural electrification (Shah, 1974).

Indonesia. In the current Plan (1974 - 79) the government has outlined a concept of Village Working Units, constituting groups of villages that cover an area from between 600 - 1000 hectares (or from one-fiftieth to one-tenth the proposed area of an agropolitan district). Within these units, agriculture and credit extension, as well as systems for processing and marketing, are to be formed. Depending on local capabilities, small-scale industry may also be developed.

Malaysia. With calls for the eradication of poverty and a restructuring of society to correct economic imbalances, a New Economic Policy was announced in 1971. Farmers were to be transferred from disadvantaged areas to regions with higher development potentials. Although the primary activity was to be farming, a series of rural cities were to be built to establish the new settlers in urban surroundings.

So far the Pahang Tenggara project is the most ambitious of the new settlement schemes: half a million people are expected in the area by 1990, many of them residing in towns. By 1974 the largest of these already had a population of 28,000 (Salih, 1974). In all, no less than 29 New Towns have been projected.

Philippines. Besides its heavy emphasis on land reform, the government is planning an acceleration of rural infrastructure development, including road networks based on farm size ratios and irrigation projects. Added to this is a push for development and reform of cooperatives with an ultimate goal of raising farm incomes and encouraging savings.

Thailand. The Second Five-year Plan (1967 - 71) declared that its objective of reducing geographical imbalances and income inequalities would be reached through direct investment in rural development. As with the Philippines and other nations, these programs include investment in infrastructure, the building up of cooperative movements, the provision of credit facilities, agricultural extension, and land development by government. These programs are being continued with a leaning toward growth center strategies for regional development.

How relevant are these policies to the theme of agropolitan development? How far do programs go in effectively reducing the contradictions created by the continued reliance on a strategy of accelerated industrialization? Though our intention is not to evaluate the programs of each nation, we may offer partial insights by noting common features:

(1) Rural development programs in Asia are inadequately funded and coordinated.
(2) Rural development is viewed as an auxiliary policy of Strategy I and not as its replacement.
(3) Rural development is conceived either on the scale of pilot experiments or as a process that occurs "spontaneously" in the hinterlands of cities that are vertically integrated into a hierarchy. The latter view is consistent with the growth center concept and is a tacit justification for the continued neglect of rural populations in policy and budgetary allocations.
(4) The command style of planning and decision making is still predominant, and there is little devolution of effective power to local communities. If any trend can be detected, it is towards an increasing concentration of decision making in central ministries.
(5) With the exception of the Philippines, land reform is receiving little attention. Yet without it, a strategy for accelerated rural development cannot succeed.

Our argument is straightforward. Without a comprehensive land reform program on a national scale, a strategy of accelerated rural development cannot succeed. But land reform cannot be separated from the simultaneous creation of agropolitan districts and the related policies of agropolitan development. Merely to redistribute land without, at the same time, undertaking the many complex tasks involved in raising agricultural productivity and in "urbanizing" the countryside, is to condemn the entire effort to failure. An agropolitan policy must thus be carried out across the board, in poor areas as well as rich, though always with due regard for local circumstances and conditions. As a result, new streams of rural to rural migration might be generated.

Where possible, they should be directed into unoccupied or sparsely populated areas to open up new land for settlement (e.g., Malaysia, Indonesia, the Philippines). The dangers of swamping the positive effects of rural development in specific localities through an influx of migrants from less developed, less productive areas must be avoided.

3. CONCLUDING OBSERVATIONS

Our original intention was to review and assess the growth center experience of Asian countries. We might easily have done so, pointing to failures and successes. But in so restricting our horizon we should simply have added another chapter to the already voluminous growth center literature (Moseley, 1974). We should not have put the question that we finally came to ask, whether the development strategy to which growth center policies are meant to contribute is also a viable strategy for the future development of Asian countries.

As we delved into the record of national accomplishments, it seemed to us that the universal adoption of Strategy I had created serious contradictions in relation to the benefits it was expected to yield. Although the numerical coefficients were different for each country, the general pattern was unmistakable. Strategy I had brought into being dualistic dependency structures that, while they had helped in achieving respectable growth rates, had also created a set of related and potentially explosive problems, including hyperurbanization, increasing rural densities, a spatial structure of dominant core and dependent periphery, widespread urban unemployment and underemployment, rising income inequalities, persistent and growing food shortages, and deteriorating material conditions in the countryside.

So long as overall economic growth could be sustained at high levels, these contradictions were perhaps not critical for the maintenance of political stability. At any rate, part of the generated surplus (or aid from outside sources) could always be used to ameliorate the worst conditions and so avoid more fundamental, structural changes in economic organization.

We then tried to place national economic growth into a world context. We concluded that the limited success of Strategy I had, in fact, been the result of a general economic buoyancy in the core regions of world capitalism that had been mediated to their periphery through international trade. By the mid-seventies, however, the world economic system was itself undergoing a major transition. As concerns the peripheral countries in Asia, this crisis was translated into higher import costs, a worsening of the terms of trade, and restricted access to world markets. In combination, these trends suggested to us that the high rates of GNP projected by national governments were most probably in error. The long-term prospect is rather for a decline in the "normal" level of economic growth to only slightly more than increases in population.

Accepting this prognosis, we then suggested that under conditions of relative economic stagnation Strategy I would become untenable. Its place would have to be taken by an alternative strategy of accelerated rural development that was oriented to human needs, a more equal distribution of economic benefits, the direct involvement of local people in the process of development.

In Part II we considered the spatial correlate of such a strategy. We called it a policy framework for agropolitan development. This envisioned creating "cities-in-the-fields" by embedding some of the key elements of urbanism in dense rural areas of limited size.

The agropolitan district appeared to us as the appropriate unit for devising a policy of spatial development through decentralized planning and decision making.

Finally, we considered some of the concrete measures which our sample of six Asian countries had already implemented and which might be seen as related to the suggested policy of agropolitan development. First and foremost was land reform. But we could find little evidence for substantial changes in patterns of land ownership. Second, a variety of recently adopted rural development programs was briefly surveyed. Here, too, we were led to conclude that none of them represented more than token efforts, and that the programs were viewed by governments as complementary to accelerated industrialization rather than as harbingers of new directions.

Our conclusions must be carefully weighed. If we are right, Asian economies will experience a deepening of the present crisis. The alternative would be to shift to a radically different strategy of accelerated rural development within the framework of agropolitan development. If we are wrong, the ultimate crisis may be avoided, even though the specific contradictions we have identified would continue. Growth center policies might then be re-examined as a means for "spreading" specific economic benefits to depressed peripheral regions within each of the national economies. This is the purpose for which they were originally devised, i.e., primarily as a means for ameliorating some of the worst side-effects of accelerated industrialization under dualistic dependency. Whether growth center policies would, in principle, be capable of achieving even this limited objective, remains an open question.

REFERENCES

Adelman, Irma (1975) Growth, income distribution and equity-oriented development strategies, *World Development* 3 (2) 67 - 76.

Ariff, K. A. M. (1973) Economic development of Malaysia: pattern and perspective, *The developing economies* 11 (4) 371 - 391.

Baldwin, William L. (1974) The Thai rice trade as a vertical market network: structure, performance, and policy implications, *Economic Development and Cultural Change* 22 (2) 179 - 197.

Bautista, Romeo M. (1973) Anatomy of labour absorption in Philippine manufacturing, 1956 - 1966, *Economic Bulletin for Asia and the Far East* 24 (2/3) 12 - 22.

Bautista, Romeo M. (1974) Employment and labour productivity in smallscale manufacturing in the Philippines, *NEDA Journal of Development* 1(1) 41 - 54.

Bose, Ashish (1971) The urbanization process in South and Southeast Asia, in Jakobson and Prakash (eds.), pp. 81 - 110.

Cline, William R. (1975) Distribution and development: a survey of literature, *Journal of Development Economics* 1, 359 - 400.

Dandekar, V.M. and N. Rath (1971) Poverty in India, *Economic and Political Weekly,* Jan., pp. 25 - 48, 106 - 146.

Davis, Kingsley (1969) *World Urbanization 1950 - 1970,* Vol. 1, University of California, Monograph Series No. 4, Berkeley, Cal.

de Haan, H. H. (1974) *The Nature and Magnitude of Underutilization of Labour in Non-Communist less Developed Countries,* Centre for Development Planning, Erasmus Universiteit Rotterdam, Rotterdam.

Emmanuel, Arghiri (1972) *Unequal Exchange: a Study of the Imperialism of Trade,* Monthly Review Press, New York.

Esmara, Hendra (1975) Regional income disparities, *Bulletin of Indonesian Economic Studies* 11 (1) 41 - 57.

Faber, Mike and Dudley Seers (eds.) (1972) *The Crisis in Planning,* 2 vols., Chatto Windus, London.

Friedmann, John and John Miller (1965) The urban field, *Journal of the American Institute of Planners* 31 (4) 312 - 319.

Friedmann, John)1973a) *Retracking America: a Theory of Transactive Planning,* Anchor Press/Doubleday, New York.

Friedmann, John (1973b) *Urbanization, Planning and National Development,* Sage publications, Beverly Hills, Cal., Chap. 5.

Friedmann, John (1975), A Spatial Framework for Rural Development: Problems of Organization and Implementation, Économic Appliquée xxviii (2-3), 519-544.

Friedmann, John and Flora Sullivan (1974) The absorption of labor in the urban economy: the case of developing countries, *Economic Development and Cultural Change* **22** (3) 385 - 413.

Gurley, John G. (1975) Rural development in China 1949 - 72, and the lessons to be learned from it, *World Development* **3** (7/8) 455 - 471.

Hansen, Niles M. (1975) *An Evaluation of Growth Centre Theory and Practice,* United Nations Centre for Regional Development, Nagoya.

Harvey, David (1973) *Social Justice and the City,* The Johns Hopkins Press, Baltimore.

Hayami, Yujiro and Vernon Ruttan (1971) *Agricultural Development: an International Perspective,* The Johns Hopkins Press, Baltimore.

Horii, Kenzo (1972) The land tenure system of Malay padi farmers, *The Developing Economies* **10** (1) 49 - 73.

IBRD (1974) *Land Reform,* World Bank Rural Development Series, Washington, DC.

ILO (1971) *Concepts of Labour Force Underutilisation,* Geneva.

ILO, UNDP (1973) *Sharing in Development: a Programme of Employment, Equity and Growth for the Philippines,* Geneva.

India, Government of, Planning Commission (1968) *Fourth Five-Year Plan, 1969 - 1974,* New Delhi.

India, Government of, Planning Commission (1972) *Draft of the Fifth Five-Year Plan, 1974 - 79,* New Delhi.

Indonesia, Government of (1969) *Indonesia's Five-Year Development Plan, 1969 - 74,* Djakarta.

Intermet (1973) *Town Drift: Social and Policy Implications of Rural - Urban Migration in Eight Developing Countries,* Final Conference on Rural - Urban Migrants and Metropolitan Development, Nov. 24 - Dec. 1, Istanbul.

Jakobson, Leo and Ved Prakash (eds.) (1971) *Urbanization and National Development,* Sage Publications, Beverly Hills, Cal.

Kerdpibule, Udom (1975) Distribution of income and wealth in Thailand, in Preteep Sondysuvan (ed.), *Finance, Trade and Economic Development in Thailand,* Sompong Press, Bangkok.

Khera, Harcharan Singh (1972) *Problems and Prospects of the Malaysian Economy,* Central News Agency, Kuala Lumpur.

Kim, An-Jae (1975) *Industrialization and Growth Pole Development in Korea: a Case Study of Ulsan Industrial Complex in the Context of Regional Development in Southern Coastal Areas,* United Nations Centre for Regional Development, Nagoya, Japan.

Kuklinski, Antoni (ed.) (1972) *Growth Poles and Growth Centres in Regional Planning,* Mouton, Paris.

Kuklinski, Antoni and R. Petrella (eds.) (1972) *Growth Poles and Regional Policies,* Mouton, Paris.

Lefeber, Louis and Mrinal Datta-Chaudhuri (1971) *Regional Development Experiences and Prospects in South and Southeast Asia,* Mouton, Paris, the Hague.

Leibenstein, Harvey (1966) Allocative efficiency vs. X-efficiency, *American Economic Review,* June, pp. 392 - 415.

Marzouk, G. A. (1972) *Economic Development Policies: Case Study of Thailand,* Rotterdam University Press, Rotterdam.

Malaysia, Government of (1973) *Midterm Review of the Second Malaysia Plan 1971 - 75,* Kuala Lumpur.

Malaysia, Government of (1974) *Economic Report 1974 - 75,* Kuala Lumpur.

McGee, T. G. (1971) Catalyst or cancers? The role of cities in Asian society, in Jakobson and Prakash (eds.), pp. 157 - 182.

McGee, T. G. (1974) *The Persistence of the Proto-Proletariat: Occupational Structures and Planning for the Future of Third World Cities,* Comparative Urban Studies Series, School of Architecture and Urban Planning, University of California, Los Angeles.

McNamara, Robert S. (1975) *Address to the Board of Governors,* IBRD, Washington, DC.

Mesarovic, Mihajlo and Eduard Pestel (1974) *Mankind at the Turning Point: the Second Report to the Club of Rome,* E. P. Dutton, New York.

Misra, R. P., K. V. Sundaram and V. L. S. Prakasa Rao (1974) *Regional Development Planning in India: a New Strategy,* Vikas Publishing House, New Delhi.

Moseley, Malcolm J. (1974) *Growth Centres in Spatial Planning,* Pergamon Press, New York.

Oshima, Harry T. (1970) Income inequality and economic growth—the postwar experience of Asian countries, *Malaysian Economic Review,* October.

Oshima, Harry T. (1971) Labor-force "explosion" and the labor-intensive sector in Asian growth, *Economic Development and Cultural Change* **19** (2) 161 - 183.

Paauw, Douglas and John C. Fei (1973) *The Transition in Open Dualistic Economies: Theory and Southeast Asian Experience,* Yale University Press, London.

Republic of the Philippines, *NEDA, 1973, Four-Year Development Plan, Fy 1974 - 77,* Manila.

Republic of Korea, Government of (1971) *Third Five-Year Economic Development Plan, 1972 - 1976,* Kyongje Kihoegwon, Seoul.

Richardson, Harry W. (1973) *Regional Growth Theory,* Macmillan, London.

Romm, Jeff (1972) *Urbanization in Thailand,* Ford Foundation, New York.

Salih, Kamal (1974) *On Urban Development Strategies in Malaysia,* UNCRD Seminar on Urban Development Strategies for Attaining Desirable Population Distribution, Nagoya, Japan.

Seers, Dudley (1970) The meaning of development, Agricultural Development Council Reprint, September.

Shah, S. M. (1974) Growth centers as a strategy for rural development: India experience, *Economic Development and Cultural Change* **22** (2) 215 - 228.

Sigurdson, Jon (1975) Rural development in China: approaches and results, *World Development* **3** (7/8) 527 - 538.

Stuckey, Barbara (1975) *From Tribe to Multi-National Corporation: an Approach to the Study of Urbanization,* Ph d. Dissertation, University of California, School of Architecture and Urban Planning, Planning Program, Los Angeles.

Sundrum, R. M. (1975) Manufacturing employment, 1961 - 1971, *Bulletin of Indonesian Economic Studies* **11** (1) 58 - 65.

Thailand, Government of (1972) *Summary of the Third Five-Year Plan (1972-1976),* National Economic and Social Development Board, Office of the Prime Minister.

Tjondronegoro, Sediono M. P. (1972) *Land Reform or Land Settlement: Shifts in Indonesia's Land Policy, 1960 - 1970,* University of Wisconsin, Land Tenure Center, Madison, Wis.

Turnham, David and Ingelies Jaeger (1971) *The Employment Problem in Less Developed Countries: a Review of the Evidence,* Development Centre, OECD, Paris.

Ul Haq, Mahbub (1972) Employment in the 1970's: a new perspective, Agricultural Development Council, reprint, October.

United Nations (1973a) Manpower growth and labour absorption in developing Asia, *Economic Bulletin for Asia and the Far East* **24** (1) 10 - 33.

United Nations (1973b) Population and food supply in Asia, *Economic Bulletin for Asia and the Far East* **24** (1) 34 - 50.

United Nations (1973c) *Economic Survey of Asia and the Far East,* ECAFE.

United Nations (1973d) *Urban Land Policies and Land-use Control Measures:* Volume II, *Asia and the Far East,* New York.

United Nations (1974) *World Economic Survey 1973,* New York.

Wallerstein, Immanuel (1974) The rise and future demise of the world capitalist system: concepts for comparative analysis, *Comparative Studies in Society and History,* September, pp. 387 - 415.

8

THE CHANGING PATTERN OF POPULATION DISTRIBUTION IN JAPAN AND ITS IMPLICATIONS FOR DEVELOPING COUNTRIES

Koichi Mera

1. INTRODUCTION

Concentration of population in a few metropolitan areas is considered as a serious problem in developing as well as developed countries. Japan is no exception. During the 30 years since the World War II, the population distribution in Japan has been shifting toward greater concentration in large metropolitan areas. One of the most striking characteristics of the Japanese experience is the rapidity of the change: during the period of fast economic growth, nearly half of the prefectures were losing population in absolute terms due to out-migration to large metropolitan areas.

There appears to have been a change in this situation recently, however. The population registration record has revealed that none of the prefectures lost population in absolute terms during 1974.[1] This is a phenomenal departure from the past trend which lasted for 18 years. This change has been preceded by a gradual decline in the number of prefectures losing population since 1970. Indeed, Japan's economy or society as a whole appears to have been undergoing substantial changes since around 1970. In terms of population distribution, some observers state that there has been a U-turn phenomenon, implying that more people started to migrate from large urban centers back to small urban centers and rural areas than vice versa. In terms of the economic growth of the economy as a whole, there has been an apparent slowing down of growth rates. This change has coincided with rapidly intensified public concern with the quality of the environment and pollution. In addition, there have been a number of other significant social changes such as an increase in concern over distribution of income, and international political and monetary disturbances, during recent years.

The purpose of this paper is, first, to examine the nature of the recent change in the pattern of population distribution in Japan and, then, to identify the factors which are responsible for the change.

Through this examination it would be possible to ascertain to what degree the behavioral knowledge we obtained earlier remains valid and how it should be modified, if at all, in view of the current developments.

[1] See Table A.1.

193

2. RECENT CHANGE AND POSSIBLE CONTRIBUTING FACTORS

The annual growth rates of prefectural populations varied widely depending upon the rate of natural increase and migration (see Table A.1). Until 1959 the growth rate was highest in Tokyo, closely followed by Osaka. Since then, prefectures adjacent to Tokyo, such as Kanagawa, Saitama, and Chiba, started overtaking Tokyo in the population growth rate, and by 1962 Tokyo became the slowest growing prefecture among the four. In the Kinki Region, the dominance of Osaka continued until 1969, but since then the neighboring Nara Prefecture has consistently maintained a higher growth rate. In addition, Osaka was overtaken by Hyogo Prefecture recently although for only one year.

In contrast to high growth rates of population within major urban regions, most prefectures in the northeast and the western regions lost their share in population in almost every year since around 1960. The results of these shifts (shown in Table A.2) can be summarized by the following:

	Population share (%)	
	1950	1970
Capital Region[a]	15.69	23.26
Osaka and Hyogo	8.62	11.85
Six northeast prefectures[b]	10.84	8.71
Seven Kyushu prefectures[c]	14.55	11.63

[a]Tokyo, Saitama, Chiba, and Kanagawa.
[b]Aomori, Iwate, Miyagi, Akita, Yamagata, and Fukushima.
[c]Fukuoka, Saga, Nagasaki, Kumamoto, Oita, Miyazaki, and Kagoshima.

This trend of population concentration can be represented by two variables defined below:

Percentage Incremental Concentration in the Capital Region (PC1)
the percentage of the annual increment of population which has been absorbed within the Capital Region comprising four prefectures, namely Tokyo, Saitama, Chiba, and Kanagawa,

Number of Rapidly Depopulating Prefectures (PC2)
the number of the prefectures which have experienced a population growth rate more than one percentage point below the national average growth rate.

These two variables are shown graphically in Fig. 1 and numerically in Table 1. They are

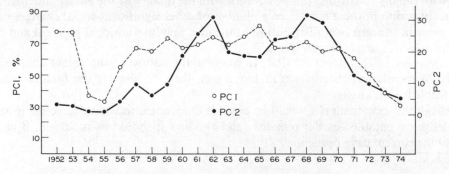

Fig. 1. Trends of population concentration, 1952-74.

TABLE 1

Indices of change in population concentration

year	Percentage incremental concentration in the capital region (PC1)[a]	Number of fast depopulation prefectures[b] (PC2)[c]
1952	31.3	26
53	30.3	36
54	27.0	6
55	26.9	4
1956	33.0	15
57	44.3	21
58	37.0	20
59	43.9	24
60	62.2	21
1961	75.9	22
62	86.4	24
63	64.4	22
64	62.1	24
65	61.7	28
1966	72.3	21
67	74.2	21
68	87.9	23
69	82.8	20
70	67.3	21
1971	49.7	18
72	44.7	13
73	39.1	7
74	35.4	3

[a]Ministry of Local Autonomy, *Population and Household Statistics, 1975*, 1975, Tokyo, Ministry of Finance Printing Office.
[b]Those having a growth rate of population which is more than 1 percentage point below the national population growth rate.
[c]Table A.1.

closely related to each other with the coefficient of correlation of 0.506. Both indices show high rates of population concentration during the 1960s and relatively low rates before and after the decade with the exception of 1952 and 1953, which had been very much influenced by the boom induced by the war in the Korean Peninsula. However, the two variables represent quite different phenomena: PC1 represents population concentration in a localized but significant urban region, and PC2 deconcentration of population from widely scattered prefectures. The close relationship of these two variables implies that most migration from any prefecture is directly or indirectly related to migration to the Capital Region.

Of these changes in the trend of population concentration, the following are considered to be possible contributing factors to recent changes: (a) intensified concern over the quality of the environment, (b) changing values in life, (c) slowing down of the economic growth, (d) diseconomies of scale in large metropolitan areas, (e) equalizing trend in income and wage levels among prefectures, (f) changing price differentials among prefectures and (g) improvement in transportation and communication.

Among the above possible factors, (a) and (b) are considered as particularly important contributing factors as the timing of emergence of the new environmental concern, and of new values, coincided well with the start of the change in the trend of population concentration. Indeed, intensified concern with the environment, which began in 1969 in the United States, induced even greater concern over the environment in Japan, culminating in the establishment of the Environmental Protection Agency in 1971. Since about that time, the government has initiated efforts for development of a net national welfare (NNW) index intended to represent the true national aggregative welfare by subtracting all costs associated with environmental costs.[2] Public opinion as represented in mass media shifted clearly from orientation to economic growth to yearning for a better living even at the cost of less economic growth.[3]

The third factor (c), the slowing down of economic growth, started in 1971, and deceleration was fast after 1973 as shown in Table 2. To some extent the deceleration must have been due to the shift in government policy from growth orientation to welfare orientation, but to a greater extent it was due to external factors such as worldwide rampant inflation, revaluation and floating of the yen, and a multifold hike in the price of oil. Generally, the economic growth rate is more volatile than the indices for increasing population concentration. But, at any rate, the pattern of the economic growth rate resembles that of population concentration, having a plateau during the 1960s as graphically shown in Fig. 2. Consequently, economic growth is considered as an important factor which has contributed to increases in population concentration.

The above hypothesis is consistent with the empirical regularity that there are economies of scale in urbanization. This finding was made not only with respect to Japan but also with respect to a number of other developed and developing countries.[4] The recent change in the pattern of migration in Japan may imply that either economies of scale in large urban centers have been replaced by diseconomies of scale or their extent has substantially reduced. These possibilities will be examined more specifically in connection with differentials in *per capita* income among prefectures.

Even in the absence of changes in values in life or degree of concern with environment, a reduction in economic incentives for migration to large urban centers may be sufficient to explain the recent change. Indeed, differentials in *per capita* personal income among prefectures have been declining since the early 1960s. Two indices have been derived for

---

[2]The Economic Deliberation Council, an advisory body for the Prime Minister, is still elaborating on this project.

[3]On the public side, the Economic White Paper for fiscal 1969 stressed the seriousness of pollution problems, and that for fiscal 1972, which was subtitled "Establishment of a New Welfare Society," stressed both the prevention of pollution and protection of the environment and explicitly disclaimed the past economic policy which was heavily oriented to high economic growth.

[4]W. Alonso, Urban and regional imbalances in economic development, *Economic Development and Cultural Change* 17 (October, 1968) 1-14, and The economics of urban size, *Regional Science Association Papers* 26 (1971) 67-83. V. R. Fuchs, *Differentials in Hourly Earnings by Region and City Size,* 1959, National Bureau of Economic Research Occasional Paper, No. 101, Columbia University Press, New York (1967). K. Mera, On the urban agglomeration and economic efficiency, *Economic Development and Cultural Change* 21 (January, 1973) 309-324, and Regional production functions and social overhead capital: an analysis of the Japanese case, *Regional and Urban Economies* 3 (May 1973) 157-186; or chapters II and IV, respectively, of *Income Distribution and Regional Development.* University of Tokyo Press, Tokyo (1975), and D. Shefer, Localization economies in SMSAS: a production function analysis, *Journal of Regional Science* 13 (April, 1973) 55-64.

measuring the degree of income disparity among the prefectures:

Range of Income Disparity (ID1)

the difference between the highest and the lowest indices of prefectural *per capita* personal income when the national average is set at 100.

Coefficient of Variation (ID2)

the unweighted coefficient of variation of all prefectural *per capita* incomes.

Per capita personal incomes of prefectures are obtainable for the period from 1955 to 1972 in two different series as shown in Tables A-3 and A-4. These two series are different not only with respect to the starting date of each year but also with respect to the method of estimation and are not directly comparable. However, with adjustments, two

TABLE 2
Growth rate of GNP, 1952 - 75

	Fiscal year basis	Calendar year basis (%)
1952	11.7	-
53	7.7	6.2
54	2.8	5.9
55	10.8	8.8
56	6.2	7.3
57	7.8	7.4
58	6.0	5.6
59	11.2	8.9
60	12.5	13.4
1961	13.5	14.4
62	6.4	7.0
63	12.5	10.4
64	10.6	13.2
65	5.7	5.1
66	11.1	9.8
67	13.1	12.9
68	12.7	13.4
69	11.0	10.8
1970	10.4	10.9
71	7.3	7.3
72	9.8	8.7
73	6.1	10.2
74	-0.6	-1.9
75[a]	1.6	1.0

[a]Projected.

Source: Japan Economic Planning Agency, *Annual Report on National Income Statistics, 1975,* Japan Ministry of Finance, Printing Bureau, 1950: for 1952 to 1973. Japan Office of the Prime Minister, Bureau of Statistics, *Monthly Statistics of Japan,* August 1975 for the 1974 calendar year based. Japan Economic Research Center, *Quarterly Economic Projections,* Nos. 29 and 30, March and June 1975 for the 1974 fiscal year based and for projected 1975 rates.

KOICHI MERA

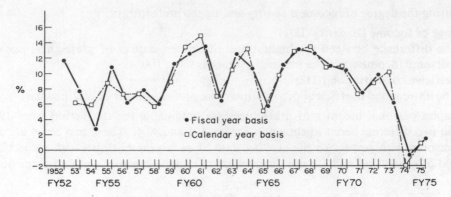

Fig. 2. Real growth rate of the Japanese economy, 1952 - 75.

series of indices have been developed and are contained in Table 3. Either series indicates substantial narrowing of the disparity in income levels among prefectures since the early 1960s. The two indices are shown graphically in Fig. 3. This declining trend in regional

TABLE 3

Indices of disparity in *per capita* personal income among prefectures

Year	Range of income disparity[a]			Coefficient of variation[b]		
	ID1[c]	ID1[d]	ID1[e]	ID2[f]	ID2[g]	ID2[h]
1955	97.3		93.9	0.19		0.18
56	102.5		99.1	0.21		0.20
57	96.7		93.3	0.21		0.20
58	94.6		91.2	0.20		0.19
59	97.1		93.7	0.20		0.19
60	97.5		94.1	0.20		0.19
1961	102.9		99.5	0.21		0.20
62	101.2		97.8	0.21		0.20
63	96.2		92.8	0.21		0.20
64	94.2		90.8	0.20		0.19
65	88.3	84.9	84.9	0.18	0.17	0.17
1966		83.2	83.2		0.16	0.16
67		80.0	80.0		0.16	0.16
68		78.5	78.5		0.15	0.15
69		78.3	78.3		0.15	0.15
70		77.9	77.9		0.16	0.16
1971		73.3	73.3		0.15	0.15
72		71.1	71.1		0.15	0.15

[a]The difference between the highest and lowest indices of prefectural *per capita* personal income when the national average is set to 100.

[b]The unweighted coefficient of variation of all prefectural *per capita* incomes.

[c]Table 4.

[d]Table 5.

[e]ID1 series from 1955 to 1965 adjusted to ID1 series from 1965 to 1972 through subtraction of a constant.

[f]Computed from Table 4.

[g]Computed from Table 5.

[h]ID2 series from 1955 to 1965 adjusted to ID2 series from 1965 to 1972 through subtraction of a constant.

income disparity is consistent with a more general finding made by Williamson with respect to developed countries.[5]

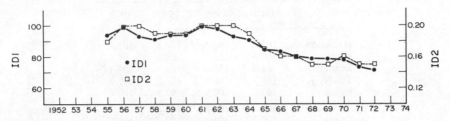

Fig. 3. Indices of income disparity among prefectures.

A narrowing trend in regional disparity is also observable in wage levels. Table 4 shows
this trend for the wage level paid to graduates of junior high schools immediately after
graduation. The table shows a general narrowing of disparity since 1960. A sudden reversal of the narrowing trend in 1972 is to a lesser extent observable in the trend of *per capita*
income disparity. As these two series move roughly in parallel, the narrowing of wage disparity is considered as a significant factor contributing to the narrowing of *per capita*
income disparity.

TABLE 4

Trend in disparity among prefectures in the average
starting wage paid to junior high school graduates

As percentage	Number of prefectures			
of Tokyo's	1960	1965	1970	1972
Below 80	30	15	6	14
Below 70	12	5	0	1

Source: Economic Planning Agency, *Chiiki Keizai Yoran
1968* and *1973*, Keizai Kikaku Kyokai, Tokyo, 1968 and 1973.

Changing price differentials among prefectures *f* is a possible factor contributing to the
recent change in the pattern of population concentration. However, available data indicate there has been no significant change in the consumer price index of prefectures relative to the national mean. This is shown for selected prefectures in Table 5.

As to improvements in transportation and communication among prefectures *g*, obviously there must have been various kinds of improvements period. It is possible to present the amount of public and private investment in this sector as a proxy for the degree of
improvement in each year, but such information will not reveal much, as what affects the
distribution of population would be the absolute levels of transportation and communication convenience rather than annual increments. Consequently this factor will be represented by a time trend variable.

---

[5] I. G. Williamson, Regional inequality and the process of national development: a description of the patterns,
Economic Development and Cultural Change 13 (July, 1965), Part 2. In this paper published ten years ago,
Japan was classified into one of the developing countries' groups having an increasing trend in regional income
disparity.

TABLE 5
Consumer price index at selected prefectural capitals

	1964	1966	1970	1972
Hokkaido	105.0	106.1	104.3	103.9
Akita	100.6	101.3	98.7	98.0
Saitama	101.9	102.4	103.9	104.1
Tokyo	108.7	109.5	108.7	109.2
Fukui	102.0	102.9	99.5	100.6
Nagoya	105.7	104.8	105.6	105.7
Osaka	107.2	106.8	107.9	106.9
Tottori	96.8	96.2	98.5	97.8
Kochi	98.8	100.2	102.3	104.2
Fukuoka	102.9	101.3	104.3	103.7
Kagoshima	100.4	101.8	101.8	102.0
Nation	100.0	100.0	100.0	100.8

Source: Economic Planning Agency, *Chiiki Keizai Yoran 1968* and *1973,* Keizai Kikaku Kyokai, 1968 and 1973, Tokyo.

3. ANALYSIS

Prior to econometric analysis of the factors described above, the relationship of the recent change to the growth pole approach is examined below.

In Japan, major policy inputs for development of less developed regions and promotion of growth poles were first provided in 1962 by the Cabinet approval of the National Comprehensive Development Plan and the enactment of the New Industrial Cities Development Act. The latter was created for implementing the growth pole strategy which is an important element in the National Comprehensive Development Plan of 1962. Thirteen areas were designated in 1964 as New Industrial Districts and six areas were designated as Industrial Development Special Zones in the same year according to the Act for Promotion of Industrial Development Special Zones enacted earlier in the same year. One New Industrial District was added in 1965 and another in 1966. Growth poles in Japan can be considered as all or some of those districts and zones designated for industrial development.

These industrial development districts and zones encompass 23 prefectures, exactly half of the total number of prefectures before reversion of Okinawa to Japanese sovereignty, and cover 94 cities *(shi)* and 288 towns and villages *(machi* and *mura).* Consequently, it would be too much to expect that all of them fared well in development during the past ten years. But, in terms of shift in the *per capita* personal income index of prefectures from 1965 to 1972 for two groups of prefectures—those having an industrial development district or zone and those without any—those prefectures having a district or zone, as a group, did not fare better than those without (Table 6). Of course, there are some success stories such as those of the Mizushima Industrial Area in Okayama and the Kashima Industrial Area in Ibaraki, both of which must have contributed to the upward shift of the respective prefectural *per capita* income index. But, such a success appears to require a particular combination of ingredients.[6]

---

[6]For a detailed evaluation of the case of Mizushima, see Fu-chen Lo, The growth pole approach to regional development—a case study of Mizushima industrial complex, Japan, United Nations Center for Regional Development, Nagoya, 1975.

The above analysis at least indicates that the government's industrial decentralization policy at selected growth poles did not materially contribute to reduction in income disparity among prefectures. In addition, it is possible to conjecture that the policy did not materially contribute to the shift in the trend of population concentration.

TABLE 6

Shift in *per capita* personal income index from 1965 to 1972

Prefectures having new industrial district or special development zone		Prefectures without either	
Prefecture	Change in *per capita* personal income from 1965 to 1972	Prefecture	Change in *per capita* personal income from 1965 to 1972
Hokkaido	-1.0	Iwate	4.4
Aomori	2.1	Yamagata	1.9
Miyagi	1.6	Tochigi	2.9
Akita	-9.5	Gunma	-0.7
Fukushima	4.1	Saitama	5.4
Ibaragi	4.6	Chiba	3.9
Niigata	-3.6	Tokyo	-10.8
Toyama	-3.8	Kanagawa	-1.0
Nagano	1.7	Ishikawa	1.7
Shizuoka	0.0	Fukui	1.9
Aichi	-2.8	Yamanashi	4.7
Hyogo	-8.0	Gifu[a]	-2.2
Tottori	6.6	Mie	4.4
Shimane	-0.7	Shiga	3.8
Okayama	6.7	Kyoto	-3.3
Hiroshima	-1.1	Osaka	-11.8
Yamaguchi	-5.0	Nara	-6.4
Tokushima	3.7	Wakayama	-0.1
Ehime	3.4	Kagawa	1.7
Fukuoka	2.0	Kochi[b]	-2.8
Kumamoto	-5.0	Saga	-6.0
Oita	2.1	Nagasaki	3.5
Miyazaki	-0.3	Kagoshima	3.0
Number of prefectures with upward shift		11	13
Number of prefectures without shift		1	0
Number of prefectures with downward shift		11	10
Total		23	23

[a]Due to the absence of the figure for 1965, the figure for 1966 was used for 1965.
[b]Due to the absence of the figures for 1965 - 7 the figure for 1968 was used for 1965.
Source: Table 5.

This conjecture can be supported by examining the relation of the distribution of public investment to the trend in population concentration. Table 7 lists the share of selected prefectures in public investment from 1955 to 1973. Only prefectures within the Tokyo and Osaka metropolitan regions are shown. It shows that there has been no declining trend in the share of public investment made in the four-prefecture Capital Region up to 1973, despite the fact that the degree of incremental concentration of population started tapering off in 1970. Therefore, it can be stated that the change in the trend of population concentration has not been induced by a shift in the geographic distribution of investment as far as the Capital Region is concerned. In the case of the Kinki Urban Region, the share in public investment started to decline in around 1969. But the change toward lesser concentration on the national scale as measured by PC2 became evident in 1966. In conclusion it can be stated that the public policy followed rather than preceded the change in the trend of population concentration.

TABLE 7
Shares in public investment of selected prefectures, FY 1955 to FY 1973

	1955	1969	1965	1967	1969	1971	1973
Capital Region							
Saitama	1.3	1.7	2.2	2.2	2.8	3.5	3.6
Chiba	2.1	2.2	3.4	3.5	4.3	4.8	4.7
Tokyo	10.8	11.7	13.0	12.5	11.5	11.1	9.9
Kanagawa	2.9	4.1	5.6	5.3	5.3	4.9	5.0
Subtotal	17.1	19.7	24.2	23.5	23.9	24.3	23.2
Kinki Urban Region							
Kyoto	2.1	2.0	1.6	1.4	1.6	1.7	1.8
Osaka	3.6	6.8	9.5	9.5	9.9	7.9	7.1
Hyogo	2.1	4.0	4.3	4.3	5.2	5.0	5.0
Nara	1.2	1.2	1.0	0.9	1.0	1.0	1.0
Subtotal	9.0	14.0	16.4	16.1	17.7	15.6	14.9
Nation	100.0	100.0	100.0	100.0	100.0	100.0	100.0

Source: Economic Planning Agency, *Chiiki Keizai Yoran, 1973*, Keizai Kikaku Kyokai, 1973, for 1965 to 1969. Division of Regional Policy, Ministry of Local Autonomy, *Statistics of Public Investment, 1975* (Gyosei Toshi Jisseki), Chihozaimu-kyokai, 1975 for 1971 and 1973. Economic Planning Agency, *Chiiki Keizai Yoran, 1968*, Keizai Kikaku Kyokai, 1968, for 1955 and 1960.

Now we proceed to an econometric analysis of the trend in population concentration. From the above screening of variables, the following are selected as possible contributing factors:

(1) Economic Growth Rate
    (a) GR1—fiscal year basis   or
    (b) GR2—calendar year basis.
(2) Degree of Regional Income Disparity
    (a) ID1—range of disparity in index,   or
    (b) ID2—coefficient of variation.
(3) Time Trend
    (a) T—year measured from 1952.
(4) Time dummy for the 1970s
    (a) TD.

Of the above, the time trend variable would represent, among others, general improvement in transportation and communication on the national scale, and the time dummy variable the recent shift in the public opinion toward environment and welfare as opposed to economic growth. The analysis has been plagued by some irregularities in some of the time series data.[7] But it was possible to obtain general characteristics of the trend of population concentration.

[7]Specifically, PC1 and PC2 are based on prefectural growth rates of population, some of which are based on fiscal years and others on calendar years as revealed in Table A.1, and ID1 and ID2 are based on calendar years from 1955 to 1964 and on fiscal years from 1965 to 1972, as revealed in Table 3.

Among alternative equations estimated for PC1, those having some significance are contained in Table 8. Equations (1) through (3) indicate that the growth rate of the economy is a significant variable which explains the variation in the trend of population concentration. The explanatory power of the variable is most significant when the economic growth rate is lagged by about one year.

When an index of income disparity among prefectures is added to the economic growth rate, the result is not improved as shown by equations (4) and (5). The result of estimation is best when the time trend variable is added. Among equations (6) through (9), equation (6) is considered to be the best in terms of the t-statistics obtained and R^2. The equation implies that there is a time trend toward greater incremental population concentration in the Capital Region (an increase of about 3 percentage points in PC1 which is the share in the incremental population increase of the region every year), an increase in the GNP growth rate intensifies population concentration, but a decrease in the range of income disparity index reduces the trend in population concentration. Comparing the two income disparity indices, it can be known that ID1 is a more meaningful index than ID2. This is understandable because the relative income level of Tokyo is more directly reflected in ID1, whereas ID2 is made up of the income levels of all the prefectures.

The significance of the time dummy for the 1970s (TD) is tested in equations (10) and (11). The results show that, if anything, there is a negative change in the trend of population concentration into the Capital Region as much as reducing PC1 by 20 percentage points, and its statistical significance is marginal. Relative to the time trend variable T, the contribution of this factor is much less conclusive.

Similar analysis was undertaken for PC2, the results of which are presented in Table 9. Generally, the results are less conclusive than those for PC1, but quite similar characteristics have been observed. First, the behavior of PC2 can also be explained, with significance, by GNP growth rates, the disparity in income levels among prefectures and to a lesser extent by a time trend. The contribution of the time dummy variable for the 1970s is less certain, but, if it does exist, it is exerting a negative effect on substantial outmigration from less-developed prefectures.

Among the 14 equations presented, equations (7) and (11) are considered to be among the best. Equation (7) states that the number of rapidly depopulating prefectures (PC2) can be explained by the GNP growth rate and the coefficient of variation of *per capita* personal incomes of prefectures, both of which are lagged by one year. Either variable contributes to increasing the number of fast depopulating prefectures, as expected. Equation (11) implies that a third factor, a time trend variable, can be added as an explanatory variable, thus the list of explanatory variables becomes similar to the one for PC1. In this case, too, there appears to be a time trend of intensified population concentration. The alternative formulation as presented by equation (12) implies that an income disparity index and a time trend alone, without a GNP growth rate, can explain PC2 to a substantial extent.

Comparing the results for PC1 with those for PC2, the following can be stated:

(1) The economic growth rate intensifies population concentration, but its impact is statistically more conclusive for population concentration into the Capital Region.
(2) Income disparity among prefectures contributes to the intensification of population concentration, and the added concentration in the Capital Region is more responsive to ID1, the range of income disparity index, while the depopulation from less-developed prefectures is more responsive to ID2, the coefficient of variation of pre-

TABLE 8
Estimated equations for PC1

Equation No.	Constant	GR1	GR2	ID1	ID2	I	TD	R^2	D - Wᵃ	Period
(1)	28.65	2.82 (2.67)ᵇ						0.25	0.77	52 - 74
(2)	18.35	3.89ᶜ (3.22)						0.34	0.96	53 - 74
(3)	27.32		3.10 (3.15)					0.33	0.94	53 - 74
(4)	60.42		3.37 (2.42)	-0.38 (-0.87)				0.31	1.07	55 - 72
(5)	66.91	2.63 (1.62)			-187.11 (-0.89)			0.21	0.85	55 - 72
(6)	-142.55	2.82ᶜ (2.34)		1.54ᶜ (1.95)		3.32 (2.49)		0.55	1.18	56 - 72
(7)	-108.54		2.63ᶜ (2.15)	1.25ᶜ (1.48)		2.80 (1.93)		0.53	1.12	56 - 72
(8)	-40.27	3.22ᶜ (3.46)			264.83ᶜ (0.89)	1.89 (1.59)		0.46	1.22	56 - 72
(9)	17.26	3.22ᶜ (2.47)				1.04 (1.48)		0.42	1.10	56 - 72
(10)	123.05	2.20 (1.34)		-0.94 (-1.45)			-20.07 (-1.30)	0.28	0.92	55 - 72
(11)	107.25	3.18ᶜ (2.41)		-0.83ᶜ (-1.42)			-20.13 (-1.62)	0.45	1.31	56 - 72

ᵃD - W is the Durbin - Watson statistic.
ᵇThe figure in parentheses is the t-statistic of the estimated coefficient directly above.
ᶜIndicates that the variable is lagged by 1 year.
Source: Computed from data presented in Table A.5 through the ordinary least-squares method.

fectural *per capita* personal incomes.

(3) There has been a consistent time trend for intensified population concentration throughout the observed period.

(4) An otherwise unexplainable shift in the trend of population concentration might have taken place since 1970, but its statistical significance is not sufficient for making a conclusive statement.

The observed time trend may be considered to represent continuous improvements in transportation and communication including the starting of operation of the New Tokaido Line, improved highway networks, the introduction of faster and more frequent airline services, and the popularization of the automatic dialing system for long-distance telephone calls. Although not conclusive, the intensified concern over the environment and a shift in value orientation among the general public from economic growth to something more humane might have had some effect on the continuing trend of population concentration.

4. CONCLUSIONS

The foregoing analysis has revealed that the recent emergence of a new pattern of population shifts, which can be characterized by a lesser degree of incremental population concentration in large metropolitan areas and a lesser number of depopulating prefectures, does not necessarily imply changes in the preferences of the population. Rather, it can be explained by continuing changes in economic variables. Specifically, the slowing down of the economic growth rate and the declining income disparity among prefectures are considered to be largely responsible for the recent change. It is to be emphasized that these two factors outweighed the continuing upward trend of population concentration which can be considered to be a result of general improvement in transportation and communication over time. Intensified concern over the environment and a possible change in values in life might have contributed to some extent to the change, but the evidence is too uncertain to conclude this.

Aside from the recent downturn of the growth rate of the economy, which might, after all, be temporary, the convergence of differences in prefectural *per capita* incomes has significant implications. First, the convergence started to appear around 1961 and continued for more than a decade in parallel with a generally high rate of economic growth. Although the convergence is associated with developed economies as found by Williamson,[8] this example demonstrates a particularly close relationship of the convergence with economic growth. As found earlier, this convergence appears to have been caused by convergence in wage rate differentials among different parts of the economy, which has in turn been caused by tightening of labor markets.

Second, it should be noted that this converging trend started well before the government's policy tools for decentralization of economic activities became available. Indeed, in terms of the share in public investment, the government has not yet adopted a policy of decentralization.

Third, the convergence of *per capita* incomes may imply the lessening of economies of scale in large metropolitan areas. However, a closer examination reveals an upward shift of the relative income level in prefectures immediately outside a metropolitan center.

---

[8] Williamson, *op. cit.*

TABLE 9
Estimated equations for PC2

Equation No.	Constant	GR1	GR2	ID1	ID2	I	TD	R^2	D - W[a]	Period
(1)	9.41	1.03 (2.74)[b]						0.26	1.33	52 - 74
(2)	11.45		0.78 (1.94)					0.16	1.15	53 - 74
(3)	6.64	1.25[c] (2.69)						0.27	0.98	53 - 74
(4)	1.77	0.31 (1.04)		0.18[c] (1.88)				0.23	1.16	56 - 72
(5)	0.22		0.44[c] (1.70)	0.19[c] (2.03)				0.32	1.05	56 - 72
(6)	1.29	0.37[c] (0.29)			90.29[c] (2.29)			0.30	1.24	56 - 72
(7)	-0.11		0.49[c] (1.95)		91.72[c] (2.50)			0.39	1.12	56 - 72
(8)	-27.47	0.19[c] (0.66)		0.46[c] (2.40)		0.53 (1.64)		0.36	1.24	56 - 72
(9)	-23.29		0.29[c] (1.05)	0.41[c] (2.11)		0.43 (1.30)		0.39	1.12	56 - 72
(10)	-16.74	0.31[c] (1.14)			168.02[c] (2.69)	0.39 (1.55)		0.41	1.36	56 - 72
(11)	-14.12		0.40[c] (1.56)		153.92[c] (2.53)	0.31 (1.27)		0.45	1.19	56 - 72
(12)	-13.98				167.66[c] (2.65)	0.42 (1.69)		0.35	1.17	56 - 72
(13)	12.48	0.25[c] (0.83)		0.08[c] (0.57)			-3.32 (-1.18)	0.31	1.49	56 - 72
(14)	6.44		0.45[c] (1.80)		59.74 (1.29)		-2.60 (-1.12)	0.44	1.42	56 - 72

[a]D - W is the Durbin - Watson statistic.
[b]The figure in parentheses is the t-statistic of the estimated coefficient directly above.
[c]Indicates that the variable is lagged by 1 year.
Source: Computed from data presented in Table A.5 through the ordinary least-squares method.

Therefore, spatial extension of metropolitan areas can be granted to exist, but evidence is seriously lacking for the argument of lessening scale economies or even diseconomies of large metropolitan areas.

The role of transportation and communication improvement in lessening income disparity deserves attention. The consistent upward trend of population concentration can be regarded as a result of improved mobility of people and better information made possible by improvement of transportation and communication services. In addition, it must have contributed to lessening of income disparity by making the distribution of factors more in line with a spatial equilibrium.

In regard to the growth pole strategy, the successful cases such as Mizushima and Kashima have two common characteristics: (1) each is located within a short distance from a large metropolis and/or along a major route of transportation, and (2) each has absorbed a large amount of investment.[9]

It is possible to derive from the above analysis several implications relative to developing countries. First, there is a fundamental conflict between high economic growth and decentralization of population. If a high rate of economic growth is to be achieved, further concentration of population into a few large metropolitan areas cannot be avoided.

However, the continuation of a high rate of economic growth would sooner or later lead to equalization of income and wage levels within the country. Then, the reduction in income disparity among regions would, in turn, prevent further concentration of population. Therefore, population concentration would be a temporary problem for developing countries.

This process, however, may take a long time. In the case of Japan, it took about 30 years, counting from the start of the postwar reconstruction period, before the concentrating trend of population became substantially reduced. The situation would not be the same with respect to developing countries. With faster rates of change observable in recent decades, the time span might be shorter. But, it would be overly optimistic to expect this whole process would complete within five or ten years.

Another option open to developing countries is, of course, to aim at a lower rate of economic growth. Rapid population concentration can be avoided by this strategy, but income inequality would persist for a longer span of time.

The growth pole strategy is obviously another opinion. To what extent this strategy ameliorates shortcomings of each of the two strategies is an open question which requires a detailed study for each case. Judging from the experience in Japan, it can be said that this strategy is effective in expanding a zone of metropolitan influence, but for satisfactorily relieving the problems of income disparity and population concentration, the strategy would require a cost which is either impossible to pay or too high to be justified.

[9]According to Lö, *op. cit.*, about $190 million of public investment from 1957 to 1969 and $2300 million of private manufacturing investment from 1960 to 1970 were made in Mizushima and according to the official development plan for Kashima, shown in *Chiiki Keizai Yoran, 1968*, prepared by the Economic Planning Agency, $750 million of manufacturing investment was anticipated.

APPENDIX

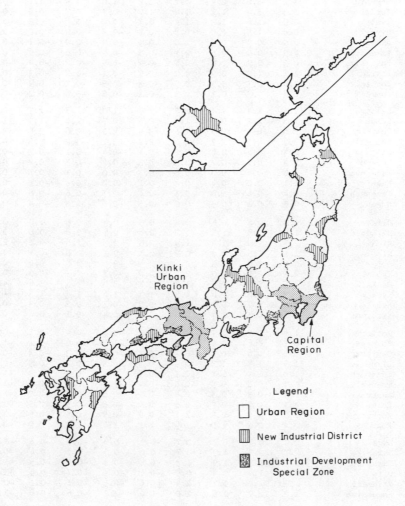

Fig. A.-1. Locations of urban regions and industrial development areas in Japan.

TABL
Population growth rate of prefectures

	Fiscal Year								Calendar Year	
Prefecture	1952	1953	1954	1955	1956	1957	1958	1959	1960	1961
Hokkaido	7.1	3.6	2.4	1.7	1.2	1.0	1.4	1.1	0.7	0.7
Aomori	1.3	3.0	1.1	1.4	1.0	0.7	0.7	0.6	0.2	0.2
Iwate	0.9	1.8	1.2	1.4	0.7	0.2	0.4	0.3	-0.1	-0.2
Miyagi	0.8	1.5	2.0	0.8	0.7	-0.1	0.2	0.2	-0.2	-0.1
Akita	0.9	0.9	0.7	1.0	0.1	-0.2	-0.2	-0.1	-0.5	-0.8
Yamagata	·0.9	-0.0	0.5	0.1	-0.3	-0.4	-0.6	-0.6	-0.6	-0.8
Fukushima	0.3	0.9	0.8	0.5	-0.1	-0.5	-0.2	-0.4	-0.9	-0.7
Ibaragi	1.1	1.0	0.9	0.0	0.0	-0.1	-0.2	-0.3	0.2	0.3
Tochigi	0.5	0.7	0.5	0.5	-0.3	-0.5	-0.4	-0.9	-0.2	-0.4
Gunma	0.8	0.3	0.1	0.3	-0.1	-0.6	-3.6	-0.2	-0.6	-0.1
Saitama	1.3	1.4	1.7	1.2	1.0	1.0	1.3	1.7	2.2	2.5
Chiba	1.3	1.2	0.9	1.2	0.6	0.7	1.0	1.0	1.2	2.0
Tokyo	6.6	6.1	2.5	1.6	3.9	4.0	3.8	3.8	3.6	3.1
Kanagawa	3.3	4.5	2.7	2.6	2.7	3.1	3.2	3.6	4.2	4.2
Niigata	0.4	0.4	0.6	0.2	-0.1	-0.4	-0.1	-0.3	-0.4	-0.4
Toyama	0.4	0.3	0.7	0.3	0.3	0.2	0.3	0.2	0.2	0.0
Ishikawa	0.6	0.4	0.0	0.6	0.3	0.0	0.1	0.1	0.2	0.3
Fukui	1.1	0.0	0.4	0.4	0.2	-0.2	0.0	-0.1	0.0	0.1
Yamanashi	0.4	0.4	1.0	0.6	-0.4	-0.7	-0.6	-0.8	-0.6	-0.4
Nagano	0.3	0.1	0.3	0.2	-0.3	-0.6	-0.3	-0.4	-0.4	-0.3
Gifu	1.3	0.6	0.6	0.4	0.5	0.4	0.6	1.0	0.9	0.6
Shizuoka	1.2	1.8	1.3	1.2	0.8	0.7	0.8	0.8	0.9	1.0
Aichi	2.7	2.6	1.9	1.9	2.3	2.3	1.8	2.1	2.6	2.9
Mie	1.1	1.5	0.2	0.2	0.1	-0.1	0.0	-0.1	0.1	0.4
Shiga	0.6	-0.0	0.3	0.1	-0.4	-0.5	-0.8	0.0	0.3	0.2
Kyoto	2.3	2.1	1.0	2.1	0.8	0.7	0.7	0.5	0.3	0.7
Osaka	4.5	5.2	2.4	1.7	3.1	3.8	3.5	3.6	4.0	4.1
Hyogo	2.9	3.0	1.6	1.5	1.4	1.6	1.4	1.5	1.7	1.9
Nara	1.1	0.9	0.7	0.5	0.0	-0.1	0.2	0.3	0.1	0.1
Wakayama	1.1	0.5	1.4	0.8	0.1	-0.4	-0.1	0.0	0.0	0.3
Tottori	1.6	0.9	0.7	0.5	-0.2	-0.6	-0.4	-0.5	-0.8	-0.5
Shimane	0.7	0.8	0.6	0.1	-0.5	-1.1	-0.6	-1.1	-1.2	-1.0
Okayama	1.5	0.6	0.8	-0.2	0.1	-0.3	-0.3	-0.3	-0.3	-0.4
Hiroshima	1.5	1.7	1.1	0.9	0.3	0.3	0.2	0.5	0.2	0.4
Yamaguchi	1.8	1.7	1.1	0.7	0.5	0.1	0.2	-0.3	-1.0	-0.6
Tokushima	0.7	0.8	0.5	-0.0	-0.4	-1.0	-0.6	-0.5	-1.0	-1.1
Kagawa	1.5	0.3	0.3	0.4	-0.1	-0.8	-0.7	-0.2	-1.0	-0.7
Ehime	1.1	0.7	0.9	0.8	0.1	-0.6	-0.5	-0.5	-1.1	-0.9
Kochi	0.8	1.2	2.8	-1.1	0.0	-0.9	-0.5	-0.6	-1.3	-1.0
Fukuoka	2.2	2.3	1.2	1.9	1.1	1.0	1.0	0.9	-0.2	-0.1
Saga	2.0	0.4	0.7	0.7	-0.1	-0.8	-0.5	-0.5	-1.4	-1.5
Nagasaki	2.7	2.3	1.5	0.7	0.6	0.0	0.5	0.4	-0.8	-1.0
Kumamoto	0.3	1.3	1.9	1.3	0.4	-0.3	-0.5	-0.5	-1.2	-1.0
Oita	1.2	1.4	1.4	0.4	-0.1	-0.7	-0.7	-0.5	-1.0	-0.9
Miyazaki	1.3	1.8	1.7	1.4	0.6	-0.3	-0.1	-0.1	-0.6	-0.6
Kagoshima	1.2	12.9	1.6	1.0	-0.2	-1.2	-0.6	-0.8	-1.2	-1.3
Nation	2.3	2.4	1.4	1.1	1.0	0.8	0.9	1.0	0.8	0.9
Number of Prefectures that Lost Population[1]/	0	2	0	3	15	27	23	24	26	25
Number of Fast Depopulating Prefectures [2]/	26	26	6	4	15	21	20	24	21	22

Notes: [1]Those having a negative growth rate.
[2]Those having a growth rate which is more than 1 percentage point below the national population growth rate.

Sources: 1 Economic Planning Agency, *Income Statistics of Prefectures: 1955-1965,* Tokyo, Shiseido, 1968, for 1956 to 1965.

E A-1
from preceding year, 1956 - 1975 (%)

							Fiscal Year					
1962	1963	1964	1965	1966	1967	1968	1969	1970	1971	1972	1973	1974
0.5	0.5	0.5	0.4	0.3	0.3	0.2	-0.1	-0.6	-0.1	0.3	0.6	1.0
-0.2	0.0	0.2	-1.0	0.1	0.4	0.2	-0.1	0.2	-0.3	0.3	0.4	0.6
-0.3	-0.4	-0.6	-1.1	-1.1	-0.3	-0.5	-1.0	0.0	-0.7	-0.1	0.1	0.6
-0.2	0.2	0.5	0.3	0.4	0.8	0.8	0.8	0.9	1.0	1.0	1.5	1.5
-1.1	-0.9	-0.8	-0.7	-0.8	-0.4	-0.6	-0.6	-0.6	-0.7	-0.1	-0.3	0.1
-1.0	-0.8	-0.7	-1.0	-0.7	-0.2	-0.3	-0.5	-1.2	-0.7	-0.3	-0.0	0.3
-0.8	-0.6	-0.5	-0.6	-0.7	-0.2	-0.4	-0.3	-0.4	-0.3	0.1	0.4	0.5
0.2	-0.1	0.2	-0.2	-0.2	0.6	0.8	1.4	1.6	1.6	1.3	1.8	1.9
0.0	0.2	0.3	0.2	0.0	0.6	0.8	1.1	1.3	1.5	1.5	1.7	1.4
0.1	0.3	0.5	0.9	0.1	0.7	0.9	0.9	0.7	1.0	1.1	1.3	1.1
3.4	4.7	5.0	6.3	4,8	5.4	5.0	4.9	5.5	5.1	5.0	4.5	3.7
2.8	2.9	3.8	4.5	2.8	4.0	4.2	5.1	6.4	4.5	4.3	4.2	3.9
2.7	2.5	1.9	1.5	1.0	1.2	1.3	0.8	0.6	0.9	0.6	0.1	0.1
4.9	4.5	4.8	7.5	3.8	4.5	4.7	4.4	4.3	4.2	3.5	2.8	2.4
-0.6	-0.5	-0.3	0.0	-0.5	-0.1	-0.3	-0.3	-0.4	-0.2	0.0	0.4	0.7
-0.1	0.0	0.0	-0.6	-0.3	0.1	0.1	0.2	0.4	0.6	0.8	0.8	0.7
0.1	0.2	0.4	-0.3	0.2	0.6	0.7	0.6	0.1	0.9	1.1	1.3	1.3
-0.2	0.1	0.0	-0.3	-0.4	0.3	-0.1	-0.7	0.0	0.4	0.7	0.8	0.8
-0.7	-0.1	-0.1	-1.1	-0.4	-0.4	0.1	0.1	-0.7	0.3	0.4	0.6	0.8
-0.2	-0.1	-0.1	-0.4	-0.3	0.1	0.0	0.1	0.2	0.5	0.5	0.7	0.7
0.8	1.1	0.9	0.4	0.3	0.9	0.9	1.0	0.4	1.0	1.2	1.4	0.9
1.2	1.3	1.3	0.8	0.7	1.3	1.4	1.0	1.5	1.3	1.4	1.5	1.2
2.8	2.8	3.0	1.9	1.8	2.4	2.3	2.4	2.6	2.5	2.2	2.0	1.4
0.5	0.6	0.5	-1.0	0.0	0.0	0.1	0.5	1.2	0.8	1.1	1.1	1.1
0.3	0.1	0.4	0.2	0.0	0.6	0.4	0.9	1.7	2.0	1.8	2.2	2.2
0.9	1.0	1.1	1.6	1.0	1.6	1.6	1.1	1.4	1.2	0.5	1.3	1.2
4.2	3.6	3.7	3.8	2.5	2.8	2.9	2.9	2.6	2.3	1.9	1.4	1.2
2.1	1.8	1.8	2.3	1.3	1.6	1.5	1.7	2.0	1.5	3.1	1.4	1.2
0.5	1.2	1.1	2.7	1.6	2.0	2.5	2.9	3.1	3.1	3.4	3.0	2.4
0.3	0.6	0.8	0.4	0.3	0.4	0.3	0.3	-.3	0.5	0.7	0.6	0.4
-0.6	-0.4	-0.5	-1.3	-1.2	-0.2	-0.2	-0.2	-0.2	0.0	0.2	0.6	0.7
-1.4	-1.4	-1.6	-2.4	-1.5	-1.1	-1.2	-1.1	-1.0	-0.9	-0.4	0.3	0.4
-0.5	-0.4	0.0	-0.2	0.2	0.8	0.8	0.9	0.9	1.4	1.0	1.1	1.2
0.8	0.9	1.1	1.1	1.0	1.4	1.7	1.6	0.9	1.7	1.9	1.3	1.3
-0.5	-0.9	-1.0	-0.7	-0.8	-0.5	-0.6	-0.2	-0.1	0.1	0.4	0.4	0.6
-1.0	-0.7	-0.8	-0.3	-0.9	-0.5	-0.7	-0.5	-0.4	-0.3	0.0	0.3	0.5
-0.6	0.1	-0.1	-0.7	-0.3	0.4	0.0	0.3	0.3	0.8	0.9	1.1	1.3
-0.9	-0.8	-0.7	-0.3	-0.6	-0.3	-0.3	-0.2	-0.6	0.1	0.4	0.5	0.8
-1.2	-0.8	-0.8	-1.2	-1.0	-0.4	-0.5	-0.8	-0.4	-0.3	0.4	0.5	0.5
0.0	-0.3	-0.2	-0.5	0.4	0.5	0.3	0.3	0.2	0.6	0.7	1.1	1.6
-2.2	-1.9	-1.5	-0.7	-0.7	-0.3	-1.0	-1.5	-0.3	-0.8	-0.4	0.1	0.8
-1.5	-1.1	-1.7	-1.6	-0.9	-0.9	-0.9	-0.9	-0.9	-0.7	-0.3	-0.1	0.7
-1.1	-0.8	-0.9	-0.9	-0.3	-0.1	-0.8	-1.1	-1.8	-0.8	-0.5	0.3	0.8
-1.1	-0.7	-1.0	-0.6	-0.8	-0.7	-0.5	-0.4	-0.3	0.4	0.0	0.5	1.0
-0.9	-0.9	-0.8	-1.6	0.1	-0.4	-0.4	-0.5	-1.0	-0.4	0.2	0.5	1.2
-1.7	-1.1	-1.1	-0.5	-1.2	-1.1	-1.8	-1.0	-1.8	-1.0	-0.4	-0.1	0.2
0.9	1.0	1.1	1.1	0.8	1.2	1.2	1.1	1.2	1.3	1.3	1.3	1.3
25	22	21	27	22	18	18	20	18	15	7	3	0
24	22	24	28	21	21	23	20	21	18	13	7	3

2 Economic Planning Agency, *National Income Account Quarterly*, 1975, for FY1966 to FY1972.
3 Ministry of Local Autonomy, *Population and Household Statistics, 1975*, Tokyo, Ministry of Finance Printing Office, 1975, for FY1952 through FY1955 and FY1973 and FY1974.

TABLE A-2
Share of Population in Prefectures 1950-1970

Prefecture	1950	1955	1960	1965	1970
Hokkaido	5.16	5.35	5.39	5.26	5.00
Aomori	1.54	1.55	1.53	1.44	1.38
Iwate	1.62	1.60	1.55	1.44	1.32
Miyagi	2.00	1.93	1.87	1.78	1.75
Akita	1.57	1.51	1.43	1.30	1.20
Yamagata	1.63	1.52	1.41	1.29	1.18
Fukushima	2.48	2.35	2.20	2.02	1.88
Ibaragi	2.45	2.31	2.19	2.09	2.07
Tochigi	1.86	1.73	1.62	1.55	1.52
Gunma	1.92	1.81	1.69	1.63	1.60
Saitama	2.58	2.53	2.60	3.07	3.73
Chiba	2.57	2.47	2.47	2.75	3.25
Tokyo	7.55	9.00	10.37	11.06	11.00
Kanagawa	2.99	3.27	3.69	4.51	5.28
Niigata	2.96	2.77	2.61	2.44	2.28
Toyama	1.21	1.14	1.11	1.04	0.99
Ishikawa	1.15	1.08	1.04	1.00	0.97
Fukui	0.90	0.84	0.81	0.76	0.72
Yamanashi	0.97	0.90	0.84	0.78	0.73
Nagano	2.48	2.26	2.12	1.99	1.89
Gifu	1.86	1.77	1.75	1.73	1.70
Shizuoka	2.97	2.97	2.95	2.96	2.98
Aichi	4.08	4.22	4.50	4.88	5.19
Mie	1.76	1.66	1.59	1.54	1.49
Shiga	1.03	0.96	0.90	0.87	0.86
Kyoto	2.20	2.17	2.13	2.14	2.17
Osaka	4.64	5.17	5.89	6.77	7.35
Hyogo	3.98	4.06	4.18	4.39	4.50
Nara	0.92	0.87	0.84	0.84	0.90
Wakayama	1.18	1.13	1.07	1.05	1.01
Tottori	0.72	0.69	0.64	0.59	0.55
Shimane	1.10	1.04	0.95	0.84	0.75
Okayama	2.00	1.89	1.79	1.67	1.65
Hiroshima	2.50	2.41	2.34	2.32	2.35
Yamaguchi	1.85	1.80	1.72	1.57	1.46
Tokushima	1.06	0.98	0.91	0.83	0.76
Kagawa	1.14	1.06	0.98	0.92	0.88
Ehime	1.83	1.73	1.61	1.47	1.37
Kochi	1.05	0.99	0.91	0.83	0.76
Fukuoka	4.24	4.32	4.29	4.03	3.88
Saga	1.14	1.09	1.01	0.89	0.81
Nagasaki	1.98	1.96	1.88	1.67	1.51
Kumamoto	2.20	2.12	1.99	1.80	1.64
Oita	1.51	1.43	1.33	1.21	1.11
Miyazaki	1.31	1.28	1.21	1.10	1.01
Kagoshima	2.17	2.29	2.10	1.89	1.67
Nation	100.0	100.0	100.0	100.0	100.0

Sources: Economic Planning Agency, *Chiiki Keizai Yoran, 1968* and
1973. (Tokyo: Keizai Kikaku Kyokai, 1968 and 1973).

TABLE A-3
Per capita personal incomes of prefectures, 1955 - 1965
(in index)

	1955	1956	1957	1958	1959	1960	1961	1962	1963	1964	1965
Hokkaido	100.0	91.4	97.8	98.9	99.0	94.9	92.0	88.1	91.3	87.4	89.2
Aomori	75.7	77.8	75.3	76.3	76.5	73.5	71.0	73.6	73.8	74.4	77.6
Iwate	71.6	71.6	70.8	68.8	70.6	69.2	68.8	71.1	72.1	73.4	76.3
Miyagi	85.1	81.5	83.1	80.6	83.3	82.9	82.6	82.4	82.5	82.1	83.6
Akita	81.1	79.0	77.5	75.3	75.5	74.4	73.9	74.8	74.9	78.7	78.9
Yamagata	81.1	79.0	80.9	80.6	81.4	82.1	80.4	79.2	79.2	79.7	80.6
Fukushima	81.1	79.0	76.4	77.4	80.4	76.9	73.9	73.6	73.8	72.9	75.9
Ibaragi	74.3	71.6	71.9	73.1	75.5	74.4	73.2	73.6	73.2	71.5	71.1
Tochigi	85.1	84.0	79.8	80.6	83.3	86.3	85.5	84.3	83.1	83.6	84.5
Gunma	81.1	76.5	75.3	80.6	81.4	79.5	80.4	81.8	83.6	87.0	84.9
Saitama	94.6	93.8	94.4	93.5	94.1	93.2	94.2	94.3	95.1	96.6	96.1
Chiba	86.5	85.2	84.3	82.8	86.3	87.2	92.8	92.5	94.0	95.6	96.1
Tokyo	158.1	163.0	159.6	159.1	160.8	159.0	165.2	163.5	159.6	156.5	153.0
Kanagawa	117.6	114.8	118.0	119.4	118.6	119.7	124.6	125.2	126.2	126.1	120.7
Niigata	87.8	85.2	86.5	83.9	84.3	82.9	80.4	83.0	82.0	84.1	82.8
Toyama	100.0	92.6	95.5	95.7	97.1	94.0	96.4	96.9	96.7	93.7	94.4
Ishikawa	95.9	93.8	91.0	98.9	101.0	99.1	94.2	94.3	91.8	91.3	91.4
Fukui	94.6	90.1	88.8	89.2	90.2	88.0	87.0	86.8	85.8	87.4	85.8
Yamanashi	78.4	79.0	78.7	79.6	83.3	89.7	88.4	84.9	85.2	87.0	88.8
Nagano	87.8	87.7	83.1	82.8	85.3	84.6	84.8	85.5	85.8	87.4	88.8
Gifu	91.9	92.6	93.3	90.3	93.1	94.0	94.2	91.2	90.7	90.3	90.1
Shizuoka	89.2	88.9	92.1	93.5	96.1	94.9	94.2	91.2	92.3	90.3	90.1
Aichi	114.9	116.0	116.9	112.9	115.7	122.2	115.9	113.8	112.6	109.2	106.0
Mie	87.8	85.2	84.3	79.6	79.4	83.8	86.2	86.8	88.0	86.5	84.9
Shiga	91.9	92.6	91.0	90.3	92.2	88.0	86.2	84.9	85.2	86.5	84.1
Kyoto	108.1	109.9	106.7	107.5	108.8	108.5	107.2	106.9	107.7	107.7	105.2
Osaka	135.1	142.0	137.1	135.5	135.3	135.0	137.7	137.7	141.5	139.6	140.1
Hyogo	118.9	127.2	127.0	123.7	113.7	106.8	105.8	105.7	102.2	103.4	102.6
Nara	95.9	95.1	96.6	103.2	101.0	96.6	100.7	96.2	95.1	97.1	94.0
Wakayama	98.6	95.1	89.9	87.1	90.2	87.2	84.1	84.9	86.9	89.4	88.8
Tottori	83.8	79.0	78.7	77.4	78.4	77.8	73.2	73.6	71.6	72.0	72.8
Shimane	82.4	79.0	77.5	79.6	80.4	78.6	77.5	74.8	71.6	73.4	75.4
Okayama	91.9	88.9	85.4	84.9	87.3	85.5	87.7	89.3	86.9	84.5	87.1
Hiroshima	89.2	92.6	94.4	93.5	94.1	93.2	91.3	89.9	88.0	90.3	90.1
Yamaguchi	90.5	86.4	87.6	88.2	88.2	90.6	86.2	86.2	83.6	84.5	84.5
Tokushima	78.4	79.0	77.5	80.6	83.3	83.8	81.9	79.9	78.7	81.2	81.9
Kagawa	98.6	100.0	95.5	95.7	94.1	97.4	97.8	95.0	94.5	97.1	99.6
Ehime	86.5	85.2	83.1	80.6	81.4	82.1	81.9	80.5	80.3	80.2	81.5
Kochi	79.7	80.2	77.5	79.6	83.3	82.9	82.6	80.0	79.8	95.2	82.3
Fukuoka	102.7	100.0	104.5	104.3	100.0	95.7	92.8	91.2	90.2	90.3	92.7
Saga	83.8	77.8	76.4	78.5	77.5	81.2	76.8	77.4	74.9	76.3	78.4
Nagasaki	83.8	82.7	79.8	78.5	77.5	70.1	69.6	71.7	70.5	73.4	78.0
Kumamoto	82.4	80.2	70.8	71.0	70.6	69.2	70.3	74.2	77.0	78.3	79.3
Oita	74.3	71.6	75.3	79.6	77.5	73.5	70.3	73.0	72.7	74.9	77.6
Miyazaki	70.3	70.4	65.2	85.1	70.6	70.9	66.7	67.3	72.1	69.1	72.8
Kagoshima	60.8	60.5	62.9	64.5	63.7	61.5	62.3	62.3	63.4	62.3	64.7
Nation	100.0	100.0	100.0	100.0	100.0	100.0	100.0	100.0	100.0	100.0	100.0

Source: Economic Planning Agency, *Income Statistics of Prefectures, 1955-1965* (Tokyo: Shiseido, 1968).

TABLE A-4
Per capita Personal incomes of prefectures, FY1965 - FY1978
(in index)

	1965	1966	1967	1968	1969	1970	1971	1972
Hokkaido	93.8	92.8	96.2	94.6	92.3	94.8	92.3	92.8
Aomori	77.1	76.5	77.3	76.5	76.8	77.7	78.2	79.2
Iwate	72.9	73.7	74.6	76.7	75.7	76.7	75.0	77.3
Miyagi	86.1	84.0	84.7	85.7	85.4	86.7	86.2	87.7
Akita	84.5	87.4	89.4	90.3	83.2	79.6	75.5	75.0
Yamagata	80.6	82.3	83.8	84.9	84.3	83.5	79.9	82.5
Fukushima	75.2	76.8	77.6	78.5	77.7	79.8	77.4	79.3
Ibaragi	77.1	77.5	78.8	80.6	80.3	83.5	82.8	81.7
Tochigi	84.5	86.7	87.0	87.5	86.7	88.1	86.5	87.4
Gunma	88.8	89.8	90.0	90.8	90.5	91.6	89.2	88.1
Saitama	100.8	100.3	99.7	102.1	104.4	108.5	103.6	106.2
Chiba	93.0	94.5	97.1	98.0	99.3	102.9	95.7	96.9
Tokyo	149.2	147.4	144.3	142.2	141.6	142.7	138.7	138.4
Kanagawa	118.6	120.1	117.7	117.7	118.4	120.0	118.5	117.6
Niigata	85.7	85.7	85.8	87.2	85.2	84.6	81.8	82.1
Toyama	92.6	92.5	92.0	91.6	90.5	91.9	89.4	88.8
Ishikawa	91.5	91.8	91.7	94.1	94.5	95.2	93.5	93.2
Fukui	85.7	86.0	85.3	86.2	87.0	88.9	86.8	87.6
Yamanashi	80.2	83.3	82.6	81.1	83.4	86.7	85.5	84.9
Nagano	84.5	85.3	84.7	83.6	84.1	85.4	86.0	86.1
Gifu	-	93.2	92.9	94.1	94.1	94.0	91.4	91.0
Shizuoka	95.7	96.6	95.3	95.1	96.7	98.5	96.1	95.7
Aichi	107.0	108.2	106.5	105.6	106.2	112.7	106.3	104.2
Mie	88.0	88.7	91.5	92.8	93.8	95.4	93.2	92.4
Shiga	88.0	89.1	89.7	92.1	92.7	93.5	91.8	91.8
Kyoto	108.5	109.6	109.1	110.2	109.3	110.0	104.5	105.2
Osaka	133.0	129.0	123.9	122.8	121.2	123.5	121.7	121.2
Hyogo	109.7	107.2	105.3	105.1	106.4	106.0	104.4	101.7
Nara	91.9	92.5	90.3	90.0	86.3	85.8	85.2	85.5
Wakayama	89.5	90.8	90.0	91.3	90.5	93.1	86.8	85.4
Tottori	77.9	80.6	81.4	80.6	81.9	83.5	84.3	84.5
Shimane	74.4	76.5	75.8	76.0	74.6	74.0	72.2	73.7
Okayama	91.5	95.2	97.1	96.7	97.6	99.4	96.5	98.2
Hiroshima	101.9	102.1	101.5	101.3	101.6	102.1	101.7	100.8
Yamaguchi	93.0	92.5	90.9	92.3	91.2	92.1	88.8	88.0
Tokushima	85.3	88.4	87.0	90.3	92.0	92.3	88.5	89.0
Kagawa	88.4	90.1	91.2	92.1	92.3	92.7	89.9	90.1
Ehime	86.1	86.7	86.1	88.8	89.4	91.2	89.7	89.5
Kochi	-	-	-	92.1	91.8	93.1	91.3	89.3
Fukuoka	94.6	95.6	95.0	94.6	95.6	97.3	95.7	96.6
Saga	85.7	84.0	79.9	82.1	82.1	80.4	78.8	79.7
Nagasaki	76.0	75.1	73.5	75.5	76.1	78.5	78.6	79.5
Kumamoto	77.1	76.1	74.6	74.2	73.2	73.7	71.6	72.1
Oita	76.7	76.5	77.0	75.7	75.7	75.6	76.9	78.8
Miyazaki	74.0	73.0	72.9	75.2	75.2	74.6	73.2	73.7
Kagoshima	64.3	64.2	64.3	63.7	63.3	64.8	65.4	67.3
Nation	100.0	100.0	100.0	100.0	100.0	100.0	100.0	100.0

Sources: Economic Planning Agency, *Chiiki Keizai Yoran, 1973* (Tokyo: Keizai Kikaku Kyokai, 1973) for 1965 to 1970.
Bureau of Statistics, Office of the Prime Minister, *Japan Statistical Yearbook, 1975* (Tokyo: Japan Statistical Association, 1975) for 1971 and 1972.

TABLE A-5
Variables used for regression Analysis

Year	PC1	PC2	GR1	GR2	ID1	ID2	T	TD
1952	31.3	26	11.7	–	–	–	0	0
53	30.3	26	7.7	6.2	–	–	1	0
54	27.0	6	2.8	5.9	–	–	2	0
55	26.9	4	10.8	8.8	93.9	0.18	3	0
1956	33.0	15	6.2	7.3	99.1	0.20	4	0
57	44.3	21	7.8	7.4	93.3	0.20	5	0
58	37.0	20	6.0	5.6	91.2	0.19	6	0
59	43.9	24	11.2	8.9	93.7	0.19	7	0
60	62.2	21	12.5	13.4	94.1	0.19	8	0
1961	75.9	22	13.5	14.4	99.5	0.20	9	0
62	86.4	24	6.4	7.0	97.8	0.20	10	0
63	64.4	22	12.5	10.4	92.8	0.20	11	0
64	62.1	24	10.6	13.2	90.8	0.19	12	0
65	61.7	28	5.7	5.1	84.9	0.17	13	0
1966	72.3	21	11.1	9.8	83.2	0.16	14	0
67	74.2	21	13.1	12.9	80.0	0.16	15	0
68	87.9	23	12.7	13.4	78.5	0.15	16	0
69	82.8	20	11.0	10.8	78.3	0.15	17	0
70	67.3	21	10.4	10.9	77.9	0.16	18	1
1971	49.7	18	7.3	7.3	73.3	0.15	19	1
72	44.7	13	9.8	8.7	71.0	0.15	20	1
73	39.1	7	6.1	10.2	–	–	21	1
74	35.4	3	-0.6	-1.9	–	–	22	1

Sources: Table 1 for PC1 and PC2.
Table 2 for GR1 and GR2.
Table 3 for ID1 and ID2.
T and TD by definition.

9

GROWTH STRATEGIES AND HUMAN SETTLEMENT SYSTEMS IN DEVELOPING COUNTRIES

Niles M. Hansen

INTRODUCTION

Those economists and planners who identify the level of *per capita* gross national product with either individual or social welfare represent a small and dwindling group. Nevertheless, while it is true that more economic wealth does not necessarily result in greater quality of life, it is equally clear that human well-being is not promoted by circumstances of involuntary poverty. Thus, the desire of developing countries to attain higher standards of living is readily understandable. What increasingly is at issue is whether the developing countries should emulate Western approaches to economic development. Until recently it was almost a universal article of faith that urbanization and capital intensive technology are the keys to development. Now it is becoming fashionable to maintain that the Western-inspired urban - industrial model may not be applicable, or at least not wholly so, to developing nations, and that this is not simply a matter of differing stages of development.

The way in which one views these questions has important implications for human settlement policies. The following sections deal, respectively, with the positive role of cities in national development, problems of strictly economic approaches to development, and the case for greater emphasis on rural areas. The final part of the paper is a critical summary of the state of the art with respect to economic development and human settlements policies for developing countries.

1. THE POSITIVE ROLE OF CITIES IN DEVELOPING COUNTRIES

Although national patterns of urbanization vary a great deal according to complex and interrelated historical, cultural, political, economic, and geographic factors, there is a direct relationship between degree of urbanization and *per capita* gross national product. For this reason alone the growth of cities in developing countries has been viewed as a positive phenomenon. However, the structure of urbanization in developing countries usually differs from that in most Western countries. The latter tend to have city size distributions that follow the Zipf rank-size rule, i.e. there is an urban hierarchy consisting of a few large metropolises, a larger number of medium-size cities, and a still larger number of small towns. (If city population size and population rank are plotted on double log paper the resulting distribution is linear.) In contrast, developing countries tend to have a "primate" city (or a very few large cities) dominating the rest of the nation in terms of both size and influence.

There is a large post war literature deploring the "dual economies" resulting from primate urban structures. In part this has been a reaction to the persistence of a colonial inheritance, but Western theories concerning human settlement patterns have contributed significantly to this position. For example, national political and economic unity have been attributed to countries with the rank-size distribution of cities just mentioned. Empirical evidence in this regard is not conclusive, but it has been argued on theoretical grounds that "depending on the economic and political circumstances in a particular country, widely different rank-size distributions may be considered as optimal. Particular rank-size distribution parameters can not give any clues that might help in the national planning decision processes" (von Böventer, 1973, p. 157).

Dissatisfaction with primate city structures is seen even more clearly in the widespread explicit and implicit acceptance of the Western hierarchical diffusion model of spatial - temporal growth and of the related growth center approach to regional development. The hierarchical diffusion model assumes that growth-inducing innovations occur in large cities or metropolitan areas and then filter down over time through the urban hierarchy; moreover, impulses of economic change also spread from urban centers to their respective hinterland areas. If this theory in fact explains how the development process works, then nations without a well-articulated urban hierarchy will find it very difficult at best to promote economic wellbeing over the whole of the national territory. Acceptance of the theory also explains why growth center policies have been so widely adopted; it follows that they are needed to fill in gaps in the hierarchy so that the filtering process can operate along with concomitant beneficial spread effects to lagging hinterlands.

An influential paper by Lasuén (1973) placed the hierarchical diffusion process in an international framework. Lasuén identified the development process with that of the generation and adoption of innovations. Nations develop according to the degree to which they adopt innovations brought forward internationally; in other words, the international development process affects nations according to the way in which particular national urban processes react to it. In the developed countries the spread of innovations has been accelerated by the existence of multi-plant firms because the filtering process works much faster in these firms than under conditions where single-plant firms are prevalent. In developing countries the plant and the firm are generally identical; the spatial spread of innovations in developing countries is relatively slow because it is a result of a host of unrelated individual decisions.

Lasuén poses the question of why adoptions occur at all in developing countries. The lack of complementary external support for innovations in developing countries is in part offset by lower risks resulting from the fact that most of the innovations have already reached the stage of standardization abroad. Moreover, the assumed innovation to be adopted is usually already well known in local markets because of imports from developed countries; the product demand is there. Finally, high costs of production resulting from small scale are not a deterrent because innovation adoptions are forced on developing countries by balance of payments difficulties and consequent import substitution policies. Significantly, innovation adopters usually are persons who previously were importers, distributors, servicers or producers of substitution goods, familiar with the marketing, financing, and technical characteristics of the product. They adopt so that they will not be driven out of business by import substitution. As a result, the spatial structure of new productive activities is nearly identical with that of the former marketing network of the product. Innovation adoptions occur where the largest previous market areas of the product were found, normally the largest city. New producers are pressed to satisfy their own local demand and cannot supply smaller towns. Eventually, however, producers spring up in other local market areas in spite of their smaller captive markets. Thus, most innovation adoptions start in the largest cities and gradually trickle down through the urban hierarchy. This is true, argues Lasuén, whether the product in question is market-oriented or resource-oriented because at this initial stage production is tied to the location of the market.

Given Lasuén's theoretical context, only two basic alternatives are open to developing countries. The first is for the largest urban center or centers to adopt new innovations before previously adopted innovations have filtered down through the urban hierarchy. The second is to delay the adoption of innovations at the top of the hierarchy until previously adopted innovations have been adopted in the rest of the country. The first choice would result in a perpetuation of economic dualism; the second would lead toward greater equality among regions, but the nation as a whole would be less developed because older and less efficient technologies would be utilized. In practice nations do not follow either of these extreme paths, but most tend to prefer a dualistic economy to one which is spatially egalitarian but retarded.

So long as the developing countries continue to adopt innovations that originate in the developed countries it is difficult to imagine that disparities between them will be closed to any marked degree in the near future. However, this does not mean that *per capita* gross national product will not grow in developing countries or that interregional disparities within these countries will not diminish. Indeed, both cross-section and time series analyses indicate that there is a systematic relation between national development levels and regional inequality or geographic dispersion. Rising regional income disparities and increasing dualism is typical of early development stages, whereas regional convergence and a disappearance of severe dualism is typical of the more mature stages of national growth and development (Williamson, 1965; see also Gould, 1970).

Japan's development illustrates that:

"There is a fundamental conflict between high economic growth and decentralization of population. If a high rate of economic growth is to be achieved, further concentration of population into a few metropolitan areas cannot be avoided.

"However, the continuation of a high rate of economic growth would sooner or later lead to equalization of income and wage levels within the country. Then the reduction in income disparity among regions would, in turn, prevent further concentration of population. Therefore, population concentration would be a temporary problem for developing countries." [Mera, 1975, p. 28 and p. 207 of this text].

Convergence of Japanese prefectural *per capita* incomes started to appear around 1961 and continued in parallel with a generally high rate of economic growth. This phenomenon appears to have been caused by convergence in wage rates among different parts of the economy, which in turn resulted from a tightening of labor markets. It is worth noting that the Japanese government had not yet adopted a policy of decentralization during this period. Moreover, there is no evidence of decreasing economies of scale or increasing diseconomies in large metropolitan areas. Rather, what occurred was an upward shift of relative incomes in other areas, usually immediately outside of metropolitan areas.

It would be rash to propose that developing countries should merely wait patiently because there is an automatic mechanism that eventually will eliminate or significantly reduce regional disparities. But alternatives already mentioned have their own problems. Rapid population concentration might be avoided by lowering the national growth rate, but this would result in lower *per capita* income and the persistence for a longer period of time of already existing disparities. The growth center strategy is another option, but as Mera points out on the basis of Japan's experience: "it can be said that this strategy is effective in expanding the zone of metropolitan influence, but for relieving satisfactorily the problems of income disparity and population concentration, the strategy would require a cost which is either impossible to pay or too high to justify" (Mera, 1975, pp. 28 - 29). More general evidence also indicates that growth center strategies are likely to be not only very costly but also ineffective. As mentioned earlier, these strategies assumed that spatial-temporal growth processes are characterized by hierarchical filtering and hinterland spread. Pred (1976) in particular has taken issue with the assertion by Lasuén and others that economic growth takes place by the trickling down of innovations through the urban hierarchy. On the basis of a vast amount of empirical evidence from developed countries he shows that the hierarchical filtering notion is deficient because it ignores the overriding significance of non-hierarchical input - output linkages and employment multiplier channels. This does not necessarily mean that hierarchical filtering does not take place internationally, between cities in developed and developing countries; here more evidence is required. However, with regard to hinterland spread effects from induced growth centers in lagging regions, there is abundant evidence from both developed and developing countries that they simply fail to appear to any significant degree (Pred, 1976; Hansen, 1975).

A final issue that needs to be considered is the role of large third-world cities as migration centers. Frequent references are made to "pseudo-urbanization" and "premature urban immigration." One of the major conclusions of a recent United Nations seminar on urban development strategies was that "An important problem in Asian cities is the presence of a large pool of unemployed or underemployed unskilled workers who have to be gradually drawn into the modern sector during the developmental process. How to keep this sector of the population within reasonable proportions appeared to be the crux of the problem in the major urban centres in developing countries" (United Nations, 1974, p. 18).

This problem is most evident in the squatter settlements that account for a large share of the populations of large- and medium-size cities in developing countries. "The inherited conventional wisdom leads to an interpretation of such settlements as physically decrepit slums, lacking in basic amenities, chaotic, and disorganized—an attitude that persists in much of the urban planning community, which tends to interpret such settlements as obstacles to good civic design" (Berry, 1973, p. 83). However, whether viewed in terms of human welfare or economic development, the growth of a large marginal urban population is not necessarily undesirable.

It cannot be denied that urban squatters have deplorable living conditions and insecure employment. Nevertheless, most migrants feel that they are better off than they were before moving to the city, where access to services—especially schools and clinics— is far better than in rural areas. Most migrants find jobs rather quickly, and advancement from the lowest occupational categories is probably widespread. Moreover, squatter settlements are not usually the first stop for the incoming migrant but are more often established by families with longer urban experience. Where squatters are not harassed by the authorities and where terrain and initial density of settlement permit, many of these settlements evolve over 10 or 15 years into stable, acceptable working class neighborhoods. In other words, squatting often provides immediate relief from the burden of rent and the threat of eviction, and it offers the longer run prospect of at least a minimum of comfort and respectability. Migration to cities also removes redundant labor from agriculture; even though productivity may be low and falling in the overloaded tertiary sector of many cities, it is still higher than productivity in agriculture. And residence in the city exposes the migrant to modernizing influences and improves his chances to acquire skills, however modest (Nelson, 1970). Because of the self-improving nature of squatter settlements the United Nations Center for Housing, Building, and Planning now stresses the acceptance and support of their longer run existence and of adequate pre-planning for their future development. Conversely, it is acknowledged that attempts to clear such settlements generally waste scarce public resources and aggravate the problems of the people concerned. Thus, the Center recommends that governments make normal urban utilities and community services available to transitional settlements, according to priorities worked out with the collaboration of the residents themselves. Better still, of course, would be planned land acquisition and development in advance of need, taking account of utility and community facility requirements as well as transportation and residential location in relation to employment opportunities (Berry, 1973).

In sum, then, it could be argued that urban-industrial growth under conditions of (hopefully temporary) economic dualism offers the best long-run hope for developing countries and that in any case feasible alternatives have not been demonstrated. For the immediate future the large cities will continue to be centers of development and links to an increasingly international economy. Although growth is slow to decentralize in developing counttries, migration enables increasing numbers of people to take advantage of the relative opportunities offered in primate cities. For the longer run there is considerable empirical evidence that regional disparities will diminish. In this perspective planners who try to inhibit, divert, or even stop growth in large cities are banal if not completely negative. Yet the voices raised against present tendencies are sufficiently numerous and respected that they deserve a hearing.

Although advocates of "more balanced growth" usually do not specify precisely what they mean by this term, it generally implies "more emphasis on rural development." Proponents of rural development usually tend to devote more attention to social and political factors than is the case in the literature emphasizing urban-industrial growth. For example, it was pointed out earlier that the hierarchical filtering model of Lasuén has been criticized in space - economy terms. However, to the extent that its descriptive aspects are a fairly accurate representation of spatial - temporal economic development processes, the world it depicts is not acceptable to many reform-minded persons in developing countries.

2. THE LIMITATIONS OF ECONOMIC ENGINEERING

Lasuén maintains that the only feasible way developing countries can absorb successive innovation clusters more rapidly is to reduce technical and organizational lags by overriding national boundaries and planning multi-national firms on a continental basis. He notes, though, that even though the countries of the European Economic Community are ready to pool their markets, they have considerable difficulty in merging their firms into multi-national enterprises. "As everybody is aware, the only really multi-national firms in the Common Market are the subsidiaries of the large multi-product multi-plant American conglomerates" (Lasuén, 1973, p. 187).

But how, under present institutional conditions, are the developing countries supposed to do better in this regard than the nations of Western Europe? Moreover, it is quite possible that the very efforts of multi-national corporations to extend their operations in developing countries can have negative results from a developmental perspective; they are part of a process which leads to the accelerated growth of a subsystem oriented toward the demands of a small privileged section of the population (in Latin America, for example, 5 per cent of the population accounts for over 50 per cent of the demand for commodities) without changing the status of the workers and peasants.

"The conditions required for world poles to develop their branches in backward countries restrict the possibilities of drastically changing the internal situation through cooperation between such countries. Such conditions therefore restrict the possibilities of allowing the productive apparatus to serve the population. In Latin America there is clear evidence that the slightest reformist attempt to change the 'internal' structures immediately affects 'external' interests and provokes a negative reaction. This reaction can take the form of 'internal' efforts to modify the internal structures again or else it can take the form of external pressure, the effect of which is not limited to the enterprises that are directly concerned." [Coragio, 1975, p. 369.]

Although these conclusions are stated in rather abstract terms, ample concrete examples of foreign private and governmental (not always independently) meddling in the internal affairs of developing countries have been reported in the press. Moreover, these initiatives, when they have originated in the West, usually have favored conservative social structures.

Generally speaking, the assumptions behind the notion that a strategy of economic polarization and dependent integration is equivalent to a development policy for developing countries has been criticized on four grounds. First, this approach erroneously assumes that there is no structural unity among social, economic, and political phenomena. This in turn implies that a strategy aiming at social objectives can be reduced to purely economic terms; social and political considerations can simply be tacked on later. Second, it assumes that international relations take place in a harmonious context. Third, the State is an idealized, autonomous element in the social system; it is regarded as apart from any real power structure. Similarly, it is assumed that a neutral, rational bureaucracy exists. Thus application of the strategy would not bring about changes in the predominant political structures. Finally, the strategy assumes that polarization mechanisms can be reproduced independently at any level. What these criticisms add up to is a contention that a theory of regional development must be embedded in a theory of social change. Without denying that the main problems of development have an economic basis, it is impossible to compose a strategy of development through "economic engineering" alone (Coragio, 1975).

3. REDRESSING THE NEGLECT OF RURAL POVERTY

Perhaps the principal criticism of the technical economics approach to development is that high aggregate growth rates and new power projects, ports, highways, and other large infrastructure projects have been largely irrelevant to the mass poverty of rural societies.

In keeping with this view is the notion that the developing countries have become overly dependent on the West because they have passed up opportunities in the agricultural sector, and particularly in small farms.

In fact a rather strong argument can be made that the small farmer has been neglected undeservedly. For example, output per acre of basic food grains in Egypt is 3515 pounds; in Taiwan it is 3320 pounds. These figures are higher than in the United States as well as in most other developed countries. Yet they reflect intensive agriculture on plots that average as little as 2 or 3 acres. If India's agriculture were organized as efficiently as that in Egypt her food grain surplus would be twice that of the total world trade of food grains in 1972. If medium-size countries such as Nigeria, Mexico, and Pakistan could double their agricultural productivity—which would still leave their yields per acre well below those in Taiwan and Egypt—the gap in the worldwide supply of food grains would disappear. Bottlenecks in the developing countries appear to account for the difference between their present situation and a steady annual increase of 5 per cent. The most important impediment is the treatment of the peasant farmer. Representative thinkers of both the collectivist left and the feudalist right have maintained that land reform favoring the individual peasant will only create a depressed peasantry, incapable of applying the knowledge necessary to increase productivity. Yet in Ceylon the rice yield has been 36 - 37 bushels an acre on farms of less than one acre and 33 - 34 bushels on larger plots. In central Thailand yields have been 304 kg an acre on holdings of 2 - 6 acres but only 194 kg an acre on holdings of 6 acres or more. Similarly, in Argentina, Brazil, Chile, Columbia, Ecuador, and Guatemala, average yields per acre have been 3 - 14 times greater on smaller farms than on larger ones. Such findings suggest that there are limited economies of scale in most farm production. But they also indicate that small-scale farmers tend to maximize output by the intensive application of labor, whereas larger farms attempt to maximize profit by using hired labor until marginal revenue equals marginal cost. But this usually results in an output which is less than that which would obtain if the aim were to maximize output (Power, 1975).

Favorable access to credit can provide an incentive to adopt technologies that otherwise would be too expensive. Farmers have traditionally depended on credit but funds from money lenders or hacienda owners have often carried interest rates of 40 per cent or more; and credit from banks and government agencies is commonly reserved for richer farmers. Moreover, good agricultural ideas are useless unless they reach small farmers. Someone needs to be on hand to provide information on improved seeds, fertilizers, rotation systems, farm implements, wells, and so forth. Preferably this person should live among village people, know their ways, and have their trust. In developed countries there is approximately one government agricultural agent for every 400 farm families; in developing countries the corresponding ratio is one for every 8000 farm families. Similarly, whereas developed countries spend $120 - $150 per year for each farm family on research, the corresponding figure in developing countries is only $2, even though evidence suggests that tropical farms applying the best methods of modern science can attain yield increases of 6 - 16 times present levels. Underlying these data is the inadequacy of agricultural topics in the education system. Schools and universities, whether established by old colonial régimes or new-nation governments, tend to regard agriculture as not worth teaching. Such neglect cannot simply be blamed on overdependence on the developed countries, though it contributes to this condition (Power, 1975).

Besides the agricultural sector, dispersed or regionally decentralized industrialization also appears to require fairly widespread rural prosperity. Otherwise local markets are not able to sustain even small-scale consumer goods production and national markets cannot be reached for technical and other reasons, including inadequate transportation means. Thus:

"industrial dispersal programs which are not justified by sufficient local demand or linked to already established industrial regions result in waste of capital and organizational resources. In the case of retarded regions and pockets of unemployment distant from industrial centres, the first planned effort must concentrate on the upgrading of agriculture. This, in turn, requires the building up of agricultural infrastructure, i.e. water control, irrigation and local transportation. If agriculture can be made to prosper, the source of a growing local demand for ancillary services and consumer goods is also established. Under such conditions, it becomes reasonable to expect that potential investors in small scale service and consumer goods industries will find the motivation to locate in dispersed and remote areas." [Lefeber, 1975, p. 291.]

But what kinds of regional policies are likely to bring about rural prosperity consistent with the objectives of greater personal and regional equity? Here the Indian case is instructive.

After the failure of widely but thinly spread efforts to generate dispersed agricultural development the Indian government launched, in 1960, an Intensive Agricultural District Program (IADP) which concentrated effort and resources in a few potentially promising areas. It was hoped that the development thus gained would spread to nonprogram areas. The results were mixed, but whatever the productivity advances, the income distributional effects ran counter to the attainment of equity objectives. Even in successful areas unemployment was not eliminated, while the number of landless persons increased because of plot consolidations and termination of tenancy. Employment increases did not match productivity increases because of the increasing capital intensity of production. Indeed, the IADP may have had the paradoxical welfare consequence of interrupting the momentum of agricultural development as a result of inadequate growth of low income demand for food and staples. To the extent, therefore, that widespread rural prosperity is a prerequisite for decentralized industrial development, the IADP approach, by increasing income differences, cannot contribute to decentralization. Here again what appears to be called for is a policy focused on raising the productivity of the average farmers rather than on benefiting farmers who already are capable and efficient (Lefeber, 1975).

4. IMPROVING ACCESS TO ECONOMIC OPPORTUNITY: A CRITICAL SUMMARY

How then can rural poor people be given greater access to economic opportunity? Imaginative thinking in this regard emphasizes greater direct involvement of local people in the development process and spatial organization in terms of functional economic areas. In the developed country context the functional economic area concept was pioneered by Fox (1967) and Berry (1967), who stressed commuting fields as the basis for delineating economically meaningful units of analysis. Possibilities for simulating in nonmetropolitan areas the greater scale and opportunities available in metropolitan areas were suggested by Thompson (1969) and expanded in more detail by Hansen (1976), who also stressed the importance of human resource development. However, these studies made explicit and implicit assumptions that are not applicable in rural areas of developing countries. The latter have no mass automobile ownership and often no real immediate possibilities for motorized public transportation systems. And the resources available are vastly smaller than those available even to lagging regions in developed countries. Nevertheless, some of the ideas in the foregoing literature have been adapted to developing countries. For example, a major penetrating analysis of rural problems in these countries concludes that:

"The goals of rational spatial policy should be the creation of truly functional economic areas, which will provide employment opportunities not merely in primary production (farming, mining, forestry, fishing) but in industry and in service activities, thus utilizing to the full the varied potential productivity of a work force. Furthermore, by creating a sense of 'community' there can be a far better protection of regional ecology than is possible if 'outside' enterprises without any local roots 'mine' the natural resources and pollute the rivers and the air. The main goal of rational spatial policy should be to improve the quality of life in a community not only by providing tasks appropriate to interests and ability but by protecting the environment, by supplying the proper educational facilities, health measures, and convenient recreational facilities. But beyond all these ends of enlightened policy should be a goal even more important: the creation of a cultural milieu that will release the largest possible amount of a community's creative power." [Johnson, 1970, p. 419.]

Johnson believes that there is nothing visionary or fanciful in these proposals because economists and geographers have the knowledge and tools to indicate appropriate policy guidelines. The real problem lies in the inability of archaic political systems to deal with contemporary socioeconomic difficulties.

Friedmann, whose influence in the planning community is considerable, has similarly argued that the development of a country is equivalent to the full realization of the creative energies of its people, and he proposes the adaptation of elements of urban places to rural areas, in the form of "agropolitan districts." Although they "may have both a town center and a dispersed village population, the key to successful agropolitan development is the treatment of each district as a *single, integrated unit*. Correlative with the idea of agropolitan development is the requirement that each unit have sufficient automony and economic resources to plan and carry out its own development" (Friedmann and Douglass, 1975, p. 42).

The richness of Friedmann's case cannot be given its proper due here, but issue may be taken with his forthright rejection of "the massive financial and technical assistance to developing countries that has been promoted as a keystone of Western liberal thought since the end of World War II" (Friedmann and Sullivan, 1975, p. 496) and his related espousal of autonomous development strategies. More specifically, Freidmann believes that Western-inspired urban-industrial growth strategies have resulted in the following "set of related and potentially explosive problems": (1) hyper-urbanization; (2) increasing rural densities; (3) a spatial structure of dominant core and dependent periphery; (4) widespread urban unemployment and underemployment; (5) increasing income inequalities; (6) persistent and growing food shortages; and (7) deteriorating material conditions in the countryside (Friedmann and Douglass, 1975, pp. 48 - 49).

Each of these propositions may be questioned. (1) The meaning of the term "hyper-urbanization" is unclear. How can it be established that a city or group of cities is too big in either an absolute or a relative sense? As discussed earlier there is evidence that moving to cities has on balance benefited most migrants. Moreover, this process has not denuded rural areas, as Friedmann's second complaint in fact indicates.

(2) If increasing rural densities and simultaneous urban growth are both problems, one cannot be solved without aggravating the other. The real problem seems to be that aggregate birth rates are too high in relation to economic growth. The West has provided medical innovations that have dramatically lowered death rates. But it also has made contraceptive means available to developing countries and urged their use. The population problem is primarily related to social factors within developing countries rather than to alien urban-industrial models.

(3) Friedmann's insightful analyses of dominant core-dependent periphery relations are well known and the phenomenon is no doubt related to dependency structures within developing countries and between them and developed countries. However, evidence cited earlier suggests that so long as overall growth can be sustained, eventually there is likely to be a convergence of levels of regional *per capita* income. Of course, even if the dualism problem is temporary, the transitional time period may still be several decades; it is difficult to counsel patience under these circumstances. On the other hand, autarchic development solutions to rural development problems, even if successful, could well require at least as much time.

(4) The problem of widespread urban unemployment and underemployment was implicitly dealt with under (1) above. Without denying the real difficulties of people living in the cities, the difficulties they would experience in the countryside are likely to be even greater. It may also be noted that if human resource development programs in rural areas are expanded in advance of employment opportunities, migration to cities may well increase.

(5) The possibly temporary nature of increasing income inequalities was discussed under (3) above.

(6) Persistent and growing food shortages are in many respects the fault of the developing countries themselves. The means exist for greatly increasing agricultural productivity but they have been neglected. In the past, urban-industrial models may have diverted attention from agriculture, but more recently there has been no lack of voices in the West pointing out the consequent lost opportunities. One danger is that the problems of distributing food may be neglected in the effort to increase yields. What appears called for is not an either - or choice between agricultural and urban-industrial modes of development but rather a judicious blending of the two.

(7) The problem of deterioration of material conditions in the countryside may be subsumed under problems already discussed, e.g. rapid population increase, dualism, and the neglect of agriculture.

The points just discussed are intended to highlight issues rather than to refute Friedmann's propositions. However, it must be emphasized that in the present international context, many of the indicated "solutions" to the developing countries' problems—and particularly those that depend on the income divergence - convergence syndrome—are posited on sustained and fairly rapid growth in the developed countries, as was the case in the 1960s. Moreover, Friedmann acknowledges that the "contradictions" of the system "were perhaps not critical for the maintenance of political stability. At any rate, part of the generated surplus (or aid from outside sources) could always be used to ameliorate the worst conditions and so avoid more fundamental, structural changes in economic organization" (Friedmann and Douglass, 1975, p. 49).

Today, according to Friedmann, the situation is fundamentally different. He believes that world capitalism is in the midst of a major transition and that the era of economic euphoria is permanently over. The negative consequences for the peripheral developing countries are seen in rising import prices, declining export markets, and deteriorating terms of trade. "We can look forward to a period when starvation will become general and endemic; when subsistence and below-subsistence survival in the countryside will no longer be overshadowed by relatively better conditions in the city; when even there, in the metropolis, the economic environment starts to deteriorate" (Friedmann and Douglass, 1975, pp. 35 - 36).

There are two major difficulties with this analysis. First, it neglects the fact of international business cycles. In other words, it assumes that the recent downturn will result in permanent stagnation rather than eventual adaptation leading to a period of recovery. Friedmann may be correct, but prophets of the doom of the West have a long and undistinguished record as predictors of the future.

Second, the political structures of developing countries are extremely inimical to the kind of autarchic rural development implied in an agropolitan or similar development strategy. In proposing such a strategy it is not sufficient to extend the analysis beyond conventional economic factors into the realm of human development. The link needed to complete the analysis is a related theory of political revolution, the kind of revolution that does not merely re-shuffle who is doing the exploiting and who is being exploited.

Meanwhile, some things can and should be done to improve welfare through a better organization of human settlement systems. These would include: (1) more attention to human resource development, (2) greater efforts to curb population growth, (3) wider and more rapid diffusion of agricultural innovations, (4) planning in terms of functional economic areas, and (5) the linking of functional economic areas by a transportation and communications policy that encourages not only more general spatial diffusion of innovations but also facilitates the movement of agricultural and light industry outputs from rural areas to large urban markets.

Economic dualism, despite all its faults, should also be tolerated insofar as it keeps gross national product growing more rapidly than would be the case under alternative strategies. As long as the divergence - convergence syndrome can be expected to operate with respect to *per capita* regional incomes, there would seem to be little point in slowing aggregate growth, i.e. in making everyone more equal by giving everyone less. However, if evolutionary processes do not significantly improve the material conditions of poor people and create more *human* settlement systems, the revolutionary "solutions"—with or without a fine theory—will become increasingly likely.

REFERENCES

Berry, B. J. L. (1967) Spatial organization and levels of welfare, paper presented to the First Economic Development Administration Research Program Conference, Washington DC.

Berry, B. J. L. (1973) *The Human Consequences of Urbanisation,* Macmillan, London.

Coraggio, J. L. (1975) Polarization, development, and integration, in *Regional Development and Planning* (edited by A. R. Kuklinski), Sijthoff, Leyden, The Netherlands, pp. 353 - 374.

Fox, K. A. (1967) Metamorphosis in America: a new synthesis of rural and urban society in *Change in the Small Community* (edited by W. Gore and L. Hodapp), Friendship Press, New York.

Friedmann, J. and M. Douglass (1975) *Agropolitan development: towards a new strategy for regional planning in Asia,* paper presented at the Symposium on Industrialization Strategies and the Growth Pole Approach to Regional Planning and Development, United Nations Centre for Regional Development, Nagoya, Japan, November 4-13, 1975.

Friedmann, J. and F. Sullivan (1975) The absorption of labor in the urban economy: the case of developing countries, in *Regional Policy: Readings in Theory and Applications* (edited by J. Friedmann and W. Alonso), MIT Press, Cambridge.

Gould, P. R. (1970) Tanzania 1920 - 63: the spatial impress of the modernization process, *World Politics* 22, 149 - 170.

Hansen, N. M. (1975) An evaluation of growth center theory and practice, *Environment and Planning* 7, 821 - 832.

Hansen, N. M. (1976) *Improving Access to Economic Opportunity: A Study of Nonmetropolitan Labor Markets in an Urban Society,* Ballinger, Cambridge.

Johnson, E. A. J. (1970) *The Organization of Space in Developing Countries,* Harvard Press, Cambridge.

Lasuén, J. R. (1973) Urbanisation and development: the temporal interaction between geographical and sectoral clusters, *Urban Studies* 10, 163 - 188.

Lefeber, L. (1975) National planning and decentralization, in *Regional Development and Planning: International Perspectives* (edited by A. R. Kuklinski), Sijthoff, Leyden, The Netherlands.

Mera, K. (1975) Changing patterns of population distribution in Japan and their implications for developing countries, paper presented at the Symposium on Industrialization Strategies and the Growth Pole Approach to Regional Planning and Development, United Nations Centre for Regional Development, Nagoya, Japan, November 4-13.

Nelson, J. (1970) The urban poor: disruption or political integration in third world cities?, *World Politics* 22, 393 - 414.

Power, J. (1975) A losing hand for third world?, *International Herald-Tribune,* December 12, p. 12.

Pred, A. (1976) The interurban transmission of growth in advanced economies: empirical findings versus regional planning assumptions, paper presented at the International Institute for Applied Systems Analysis, Laxenburg, Austria, January.

Thompson, W. R. (1969) The economic base of urban problems, in *Contemporary Economic Issues* (edited by N. W. Chamberlain), Richard D. Irwin, Homewood, Illinois.

United Nations Center for Regional Development (1974) *Urban Development Strategies in the Context of Regional Development,* Nagoya, Japan, UNCRD.

von Böventer, E. (1973) City size systems: theoretical issues, empirical regularities and planning guides, *Urban Studies* 10, 145 - 162.

Williamson, J. G. (1965) Regional inequality and the process of national development: a description of the patterns, *Economic Development and Cultural Change* 13, Part 2, 3 - 45.

10

DEVELOPMENT POLES: DO THEY EXIST?

BENJAMIN HIGGINS

The idea of using development poles as building blocks for regional and national development plans is currently enjoying an increasing vogue. There is probably not a major retarded region anywhere in the world where some planners or politicians have not proposed the creation or strengthening of one or more *pôles de croissance* as a solution to its economic and social problems. Increasingly, too, both politicians and planners are attracted to an urban-based approach to national development planning, proceeding from a planned urban structure to the consequent pattern of regional development, and aggregating regional plans to obtain a national plan. The result may then be compared with national goals, and if there are discrepancies, either the planned urban structure or the national goals might be modified. Thinking along these lines can be found in high places in Malaysia, Indonesia, Thailand, the Philippines, South Korea, Brazil, Mexico, Nigeria, Côte d'Ivoire, Niger, and other countries with serious regional discrepancies.

What lies behind this thinking is still, for the most part, a very simple model. François Perroux, in his original presentation of the concept of *pôles de croissance,* remarked that growth is not spread uniformly among sectors of an economy, that certain sectors are concentrated in certain places, and so growth is concentrated in certain places. Since the industrial revolution, at least, a large share of these "leading sectors" have been found in cities, and with the passage of time, in increasingly large cities. Some at least of these leading sectors have spread effects *(effets d'entraînement)* raising income and employment in some larger region. These enterprises are called *entreprises motrices* or propulsive enterprises. Significant aggregations of propulsive enterprises constitute a *pôle de croissance,* which serves as the generator of growth for the whole region. From this highly descriptive theory it is an all too easy step to a policy conclusion: where a region is retarded, it must lack a *pôle de croissance;* and if market forces do not assure the creation of such a pole, one must be created by positive government intervention. The next step is a bit longer: if a nation is underdeveloped it lacks an adequate system of development poles and growth centres; and if the market seems unlikely to create an urban hierarchy which will generate satisfactory regional and national development, such a hierarchy must be created by policy.

Such policy conclusions are clearly much too simplistic; Perroux himself never stated policy recommendations in quite so simple a form. Do we really know what we are doing in using development poles and growth centres as building blocks for regional and national development?[1] In this paper we shall first try to lend some additional precision to the concepts of development pole, growth center, propulsive region, etc. We shall next examine some of the related concepts introduced by Perroux and his followers. Finally, we shall suggest an alternative approach.

DEFINITIONS

The original concept of a development pole as presented by François Perroux was an aggregation of propulsive industries, generating spread effects (favourable impact on income and employment) in some larger region. It is therefore convenient to begin our definitions of basic concepts with "propulsive industry". We shall say that an industry B is propulsive with respect to industry A if

$$I_A = f(I_B) \text{ and } \frac{\Delta I_A}{\Delta I_B} > 0, \tag{1}$$

where I_A is investment in industry A, and I_B is investment in industry B. We might also express this relationship as

$$I_A = a I_B \text{ and } \Delta I_A = a \Delta I_B. \tag{2}$$

Contrary to the original formulation of Perroux, it is not possible to discern propulsive industries by their relative rate of expansion. If a propulsive industry is a particularly powerful generator of spread effects, or if the other industry is a strong reactor, it is possible for the rate of expansion in the "growth industry" A to be higher than the expansion of the propulsive industry B, even though it is the propulsive industry that generates the expansion process. With t as time, if

$$a > 1, \text{ then } \frac{dI_B}{dt} > \frac{dI_A}{dt}. \tag{3}$$

Since a "development pole" is defined as an aggregation of "propulsive industries", it follows that its rate of growth may be lower than the growth of cities whose expansion depends basically on investments initially taking place in the development pole.

Investment in a development pole affects other cities and regions in various ways. The impact may be expressed in terms of investment, income, employment, population, level of technology, welfare, etc. For the moment, however, we shall measure the impact in terms of investment I. We shall assume that regional income and employment rise with I. We shall also assume for convenience that welfare can be measured by *per capita* income, modified however one wished by use of social indicators or shadow prices, to take care of objectives regarding income distribution, education, health, nutrition, environmental protection, etc., which are not accurately reflected in national income figures with standard methods of national accounting.

---

[1] L. Corragio, speaking of growth poles, rightly refers to "the slow waste of the term through over use", and states that "an apparently promising concept has produced only scanty results". However, in trying to clarify the concept, instead of trying to make it operational, he focuses on the relation between polarization and "dominance" in the Perroux theory, and concludes that the concept is an apology for capitalists' imperialism: "Thus Perroux seems to be particularly concerned in convincing the dominated countries that their only way of development lies in their coupling more firmly to this same system of capitalist domination", (L. Corragio, Towards a revision of growth pole theory, in A. Kuklinski, *Polarized Development in Regional Policy and Regional Planning*, Mouton, The Hague, 1974, chapter 7). We shall return to this question later. For an opposing view, see B. Higgins, Pôles de croissance et pôles de développement comme concepts opérationnels, *Revue Européenne des Sciences Sociales (Cahiers Vilfredo Pareto)*, No. 24, April 1971.

DEVELOPMENT POLE

We shall consider that each region r is composed of an urban center u and a peripheral region r'.

Thus
$$r = u + r'. \tag{4}$$

We shall then say that u is a development pole if

$$I_{r'} = I_1(I_u)$$

and

$$\frac{\Delta I_{r'}/I_{v'}}{\Delta I_u/I_u} = \frac{I_u}{I_{r'}} \cdot \frac{\Delta I_{r'}}{\Delta I_u} > 0. \tag{5}$$

Normally an increase in investment in the periphery will raise income and employment there. That is, investment in the pole generates growth in the entire peripheral region. If the expression in equation (5) is greater than unity, the city is a "dominant" development pole. A 5 per cent increase in investment in the pole brings a more than 5 per cent increase in investment in the peripheral region. If it is greater than zero but less than one, the city is a "subdominant" development pole. Once again, if the sum of the a's relating to investment in the development pole to investment in other cities in the system is greater than one, the growth of the development pole will be lower than the growth of the region as a whole.

GROWTH CENTRE

We will define a city j as a growth centre if $I_j = I_2(I_u)$ and

$$\frac{\Delta I_j/I_j}{\Delta I_u/I_u} = \frac{I_u}{I_j} \frac{\Delta I_j}{\Delta I_u} > 0. \tag{6}$$

That is, the percentage change of investment in the city, as a result of investment in the development pole, is positive. If the expression in equation (6) is greater than unity we will say that the city is a "strong" growth centre. If it is greater than zero but less than one, we will describe the city as a "weak" growth centre. Implicitly, we are imagining that there is some multiplier relationship between investment in the city j and income, employment, population growth, technological progress, etc., in the city, so that expansion will take place in terms of all these variables, whenever investment in the city increases.

PROPULSIVE REGION

It is possible that the initial force for expansion is generated, not in a city but in a non-urbanized region, with agriculture, forestry, fishing, or mining as the principal economic activities. We shall define a region as "propulsive" if $I_u = I_3(I_{r'})$ and

$$\frac{I_{r'}}{I_u} \frac{\Delta I_u}{\Delta I_{r'}} > 0, \tag{7}$$

that is, with a positive percentage change of investment in the region there will be a positive percentage change of investment in some urban centre or centres. If the expression in equation (7) is greater than unity (the percentage increase in investment in the urban center is greater than the percentage increase of investment in the region) we will say that the region is a "strong" propulsive region. If it is greater than zero but less than one we will say that it is a "weak" propulsive region.

Because of the relationship between migration and investment we can also conclude that if the region is propulsive, and using P for population,

$$\frac{P_{r'}}{P_u} \frac{\Delta P_u}{\Delta P_{r'}} > 0. \tag{7a}$$

Growth of population in the region brings population growth in the urban centre as well. Clearly, the urban centre of a propulsive region is closely related to the Christaller concept of "central place". For a "strong" propulsive region the expression in equation (7a) may exceed unity; that is the percentage increase in population of the urban centre will exceed the percentage increase in population of the region itself.

CENTRE OF ATTRACTION

There remains the question of the impact of growth of a development pole or a growth centre on the population density of the surrounding region. We will say that a city is a centre of attraction if $P_{r'} = p(I_u)$ and

$$\frac{I_u}{P_{r'}} \frac{\Delta P_{r'}}{\Delta I_u} > 0, \tag{8}$$

that is, expansion in the urban centre generated by investment in that centre leads to a reduction of population in the peripheral region. If the elasticity expressed by equation (8) is greater than minus one (greater than unity in the negative direction) we shall say that the city is a "strong" centre of attraction, and if it is between zero and minus one, it is a "weak" centre of attraction.

It is apparent that a city may be both a development pole and a centre of attraction. That is, economic expansion of the city may raise the level of investment and also the level of *per capita* income and welfare in the peripheral region by reducing the population pressure in the region, permitting larger holdings of land per family, improvements in agricultural techniques, etc. A "development pole-centre of attraction" could conceivably have unfavourable effects on welfare of the region if the best-trained, most capable people are attracted to the city, while the investment generated in the region is either low productivity or highly capital intensive. However, cases where total investment in the region goes up, population is reduced, but welfare goes down, would be rare.

If the elasticity of equation (8) is positive, we will say that the city is a *diffusion centre* (to avoid calling it a "repulsive city"). In this case investment in the city increases population density in the peripheral region.

Probably most people, or at least most politicians, will be most pleased when a city turns out to be both a development pole and a diffusion centre. That is, investment in the city will raise *per capita* incomes, employment, etc., in the peripheral region, and will raise population densities there as well. Some people are always unhappy if rural - urban migration is the only way of raising the level of welfare of the rural population. Some people dislike even migration from small towns to large cities. However, unless one attaches a high shadow price to rural or small town life as such, a development pole which is also a centre of diffusion is not obviously preferable to a development pole which is a centre of attraction. There may, of course, be diseconomies of scale in terms of pollution, congestion, etc., but these factors need separate analysis.

HOW MANY DEVELOPMENT POLES?

A somewhat complicated conceptual problem is whether or not to allow for two-way interactions among cities in the definition of development poles. Perroux himself was adamant on this point. He insisted that the interaction must be unidirectional and non-symmetrical. If two cities generate favourable interactions on each other, then, in Perroux's terminology, neither of them is a true development pole. Similarly, if

$$\frac{\Delta I_A}{\Delta I_B} > \quad 0 \text{ and also} \quad \frac{\Delta I_B}{\Delta I_A} > 0,$$

both industries acting upon each other, neither is a true "propulsive industry". There may be two cities in one region, both of which generate spread effects to the region but which do not sustain each other's growth. In other words for both of them to be development poles the relationship between them must be essentially competitive rather than complementary.

At first blush this definition seems inconvenient and unnecessarily restrictive. Yet if we permit a city to be defined as a development pole provided that its expansion has positive effects *somewhere,* even though the city may itself be responding to investment in another city, the concept of development pole becomes virtually meaningless, and it is almost impossible to distinguish development poles from growth centres. Any city might then be a development pole. One possibility would be to define a city as a development pole if the expression in equation (5) is greater than one for the impact of investment in the city on the rest of the region, while the elasticity of the response of that city to investment anywhere else in the region is less than one. The inconvenience of this definition would be that we might then end up with no development poles in a particular regional or national economy, even though one or two large cities were in fact generating positive and substantial effects on the growth of employment, *per capita* income, etc., elsewhere in the economy.

A true development pole must have some true propulsive enterprises that generate spread effects through investment, which is not to any significant degree a reaction to investment and related growth which has already taken place elsewhere in the system. Thus

$$\frac{\Delta I_A}{\Delta I_B} > 0 \quad \text{but} \quad \frac{\Delta I_B}{\Delta I_A} = 0,$$

and a development pole contains a collection of enterprises of the B type that are, *sui generis,* innovating enterprises. In reality any city will have *some* enterprises which expand in reaction to events elsewhere in the region. But while we may not wish to insist that

$$\frac{I_{r'}}{I_u} \frac{\Delta I_u}{\Delta I_{r'}} = 0$$

for the city to be a "pole", we must insist that it is "low", perhaps less than 0.5. The essential characteristic of a development pole is the domination of its economy by innovating enterprises of the B type, which make investments in terms of the future, and not in response to recent growth of their market.

Thus Perroux's insistence that relations between a propulsive enterprise and other enterprises, and thus between a development pole and its region, must be unidirectional and
non-symmetrical, is well founded. This restriction is necessary to make sense out of the
concept of development pole. In other words, a propulsive enterprise must be one in
which some investment is taking place which is not "induced"; that is, it is not related to
recent increases in profits or sales. It is here that the relationship between Perroux and
Schumpeter comes in: a propulsive enterprise is an innovating enterprise. Investments
are made in anticipation of future success of the innovation—not because of past success
of a routine operation. What Perroux did was to put Schumpeter's concept of innovations
into space, pointing out that innovating, propulsive enterprises tend to be concentrated in
certain urban centres. This concentration of propulsive enterprises makes these urban
centres development poles. Moreover, Schumpeter's concept of "clusters of followers",
who appear after the success of the innovation is clear, together with his concept of secondary effects, is closely akin to Perroux's *effets d'entraînement;* here again, Perroux has
put the Schumpeter concept into space, specifying *where* the clusters of followers and
expansion of related enterprises takes place.[2]

A simple equation will serve to illustrate the point. Let Y be income, K_s the supermulti-
plier, I_i induced investment, I_r investment in discovery and exploitation of new resources,
K the stock of known natural resources, I_t investment in discovery and application of new
technology, and T the level of technology. Then in any economy

$$Y = K_s \Delta[I_i(\dot{Y}) + I_d(\dot{K}) + L_t(\dot{T})].$$

Now what the development pole concept does is to put these growth forces into space.

---

[2]In Chapter 8 of A. Kuklinski (ed.), *Polarized Development in Regional Policy and Regional Planning,*
Mouton, The Hague, 1974, Kosta Mihailovich goes to some lengths to distinguish Perroux's theory of *pôles de
croissance* from Schumpeter's theory of innovations. Yet Perroux has always acknowledged his debt to Marx.
What seems to bother Dr. Mihailovich is Schumpeter's theory of entrepreneurship, which he takes as an apology
for private enterprise. That is not quite true. Schumpeter certainly admired and enjoyed the kind of society
produced in capitalist countries, especially the European ones, at the turn of the century. Yet he was Minister
of Finance in a socialist regime in Austria, and in his *Socialism, Capitalism and Democracy* he stated explicitly
that the socialist formula is superior to the capitalist one. It should also be said that late in his career he advocated
the corporative state (maintaining its basic Catholic philosophy and eliminating its fascist trappings) as a middle
way likely to work better than either. Schumpeter was a very complex personality and an extremely independent
thinker. The present writer knew him well during three years at Harvard, but always found him something of an
enigma. Any attempt to pin labels on Schumpeter is futile.

What concerns us here, however, is that whatever Schumpeter's personal taste in social systems may have been,
his theory is neutral. The crucial role of entrepreneurship and innovation in economic development is not tied to
the capitalist system. Socialist countries, too, have need of new techniques, new products, new resources, and
new organizational systems; and the men who see and seize the opportunity to introduce these "ways of doing
things differently", bring together the factors of production in order to do all that, and organize them into effective enterprises, play a significant role in economic progress in any society and tend to be rewarded for this role
one way or another.

On one point Mihailovich is clearly wrong in his interpretation of Schumpeter, where he says that "Schumpeter's
theory was modelled for a system of unrestricted competition". Not so. On the contrary, an essential element
of the Schumpeter model, which distinguished him from his contemporaries and sometimes got him into conflict
with them, was precisely his insistence that the possibility of creating a monopoly based on an innovation is the
key incentive to entrepreneurial endeavour within a capitalist system. Monopoly is thus essential to economic
growth. The relation of this theory to Perroux's concept of "dominance" is apparent; but once again Perroux
put his concept into space while Schumpeter did not.

It follows from the above that L. Corragio's denunciation of Perroux's theory of *pôles de croissance* as an
apology for capitalist imperialism is also off the mark (chapter 7 of the same volume). Certainly, some of
Perroux's writings, including his opening chapter of the Kuklinski volume, have that ring. But the concept of
development poles and growth centres as instruments of policy is politically and ideologically neutral.

$I_d(\dot{K})$ will occur mainly in propulsive regions. $I_r(\dot{T})$ takes place in development poles. Induced investment might take place anywhere, but it will take place in growth centres as well as in propulsive regions and development poles, and as pointed out above, if the growth centre is a strong reactor, its growth may be faster than that of the development pole itself.

In reality we will find few enterprises which are engaged exclusively in research and innovation; some of their investment will be induced, related to past increases in profits and sales. Thus to distinguish propulsive enterprises from others we shall have to define propulsive enterprises as those where at least x per cent of their investments are in research and development leading to innovations. By the same token, no city consists of propulsive enterprises alone, and we should have to define a "development pole" as a city where y per cent of the enterprises are propulsive. No doubt the x and the y could be determined empirically in any particular country; but the concept of development pole begins to become a bit blurred.

With these definitions there must be at least one development pole or one propulsive region in every system if growth is to take place in that system. Natural-resource-based development will be generated by a propulsive region, with the causal flow from the rural areas to the cities. Human-resource-based expansion will be generated by development poles. Historical experience indicates clearly that higher levels of welfare are attained through human-resource-based development than through natural-resource-based development. It also indicates that sooner or later every economy, whether national or regional, must make the shift from natural to human-resource-based development if continuing growth is to be assured.[3] However, the propulsive region or development pole need not be inside the borders of any particular region or even inside the borders of the country. Regional and national borders are sometimes political or historical accidents. Several cities may serve simultaneously as development poles for the same region. Nor is the level of welfare necessarily higher within the development poles or the propulsive regions than it is in the growth centres.[4]

ECONOMIC SPACE

Perroux has always been insistent on the importance of the concept of "economic" as opposed to "geographic" space. The spread effects generated by a particular development pole may not be felt primarily in the peripheral geographic region of which it is the centre, but may be diffused throughout the world. Conversely, a geographic region's true

---

[3]This argument has been supported in several publications including my chapter in Antoni R. Kuklinski (ed.), *Growth Poles and Growth Centres: Hypotheses and Policies,* Mouton, The Hague, 1972.

[4]Corragio *(op. cit.)* suggests another term which may be useful where spread effects *(effets d'entraînement)* are subject to *filtration* to the world outside the target (peripheral) region, while the backwash effects *(effets de blocage)* are concentrated within the target region, the activity (or urban centre based on it) constitutes an "enclave within the region". No doubt dynamic enterprises often have more impact outside their peripheral region than inside it—the mining enterprises in Mauritania, for example. But surely cases in which an activity actually *reduces per capita* income or increases unemployment in the target, peripheral region are rare. They may reduce *total* income and employment in the peripheral region by serving as a strong centre of attraction, but that is not necessarily undesirable. Sometimes an "enclave" will reduce *per capita* income in the hinterland without reducing *total* population in the region by attracting capital and the better trained, more ambitious people into the "enclave"—Recife and Fortaleza in Northeast Brazil, perhaps. Perhaps we could reserve the term "enclave" simply for cases where investment raises welfare outside the region (city and hinterland combined) more than it raises welfare within the region (city and hinterland combined).

development pole may lie outside its borders; the development pole for the retarded north-east region of Malaysia may not be Kota Baharu, Kuala Trengganu, or even Kuantan (the capital cities of the region), but Kuala Lumpur, or Singapore, or even Bangkok or Tokyo. Walter Prescott Webb, it will be recalled, spoke of the whole of the New World as a development pole (or perhaps a propulsive region) for the whole of Europe through-out a "three hundred years' boom". Perroux himself has recently reiterated his point that even today Latin America's true development poles lie in Europe rather than within Latin America itself.[5]

All this may be true as a description of fact, and it was probably necessary for Perroux to underline the point in order to counter simplistic and unrealistic models in which it was assumed, explicitly or implicitly, that *all* spread effects of investment in a development pole are felt within its "own" geographic region or hinterland. No doubt Perroux wanted to get away from the concept of cities as "central places", essentially market towns *created by* their peripheral region. However, the inclusion of "economic space" in the concept of "development pole" makes it virtually useless from a policy point of view. Add "econo-mic space" to "development pole" and what do we have? A statement that within the global economy there is a network of interrelations and interactions, *effets d'entraînement* flowing mainly from cities to other cities or to rural areas, but in part from rural areas to cities, and taking the form of movements of goods, natural resources, capital, people, technological knowledge, and skills.

It is, of course, extremely useful to have empirical knowledge as to what these flows are for any country or region. But when spread effects are generated from centres outside the geographic area of control of the authority wishing to accelerate growth of a retarded region, the knowledge can affect regional development policy only in very roundabout ways. Suppose the Malaysian government discovers that investments in Tokyo, Bangkok, Singapore, and London will result in some spread effects trickling down to the Malaysian northeast. What then? The Malaysian authorities are certainly not going to undertake investments in all these cities as a device for improving economic and social conditions in their own northeast.

When planners or politicians talk of the creation or expansion of growth centres or development poles as a device for raising productivity and incomes in a retarded region, they are obviously not talking of investing in several major world centres outside their own country. They are usually not even thinking of investing in cities within the country but completely outside the region. No one talks of making Calcutta a stronger "develop-ment pole" in order to solve the problems of southern India. Some people do talk of making Montreal a stronger development pole to solve problems in Quebec of which it is the major urban centre. If we are concerned with reducing regional disparities, concentra-tion on growth centres or development poles within the geographic region towards which the policy is directed is almost always justified; it is rare, indeed, that investment in a development pole outside the retarded region will have more impact on income and employ-ment in the retarded region than in the pole itself, or even in its own peripheral region. Investment in Kuala Lumpur is far more likely to increase than to reduce gaps between the advanced state of Selangor and the retarded states of Kelantan and Trengganu; and invest-ment in Colombo may very well widen the gap between Colombo and Gal Oya. There are usually leakages all along the way, and the more remote the region from the pole, the

---

[5]François Perroux, *Multinational Investments and the Analysis of Development and Integration Poles,* Cahiers d'ISEA, Serie No. 24, 1973.

more leakages there are and the less likely is investment in the pole to reduce gaps between a retarded region and more prosperous regions. It is conceivable that some kind of investment in Tokyo will raise income and employment in Kuantan, but it is likely to raise income and employment in Kuala Lumpur more, and to raise income in Tokyo more still.

If we are to retain the concept of growth centres and development poles as building blocks in the preparation of regional and national development plans, then it might be better to do away with the concept of economic space and consider quite simply the relationship between investment in an urban centre and the creation of income and employment in the larger geographic region of which the urban centre is a part. That does not mean that relations with other parts of the world will be ignored but only that these relations will not be considered part of development pole policy. We may have to choose between retaining the concept of development pole as a major instrument of development policy and the concept of development poles being set in economic space rather than in geographic space.

CENTRES OF ATTRACTION VERSUS CENTRES OF DIFFUSION

This dilemma brings us back to another, and fundamental, aspect of the development pole concept: the distinction between development poles that are centres of attraction and those that are centres of diffusion. We have known for a long time that technological progress, resource discovery, and structural change are at the core of the development process. The development pole concept has the merit of allocating these aspects of growth in space. Cities are necessary both to the process of technological progress and to structural change, since industries and services, and particularly sophisticated industries and services, are concentrated in cities. But is there nothing more to growth pole theory than that? If all development poles were centres of attraction, the growth of cities would simply be an adjunct of structural change; the primary sector is in the countryside, the secondary, tertiary, and now the quaternary sectors are in cities. Technological progress is generated in cities and structural change moves people to cities, so that development is accompanied by relative growth of the urban sector.

Would the development pole concept be worth retaining if it involved no more than that? Note that in the process described in the preceding paragraph it is development that creates the poles, not the poles that generate the development. Perhaps innovators like to live in cities, but it is not clear that they all like to live in large cities, nor that they would stop innovating if policies were designed to diffuse industrial and service activities. Here the policy proposal "Make Kuantan a development pole in order to resuscitate the Malaysian Northeast" means simply "Make some industrial and service investments in Kuantan in order to draw people to the city from the countryside, and let's hope some of the investments will lead to innovations". To say that is to say no more than "let's try to raise productivity of the Malaysian east coast". It is likely to mean in practice: "Let's move some of the developmental investment from Kuala Lumpur to Kuantan." But it is obvious that if developmental investment is redistributed, income and employment will also be redistributed. The concept of a "pole" as the *generator* of development has disappeared.

And so we come to "development poles - centres of diffusion". It is likely that most politicians, and perhaps even most planners, when they speak of creating development poles to turn a retarded region into a prosperous one, really have in mind creation or

expansion of urban centres that will raise incomes and create employment for people
where they are, elsewhere in the region, and do not have in mind solving the problems of
the peripheral region by emptying it.

Should we then confine the concept of development pole to those urban centres which
are also centres of diffusion, as well as having *y* per cent of its enterprises propulsive and
generating increases in income and employment in the region as a whole through investment in these enterprises? Certainly, we should then have a clear definition of development poles. But how many such urban centres exist? Historically regions have created
cities, not the other way around, and the number of cases in which investment in a pole
raises income, employment, *and population* in the peripheral region are probably rather
rare.

Since true development poles seem to be so rare a phenomenon, one might ask: How
did the concept ever come into existence, let alone acquire such a vogue? Let us remember
that Perroux first introduced his concept of *pôle de croissance* in 1950, when France—
western Europe in general—had not yet recovered entirely from World War II; the west
Europe that Perroux had in mind at the time was essentially western Europe of the 1930s.
And that was a Europe which was still dominated by "propulsive enterprises" based on
exploitation of natural resources—iron and steel, heavy chemicals, textiles, pulp and
paper, etc. It was also a Europe where communications were primitive in comparison to
those of today, and when the railroad was the main form of inter-urban transport. In
such a Europe many cities were indeed *regional* centres, with industries located where they
were in order to use *nearby* raw materials and sources of energy, or to serve a regional
market. In such circumstances it is indeed possible that investment in the city will create
both income and employment in the peripheral region. If a steel mill expands, employment is created and income generated in nearby coal and iron mines; if the paper mill
grows, the number of jobs in nearby forests increases, etc.

It should also be recalled that in 1950 the concept of a truly "managed" non-socialist
economy was still foreign to most economists. Policy was largely a matter of "patching
the market", and "planning" meant planning infrastructure and making projections for
the rest of the economy. Thus Perroux and his followers were looking for single, simple
forms of intervention which would make the market work better, while leaving most of
the jobs of development to the market, Perroux himself has largely abandoned this exces-
sively simplistic approach and recognized the need to plan *the whole urban structure* in
order to be sure of achieving the desired result.

A STAGE THEORY OF URBAN-REGIONAL INTERACTIONS

These observations suggest a "stage theory" with regard to the role of development
poles in regional and national economic development. In the early stages of development,
when the bulk of the population is engaged in agriculture, it is the propulsive region that
creates the city. Growth of population and output in the countryside generates growth of
the urban centre as a market and source of services; the city is a "central place". As development proceeds, with the usual structural change, the relative share of the primary sector
in total employment shrinking and the share of industry and services expanding, a threshold is crossed where most of the population is urban. If at that stage the leading industries are natural-resource or energy oriented, and if industrial location is determined in
large measure by readiness of access to raw materials and energy, then indeed the urban

centre may become a true development pole. Also, as Lasuén has suggested, in this phase, with shifts in importance of particular industries and thus of particular kinds of natural resource, there will be changes in relative importance and size of cities and shifts in rank. As development proceeds still further, however, and development becomes increasingly human-resource based, the propulsive enterprises more scientifically oriented and more footloose, typified ultimately by the multi-product, multi-national firm, the link of the urban centre with the surrounding countryside is broken. The propulsive enterprises will operate in an ever wider economic space, both in purchase and sale of goods and services, and in the purchase and sale of technology. Even small industrial towns with fairly advanced technology (as in the case of eastern Ontario) cease to serve as development poles for their own region and operate in an economic space that is virtually worldwide. Also, according to Lasuén, the urban hierarchy becomes more rigid and there are fewer shifts in rank.

In this phase, too, the major metropolitan centres, which may have been development poles in phase two, become increasingly "central places", providing services to a wider "region" which now, however, no longer consists of the surrounding or any other countryside, but of an entire urban hierarchy, in which some cities will be in the same country and some in other countries. What becomes of Perroux's asymmetry? Does growth of Tokyo cause growth of Seoul, Singapore, Taipeh, and Hong Kong, or does growth of these cities cause growth of Tokyo? In fact there is a two-way flow. As a centre of innovation Tokyo sells technology and know-how and helps to get manufacturing going in lesser cities, but in turn the growth of these cities increases the demand for services and specialized equipment that Tokyo can provide. The asymmetry on which Perroux rightly insisted thus becomes difficult to preserve, and a meaningful, operational concept of development pole becomes hard to maintain. Instead of one-way flows of spread effects we are confronted with a complex feedback system. Perhaps we should abandon the development pole growth centre concepts and retain the theoretically more precise, although operationally less useful, concept of economic space.

If this stage theory is correct, it requires a new look at the question of the relationship between generation of spread effects and city size. Innovation may be concentrated in large cities, although not exclusively. Metropolitan centres may generate spread effects in the form of diffusion of technology. But in today's world the cities which create income and employment in their peripheral region are likely to be smaller cities, since these are the ones where natural-resource-based industries are likely to predominate. To take the Malaysian example, Kuala Lumpur is not yet a development pole even in the sense of being a major centre of innovation. It may serve as a "funnel" through which technological advance is poured and then diffused throughout the country, but the technology is still largely borrowed from abroad. The centres of innovation are elsewhere. Moreover, the industrial growth in the Klang valley does not create much income or employment in the surrounding countryside. Even the recent industrial growth in Kuantan, consisting in important degree of footloose enterprises not dependent on local raw materials, cannot be expected to have a major impact on income and employment in the northeast of Malaysia; certainly there is no reason to believe that the problem of poverty and underemployment in Kelantan and Trengganu can be solved merely by continued growth of Kuantan, although Kuantan may serve as a centre of attraction for some of the population of nearby states. On the other hand, Bukit Ridan, the central city for the region of Pahang Tenggara, may well become a development pole for the region by the time it achieves a population above

100,000 people. That is to say, in Bukit Ridan it is likely that many, if not most, of the industrial enterprises established will be located there in order to make use of natural resources produced within the region. The same may be true in some degree of Johore Baharu in relation to Johore Tenggara.

Our scepticism regarding the general applicability of the "development pole" approach to reduction of regional disparities and acceleration of national economic development does not mean, therefore, that it has no applicability at all. It does mean that we cannot hope to solve the problems of all retarded regions merely by attracting some number of industrial enterprises, no matter how productive and how dynamic, to some city within the region.

IS THE GAME WORTH THE CANDLE?

At this point one begins to wonder whether the game is really worth the candle. Is it really worth so much effort to preserve the concept of development pole? What concerns us as planners is the impact of investment in one place on income and employment in other places. If we have that information, the distinction between development poles and growth centres, propulsive regions, reactor regions, etc., becomes somewhat irrelevant. It is the interactions themselves that count, not the definitional distinctions. In short, we might do better to keep the concept of "economic space" and abandon the concept of development poles rather than abandoning "economic space" in order to preserve the concept of development poles.

URBAN STRUCTURE AND QUALITY OF ECONOMIC ACTIVITY

Does a hierarchy of size mean a hierarchy of quality? It is well known that in almost every country there are thresholds of city-size below which certain types of manufacturing and service activities do not ordinarily appear. But not much is known about possibilities of changing these thresholds by positive government action. Are high-quality industrial and service activities *necessarily* limited to large urban centres? One could think of three policy options:

(1) The "early Perroux" approach. Here the major urban centres would be encouraged as development poles with the expectation that "spread effects" would be generated in the region as a whole, more or less automatically, in such a way as to assure satisfactory development of the region. Two questions arise: Can we be certain that the spread effects will be automatic? and Can we be sure that they will be concentrated in the region of which the metropolis is the centre?

(2) The second approach might be characterized as the "late Perroux" or "Lasuén" approach.[6] Here it is recognized that the generation of spread effects may not occur automatically. While the metropolitan centre would be treated as a development pole there would also be positive measures to strengthen "growth centres" as reactors to investment in the pole, and to make sure that the transmission lines are there, open, and of adequate capacity.

(3) Under the third policy option, instead of relying on the metropolitan centre, a number of cities, or perhaps all cities of any size, would be encouraged as growth centres.

[6] F. Perroux, Multinational investments and the analysis of development and integration poles, reprint from *Economies et Sociétés Cahiers de l'ISEA*, Serie F. No. 24, pp. 842 - 4; and J. R. Lasuén, On growth poles, *Urban Studies* 6 (2), June 1969.

The difference between policy (2) and policy (3) might be illustrated by an example. Under policy (2), IBM might establish a major plant in the metropolitan centre, with subcontractors for particular components in smaller towns of the region. Under policy (3) on the other hand, there would be a major IBM plant in some small town itself. It could be that the immediate impact on income and employment would not be very different under policy (2). However, the quality of development in the smaller towns, especially in terms of capacity to generate innovations, would be very different indeed. The current view is that sophisticated, scientifically oriented, "footloose" enterprises of today cannot be attracted to cities which do not have a wide range of scientific activities, plus cultural and recreational activities of high level. If such is the case, it may be that option (3) is impossible, or at least, possible only at a very high cost in terms of subsidies and incentives.

However, it cannot be said that the impossibility of attracting high productivity and rapid growth enterprises to small towns has been established beyond a doubt, particularly if the smaller towns are part of a larger urban structure that includes some cities with the characteristics of a development pole. Thus one finds both sophisticated manufacturing enterprises and quaternary services in such cities as Palo Alto, Santa Barbara, Santa Monica, Austin (Texas), Nashua (New Hampshire), etc. However, these are not really small cities, and they all have special advantages. Most important, each of them is linked to a much larger city serving as a true development pole (Austin to Houston, Santa Monica and Santa Barbara to Los Angeles, Palo Alto to San Francisco, etc.). It is doubtful that the question can be settled on purely theoretical grounds. Only a careful study of individual urban centres will yield useful results.

GENERATORS, TRANSMISSION LINES, REACTORS

The importance of looking at the whole matrix of interactions, rather than arriving at some definitions and then trying to fit cities and regions into categories based on these definitions, and finally to create "development poles" and "growth centres" where they do not exist, is underlined by the growing recognition that new urban economic activities, no matter how dynamic they may be, do not automatically generate *effets d'entraînement* to the peripheral region. It is not enough to have generators of spread effects; there must also be transmission lines *within the target region,* they must be strong enough to carry the load, and they must be open. There must also be reactors at the other end of the transmission lines with adequate capacity to translate the transmitted economic energy into new economic activity. This point has recently been recognized by Perroux himself.[7] He states that "a growth pole or development pole is a growth industry *coupled* with its surrounding environment" (p. 842). Links must already exist or must be provided or organized, if spread effects are to appear. "But for this pole to constitute the nucleus of widespread development . . . connections, or intermediate elements, must be established between the pole and the regional or national economy [and] institutions should exist that make possible . . . the distribution of the incremental product in the form of additional incomes" (p. 844). He suggests that in LDCs where the transmission lines do not yet exist, there may be only "development of poles" and not true "development poles".

It is precisely here that our knowledge is most inadequate. To be sure, we know that interactions are reflected in movements of goods and services, of capital, of people, and in

---

[7] Perroux *op. cit.;* reprinted in Kuklinski, *op. cit.*

diffusion of technology. What we do not know is the precise mechanism by which these movements take place. Meanwhile those of us who are actively engaged in planning might try to fill in, for whatever region or country is our concern, a matrix similar to that shown in Table 1. This table is of course grossly oversimplified; we would like it broken down

TABLE 1.

Urban interaction matrix

	Kuala Lumpur			Investment in Penang			Kuantan			..., etc.
Reaction in	Prim.	Sec.	Tert.	Prim.	Sec.	Tert.	Prim.	Sec.	Tert.	
Kuala Lumpur Primary										
Secondary										
Tertiary										
Penang Primary										
Secondary										
Tertiary										
Kuantan Primary										
Secondary										
Tertiary										

for, say, three-digit industries; and we would like interactions in terms of migration, diffusion of technology, etc., as well as in terms of investment. But the idea is clear. If anyone protests that such information is seldom available, my reply would be threefold: without such information we cannot distinguish development poles, growth centres, etc., anyway; where no numbers exist even X's are helpful; and the recognition that it is this kind of interaction that we really need to know, as a basis for planning, could save a good deal of time and energy which might otherwise be dissipated in efforts to define concepts more clearly, quarrels about "optimum size of cities", debates over ideological implications of the concepts, and the like. Fundamentally, the development - pole growth centre idea, when applied to concrete policy decisions—in socialist and non-socialist economies alike—boils down to two questions:

(1) What are the manufacturing and services enterprises that we can hope to lure or push into urban centres of various types and sizes in retarded regions, and what is the net cost in terms of investment in infrastructure, subsidies, or inefficiency?

(2) What will be the impact on income, employment, income distribution, etc., within the region, and what will be the impact outside the region?

Probably we needed the whole debate on development poles and growth centres to bring us to this simple formulation of the problem. But from now on let us tackle the real problem and not be led astray by slogans, however attractively phrased.

11

GROWTH POLES AND REGIONAL POLICY IN OPEN DUALISTIC ECONOMIES: WESTERN THEORY AND ASIAN REALITY*

FU-CHEN LO and KAMAL SALIH

The desire to catch up with the advanced nations of the West, including Japan, is so strong and the arguments concerning the so-called advantages of being a late-comer so convincing, that many developing countries have been persuaded to copy Western approaches to economic development in an almost indiscriminate manner. Some of these ideas, which have dominated thinking among Third World development planners for over two decades past, include the strategy of economic growth through accelerated industrialization; the necessary and concomitant process of urbanization and the positive role of cities in economic development; capital intensive technology as the optimum choice of technique; centralized planning; and the various notions of the vicious cycles of under-development. Lately, however, dissident voices in the West no less than in the rest of the world have been raised against this dominant paradigm. The basic argument is that conditions in Asia and the Third World are different from the West at the same stage of development, that Asian experience in the past two decades has shown the Western-inspired approaches to be not completely applicable, and that this is not solely the function of the stage of development.

Changing modes of thought and an alternative paradigm of development appear to be emerging, though the details are not yet clear.[1] This reorientation incorporates new concepts such as the complementary if not primary goal of distribution in addition to growth as one of the basic objectives of economic development; the quality of life as a major concern in the light of the fact of limits to growth; agricultural development as the parallel requisite if not the prerequisite to accelerated industrialization; labour-intensive technology and the role of small- and medium-scale industries; the complementarity of rural and urban development; the idea of popular participation and self-reliance in planning; and the theory of mutual dependency in the new economic order. It should be emphasized that these reconsiderations are not so much the total rejection of Western ideas as the search for more appropriate approaches to an Asian development strategy.

*The authors gratefully acknowledge the assistance of Khoo Yoke Kuan and Thasanai Phiriyavithayophas in the preparation of this paper.

[1]For a discussion of the concept of and the need for alternative paradigms of development, see P. Streeten, The concept of "alternatives", and L. Lefeber, On the paradigm for economic development, both in *World Development* 2 (1) (1974).

243

In regional development policy and planning, perhaps no other approach, aside from the idea of regional planning itself, had captured the imagination and interest of policy makers and planners in the developing.countries more than the growth pole or growth centre approach.[2] This paper seeks to re-examine some of the assumptions of the theory in the light of the Asian development experience, considering alternative reformulations which would be consistent with Asian conditions. This exercise, of course, must necessarily recognize the differing internal perceptions of regional problems in each country and the different options open to it in designing its regional policy. There is, however, sufficient commonality in their experiences to suggest an alternative to the accepted Western approach. By treating the problems of industrial development, urbanization, and labour absorption in a common framework, it may be possible to examine the new policy issues in a more meaningful fashion.

In this paper first of all we attempt a characterization of Asian economies as they had evolved from the colonial period, discussing some of the problems of industrialization in the post-colonial transition. Then we consider the resultant patterns of urbanization and industrial development in these countries. We offer some partial evidence of different spatial manifestations of urban - industrial growth which have led the countries concerned to adopt the growth pole approach as a stategy to solve these problems. After a brief critique of the assumptions of this approach, we introduce a concept of comparative urban efficiency as an explanation of the failure of the concentrated decentralization strategy adopted by these countries. This will allow us to re-examine the role of growth centres in solving the fundamental issue of labour absorption in Asian economies and to explore alternative complementary strategies within the broader framework of balanced urban - rural regional development.

1. ASIAN ECONOMIES AS OPEN DUALISTIC SYSTEM AND THE PROBLEM OF INDUSTRIALIZATION

While they may differ in terms of size, population growth, resource endowment, man/ land ratio, and the pressure on land, Asian countries, except for a few with closed political systems, may be characterized generally as open dualistic in economic structure.[3] Their economies are heavily dependent on foreign trade as well as on foreign aid and investments for their growth. Structurally, they exhibit a modern primary export and industrial enclave isolated from the rural, traditional, agricultural sector. These sectors are linked to each other and to the outside world by trade. Modern primary product exports flow from the commercial agricultural sector to the foreign sector. The earnings of this export are used to pay for the importation of manufactured goods by the non-agricultural sector. The non-agricultural sector in turn supplies industrial consumer goods

---

[2]We are not going to engage in any semantic discourse on the distinctions between these two terms here but will throughout the paper use them interchangeably.

[3]See D. S. Paauw and J. C. Fei, *The Transition in Open Dualistic Economies: Theory and Southeast Asian Experience,* Yale University Press, (New Haven, Conn.: 1973); Hla Myint, *Economic Theory and the Underdeveloped Countries,* Oxford University Press, (New York; 1971); and B. Higgins, *Economic Development,* rev. ed., Norton, (New York; 1968), esp. pp. 224-326. Early discussions of dualistic economies include J. H. Boeke, *Economics and Economic Policy of Dual Societies,* International Secretariat, Institute of Pacific Relations, (New York; 1953); W. A. Lewis, Economic development with unlimited supplies of labour, *The Manchester School,* May 1954. Newer formulations are found in J. C. Fei and G. Ranis, *Development of the Labor Surplus Economy,* Irwin for the Economic Growth Center, Yale University, (Homewood, Ill., 1964).

and commercial services to the corporate agricultural sector. The surplus generated by the corporate agricultural sector was either repatriated or utilized in capital formation in the modern agricultural and non-agricultural sector. The traditional non-corporate agricultural sector remains, however, isolated from the modern sectors and continues to exist at a subsistence level.

In response to this colonial pattern, politically induced by pressures against the neglect of the rural areas, economically necessitated by the secular deterioration of the terms of trade of primary agricultural products relative to manufactured goods, and spurred by political independence from the colonial governments immediately after World War II, these countries have reoriented their strategy along two policy dimensions. First is the measure to keep the surplus from the agriculture export sector within the country instead of allowing it to be repatriated as it was in the colonial period. Second, is the measure to channel this surplus into the manufacturing industrial sector and rural agriculture sector rather than the export agriculture sector as before. The patterns of economic growth of the open dualistic economies in Asia after the war are thus more or less characterized by the extent to which these two policies are pursued in the respective countries. Paauw and Fei divided the patterns of growth of the Asian countries after the war into two types. The first is classified as economic nationalism, into which category fall such countries as the Philippines, Taiwan, and the Republic of Korea. Countries falling into the second type are classified as neo-colonialism, e.g. Thailand and Malaysia. Indonesia and a number of other countries fall roughly in between these two sets.

The characteristics of economic nationalism are that population pressure in the country is usually high and natural resources endowment poor. The potential for growth of land-based exports is small. The income generation through land-based exports is not sufficient to keep pace with the growth of population. Thus the necessity to adopt more aggressive measures of industrialization is greater. On the other hand, the countries that are classified as neo-colonialism have lower population pressure, where the natural resource endowment and the potential for growth of land-based export, though declining, are still expected to play a major role in economic development. Thus the necessity of forced industrialization is less, allowing the government to pay more attention to rural development. It is clear also that the social and political conditions in these countries play a significant part in determining their respective industrialization policies.

In the colonial period most of the manufactured products were imported while the non-agricultural sector played only a minor role by supplying industrial and commercial services. Indigenous capital, entrepreneurship, and skilled labour, which are necessary for the development of manufacturing industries, were nearly non-existent. The industrialization policy of Asian countries thus can be considered as an effort to overcome this deficiency.

The first stage of transition from a primary agricultural export economy to an industrialized economy usually consisted of import-substituting industry, especially in the production of consumption goods. Elaborate structures are devised to encourage import-substituting industry. The necessity of importing capital goods from developed countries for capital formation in the first stage of industrialization, however, caused the level of investment to be severely constrained by the capacity to import. Since foreign exchange

---

[4]For a detailed study see D. Felix, The dilemma of import substitution: Argentina, in G. F. Papanek (ed.), *Development Policy: Theory and Practice,* Harvard University Press (Cambridge, Mass., 1968), and H. J. Bruton, The import-substitution strategy of economic development: a survey, *The Pakistan Development Review,* 1971.

earnings from primary products export are limited, to increase the supply of investment goods requires an import capacity squeeze on consumer goods import. Furthermore, the market for consumer goods is available and the production technique is relatively simple. The first stage of transitional growth was quite successful in many countries. A high growth rate of *per capita* income had been achieved and the import dependency ratio of various sectors, especially consumer goods, had been declining.

But the dynamism of import-substituting industrialization diminished once the consumer goods phase of import-substituting has been fully carried out. Many reasons can be given.[4] First of all, the import dependency ratio of consumer goods, although it has been declining, has reached a floor and cannot be further decreased. At the same time, the import mix shifts to one of fuels, industrial materials, essential foodstuffs, and capital goods required by the industrial consumer-oriented sector. Secondly, as the consumer goods phase of import-substituting industrialization is succeeded by a predominantly capital and intermediate goods phase, the capital intensity of import-substituting projects rises, resulting in a rising import content of investment and causing the level of investment to be more severely constrained by the capacity to import. Thirdly, the projects tend to require increasingly large markets in order to reach minimum efficient scales, so that the ability of import-substituting industry to induce investment is progressively weakened by the thin domestic market.[5]

For the further growth of national income, these difficulties have to be overcome. However, these difficulties cannot be surmounted by further exploitation of the primary agricultural sector to finance the necessary import for import-substituting industry. This is because the structure of foreign exchange earnings from primary products export, which were used to finance industrialization in the first stage, is no longer viable in the second stage due to the increase of imports required for further industrialization and the secular deterioration of the terms of trade. Expansion of the primary agricultural export sector is constrained in some countries, on the other hand, by the landbase constraint and competing policy choices. In addition, the relative underdevelopment of the traditional agricultural sector implies that the internal domestic market cannot expand enough to counterbalance the diminution of the foreign exchange reserves needed for capital development. The manufacturing sector thus has to finance its own growth through its own exports. Hence it might be inappropriate, in some cases not feasible, for Southeast Asian countries (except Taiwan and the Republic of Korea) to carry further import-substituting industrialization into a capital and immediate goods phase before they increase substantially the share of manufactured products in their total exports.

There are two possibilities for these countries. First is what is being carried out in the Republic of Korea and Taiwan now; that is, to turn the industrial sectors which were started as import-substituting industries into export industries, such as textile products, electrical appliances, and miscellaneous light industries. Second is what was suggested by Myint as a strategy of "export substitution" in his report to the Asian Development Bank.[6] By export substitution, Myint meant substituting the existing exports of raw materials by the exports of processed and semi-processed materials. Given the range and volume of Southeast Asia's primary exports, there would seem to be considerable scope for increasing the degree of processing done locally in a wide variety of mineral, timber, and agricultural

[5]Felix, Dilemma of input substitution, *loc cit.*

[6]Asian Development Bank, *Southeast Asia's Economy in the 1970's,* Praeger, New York, 1972.

products. What Myint has suggested can be regarded as *vertical* diversification particularly suited to resource rich countries. However, processing of raw materials for export has its own limitations, particularly at a certain later stage when it requires considerable technology and market development. In contrast to this, the Republic of Korea and Taiwan, in particular, have followed what one may call a *horizontal* diversification approach in that the import substitution takes place from light consumer-oriented industries, for instance, textiles, and then in the second stage it became export-oriented from which the foreign exchange earnings become the catalyst for further new import-substitution industries in a mutually reinforcing fashion.

To summarize, Asian countries generally had adopted a strategy of industrialization as a measure for decolonialization. The first stage of industrialization is import substitution in nature, and for almost all these countries it is financed by the foreign exchange earnings from the export of primary products. Under the conditions peculiar to open dualistic economies as represented by these countries, however, import-substitution industrialization cannot be sustained indefinitely. One of the necessary conditions for the further growth of income *per capita* and further advance into the second stage of industrialization is, therefore, success in expanding the export of manufactured products.

One point which should be noted is that we have not taken foreign aid and foreign investment into consideration here. If we take this into account, the need to expand manufactured products export to finance the second stage of industrialization might be postponed for a certain period. However, the impacts of these external sources of industrial finance may not be necessarily either predictable or desirable. The question is complex and requires further discussion.

Several questions of policy have, however, arisen. Dualistic economic development through the above strategy of industrialization has generated severe regional disparities in income and welfare and it has given rise to extreme primacy in urban development. Given the high rates of urban and rural population increase, given a choice of techniques for industrialization, which tends to be biased towards the capital-intensive corporate sector, and given deteriorating man/land ratios and declining agricultural productivity, which forces switching of agricultural production to more capital intensive methods, the major question in Asian development policy has now become how to cope with labour absorption under premature urban immigration. For regional policy this must mean how to allocate labour absorptive capacity between urban and rural areas and among regions in order to promote a fair sharing of development.

2. POPULATION PRESSURE, URBANIZATION TRENDS, AND LABOUR ABSORPTION IN SELECTED ASIAN COUNTRIES

Population pressure in Asian countries varies in degree. The central issue is its pressure on the land and available resources. As shown in Table 1, population density is not necessarily high among the less-developed countries in Asia. However, the pressure on land can be a problem and is reflected in the man/land (cultivated land only) ratios (row 2). For example, in the case of Indonesia, although the population density is very low, namely 64 persons per km^2, the man/land ratio has reached 1147 persons per km^2, while 88 per cent of the population remains in the rural sector. If further we refer to Table 2 which shows rates of labour absorption by sectors, it is evident that from 1961 to 1971 the rural sector had absorbed 25.9 per cent of the increase in the total labour force, while 51.1 per cent was due to the tertiary sector (most of these people may be assumed to have gone to the urban informal sector) and 23 per cent to the industrial sector. The Philippines is another example, with an 11.2 per cent urbanization rate (Table 1), while 45.6 per cent (Table 2) of the additional labour force had been absorbed in the tertiary sector (again possibly into the urban informal sector).[7] In the case of the Republic of Korea, with 54 per cent of its population ubanized by 1970 (Table 1), 44.3 per cent of the labour force increase between 1960 and 1970 was absorbed in the industrial sector (Table 2). Thailand, on the other hand, with rich agricultural land indicated that only 12 per cent of its population was urbanized (Table 1) and that from 1960 to 1970, 62 per cent of the labour force increase was absorbed in the rural sector (Table 2).

TABLE 1.
Population densities, man/land ratios, and urbanization levels
of selected Asian countries, 1970

	Indonesia	Thailand	Philippines	Malaysia	Republic of Korea	Japan
Population density per km²	64	70	127	32	320	280
Man/land ratio per km² (cultivated land only)	1147	317	446	302	1381	1838
Percentage urban population	12	12	32	29	54	72
Percentage rural population	88	88	68	71	46	18
Population growth rate, 1960 - 70 average	2.1	2.7	3.1	2.6	1.8	1.1
Urban population growth rate, 1970	3.2	5.0	11.2	3.1	5.3	1.9

Sources: Hiroshi Miura, Tonan Ajia no ningen teiju keikaku (The human settlement programme in Southeast Asia), *Chiiki kaihatsu* (Regional development) **132** (1975) 1-24. Economic Commission for Asia and the Far East (ECAFE), *Statistical Yearbook for Asia and the Far East*, United Nations, Bangkok, 1973.

However, it is not necessarily true that high population pressures imply rapid urbanization. It is a striking fact, as shown in Fig. 1, that the urbanization trends, historically (Fig. 1a) or in a cross-national manner (Fig. 1b), have shown almost no relation to population density; but a close correlation exists between urbanization and the stages of development or *per capita* income level, which can be viewed as indicative of the degree of industrialization.[8]

The process of industrialization, as indicated in the previous section, has stimulated import-substitution industries and export diversification. By comparing the experiences of the Republic of Korea and Malaysia in terms of the contrasts in population pressure and resource endowment, the spatial pattern of urbanization can be analysed more meaningfully.

---

[7] See also International Labour Office (ILO), *Sharing in Development: A Programme of Employment Equity and Growth for the Philippines,* Geneva, 1974.

[8] Several studies have attempted to show this relationship, e.g. B. J. Berry, City size and economic development: conceptual synthesis and policy problems, with special reference to South and Southeast Asia, in L. Jakobson and V. Prakesh (eds), *Urbanization and National Development*, pp. 111 - 55, Sage, Beverly Hills, 1971, vol. 1.

TABLE 2
Labour absorption by sector in Asia, 1950 - 60, 1960 - 70

	Total	Primary	Industry	(In millions) Tertiary
Asia				
1950	75,576	59,287	5,106	11,183
1960	92,349	70,371	7,047	14,931
Labour increase	16,773	11,084	1,941	3,748
Percentage share	100	66.0	, 11.6	22.4
Annual growth rate (percentage)	2.02	1.73	3.27	2.93
				(In thousands)
Indonesia				
1961	34,578	23,516	2,526	8,536
1971	40,100	24,946	3,795	11,359
Labour increase	5,522	1,430	1,269	2,824
Percentage share	100	25.9	23.0	51.1
Annual growth rate (percentage)	1.49	0.59	4.15	2.90
Thailand				
1960	13,837	11,334	569	1,933
1970	16,850	13,202	951	2,698
Labour increase	3,013	1,868	381	764
Percentage share	100	62.0	12.7	25.3
Annual growth rate (percentage)	1.99	1.54	5.26	3.39
Philippines				
1960	8,536	5,162	1,038	2,336
1970	12,297	6,332	1,916	4,049
Labour increase	3,761	1,170	877	1,713
Percentage share	100	31.1	23.3	45.6
Annual growth rate (percentage)	3.96	2.06	6.31	5.65
Malaysia				
1957	2,165	1,245	262	658
1970	2,871	1,359	367	1,145
Labour increase	706	114	105	487
Percentage share	100	16.2	14.9	68.9
Annual growth rate (percentage)	2.19	0.68	2.63	4.35
Republic of Korea				
1960	7,036	4,620	531	1,885
1970	10,378	5,157	2,009	3,211
Labour increase	3,341	537	1,478	1,326
Percentage share	100	16.0	44.3	39.7
Annual growth rate (percentage)	3.96	1.10	14.27	5.47
Japan				
1960	44,610	14,490	12,380	17,740
1970	50,860	8,860	17,910	24,090
Labour increase	6,250	-5,630	5,530	6,350
Percentage share	100	-90.1	88.5	101.6
Annual growth rate (percentage)	1.3	-4.8	3.8	3.1

Sources: ILO, *Labour Force Projections, 1965-1985,* Part 1, *Asia,* Geneva, 1971. ILO, *Yearbook of Labour Statistics,* Geneva, 1974. Bureau of Statistics, *Japan Statistical Yearbook 1971,* Office of the Prime Minister, Tokyo, 1972.

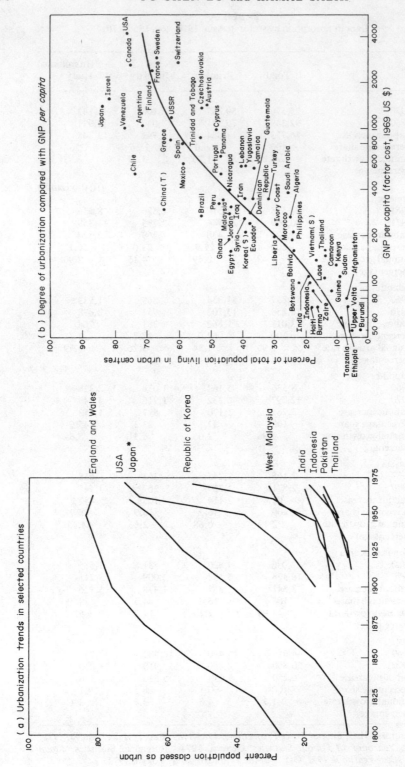

Fig. 1. Urbanization trends and cross-sectoral GNP *per capita*.

Source: International Bank for Reconstruction and Development (World Bank), *World Bank Operations: Sectoral Programmes and Policies*, Baltimore, Johns Hopkins, 1972, p. 475.

*see p. 13 n. 6

It is first possible to decompose the sources of industrial growth due to (i) domestic demand expansion, (ii) import substitution, and (iii) export expansion. Results are summarized in Table 3.[9]

The results show that industrial growth in Malaysia was strongly supported by import substitution from 1963 to 1968. However, in the 1968 - 71 period, domestic demand expansion was the major driving force behind industrial growth. One should note that the value of gross export of rubber and tin during this period was a dominant component in Malaysia's GDP, being more than 30 per cent of GDP. In other words, the strong domestic demand was supported by primary product export. On the other hand, the newly introduced import substitution consumption-oriented industries by this period may have saturated the domestic market. In the Republic of Korea, on the other hand, import substitution started in the 1955 - 8 period and export expansion gradually gathered momentum from 1963. In the 1968 - 72 period export expansion has contributed 30.8 per cent to the growth of the manufacturing sector.

If we compare the urban population growth by size class of cities of Malaysia and the Republic of Korea in the 1960 - 70 period (Table 4, last column),[10] it is evident that in West Malaysia the city size of 0.5 - 1 million (primate city) and 10,000 - 20,000 cities have enjoyed the highest growth rates, which may have reflected the concentration of import substitution industry in the primate cities and the rapid growth of newly developed resource frontier towns.[11] A similar pattern can be found in the case of Indonesia, that during the same period we observed high growth rates in the large cities and 10,000 - 20,000 size resource frontier towns. In contrast, having no primary export or resource frontier, the case of the Republic of Korea shows that cities over 1 million population have enjoyed 6.6 per cent annual growth rates in the 1955 - 60 period and 8.6 per cent in the 1960 - 71 period. Interestingly enough, in the second stage (1960 - 71) the second-rank and third-rank cities began to enjoy higher urban growth, with the lowest rank cities declining during the same period. This may have implied that import substitution as well as export-oriented industries first concentrated in the primate cities and gradually decentralized to the second-rank cities, and so on.

It appears that in the post-war industrialization in the open dualistic economies, the import substitution and export-oriented industries tend to support primacy development.

---

[9]The table was prepared by applying a technique used by Chenery, Hoffmann, and Tan. The domestic demand is defined as:

(1) $D = X + M - E$, where D, X, M, E are domestic demand, domestic supply, import, and export, respectively.

Define $u = \dfrac{M}{D}$, $e = \dfrac{E}{D}$, $x = \dfrac{X}{D}$.

(2) $X_1 - X_0 = D_1 (u_0 - u_1) + D_1 (e_1 - e_0) + x_0 (D_1 - D_0)$.

The logic behind equation (2) is that the growth of output of a certain commodity is attributed to the growth of domestic demand $[x_0(D_1 - D_0)]$, change in import ratio $(u_0 - u_1)$, and change in export ratio $(e_1 - e_0)$. H. Chenery, Patterns of industrial growth, *American Economic Review* **50** (4) (1960), and L. Hoffmann and Tan Tew Nee, Pattern of growth and structural change in West Malaysia's manufacturing industry, *Kajian Ekonomi Malaysia* **8**, (2) (1971).

[10]One has to be careful about the comparison of growth rates due to industrialization since the choice of size class may effect the calculation of the growth rates

[11]B. Higgins, Regional interaction, the frontier and economic growth, in A. Kuklinski (ed.), *Growth Poles and Growth Centres in Regional Planning*, Mouton, Paris and The Hague, 1972, pp. 263 - 302.

TABLE 3

Sources of gross output growth: Malaysia and the Republic of Korea

	$x_1 - x_0$	Domestic demand expansion (%)	Import substitution (%)	Export expansion (%)
Malaysia				
1963 - 8				
Consumption goods	369,082	45.6	40.8	13.7
Intermediate goods	535,243	41.2	44.2	14.6
Capital goods	191,229	29.6	74.0	-3.8
Total	1,095,554	40.2	48.7	9.2
1968 - 71				
Consumption goods	227,180	69.0	12.1	19.0
Intermediate goods	340,818	88.6	7.2	4.2
Capital goods	196,095	102.3	3.9	5.4
Total	764,092	96.8	-1.2	4.8
1963 - 71				
Consumption goods	596,262	47.2	35.3	17.5
Intermediate goods	876,062	47.3	39.0	13.6
Capital goods	387,324	43.9	62.1	-5.9
Total	1,859,646	50.0	39.2	10.0
Republic of Korea				
1955 - 8				
Consumption goods	10,802	99.3	-1.5	1.5
Intermediate goods	15,596	75.5	23.8	0.5
Capital goods	9,297	17.5	82.7	0.0
Total	35,695	71.3	28.1	1.6
1958 - 63				
Consumption goods	107,137	96.2	-1.7	6.0
Intermediate goods	60,348	84.9	8.7	6.4
Capital goods	44,398	117.7	-23.0	5.0
Total	211,883	103.1	-8.9	5.6
1963 - 8				
Consumption goods	218,107	80.8	-8.7	27.7
Intermediate goods	194,008	81.1	10.7	8.1
Capital goods	124,780	135.1	-39.2	4.4
Total	536,895	103.6	-18.7	15.1
1968 - 72				
Consumption goods	400,377	72.0	1.6	26.3
Intermediate goods	204,541	83.0	1.5	15.5
Capital goods	115,351	43.1	-7.8	64.6
Total	720,269	63.6	5.7	30.8
1963 - 72				
Consumption goods	618,484	71.0	-3.9	32.7
Intermediate goods	398,549	77.0	8.9	14.1
Capital goods	240,131	95.5	-29.2	33.9
Total	1,257,164	81.4	-8.5	27.1

Notes: The values of $x_1 - x_0$ are thousand Malaysian dollars for Malaysia and
million won for the Republic of Korea. Furthermore, the values for the
Republic of Korea are in 1970 prices.

Consumption goods: food manufacturing, beverage manufacturing, tobacco, textile manufacturing, footwear, clothing and other wearing apparel, furniture and fixtures, paper and paper products, leather and leather products.

Intermediate goods: wood and cork products, rubber products, industrial chemicals, products of petroleum and coal, nonmetalic mineral products, basic metal industries (excluding tin processing for Malaysia).

Capital goods: metal products, machinery (except electrical machinery), electrical
machinery, transport equipment.

TABLE 4.
Urban population growth by size class of cities of
selected Asian countries

City size	% distribution 1970	Compound growth rates/ann.		
		1930 - 40	1950 - 60	1960 - 70
Japan	27.9	10.7	5.8	2.3
1,000,000 +	27.9	10.7	5.8	2.3
500,000 - 999,999	6.1	-1.6	0.5	9.7
100,000 - 499,999	37.6	7.7	6.7	0.1
50,000 - 99,999	16.0	1.9	5.7	1.3
20,000 - 49,999	12.5	1.5	9.3	-1.6
10,000 - 19,999	0.05	1.0	5.6	-0.3
	100			
	1971		1955 - 60	1960 - 71
Republic of Korea				
1,000,000 +	54.6	n.a.	6.6	8.6
500,000 - 999,999	7.3	n.a.	-	5.3
100,000 - 499,999	15.2	n.a.	-1.7	5.2
50,000 - 99,999	10.0	n.a.	3.8	1.7
20,000 - 49,999	12.2	n.a.	12.2	-0.5
10,000 - 19,999	0.8	n.a.	-14.2	-8.3
	100			
	1970		1947 - 57	1957 - 70
West Malaysia				
1,000,000 +	-	n.a.	-	-
500,000 - 999,999	21.6	n.a.	-	5.2
100,000 - 499,999	30.4	n.a.	6.6	0.8
50,000 - 99,999	22.7	n.a.	9.2	4.5
20,000 - 49,999	13.4	n.a.	2.4	-1.7
10,000 - 19,999	11.9	n.a.	8.5	4.3
	100			
	1971	1930 - 54	1954 - 61	1961 - 71
Indonesia[a]				
1,000,000 +	49.3	-	11.3	6.5
500,000 - 999,999	12.6	5.0	-2.3	2.4
100,000 - 499,999	29.6	4.0	4.7	0.8
50,000 - 99,999	6.7	1.7	3.0	-1.0
20,000 - 49,999	1.5	-3.0	0.5	-0.4
10,000 - 19,999	0.2	-7.0	-19.7	9.4
	100			

Notes: n.a. = not available as figures for more than 1 year are not known.
[a]Calculated figures are for municipalities or *kotamadya* only.
Sources: Bureau of Statistics, *1970 Population Census of Japan,* Office of the Prime Minister, Tokyo, 1971. Kim Hyun Ok, *1972 Municipal Yearbook of Korea,* Ministry of Home Affairs, Seoul, 1973. "Urbanization in Peninsula Malaysia, Appendix A: Population distribution and growth patterns", Special Projects Section, Economic Planning Unit, Kuala Lumpur (unpublished data). Sugljanto Soegijoko, Urban areas in Indonesia: a survey towards the urban development strategy for Indonesia, paper presented at the Senior-level Seminar on Urban Development Strategies in the Context of Regional Development, UNCRD, Nagoya, 1974.

Some countries, for instance the Republic of Korea, have begun to experience decentralization to the second-rank cities. On the other hand, in those countries with rich resource frontiers particularly, the exploitation of the primary export sector has led to the development of resource frontier towns, which phenomenon is reflected in the high growth rates of low-rank cities in these Asian countries.

Tables 5 and 6 show primacy industries or urban concentration coefficients (last column) calculated from six selected countries in Asia including Japan (as a developed country for comparison). Table 5 was calculated by using El-Shakhs's method and the formula used in Table 6 was formulated by Subramanian.[12] The primacy index in Table 5 shows an increasing primacy trend in all the Asian countries referred to except Japan. In Japan the

TABLE 5.
Degree of primacy for six countries in Asia

	Population of city					
Country	First largest	Second largest	Third largest	Fourth largest	Average size of fifth city	Primacy index values
Republic of Korea						
1955	1,574,868	1,049,363	457,331	317,967	48,924	0.72144
1960	2,445,402	1,163,671	675,644	401,473	45,428	0.75021
1971	5,850,925	1,943,958	1,132,589	671,053	60,372	0.77620
Japan						
1920	2,173,201	1,252,983	608,644	591,323	193,404	0.58829
1930	2,453,573	2,070,913	907,404	787,616	311,597	0.56505
1950	5,385,071	1,956,136	1,101,854	1,030,635	211,652	0.65795
1960	8,310,027	3,011,563	1,591,935	1,375,710	228,281	0.69744
1965	8,893,094	3,156,222	1,935,430	1,788,915	237,696	0.68125
1970	8,840,942	2,980,487	2,238,264	2,036,053	256,378	0.66071
Malaysia						
1947	189,100	176,000	80,900	54,500	43,930	0.44405
1957	332,800	234,900	125,700	75,600	45,775	0.54976
1970	545,300	269,200	248,000	136,200	51,305	0.59573
Indonesia[a]						
1920	306,310	193,190	158,036	134,285	46,757	0.51489
1930	533,015	341,675	217,796	166,815	56,986	0.58660
1954	1,851,531	926,471	805,071	369,996	111,433	0.65954
1961	2,906,533	1,007,945	972,566	503,153	131,635	0.66388
1971	4,576,009	1,556,255	1,201,730	646,590	154,468	0.70110
Philippines						
1970	1,330,788	754,452	392,473	347,116	112,665	0.60283
1970[b]	4,363,387	392,473	347,116	199,901	110,000	0.59140
Thailand						
1968	2,718,794	84,105	76,223	50,948	30,211	0.55717

[a]Figures are for *kotamadya* only.
[b]Metropolitan Manila population is used for the first largest city.
Notes: The size of the fifth city is the average size of all cities above 20,000 excluding the four largest cities. Average size of the fifth city in Japan applies for all cities above 100,000 excluding the four largest cities.

[12]Salah El-Shakhs, Development, primacy, and systems of cities, *Journal of Developing Areas* 7 (1972) 11-26; M. Subramanian, An operational measure of urban concentration, *Economic Development and Cultural Change* 20, (1) (1971) 105-16.

TABLE 6.

Urban concentration coefficient of selected countries in Asia

Country	Population of localities (thousands)	Percentage population in localities of:									Estimated percentage population in each interval	Concentration coefficient[b]
		20,000	Biggest city[a]	20,000 - 100,00	100,000 - 500,000	Biggest city[a]	500,000 2,500,000	Biggest city[a]	2,500,000 12,500,000	Biggest city[e]		
Japan												
1920	10,020.0	—	—	32.6	21.2	—	46.2	2,173,201	—	—	20.4	61.06
1930	15,363.7	—	—	28.2	22.3	—	49.5	2,453,573	—	—	20.1	60.14
1940	27,494.2	—	—	22.6	25.1	—	15.8	—	36.5	6,778,804	17.8	57.37
1950	31,203.2	—	—	31.7	32.5	—	18.6	—	17.3	5,385,071	18.3	54.88
1960	59,333.2	—	—	36.3	32.5	—	12.1	—	19.1	8,310,027	17.4	62.81
1965	66,918.6	—	—	31.7	34.3	—	16.1	—	18.0	8,893,094	17.3	55.83
1970	74,853.3	0.05	—	28.4	37.6	—	18.2	—	15.8	8,840,942	17.3	51.81
Republic of Korea												
1955	7,287.6	9.1	—	33.6	21.3	—	36.0	1,574,868	—	—	21.2	45.46
1960	9,471.3	3.3	—	36.5	15.0	—	45.2	2,445,402	—	—	20.1	63.68
1966	12,369.2	1.3	—	27.9	17.3	—	22.7	—	30.8	3,805,261	19.0	57.84
1971	16,400.4	0.8	—	22.2	15.2	—	26.0	—	35.7	5,850,925	18.1	58.39
West Malaysia[c]												
1957	2,031.1	30.1	—	36.8	34.1	332,800	—	—	—	—	26.7	27.69
1970	3,003.8	25.9	—	30.4	25.5	—	18.2	545,300	—	—	24.7	24.67
Indonesia[d]												
1920	1,882.4	10.7	—	41.7	47.6	306,310	—	—	—	—	27.1	59.78
1930	2,942.8	6.9	—	36.4	38.6	—	18.1	533,015	—	—	24.8	60.46
1954	10,618.3	0.5	—	38.1	27.6	—	33.7	1,851,531	—	—	20.8	61.23
1961	10,814.5	0.3	—	12.4	37.5	—	23.0	—	26.9	2,906,533	19.6	72.86
1971	14,852.9	0.2	—	8.2	29.6	—	31.1	—	30.8	4,576,009	18.6	76.11
Philippines[e]												
1970	11,444.9	n.a.	—	39.5	22.4	—	—	—	38.1	4,363,387	23.0	70.25
Thailand[f]												
1968	4,845.8	18.5	—	25.4	—	—	—	—	56.1	2,718,794	19.8	101.56

Sources: Population figures are obtained from the following sources: *1970 Population Census of Japan*, Vol. 1, *Total Population*, *1972 Municipal Yearbook of Korea*. *Urbanization in Peninsula Malaysia*, Appendix A. Suo Soegjioko, *Urban Areas in Indonesia*, table 2. E. Yambot (ed.), *Philippine Almanac Handbook of Facts*, (Philippine Almanac Printers, Quezon City, 1973), National Statistical Office, *Statistical Yearbook, Thailand, Number 29, 1970 - 1971*, Office of the Prime Minister, Bangkok, 1971.

[a] Size of city in actual numbers.

[b] The concentration coefficient is the sum of the absolute values of the differences between the actual and the estimated values in each size interval.

[c] Calculation of urban population starts from 5000 size for both years.

[d] Indonesia's urban population includes all the *kotamadya* (or localities given the status of city only.

[e] The calculation considers Metropolitan Manila as the biggest city and the urban population as 50,000 and above.

[f] Thailand's coefficient is over 100, the highest. This unusually high value may be due to the extremes in size class distribution, Bangkok - Thonburi being 2.7 million and no localities within the two size classes, 100,000 - 500,000 and 500,000 - 2,500,000.

primacy index reached its peak during the 1960 - 5 period and has declined since then, which coincides with the pattern of regional *per capita* income disparities in the same period[13] (reflecting the consistency of El-Shakhs's observation on city size distribution and Williamson's divergence and convergence of regional income disparities).[14]

Table 6 gives similar results except that Subramanian's formula gives more detailed coverage of the lower-rank cities and shows extremely high primacy indices for Thailand, the Philippines, and Indonesia, and suggests that the Republic of Korea was beginning to show decreasing primacy in the 1960 - 6 period.

The patterns of urbanization due to the industrialization strategy in each country vary in Asia according to the resource endowment and population pressure on agricultural land. The impact of varying strategies on employment, given the conditions in each country, are reflected in the patterns of labour absorption of the sectors in the economy. In spite of the differences in level of economic development, however, there appears to be a manifest asymmetry in the relationships between urban and rural areas which leads to concentrations of population and investible resources in the major urban regions. Of course, this can be expected from the fact that the industrialization strategy adopted by these countries has tended to be biased toward the larger cities. However, the asymmetrical rural - urban relationship arises also from the conditions in rural areas derived not merely through land pressure but also out of increasing rural welfare.

Increasing population pressure in rural areas can be accommodated in several ways. For resource-poor countries, industrial expansion, as we have seen in the cases of South Korea and Japan, is the outlet for the labour force problem. For resource-rich countries, where the man/land ratio (and possibly population density) is low, expansion of the frontier is the major source of accommodation. Where the land frontier is non-existent or has been exhausted, or when various socio-political conditions internal to the economy prevent expansion of the frontier, absorption of labour may be accommodated through further land subdivision and/or in the second instance through work sharing. This process is controlled by various cultural and ecological relations and factors. However, continued pressure on rural land will lead subdivision to the lower limits of economic farm size, with declining agricultural productivity, while work sharing may lead to a point where the limited capacity for substitution of labour for capital results in equally declining productivity of land and labour.

The responses to these two (of many) problems arising from the labour force explosion can be several, but land consolidation (or land reform) and farm mechanization (substitution of capital for labour) might be suggested. In these instances, however, if the programme is not conducted properly a geographic displacement of labour towards urban areas will occur. When this process of agricultural development is not consistent with the industrialization strategy, a critical labour absorption problem arises which, in the absence of appropriate policy, can lead to a persistent urban - rural involutionary trap. A proper analysis of alternative development strategies is therefore necessary, some of which will be considered in greater detail in section 6. In Asian regional planning the role of growth poles and supporting regional policy, including rural development, must be carefully examined in this light.

---

[13]See UNCRD, *The Growth Pole Approach to Regional Development: A Case Study of Mizushima Industrial Complex, Japan,* Nagoya, 1975, table 3, p. 33.

[14]J. G. Williamson, Regional inequalities and the process of national development, *Economic Development and Cultural Change* **13** (1965) 3-45.

3. GROWTH POLE STRATEGY: THE APPLICABILITY OF
WESTERN THEORY

In regional planning in Asia the uniformity with which the growth pole strategy is adopted (in some cases implemented), in spite of the differences in the problems of each country, is remarkable. It is not certain however that the strategy will meet with uniform success. Whether this is due to differences in the national conditions discussed above or to difficulties in the theory itself is not entirely clear. To the extent that labour absorption is one of the fundamental questions of the economic development of Asian countries, in particular of the less-developed ones, the received growth pole doctrine and the strategy derived from it will have to be re-examined. It is our thesis that under Asian conditions this growth pole theory at best can be only a partial one, even if accelerated industrialization is its prime objective.

The theory of growth poles dates from the theory of *pôles de croissance* proposed by Perroux of France in the 1950s and has been elaborated further by Friedmann, Rodwin, and others in the form of "concentrated decentralization" since the 1960s. In Asia, Japan's new industrial cities development policy, Malaysia's locational incentive measures for industrial estates, Korea's industrial cities development measures for decentralization, India's rural growth centre programme, and Iran's industrial pole strategy are just some examples of the application of this strategy. These policies and projects are aimed either at establishing growth poles to promote decentralization of population and industrial activities from the over-urbanized area or at establishing a large-scale import-substitution/export-oriented industrial complex to promote rapid industrialization. At the same time, however, they are expected to play a role as regional core cities providing the driving force in regional development, in particular the reduction of regional disparities.

As development proceeds along the above lines, the following questions have arisen in the context of Asian developing countries: (1) under a market-oriented economic system, decision making by private enterprise does not ensure that industrial activities will be located as expected in the decentralized growth poles; (2) even though the growth pole itself might be successful in attaining self-sustained growth, the modern industries located in the growth pole might not be able to contribute at all to their hinterlands. In other words, the linkage between industries located therein and the economic structure of the surrounding peripheral area comes into question. These questions, of course, are related to the stage of industrial development and the industrial policies of the respective developing countries.

The dissatisfaction with the growth pole theory as received is, however, not merely contextual. A number of theoretical and practical difficulties have been raised amongst writers in the field.[15] The theory relies heavily on the notion of leading industries with forward and backward linkages within the economic system and on the empirically supported fact that the spatial juxtaposition of those industries leads to the creation of agglomeration economies which induce increased locational efficiency at these central locations. Further, it accepts that these urban concentrations are merely short-term phenomena necessary for accelerated industrial growth and economizing on urban infrastructural expenditure. Also in the long-run, due to declining marginal returns to labour and capital in the large

---

[15]An excellent review of the theory can be found in J. Friedmann, Specific recommendations on regional planning in the rural - urban context in Thailand, mimeographed, Memo No. 6 to the NESDP, Bangkok, March, 1975. See also J. R. Lasuén, On growth poles, *Urban Studies* **6** (2) (1969) 137-61, and D. F. Darwent, Growth poles and growth centres in regional planning: a review, *Environment and Planning* **1** (1) (1969) 5-31.

cities, a process of spatial convergence will lead to the regional equalization of *per capita* incomes. Extensions of the theory suggest that this process occurs within an equilibrium locational matrix of central places distributed roughly in lognormal fashion according to size. Within this spatial organizational framework, hierarchical diffusion processes and net-spread effects into the hinterland of the growth poles become important. From the policy point of view the failure of market forces to generate the trickling-down process underlying the theory and political pressures arising from conflict between the core region and the periphery have led to the idea of planning of growth poles in a controlled spatial development context in cases where the regional system is not fully integrated. This unforgivably brief description is thus the current state of the theory as received by the developing countries. The theory provides the major rationale for their adoption of the strategy.

In the attempt by Asian planners to apply this approach to solve their regional problems, a number of theoretical and practical difficulties have arisen which need to be resolved. The argument that the trickling-down process does not work in cases of spatially segregated "factor" markets (leading to wage stickiness particularly, a characteristic of dualistic economies) implies the need, according to the theory, to restructure the city system toward some "norm" of lognormality. Aside from the practical problem of identification of growth poles (to fill in the "break", so to speak), this necessitates a notion of optimum size of cities. It further implies that an equality exists between private and social costs in the location decisions of firms. It has been argued, however, that the theory of optimum city sizes is no longer tenable and that the question is a meaningless one.[16] At best there can only be a range of such sizes which could sustain autonomous growth pole development.[17] We are not sure, however, that these criticisms of optimum city size really mean that the growth pole idea has reached a theoretical impasse from which we cannot extricate ourselves in order to make it more useful from the policy point of view. We hope to argue later that the question is incorrectly posed, and that shifting the question of the optimum size of a city, or of the self-sustaining size of growth poles, to a consideration of relative sizes (meaning a consideration of the city system as whole), will lead to a more useful formulation.

A more serious indictment of the growth pole approach in relation to Asian regional development and planning, however, is its low labour (as against capital) absorptive capacity. By focusing on it as a mere tool of accelerated industrialization heavily dependent on the foreign sector, the programming of growth poles has led to concentration on capital-intensive large-scale technology, which will increase industrial production but not employment (in absolute as well as relative terms).[18]

However, especially in the developing countries where surplus labour is a universal phenomenon, it is necessary to consider explicitly the question of employment possibilities in the non-agricultural sector and the employment absorption effect of the growth pole when discussing growth pole development policy. Because the rate of employment absorp-

---

[16]W. Alonso, The economics of urban size, *Regional Science Association Papers* **26** (1971) 67-83.

[17]H. W. Richardson, Optimality in city size, system of cities, and urban policy: a sceptic's view, *Urban Studies* **9** (1972) 29-48.

[18]There has been some shift e.g. Wilbur R. Thompson, from the earlier emphasis on input - output relations in the vertically integrated industrial structure of geographic growth poles to consideration of a "nebulous universe of small, differentiated firms, or different industries, (which) could coalesce into a large dynamic center by way of external linkages of psychological, social, cultural, institutional character". (See Lasuén, "On growth poles", *loc. cit.*) These possibilities have not been thoroughly explored, but they may be of critical importance in Asian countries.

tion in the modern industrial sector, which is occupied by the large-scale establishments, is always lower than that of the population increase, rural surplus labour, pushed out of the rural areas, flows to metropolitan or industrialized areas, but cannot be absorbed by the modern industrial sector. As a result it forms a large social strata of semi-unemployed (disguised unemployment) engaging in low productive or premodern activities and forming and living in slums. In short, the pattern of industrial development in selected Asian countries outlined above has engendered a pattern of spatial duality, reflecting specific population pressures and resource situations in each country and its stage of economic development. Naturally the adopted industrialization strategy has tended to benefit the urban sectors, primarily the primate cities in the case of import substitution industry, and the smaller towns in the case of resource exploitation industrialization. In terms of employment generation, however, the contribution of post-colonial import-substituting industrialization in the developing countries of Asia has been rather sluggish.[19] The process of Asian urbanization, characterized by T. G. McGee as "pseudo,"[20] thus resulted from premature rural - urban migration and limited industrialization in extreme duality in the primate city[21] and continued underemployment in the rural areas.[22]

Given the high population growth rates anticipated in Asia, given forecasts that show that over half of the world's population by the end of the century will be in Asia and that over half of this number, furthermore, will be in cities of over a million,[23] and given the long-run asymmetry of rural - urban relations under current structural conditions, the question of labour absorptive capacity, which currently concentrates only on a few cities, becomes a critical issue.[24] The growth pole approach by its nature cannot alone cope with

[19]The term "import reproduction" is perhaps more accurate than "import substitution". As suggested by Keith Marsden, import substitution describes the process by which a foreign article is replaced by a domestic article which satisfies the same consumer desire but uses local inputs, whereas import reproduction involves producing the same article domestically without adapting to local factor prices or inputs. Thus the contribution to employment creation is low because the strategy relies on foreign technology and the price-distorting policies needed to support it. The distinction is cited in J. Weeks, Policies for expanding employment in the informal urban sector of developing economies, *International Labour Review* 3 (1) (1975) 8.

[20]See some of his writings in *The Urbanization Process in the Third World: Explorations in Search of a Theory,* Bell, London, 1971.

[21]See, for example, ILO, *Employment, Incomes and Equality: A Strategy for Increasing Productive Employment in Kenya,* Geneva, 1972; K. Hart, Informal income opportunities and urban employment in Ghana, *Journal of Modern African Studies,* March 1973, pp. 61-89; and Armstrong and McGee, Revolutionary theory and the third world city: a theory of urban involution, in McGee, *Urbanization Process in the Third World.*

[22]The literature on this problem is quite long and the subject controversial. For a short discussion, see Higgins, *Economic Development,* esp. pp. 318 - 26. Interesting expositions relevant to Asian conditions include C. Geertz, *Agricultural Involution: The Process of Ecological Change in Indonesia,* University of California Press, Berkeley, 1963; E. Boserup, *Conditions of Agricultural Growth: The Economics of Agrarian Change under Population Pressure,* Allen Unwin, London, 1972; and Ajit Kumar Dasgupta, Disguised unemployment and economic development, in *Planning and Economic Growth,* Allen Unwin, London, 1965.

[23]K. Davis, *World Urbanization 1950 - 1970,* Vol. 2, *Analysis of Trends, Relationships, and Development,* University of California, Institute of International Studies, Berkeley, 1969.

[24]In the case of urban labour absorption, see the discussion in J. Friedmann and F. Sullivan, Labour absorption in the urban economy: the case of the developing countries, *Economic Development and Cultural Change* 22 (3) (1974) 385-413; and T. G. McGee, *Persistence of the Proto-proletariat: Occupational Structures and Planning for the Future of Third World Cities,* University of California, School of Architecture and Urban Planning, Los Angeles, 1974. On the agricultural sector, see H. T. Oshima, Labor-force "Explosion" and the labor-intensive sector in Asian growth, *Economic Development and Cultural Change* 19 (1971) 161-83. See also ILO, *Sharing in Development.*

this problem. In the Asian situation, therefore, wherein the growth pole approach creates a tertiary sector as a side effect—manufacturing productivity (industrial efficiency) being its prime goal—probably the side effect will become the main effect.

In order to ensure the effectiveness of a growth pole development policy as a decentralization strategy for the over-congested city in Asia, it is necessary to consider growth pole development as a measure to cope with "premature" rural - urban migration. In this context, India's rural area growth pole policy and Thailand's re-emphasis on its rural service centre policy (purported to provide rural surplus labour with employment opportunities to solve the problem of poverty in the rural area) are based on the recognition that industrialization following the conventional import substitution policy is limited for absorbing rural surplus labour. These rural growth centre policies aim to promote the location of small- and medium-scale industries which utilize agricultural products as raw materials in the rural area. This will increase the value added of as well as the demand for agricultural products, leading to an increase in income and employment opportunities in rural areas.[25] This in turn will induce small and service industries oriented toward local markets to locate in rural areas and eventually reach self-sustaining levels of growth. In this sense, growth pole development is significantly related to the problems of industrial structure and income distribution both in the city and rural areas.

A reformulation of the theory of growth poles in labour absorptive terms, that is in reference to human resource rather than mere natural resource utilization, is thus called for. There is at the moment a paucity of regional planning concepts that treat the economic duality of Asian cities, which arises from premature urban immigration, in its broader regional context which includes the structural rigidities which are present in the surrounding rural hinterland. Growth pole theory, in a similar fashion to the earlier urban economic base concept, has so far treated the city as a unitary phenomenon. To improve the applicability of the theory of growth poles, this must be revised and the concept of urban efficiency, so fundamental to the theory, be disaggregated and handled in a comparative framework.

4. REHABILITATING THE GROWTH POLE IDEA: A CONCEPT OF COMPARATIVE URBAN EFFICIENCY

The growth pole approach in its theory as well as applicability to the solution of the primacy problem has rested on the assumption that there is an efficient size of a city. The industrial decentralization issue and the attempt to solve regional disparities arise primarily from some notion that the primate city is too big. It is thought that programming of a city at some minimum threshold size for self-sustained growth (i.e. a growth pole) will lead to regional convergence of income. The theory of optimum city sizes has, however, been challenged as mentioned above. It has been argued that there is not a unitary conception of optimum city size, but that this varies with city function and time and also with different points of view, for example, that of the firm, the household, or the community.[26] While the previous over-emphasis on urban infrastructure costs as a measure of efficiency has been replaced by the notion of productivity (no matter how simplistic the measure-

---

[25]See ILO, *Sharing in Development*.

[26]Richardson, Optimality: a sceptic's view, *loc. cit.*

ment is), the most damaging criticism is the case when there is divergence between private and social costs and benefits in urban location.[27] Since in the real world this divergence exists as a matter of fact and dynamic external (agglomeration) economies serve as the primal process in the development of growth poles, the rational basis for the approach in regional development planning that aims at decentralization from primate cities appears to be destroyed.

We want to suggest that the question of optimum city sizes, as alluded to by many writers, is posed incorrectly, and to show a way to formulate it in order to rehabilitate the usefulness of the growth pole theory in the face of the criticisms discussed above. In the next section we introduce in brief the notion of comparative urban efficiency and discuss how a disaggregated approach to the optimum city size problem answers many of the conceptual questions posed about Asian regional policy, in particular the problem of labour absorption.[28]

4.1. Economics of Urban Size and Comparative Efficiency

In formulating the notion of comparative urban efficiency it is convenient to use Alonso's economic theory of city size. Regarding the city as an aggregate production unit, he obtained the urban cost and production curves shown in Fig. 2a. From the assumption that average productivity increases (linearly) with urban size, Alonso concludes that the minimum cost size P_a is meaningless. He suggested that more important is the question of the difference between optimality from the point of view of the whole nation P_c and that of the residents or firms located in the city P_b. The difference, of course, arises from the divergence between social and private costs and benefits.

The critical question seems to us to be why a city can and does continue to grow beyond both the national and the local optimum. That is a question relating to the primacy problem in developing countries as well as the metropolitan problem in advanced economies (whole city size distribution is presumably rank-size). From the Alonso framework (Fig. 2a) this instability of urban size in fact occurs within a whole range of city sizes where the average productivity AP exceeds average cost AC, roughly where agglomeration economies exist. The range of spontaneous growth begins from the minimum threshold size P_d to a possible maximum of P_z.[29] In this context there are three policy dimensions of urban and regional planning; (i) how to induce the growth of towns below P_d to the threshold of spontaneous self-sustained growth, what we might call the agropolitan problem; (ii) how to control the growth of the larger cities beyond P_b, that is how to manage the problem of declining urban efficiency,[30] this we may call the metropolitan problem for developed countries or the primacy problem for the less developed countries; and (iii) how to programme the development of intermediate-size cities to prevent the growth of primate cities, that is the growth pole problem (see Fig. 2).

---

[27]Alonso, Economics of urban size, *loc. cit.*

[28]The complete formulation and development of the arguments cannot be presented here for lack of space but will be published in a separate paper under preparation by the authors.

[29]Of course, the existence of this upper limit depends on the shape of the average urban productivity curve.

[30]Richardson, in reviewing the theory of optimum city size, has suggested in fact that we should now shift our attention to the question of intra-metropolitan efficiency. See Optimality: a sceptic's view, *loc cit.*

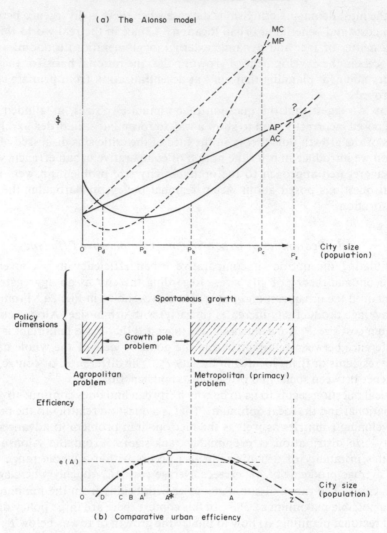

Fig. 2. Economics of urban size and comparative efficiency.

In reformulating the question of optimum city size for our purposes here, our point of departure is to consider the urban efficiency curve derived from substracting the *AC* curve from the *AP* curve in Alonso's model (the curve *DZ* in Fig. 2b). The efficiency curve *DZ* takes the shape of an attenuated inverted-U form, suggesting an "optimum" size for the firm (or household) at the maximum point.[31] However, this is not crucial to our argument: a city continues to exist and grow so long as efficiency is non-negative. What is important is that in considering the comparative advantages of an agglomeration economy

[31]A recent study shows some interesting observations of such efficiency curves, estimated for manufacturing sectors in the United States, which take this second order form. Tatsuhiko Kawashima, Urban production functions and economies of urban agglomeration: optimum urban size and urban-agglomeration-oriented industries, in *Eighteenth North American Meeting,* Regional Science Association, Michigan, 1971. Compare this with L. Sveikauskas, The productivity of cities, *Quarterly Journal of Economics* **83** (3) (1975) 393 - 413, who uses a log-linear form, but with less satisfactory results, applied to similar manufacturing data. The proper specification and estimation of this function is quite critical for the subsequent discussion.

for industrial location in a system of cities, it is quite conceivable that decentralization of such industrial activities will not take place if the agglomeration economy of the smaller cities, presumably in the less-developed region, still remains comparatively smaller. This is true even in a case in which the growth of a large metropolitan region exceeds the "optimum" size of the city in terms of a maximum agglomeration economy for a certain type of industry. This is the concept of comparative efficiency (illustrated by Fig. 2b).

Consider, for example, in Fig. 2b a primacy situation involving cities *A, B,* and *C* with the first as the primate city. The primate city *A,* which is larger than the optimum size P_b from the firm's point of view, is however more efficient than city *B,* whose efficiency measure falls below $e(A)$. The growth pole approach in terms of "concentrated decentralization" can be effectively implemented if the efficiency of a new pole, such as A^*, is programmed at a higher level than that of the primate city *A.* Such a city, of course, can be city *B* (or both *B* and *C* together) which has been induced by deliberate government policy to expand to size A^* with an "efficiency" level competitive with that of the primate city. In the absence of such a situation, the gap being larger between *A* and the other cities, the primate city will continue to grow. This formulation of urban efficiency is quite robust; it depends solely on a pairwise comparison of efficiency with the primate city, not on any distribution of city sizes.[32]

The formulation of comparative efficiency is quite central to the problem of seeking a link between the pattern of development of city size distributions with the level of economic development as found by El-Shakhs,[33] and the pattern of regional convergence and divergence observed by Williamson.[34]

4.2. *Urban Sectoral Efficiency and Urban Labour Absorption*

In terms of examining the problem of labour absorptive capacity of growth centres, a breakdown of the urban efficiency curve by sectors is most useful. It should be noted that the belief that the largest cities may still be most efficient is true only for all aggregated economic activities.[35] We noted earlier that for different functions of cities there may be different optimum sizes. For simplicity we may assume that there are two sectors—manufacturing (which includes, for convenience, skilled labour as well) and the tertiary or service sector. A consistent set of urban sectoral efficiency curves may be depicted as in Fig. 3.

The efficiency curves are constructed on a number of plausible assumptions. The manufacturing sector curve takes the form of an inverted U and is supported by some

---

[32]Richardson has said that one of the most difficult problems in the concept of optimum city size and city size distribution is how to compare which distribution is more efficient, even though it is generally agreed that the rank-size distribution is an efficient one. Some of these questions are discussed more fully in the paper under preparation.

[33]El-Shakhs, Development, Primacy, and Systems of Cities, *loc. cit.*

[34]Williamson, Regional Inequalities, *loc. cit.* This subject is elaborated a little further in UNCRD, *The Growth Pole Approach to Regional Development.*

[35]Koichi Mera, On the urban agglomeration and economic efficiency, *Economic Development and Cultural Change* **21** (1973) 309-24. Mera hypothesizes that the total efficiency of cities increases continually with the size of city. Using this formulation, Sveikauskas tested this hypothesis with manufacturing data only obtaining a rather poor fit.

empirical evidence.[36] This curve is not necessarily the same as *DZ* in Fig. 2a, but the minimum threshold size for manufacturing may still hold. The tertiary sector curve is drawn beginning at intercept zero to reflect a direct relationship with increasing population size of the city: the larger the population served, the more efficient the tertiary sector (a claim supportable perhaps by the theory of central places). Further, we should note that the two curves are complementary (the complementarity of basic and non-basic sectors!). However, the domination of one sector over another in any one city cannot *a priori* be excluded.[37]

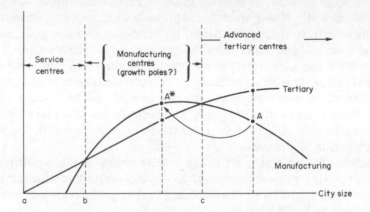

Fig. 3. Sectoral efficiency curves.

The dominant sector, however, may characterize the city structure and function: cities in the range (a - b) are essentially central places, though the larger ones in this class may have some manufacturing (see Fig. 3); those between (b - c) are manufacturing cities, the potential growth centres, with a substantial tertiary sector; and, finally, the upper level cities where manufacturing efficiency is already on the decline and the tertiary sector, perhaps of a more advanced form (but could include also informal sector activities), is more important.

These observations are consistent with the findings of a recent study on urban develop-

---

[36]See Tatsuhiko Kawashima, Urban production functions and economies of urban agglomeration: optimum urban size and urban-agglomeration-oriented industries, paper presented at the Eighteenth North American Meeting, Regional Science Association, Michigan, 1971.

[37]These hypotheses may, however, be tested empirically by examination of urban density functions in cities of different sizes. If we define efficiency as productivity net of rent per unit square of urban land, then at the urban sizes of b and c (Fig. 3), there should be an intersection of their manufacturing and tertiary density curves. See E. M. Hoover, *An Introduction to Regional Economics,* Knopf, New York, 1971 and E. S. Mills, *Studies in the Structure of the Urban Economy,* Johns Hopkins, Baltimore and London, 1972. It has been indicated that not only does the density of economic activity tend to increase with the size of city but also that the resulting competition between types of economic activity, in terms of productivity per unit of land, may exclude those extensive land-use activities with low productivity per unit of land due to the high cost of location. In particular, once a city grows to a certain stage, it may become uneconomical for manufacturing activities that require considerable land acreage. The tertiary sector, with high productivity per unit of land, will gradually take its place. Consequently, for the manufacturing sector, efficiency of production will increase initially with city size because of juxtaposition economies till that city reaches a size at which diseconomies of agglomeration, particularly increased land costs, cause a decrease in the efficiency of production and become less than the productivity of land for tertiary sector utilization.

ment in three Asian countries.[38] Dividing urban employment into a manufacturing sector (MNF) and two tertiary sectors, consumer-oriented tertiary (COT) and producer-oriented tertiary (POT), the study found that:

    (a) cities below 100,000 population have the highest proportion of employment in the MNF sector yet with a relatively low rate of growth of total employment;

    (b) cities with a population between 100,000 and a quarter of a million have a high rate of growth of MNF matching with a high rate of growth of the COT sector, with consequently high rates in total urban employment;

    (c) cities with a population between 250,000 and 500,000 are characterized by an increasing rate of growth of the POT sector, but employment is still influenced predominantly by the high growth rate of the COT sector;

    (d) million plus cities are characterized predominantly by the POT sector.

The problem with Asian cities, outside of Japan, is probably the fact that most of the POT activities reside mainly in the primate city, together with a continually large proportion of informal sector activities (perhaps incorporated in the COT sector).

This last point may be illustrated by using Fig. 3. If a growth pole A^* is built in the (b - c) range, a comparison of relative urban manufacturing efficiency with the existing primate city A will lead to decentralization of some industrial activities to A^*. However, the comparative efficiency on the tertiary dimension between those two cities still suggests a higher labour absorptive capacity for the primate city A. Thus labour released from rural areas under premature rural - urban migration may continue to locate in the major cities. Given the observed nature of major dualistic Asian cities and the manner in which the growth centres in some countries are being planned, the above reasoning is sufficiently testable and will probably be borne out.

To this extent, introduction of the notion of comparative sectoral efficiency rather than an aggregate measure of productivity of cities allows us to conclude that in addressing itself to the problems of labour absorption in Asian countries, the growth pole approach in the industrial complex sense can at best be only a partial strategy. It is necessary for accelerated industrialization, if this is the objective, but not sufficient for overall regional development, if other objectives such as employment attain high priority. The approach, however, should not be completely rejected but adapted and used in conjunction with other possible approaches.

5. BALANCED RURAL - URBAN DEVELOPMENT: ALTERNATIVE FRAMEWORKS AND REGIONAL POLICY ISSUES

We have sought to show that the growth pole approach, if properly formulated, is useful in the case of accelerating industrialization and urbanization. However, in considering the fundamental problem of labour absorption in Asian economic development, the approach by itself is of limited value but has to be complemented by other approaches. As long as the economies of Asian countries remain import-substitution oriented, labour absorption in the corporate sector will continue to remain low. Further emphasis on plantation agriculture, the extraction of raw materials, and the building of upward-multiplier large-scale industry will fail to accommodate a large proportion of the population in the rural underdeveloped regions of the various Asian countries. In many of these countries this has become an acute political issue in regional development.

---

[38]UNCRD, *Role of Cities in Attaining a Desirable Population Distribution in the Context of Rapid Urbanization, Findings from Three Asian Countries: Synthesis,* Nagoya, 1974 (hereafter cited as *Synthesis*). The results on urban sectoral employment were based only on the Japanese experience.

Many countries have adopted rural-oriented development strategies in order to accelerate the expansion of rural welfare. The rural works programme and the integrated rural development strategy are two examples. Under rapid population expansion and deteriorating man/land ratios, the agricultural sector will only be able to absorb labour up to a limiting capacity of its substitution for capital in order to increase further agricultural productivity. The experiences in this regard indicate mixed results.[39] In particular there has been a neglect of the urban function and the role of lower-order centres providing production, processing, and marketing services.

Some newer thinking on choices of alternative development strategy has been forthcoming recently in line with the reorientation of the prevailing development ideology in the Third World. A greater concern for social justice and employment goals has developed not only among international aid agencies but also among governments. The question Development for what? has shifted attention away from growth-only policies and dependency and towards greater equality and self-reliance as immediate goals.

The response to labour absorption as the prime objective of Asian development planning can proceed along several dimensions. Increasing premature rural - urban migration in Asia and other Third World economies can be accommodated in the urban informal sector. The major policy questions are then how to expand employment opportunities in this sector and how to expand the corporate sector into the urban informal to take advantage of surplus labour and the organizational capacity of individual and family enterprises.[40] A more accommodating official position with respect to such activities rather than coercive action to remove hawkers, squatters, etc., from the Asian city has also been urged.[41] This strategy must, however, be placed in its regional context lest the city becomes overwhelmed by extra-urban processes beyond its control.

Mobilization of the rural sector can be sought in "a balanced, persistent, and sustained fashion . . . so that the rural economy can hold its people in productive employment, absorb a substantial proportion of the inevitable increments in population and generate the rural surpluses of which it is capable and which are needed by the rest of the economy . . . [which means] the simultaneous growth of primary and secondary food production and of rural industry and services in a mutually reinforcing and self-feeding fashion."[42] The outlining of regional policy in this context is one of our major tasks.

A third dimension involves the role of small-scale industries and the choice of technology in the industrialization programme. It is noted that technological choice can be an important instrument of employment policy in developing countries although many issues have yet to be solved including institutional problems and duality.[43] This may not neces-

---

[39]On a critique of integrated rural development strategy, see V. W. Ruttan, Rural development programs: a skeptical perspective, in J. Friedmann (ed.), *New Concepts and Technologies in Third World Urbanization*, University of California, School of Architecture and Urban Planning, Los Angeles, 1974. For an example of a rural works programme, see Y. B. de Wit, The Kabupaten programme, *Bulletin of the Institute of Indonesian Economic Studies*, March 1973, pp. 65-85.

[40]Weeks, Policies for expanding informal employment, *loc. cit.* J. Friedmann and F. Sullivan, *Labour Absorption in the Urban Economy*, and McGee, *Persistence of Proto-proletariat*.

[41]See, for instance, McGee, Hawkers in selected Asian cities: a comparative study, mimeographed, 1975, and A. Laquian, *Slums Are for People*, University of Hawaii Press, Honolulu, 1971.

[42]ILO, *Sharing in Development*, pp. 28-29.

[43]A. Sen, Employment, institutions and technology: some policy issues, *International Labour Review* 112 (1) (1975) 45-73. See also F. Stewart, Technology and employment in LDCs, *World Development* 2 (3) (1974) 17-46, and K. Marsden, The role of small-scale industry in development: opportunities and constraints, in J. Friedmann (ed.), *New Concepts and Technologies in Third World Urbanization*, pp. 55-91.

sarily be used merely in the production of consumer-oriented commodities but also in production of producer-oriented goods.[44] The promotion of small-scale industries leads to some degree of foot-looseness which may easily lead to decentralization to rural areas. Again, such reorientation of policy must be integrated with the other approaches mentioned above.

In the context of these reorientations, new formulations of regional policy appropriate for the open dualistic economies in Asia have to be devised. Several new approaches should be explored. A so-called agropolitan strategy is emerging in the literature aimed at the acceleration of rural development through urbanization of the rural sector.[45] Agropolitan development seeks to create the territorial basis for a new balanced strategy incorporating industrial and agricultural development within new agropolitan units in ways which promote the symbiosis of urban and rural processes. Various measures to sustain agropolitan development such as a new policy for spatial development in Asia have been suggested.[46]

This new approach cannot, however, be isolated from the growth pole approach, just as the latter cannot be adopted as the sole strategy for regional industrial development. The possible links between agropolitan and growth centre development, reflecting the links between agricultural and industrial growth, must be explored within the Asian context. Our evaluation of the growth pole idea has sought to suggest that the strategy must include some mechanisms for increasing its capacity to absorb labour. Lasuén had suggested that this may be possible if developing countries, in order to accelerate their growth, can deliberately reorganize their business organizations into diversified corporate structures which diminish the exigencies of a polarized strategy.[47] This may be done first through the retailing, wholesaling, banking, and services sectors. Coupling of small-scale establishments with larger enterprises (in some countries, perhaps, involving public corporations and more active government intervention)[48] into multifirm multilocation undertakings is possibly one way to mobilize the urban informal sector as well as other unincorporated activities likely to occur in both metropolis and agropolis.

What is emerging out of these concerns is an increasing awareness that rural and urban problems cannot be treated separately and that relations between the two must be explored, especially the linkages between rural and urban areas and possible disequilibria between them. This arises from the inherent asymmetry of urban - rural relations under the prevailing conditions in Asia. The economic rationale for the one-way flow of investible resources as well as of labour to major urban areas lies not merely from pressure on rural

----

[44]H. Pack and M. Todaro, Technical transfer, labour absorption and economic development, *Oxford Economic Papers,* November 1969. See also K. J. King, Kenya's informal machine-makers: a study of small-scale industry in Kenya's emergent artisan society, *World Development* 2 (4 and 5) (1974) 9-28.

[45]C. L. Salter, Chinese experiments in urban space: the quest for an agrapolitan China and R. Murphey, Comments, in J. Friedmann (ed.), *New Concepts and Technologies in Third World Urbanization,* pp. 101-27.

[46]J. Friedmann, *op. cit.,* see chapter XV.

[47]Lasuén, On growth poles, *loc. cit.,* pp. 37-39. One possible bottleneck in this regard probably will be in the availability of appropriate decision-making resources, cf. A. O. Hirschman, *The Strategy of Economic Development,* Yale University Press, New Haven, Conn., 1958. UNCRD, *Synthesis,* brought out the importance of central managerial functions of cities and suggested that the decentralization of second level managerial functions may act as an initial stimulus towards some form of economic reorganization in cities.

[48]See, for instance, Kamal Salih, Urban strategy, regional development, and the new economic policy.

support systems but also on the attractions of the urban area. While there is a balance between push and pull factors, the implications of prospective rapid urbanization cannot be ignored.[49] Creation of urban employment opportunities alone (through growth centre development, for instance) cannot guarantee against increasing unemployment in urban areas, without urban - rural differentials (wages, amenities, basic minimum needs, etc.) being reduced.[50] It appears thus that how to achieve a balanced rural - urban strategy of development is central to regional development planning. The empirical basis for this reorientation from the accepted doctrines in regional policy, particularly of the Western type, is at the moment inadequate and its foundation must be based on a sounder theoretical framework which incorporates the particular conditions of Asia.

6. CONCLUDING REMARKS

The post-colonial development of many countries in Asia has been marked by the varying success of import substitution as a strategy of industrialization. This pattern of economic development is supported by a continuation of resource exploitation started during the colonial period and a widening of the primary resource sector, financed by new international arrangements which in recent years have begun to be based on greater indigenous investment participation and control. While increasing economic nationalism is being pursued, Asian development policies have persisted in their orientation to growth and in their adoption of the strategy of accelerated industrialization as the main driving force of economic development in order to catch up with the advanced countries of the West. As a consequence a vast majority of their population has remained in poverty and does not participate meaningfully in the development process, while income disparities continue to increase.

In its spatial context, this pattern of Asian development has led to extreme polarization of economic activities in a few regions and the growth of primate cities, leaving the rural areas largely neglected. As a result the problem of regional disparity of development has become a key issue in policy formulation for subnational development planning. This is particularly true when polarization of development in the developed region(s) continues to such an extent that, for instance, growth of *per capita* income in the other subnational regions lags far behind that of the developed region(s). This disparity sometimes is further compounded by the depopulation of lagging regions and massive in-migration into the overcongested developed regions which aggravates the already serious urban problems and increasingly high costs of public services. At this juncture a decentralization policy and a balanced growth concept seem to be not only necessary economically but also desirable politically. The adoption of these often leads to the policy question of spatial allocation of scarce resources, mainly capital investment, among the regions in a developing country. Today, decentralization of industrial activities, particularly from capital regions, is an urgent problem for a great many developing countries in Asia.

After two decades of theoretical development and voluminous empirical studies, the growth pole approach, in a broad sense, has become a vital tool of public policy for

---

[49]G. W. Jones, The implications of prospective urbanization for development planning in Southeast Asia, *SEADAG Papers,* Southeast Asia Development Advisory Group, New York, 1972.

[50]M. P. Todaro, A model of labor migration and urban unemployment in less developed countries, *American Economic Review* **59** (1969).

regional economic development. It is worth noting that the growth pole (centre) concept has been integrated into national development policies as shown in numerous national planning documents and the planning legislation of Asian countries. Either it has been applied as a decentralization policy to cope with the phenomenon of polarization in large metropolitan areas or it has been utilized as a strategic public investment policy in the establishment of industrial core regions. In particular, the use of seashore areas in the development of industrial estates and of import - export processing zones has attracted increasing attention in the Asian countries. In this regard, too, the growth pole strategy is utilized as an instrument in the implementation of a national industrial location policy and as a strategy of nationwide regional development.

In this paper we have attempted to show that the growth pole approach, while continuing to be the major thrust of industrial strategy in the region, must be adapted to suit the special conditions of Asian development. In line with the need to broaden the focus of development policy from the maximization of economic growth toward a greater sharing of development, and given labour absorption as the fundamental issue of development planning, we have sought a reformulation of the growth pole approach in two directions in order to increase its applicability to Asian countries. First, by introducing a concept of comparative urban efficiency, the problem of programming growth centres in order to decentralize industrial activities from the primate city or the core region reduces to a consideration of increasing their comparative advantage over that of the primate city, without having to determine their optimum size, which latter has been the major theoretical weakness of the theory. Second, by disaggregating the notion of total efficiency of cities into its sectoral components, we showed that the growth pole approach may lead mainly to the decentralization of manufacturing firms (particularly of the large-scale capital intensive type), but does not necessarily reduce the flow of rural migrants into the primate cities. The growth pole approach, being urban-oriented and creating weak links between the pole and its rural hinterland, is thus only a partial approach.

It is thus suggested that the approach be integrated with other complementary strategies in a broader regional policy framework. The several emerging ideas that are useful in the Asian context include the new agropolitan approach, which is aimed at revitalizing the rural environment through seeking a symbiosis of industrial and agricultural development. The suggested shift to accelerated rural development as a prime mover of Asian development is complemented by the role of small- and medium-scale industries, appropriate economic organizational innovations, and a change to a more positive attitude toward the informal sector in Asian primate cities. In all these reconsiderations, what appears to be needed is a more balanced approach toward urban and rural development in Asian regional planning.

The rethinking we suggest in this paper depends greatly upon the political conditions and the development ideology prevailing in Asian countries. While promoting the idea of a new framework for Asian regional policy, we hasten to add also that these countries must themselves evolve their own approaches based on their own experiences, resources, and perceptions. There is no pretence to completeness or finality in our own thinking, but the reorientations needed to solve Asian development problems cannot be postponed further.

INDEX